C.L.R. James in America in the 1940s.

AMERICAN CIVILIZATION

BY

C.L.R. JAMES

EDITED AND INTRODUCED BY
ANNA GRIMSHAW AND KEITH HART

WITH AN AFTERWORD BY ROBERT A. HILL

BLACKWELL
Cambridge MA & Oxford UK

Copyright © The Estate of the late C.L.R. James, 1993;
Introduction copyright © Anna Grimshaw and Keith Hart, 1993;
Afterword copyright © Robert A. Hill, 1993

First published 1993

Blackwell Publishers
238 Main Street, Cambridge, Massachusetts 02142, USA

108 Cowley Road, Oxford OX4 1JF, UK

Library of Congress and British Library Cataloguing-in-Publication Data
A CIP record for this book is available from the British Library.
ISBN 0-631-18908-4   ISBN 0-631-18909-2 (pbk.)

Typeset by Jim Murray of *Cultural Correspondence,* New York
Printed in the United States of America

". . . my ultimate aim, and my book on Melville is merely a preparation for it, is to write a study of American civilization."

C.L.R. James
Mariners, Renegades and Castaways:
The Story of Herman Melville
and the World We Live In

CONTENTS

      [   ]   Untitled in the original

Acknowledgments

The editors would like to thank Peter Clarke, Jeremy McBride, Graham McCann, Andrew McLaughlin, and Alison Rooper for their friendship and support. We are greatly indebted to Simon Prosser for insuring that C.L.R.'s masterpiece made it into print at last. Jim Murray's contribution to its publication goes far beyond what can be acknowledged here.

Every effort has been made to trace all copyright holders, but if any has been inadvertently overlooked, the editors and publishers will be pleased to make the necessary arrangements at the first opportunity.

Anna Grimshaw and Keith Hart

American Civilization:
An Introduction

I. PREFACE

C.L.R. James is one of the greatest writers and activists in the Marxist tradition. His vision of the movement of world civilization encompassed his own experience of the Caribbean (where he was born), Europe, America, and Africa. The crux of his development as an original thinker was the first period he spent in the United States (1938–53). Towards the end of that period James produced a book-length manuscript entitled *Notes on American Civilization*. This document, published here as *American Civilization*, is in many ways the most wide-ranging expression of his thought, the indispensable link between his mature writings on politics and his semi-autobiographical masterpiece, *Beyond a Boundary*.[1]

James completed his long essay on American civilization in early 1950, at a time which he felt was critical for the future of human society. Its central theme was the struggle of ordinary people for freedom and happiness, a struggle which he found to be most advanced in America. At the same time James recognized that the forces mobilized to repress these popular energies had never been so developed, or so brazenly employed, as in the twentieth century.

American Civilization was an expression of a great surge of energy and imaginative vision as James, at the peak of his intellectual powers, responded to historical circumstances and launched himself on an extensive program of writing. His concern was with no less than the conditions of survival of modern civilization. James's work on the manuscript was abandoned as he became swept up in a fight to avoid deportation. After his enforced departure from America in 1953 he never again found the circumstances in which to complete the original work he planned.

C.L.R. James died in Brixton, London in May 1989. His death came as popular forces exploded across China and Eastern Europe to challenge some of the most brutal and oppressive bureaucratic state formations in modern history. These outbursts were a watershed in political resistance, a vivid reminder of the presence and power of ordinary people in the struggle for civilization.

At the same time, too, they constituted a unique experience in terms of mass communications. This movement of the people was a world event like no other. Television beamed around the globe pictures of the confrontation between the forces for freedom and those of repression; and the images were stark and unforgettable – the Chinese youth standing before the tank as it rolled into Tiananmen Square, crowds swarming onto the Berlin Wall, the appearance of Havel and Dubcek in front of thousands in Wenceslas Square, the fierce battle fought on the streets of Bucharest, and the long-awaited moment of liberty as Nelson Mandela walked through the gates of a South African jail.

We live in one world; and, in many of its essential features, it is the world James foresaw in *American Civilization*. He understood the modern era to be a moment in the history of humanity which would result either in the total reorganization of society by ordinary men and women (socialism) or the continuing degradation of civilization as manifested in the public violence of fascism, the Stalinist state and the threat of nuclear war (barbarism). James drew attention to the subjective and objective features which together were, for him, what made the twentieth century distinctive. The development of industry, urban growth, and the tremendous expansion of mass communications had given ordinary people a coherence, concentration, and awareness they had never known before; moreover, this sense of collective purpose was becoming increasingly universal. But, at the same time, this capacity for popular self-expression and self-organization came up against the enhanced powers of rule from above, embodied in the modern state apparatus and in bureaucratic organization more generally. As the struggle intensified, James saw that it reverberated through all areas of life, including the most personal relations between men and women.

James's particular insight into the twentieth century drew self-consciously on his own life experience, containing as it did several distinctively new currents of the twentieth-century world. First of all, he was black and he had grown up at a time when imperialist war had projected black and colonial peoples onto the world stage as a potential revolutionary force. His participation in Europe's intense political struggles during the 1930s and his involvement with the movement for colonial freedom gave him a unique insight into the crisis of European hegemony and the interrelation between struggles in the metropolitan countries and the colonized areas.

But this was not all. James's move to the United States in 1938 opened his eyes to the specific contribution to be made by the people of America to the global struggle for a new society. It was this transition from Europe to America that holds the key to James's revolutionary vision. He saw early on that the Second World War represented an opportunity for America to launch its bid for world dominance at the expense of European imperialism. By the end of his fifteen-year stay, a world system based on competition between the two new superpowers of the United States and the Soviet Union – the Cold War – had arisen to terrorize mankind with the threat of nuclear annihilation.

Reading James's 1950 manuscript some forty years after it was drafted, it is possible to find there anticipations of a world to come. He drew attention to political developments which subsequently unfolded within America itself, notably the civil rights and feminist movements. Moreover, he highlighted the contradiction between bureaucracy and the people, a central feature of the modern crisis which now stands more fully revealed in the aftermath of Stalinism's failure. The remarkable prescience of *American Civilization*, however, was not fortuitous. James wrote his study at a critical time when America was asserting its world leadership with consequences as far-reaching as those unleashed a century earlier by the Civil War. His analysis caught some of the deeper currents of modern history; and, following his own approach to the work of great artists and writers, we can understand its originality to have been forged in a moment of transition, as one historical era gave way to another. James's creative innovation in this text was revealed not just in the content but also in the unfinished form of the writing itself, which sought to bridge the gap between the world of books and the lives of ordinary Americans.

The unraveling of the postwar order as a result of the collapse of Stalinism reopens all the questions that James posed four decades ago. *American Civilization* has immense significance, both as a penetrating account of the world in 1950 and as a powerful source of critical insight into the entire postwar era, illuminating as it does the century which now draws to a close.

II. THE PLACE OF *AMERICAN CIVILIZATION* IN JAMES'S LIFE AND WORK

C.L.R. James arrived in the United States at the end of 1938. Behind him were six years of intensive political activity in Europe and a substantial body of writings. The major texts of this prewar period – *World Revolution, The Black Jacobins,* and *The History of Negro Revolt*[2] – reflected the direction in which James's ideas were developing; specifically his attempt to integrate the struggles of black and colonial peoples into the revolutionary concerns of European Marxism. They also contained the seeds of his future work – work, both practical and theoretical, which he brought to maturity during his fifteen-year stay in America.

It would, however, be mistaken to think of James as having only been made by his experiences of Europe. When he left his native Trinidad for England in 1932, he was 31 years old, mature and educated, widely read in the classics, in European history, and literature. He was a published author of fiction and a sports journalist of note. Furthermore, James's method and his perspective were already formed, having evolved during his early years; and both were encapsulated in his appreciation and understanding of the game of cricket.

As a young boy, James watched cricket from the window of his house. His attention was caught by different players with their distinctive styles; he talked extensively to cricketers; he studied technique and played himself to a good standard; he built up his own library of newspaper clippings and collected books which enabled him to trace the evolution of the game. In this way he developed a sure grasp of history; but it was combined with a strong visual memory and sensitivity to the uniqueness of individuals within particular social contexts. These elements and the thoroughness with which James approached questions in cricket became the hallmark of all his subsequent work. For James, cricket was a metaphor for the world and at the core of its interpretation lay a method combining history with keen personal observation.

James's youth was not marked by any explicit political interest; but he reached adulthood during a period of considerable change and unrest in the island's colonial society. As he wrote subsequently, "Cricket had plunged me into politics long before I was aware of it. When I did turn to politics I did not have much to learn."[3] Cricket clubs in Trinidad expressed the prevailing principles of social stratification, with divisions based on wealth and color. James, a member of the black middle class, chose to join the leading club of the brown-skinned elite. He later regretted this political decision on the grounds that it distanced him from the creative energies of the Caribbean people. These were exemplified in the exciting styles of cricket played by Trinidad's lower-middle-class blacks, most notably by the great all-rounder, Learie Constantine.

Nevertheless, it was Constantine, with his pragmatic political sense and his experience of touring abroad as a professional cricketer, who began to question James's bookish notions of the world. It was also Constantine who invited James to join him in England, to collaborate on the writing of his cricket memoirs. But, by the end of the 1920s, James's perceptions were being changed by other forces. He could not ignore the restlessness of the Trinidad people in the years after the First World War; and he was, like everyone else, closely following the activities of Captain Cipriani.

Cipriani, a local man, achieved prominence during the war as a champion of West Indian soldiers serving abroad. When they returned, these men were expected to settle back into the old structures of colonial authority. But this was impossible, given their experience of war combat, their struggles against discrimination and segregation, their encounters with the ferment of revolutionary ideas (some of which crystalized in Garvey's Back to Africa movement). The strong bond forged between Cipriani and the men formed the basis for a political movement which took off after their return to Trinidad. It was a time of heightened crisis, punctuated by massive strikes, particularly that by dockworkers, and rioting in Port of Spain which had to be suppressed by military force.

For Cipriani the war had proved beyond doubt the capacity of the West Indian people for self-government; and he articulated the frustration and general dissatisfaction with Crown Colony government. James was in active sympathy and he prepared to write a biography of Cipriani. Moreover, during the period of growing agitation against the colonial regime, he was writing short stories celebrating the vitality of the ordinary men and women of Trinidad.

James was part of a literary circle whose members, prominent among them Albert Gomes, Alfred Mendes, and Ralph de Boissiere, founded two journals: *Trinidad* (1929–30) and *The Beacon* (1931–3). These publications provided an outlet for poetry and fiction; and they acted as a forum for debate on matters of art, culture, and philosophy. The five short stories published by James between 1927 and 1931[4] reflect the leanings of this group of writers towards life in the urban slums, known as "barrackyards." The themes and characters he chose, however, were not dictated by conscious political considerations or by an explicit desire for social realism. Rather, they grew naturally out of the material available to him as a writer and observer in Trinidad.

Barrackyard life, vibrant and unexplored, was a creative source, native to the Caribbean. Through its discovery, James and his contemporaries began to break the hold of the English tradition over the subject matter and cultural sensibility of colonial writing. Their work, located in the conditions of the Caribbean, laid the foundations for a distinctive body of literature, a genre consolidated and expanded by a later generation of writers such as V. S. Naipaul, George Lamming, and Wilson Harris.

In the spring of 1932 James left behind the confines of Trinidad's colonial society and embarked for England in the hope of joining the cosmopolitan circle of London's Bloomsbury as a writer. He carried with him a novel, *Minty Alley*,[5] and a draft of his biography of Cipriani. But his career in Britain soon took a different course from the one he expected: "I arrived in England intending to make my way as a writer of fiction, but the world went political and I went with it."[6]

London's intellectual atmosphere was dominated by political debate, especially over the events of 1917, the formation of a Workers' State in the Soviet Union and the emergence of Stalinism. But, in an economic climate of depression, the early optimism had begun to dissipate. The growing fascist threat weighed down over a turbulent Europe.

James's first taste of radical politics came soon, when he moved to Nelson, the militant Lancashire textile town, nicknamed "Little Moscow," which employed Learie Constantine as a professional cricketer. Industrial unrest throughout north-east Lancashire culminated, during August, in an all-out strike which brought cotton manufacturing to a virtual standstill. James found himself caught up in the events. He took part in the public meetings, the demonstrations, and the discussions which spilled over into people's homes.

It was in this atmosphere that he completed his biography of Cipriani; and, with Constantine's financial help, it was published by a small Nelson firm in September 1932. It was abridged a year later by Leonard Woolf as *The Case For West Indian Self-Government.*[7] Its publication, however, marked the end of the first phase of James's life, one situated firmly in the formative conditions of his Caribbean youth.

James learned a great deal from his stay in Lancashire, witnessing the day-to-day struggles of its working-class communities; finding, too, considerable interest among them in the colonial question. He and Constantine became widely known as spokesmen on the West Indies; and, in the process of explaining social conditions there, they learned about themselves and were able to clarify their own political position.

It was while living in Nelson that James first became acquainted with Marxism. He read Trotsky's *The History of the Russian Revolution* (1931); and later he began to study the work of Marx, Engels, and Lenin. He quickly dispensed with the literature being produced by Moscow and its British agent, the Communist Party; and he developed a Marxist position which was implacably opposed to the Stalinism of the Soviet Union. James joined the nascent British Trotskyists, many of whom were at that time operating within the Independent Labour Party (ILP).

For the next two years James was primarily concerned with the possibilities of revolution in Europe; and he was immersed as a writer and political activist in Britain's radical left-wing movements. His approach to questions of politics was distinctive. It stemmed, in part, from the fact that he had mastered European history and literature before he studied the principal works of the Marxist tradition. This was in contrast to many who ventured into history only after reading Marx. James's historical perspective, laid down in the West Indies, and the method he developed through his study of cricket, the rigor and thoroughness with which he handled material, marked every aspect of his political career in Britain. He quickly became one of the spokesmen of the British Trotskyist movement and his enhanced public profile as a cricket reporter on the *Manchester Guardian* brought increased respect to the Marxist Group, of which he was the leader.

James's work on revolutionary movements in Europe taught him the importance of international working-class collaboration; and this lay at the heart of his response to the Italo–Ethiopian crisis of 1935/6. After Mussolini's invasion of the last independent African state, James supported a motion at the ILP's annual conference calling for workers' sanctions against Italy instead of the government's League of Nations sanctions. The party's pacifist members refused to accept the conference's endorsement of the resolution, on the grounds that it might precipitate war. Many members, including James, broke with the ILP on this issue. It was a harsh lesson in the equivocation of the organized left and the labor movement.

At that time the widely held view of radicals was that the revolution had to take place first in Europe; only then would its leaders be able to grant the subjects of the colonies their freedom. James rejected this view, since he knew from history and from his own experience the great potential of the so-called "backward" peoples. He wrote at the time: "Africans must win their own freedom. Nobody will win it for them. They need cooperation, but that cooperation must be with the revolutionary movement in Europe and Asia."[8]

The Italo–Ethiopian crisis turned James decisively towards Africa. It gave focus to general questions concerning leadership and the masses in revolution and the relationship between the European left and the colonial world. He had already begun to explore these questions in his study of the slave revolution in San Domingo.

James's work on these issues was strengthened in 1936 by the arrival in London of his boyhood friend, George Padmore. After being recruited by the Kremlin to head the Profintern's Negro Bureau, Padmore broke with Moscow over its changing line on the colonies. In the context of the Soviet Union's attempt to make an alliance with Britain and France against Germany, Italy, and Japan, Padmore had been instructed to cease his anti-imperialist organizing against Britain and France (who had the most colonies in Africa) and direct his political efforts against the very powers that had no African territories. Padmore brought to England his considerable skills, his international perspective, and his knowledge of how to build a political movement. He helped to reorganize the International African Friends of Abyssinia, a committee set up by James, Amy Ashwood Garvey, Jomo Kenyatta, and other blacks. It became known as the International African Service Bureau with Padmore as chairman and James as the prospective editor of its journal, *International African Opinion*.

James's activities in the prewar period connected him to a long line of immigrant radicals who had played a distinctive role in British political life. These people often advocated broad ideals (such as colonial freedom) while, at the same time, also inserted themselves into the struggles of local working-class communities. James was conscious in particular of those Irish and Indian radicals whose struggle for freedom was then more advanced than that of the radical Pan–African movement he was instrumental in organizing.

The different threads of James's political activity and historical writing during the years 1932–8 came together in the three books he published towards the end of his stay in England.

The first, *World Revolution* (1937), was a history of the Communist International, considering in detail the foundation and development of the Soviet Union. James examined the part played by key figures (Lenin, Trotsky, Stalin) in the Russian Revolution and its aftermath; and he firmly linked the fortunes of the newly created Workers' State to the fate of the revolution in Europe. He showed the far-reaching consequences, for both the Soviet Union and the international revolutionary movement, of Stalin's 1926 pronouncement: "Socialism in One Country."

World Revolution was not particularly original; but James's revolutionary Marxist position opposed to Stalinism was badly needed at that time by Trotskyists and their sympathizers on the left. It was the first systematic work on the Russian revolution in English written from a Trotskyist viewpoint. James had access to the plentiful material available in French. He was already engaged in translating Souvarine's monumental biography of Stalin (published in 1939); and he had long been fascinated by France's revolutionary history. This comprehensive study of the Communist International appeared in a climate of confused rhetoric among intellectuals about the status of the Soviet Union. It dealt with the recent defeat of the workers' movement in France and Germany; and it faced squarely Stalin's role in undermining the struggle against fascism in Spain.

The method James employed to understand the Russian Revolution, focusing on its international aspect and on the special role of leaders and masses in revolutionary situations, marked a second book published a year later. *The Black Jacobins* (1938) was an account of the San Domingo revolution of 1791–1804, the only successful slave revolt in history. It was written with the coming struggles in Africa and the colonial world clearly in mind. In both cases the relationship between the metropolitan center and the colonies was critical to an understanding of the course of local rebellion and resistance. James's explicit aim, here and in *A History of Negro Revolt* written at much the same time (1938), was to document the history of populations exploited by colonial powers over centuries, but who were denied a place, except as passive subjects, in the official accounts.

The slaves of San Domingo moved in the wake of the French Revolution. At the same time, however, their island's wealth was central to the challenge posed by the French bourgeoisie to the old forms of authority. Although illiterate and led by an ex-slave Toussaint L'Ouverture, this black mass constituted a formidable revolutionary force. The sugar plantations were then the most advanced mechanism of industrial production in the western world. This lent organizational structure to the slaves as they successfully fought off the colonial powers, France, Britain, and Spain. The slaves won their freedom and eventually their independence with the creation of the state of Haiti in 1804.

At the heart of *The Black Jacobins* lay the figure of Toussaint L'Ouverture. James's analysis of his career as a revolutionary leader and of his successor, Dessalines, echoed the portraits of Lenin and Stalin in his history of the Communist International. The problem of power in moments of transition was a theme explored by James in the two books. In both the Russian and San Domingo revolutions "backward" or peripheral populations were catapulted to the forefront of the advanced movements of the day.

The originality of *The Black Jacobins* derived from James's fusion of Marxism with the colonial struggle of blacks in the New World and Africa. This perspective also informed *A History of Negro Revolt*, a synoptic review of the intimate link between industrial capitalism and black resistance over two centuries. Here he showed how the American Civil War in the nineteenth century and the coming African decolonization struggle in our own time were crucial to international capitalist development.

Many black radicals merely tacked Marxist rhetoric onto their primary preoccupation with national emancipation; whereas most European radicals saw colonial struggles as inherently secondary to their own revolutionary initiatives. For James the two strands were interwoven; and, as he remarked in the context of the San Domingo slave revolution, "People do not just win freedom for themselves; but they expand the struggle for freedom worldwide."[9]

The three texts James published in 1937/8 set the context for his future work. When he visited America shortly afterwards, he was a leading international figure of the Trotskyist movement and a distinguished commentator on revolutionary Marxism and the struggle for black freedom. He intended to stay in the United States only for a few months, but he ended up staying fifteen years, when he was forced to leave, protesting vigorously. So, although he was not aware of it when he went, America became the crucible of his mature life's work, inseparable as a vital historical and social context from his personal development both as a creative writer and political activist. It was in America that James reached a new and original conception of political life. It was encapsulated in his manuscript, *Notes on American Civilization*.

James was invited to the United States by the Trotskyist Socialist Workers Party (SWP). He arrived in October 1938 and immediately embarked on an extensive speaking tour which took him across America – from the East Coast, through the Midwest and then to California. Having already escaped the confines of a small Caribbean island, he was now freed from the claustrophobia of a decaying Europe. This journey was the beginning of a new stage in James's life. At the end of his stay in America he wrote: "I remember my first journey from Chicago to Los Angeles by train – the apparently endless miles, hour after hour, all day and all night and the next morning the same again, until the evening. I experienced a sense of expansion which has permanently altered my attitude to the world."[10]

James addressed American audiences on the decline of the British Empire, the approaching war in Europe and the race question. At the end of this tour he held discussions with Trotsky at his headquarters in Coyoacan, Mexico. During April 1939, Trotsky, James, and a handful of comrades worked out the SWP's strategy for relations with blacks. James insisted that the organized revolutionary movement should recognize that the blacks' struggle was for basic democratic rights rather than socialism as such.

The consequences of James's tour were far-reaching. He left Mexico with serious doubts about Trotsky's interpretation of events in Russia and Europe; and his journey, particularly his return to New York, traveling by bus through the old South, gave him valuable firsthand experience of the race problem in the United States. The themes which defined James's work for the next decade and a half were already emerging at this stage – the revolution in Europe, the black question and the situation of American workers or, as he put it, "the pressures on the workers and their violent reaction against these."[11] In order to clarify his position as a Marxist on the key issues raised by these questions, James undertook a serious study of philosophy, while being engaged in intensive political activity, especially in black communities. His theoretical investigations and political work fed directly into each other. Both lie at the heart of the original synthesis, his new political vision, reached in the 1950 manuscript.

James, the activist, began by speaking to America's black communities on the pressing issue of the day – their response to the impending war. In the context of Roosevelt's call for Americans to defend democracy in Europe, James reminded blacks of their own lack of freedom and basic democratic rights in the United States. Drawing on historical precedents, he recognized the tremendous threat blacks, employed at the heart of the American capitalist machine, could pose to the government. He emphasized that this threat was magnified not only by their potential alliance with white workers, but also by their links with the millions of colonial peoples resisting imperialism worldwide.

Later, during 1942, James traveled among the rural black communities of Missouri and he learned a great deal through his participation in the sharecroppers' fight for better wages. Writing in 1943, he described this as going "into the wilderness for ten months – a tremendous experience involving thousands upon thousands of workers, black and white, and much traveling over hundreds of square miles."[12]

The more deeply he penetrated into the lives of America's blacks, both the industrial workers of the northern cities and the agricultural laborers in the south, the more certain James became of the key role they would play in America's future. In the most advanced society of the day the blacks were the most exploited and oppressed section of the population. Their struggle, rooted in the history and day-to-day experience of a stark inequality, had an independent vitality and developing organic political perspective of its own. For James the black question lay at the core of the American question. It encapsulated the central contradiction of a society whose original ideals of freedom and equality were, in the twentieth century, crushed at every turn by the coercive power of industrial capitalism. James's work on the position of blacks within the United States led him directly into the question of the revolution in America.

· The challenge of the New World was the bridge into the other main body of work James carried out in America during his fifteen-year stay. This consisted of theoretical investigations stimulated initially by the ideological confusion which followed the Hitler–Stalin pact in 1940. The SWP was soon split by this development. The split, which was led by Max Schactman and others, involved a very large minority of the SWP and the majority of the Trotskyist youth. James supported the minority position, which rejected Trotsky's advocacy of "the unconditional defense of the USSR" and the class character of the Soviet Union as "a degenerated workers' state." The minority quickly organized itself in May 1940 into the Workers Party (WP), under the leadership of Max Schactman. James's theoretical contribution to the new formation was soon displayed when the WP's official organ, the *New International*, devoted its special July 1940 issue entirely to publishing his analysis of "Capitalist Society and the War."

Much of James's work was carried out within the WP with a small handful of collaborators in a group formed after the split. It was a group marked more by its disciplined search for a coherent Marxist position than for its attachment to any of the parties on the left. Two of his closest associates were women – Raya Dunayevskaya, Trotsky's former secretary, and later Grace Lee, a philosophy Ph.D. from Chicago. James's decision ultimately to extend his stay in America beyond the legal limit of his visitor's visa was greatly influenced by Raya Dunayevskaya who convinced him that he should stay and start a political organization which became known as the Johnson–Forest Tendency.

In the mid-1940s James did for Marxism in America what Lenin had done for Marxism in Russia, namely to adapt the methods and concepts of Marxism to US history. He held, following Marx, that American events such as the War of Independence and the Civil War had had profound consequences for relations between the classes in Europe. Now the Second World War had launched the United States into a bid to replace Europe as the main imperial power. This meant that the American people were projected onto the world stage as a new historical agent. James recognized, as had Lenin and

Trotsky before him, that the workers' soviets of the Russian Revolution had introduced a new political form, one which pointed to the future. Its introduction to the United States would require what he called "the Americanization of Bolshevism" – a program of political education which James and his group planned to make the basis of its organizational work. (See Appendix). The industrial climate after the Second World War lent considerable encouragement to such a program, particularly the great wave of strikes which took place in 1946 and afterwards. But by the end of the decade this revolutionary moment appeared to have passed.

One of the prime tasks of the Johnson–Forest Tendency from its inception was to examine the nature of the Soviet Union. But once James began to analyze the history of the Soviet Union and its relationship to the development of capitalism, he found himself being drawn deeper into questions of Marxist theory and Hegelian dialectic. He and his collaborators published the conclusions of their extensive theoretical and practical work towards the end of the decade. An important pamphlet, *The Invading Socialist Society,* was later followed by *State Capitalism and World Revolution,*[13] which was presented to a congress of the Fourth International in 1950. Meanwhile, James circulated, in the form of letters written from Reno, Nevada in 1948, the results of his own work on method *(Notes on Dialectics).*[14]

State Capitalism and World Revolution contained as its main theme the notion that Stalinism was the last stage of capitalist development world-wide. Although hostile to private property capitalism, the Stalinist bureaucracy of the Soviet Union was just as committed as the western bourgeoisie to the maintenance of a regime of wage slavery. For the sake of accumulation through increased labor productivity, state monopoly capital subjected workers to an extreme rationalism, otherwise known as The Plan, which differed only in degree from the industrial tyranny of American capitalism. The book's inspiration was Lenin's last writings after 1917; and it ends with the observation that the political deficiencies of the revolutionary movement in 1950 were substantially philosophical.

In *Notes on Dialectics*, James set out to teach his followers how to use Hegel's *Science of Logic*. Dialectical reason, he explained, was a way of thinking which reflected the movement of the object of thought, the world in which we live. Analytical thinking and common sense can only identify what is or has been; but, the dialectic, in contrast, enables us to imagine a different future by combining speculation with knowledge in the context of action. James applied this method to the history of the international labor movement, beginning with the French Revolution. He showed that Trotsky's thought never moved with history, remaining trapped in the circumstances of the Russian Revolution and its immediate aftermath. This was nowhere more clearly exposed than in the Leninist notion of the revolutionary vanguard party. James concluded that the next decisive stage in history would be the overthrow of the rule of the Party itself and the emergence of the people against the structures of government bureaucracy.

Having decided that Trotskyism was not just wrong in its ideas, but fundamentally wrong in its method, James broke with the Trotskyist movement. In doing so he was also ready to break with the old European forms of political life, which he had come to see as irrelevant to America and an impediment to world development. For he had long been engaged in the process of seeking to understand American society. The basic premise of his investigations was clear: "From the first day of my stay in the United States to the last, I never made the mistake that so many otherwise intelligent Europeans made of trying to fit that country into European standards. Perhaps for one reason – because of my colonial background – I always saw it for what it was, and not for what I thought it ought to be. I took in my stride the cruelties and anomalies that shocked me and the immense vitality, generosity and audacity of those strange people."[15]

Following his arrival in 1938, James rapidly immersed himself in a study of American history and literature, but he also paid serious attention to the popular arts of the American people. He read detective novels and comic strips; watched B movies and followed the careers of Hollywood film stars. He became a "neighborhood man," observing closely the daily lives of men and women, their social relations, their living space, their routines of work and leisure. Between July and October 1944 James published two important political essays on the American question ("The American People in 'One World': an Essay in Dialectical Materialism," *New International,* July 1944, and "Education, Propaganda, Agitation: Post-war America and Bolshevism," October 1944); but taken as a whole his political journalism as a member of the Johnson–Forest Tendency contained few hints of his much larger project on American civilization.

The fullest evidence of his original approach to America as a civilization was to be found elsewhere, in the remarkable correspondence that he maintained during these years with Constance Webb. Here, not bound by the terms of left-wing polemics, James ranged widely over questions of politics, art, music, and culture. The letters suggest that, through his friendship with Constance Webb, he sought to grasp the key to American society – the independence and vitality of its people. She was a representative of twentieth-century America: young, free-spirited, aware but uneducated in the European sense; struggling to find an integrated life, a struggle sharpened by her experiences as a woman (a section of the population whose lack of freedom and equality James likened to the experiences of America's blacks).

Drafted with great vigor and speed in 1949–50, *Notes on American Civilization* represents, in both its style and content, the crux of James's development as a political thinker and activist. It stands between his major theoretical works of the 1930s and 1940s and the broader perspective of his later years, encapsulated in the classic *Beyond a Boundary* (1963) which contains all the elements of his mature (and unique) vision of humanity.

American Civilization constitutes a decisive break with the European tradition, what James called "old bourgeois civilization" with its oppositions between art and culture, intellectuals and the people, politics and everyday life. In it he sought to fuse the different elements – history, literature, political struggle, popular art, and detailed observations of daily life – into a dense work of startling originality. James was seeking to grasp the whole at a particular moment in history; and yet, at the same time, the movement of the narrative, the shift from established literary sources to the lives of ordinary men and women, reflected his understanding of the general dynamic of history. In short, he aimed to distill the universal progress of civilization into a specific contrast between the nineteenth and twentieth centuries. The culture of the intellectuals was giving way to the emergence of the people as the animating force of history.

What James had discovered was that it was in the United States that the question he considered to lie at the heart of the civilization process itself – the relationship between individual freedom and social life – was most starkly posed. He understood the movement of the modern world to be one of increasing integration. The growing interconnectedness of things through the expansion of communications, the centralization of capital, the accumulation of knowledge, and the breakdown of national boundaries was mirrored, in his view, by the increasing sophistication and awareness of the human subject. But, conversely, never before had the individual personality been so fragmented and restricted in the realization of its creative capacities. For James, this was the core of the modern crisis. He uncovered in America an intense desire among people to bring the separate facets of human experience into an active relationship, to express their full and free individuality within new and expanded conceptions of social life. This he called "the struggle for happiness."

James was conscious of the struggle within his own life, for he too was seeking integration. As he wrote to Constance Webb: "I feel all sorts of new powers, freedoms etc. surging in me. . . . We will live. This is our new world – where there is no distinction between political and personal any more."[16] Unfortunately for James the distinction was etched deeply within his own personality; and it had become reinforced over many years by his involvement in the revolutionary movement. By the late 1940s the tensions between his political role in the Johnson–Forest Tendency and his personal commitment to a shared life with Constance Webb were acute. His study of American civilization may be interpreted as an attempt to resolve that contradiction.

It was the first work that he planned in an ambitious program of writing which would address a more general audience on the modern crisis of civilization. But the uncertainty of James's position in America meant that the project quickly became fragmented and he did not again find the conditions to enable him to complete his original plan of work.

Never having acquired a resident immigrant visa, James was served with a deportation order by the Immigration and Naturalization Service (INS) in 1948. After two years of legal hearings before the INS, the order for his deportation was upheld. It was the height of the Red Scare; and James sought to gain support for his case by delivering public lectures on American literature, in particular on the great nineteenth-century writer, Herman Melville. These formed the basis of a critical study, *Mariners, Renegades and Castaways: The Story of Herman Melville and the World We Live In;*[17] but, although it was sent out to every Congressman and others who might influence James's case, he finally lost his appeal against deportation and the book has only recently reached a wider audience. The American civilization project was transformed into a collective enterprise of the Johnson–Forest Tendency as a part of James's struggle to remain in the United States.

In its themes and preoccupations *Mariners, Renegades and Castaways* was clearly taken from the more comprehensive study of America which James had already begun. Writing with explicit reference to the barbaric, totalitarian regimes of Hitler and Stalin, but mindful also of American trends, James addressed ". . . the obvious, the immense, the fearful mechanical power of an industrial civilization which is now advancing by incredible leaps and bringing at the same time the mechanization and destruction of human personality."[18]

For James the question had been posed a century earlier by Melville in *Moby Dick*, his tale of the *Pequod*'s ill-fated voyage in search of the great White Whale. James took the ship to be a microcosm of the newly emerging industrial society; and he discussed the different characters and the dynamics of their relations as they unfolded within the novel's narrative structure. He began with the towering presence of Captain Ahab, the embodiment of a wholly new human type, the captain of industry and ultimately the modern totalitarian dictator, a man prepared to bring about the ruin of civilization in the pursuit of his own personal ambition.

Counterposed to this destructive force was the ship's crew, its members being representative of the ordinary people of the world. Melville showed them at work inside the whaling ship. His description of the intricacy of their tasks, their skills, their cooperation and sense of community strongly appealed to James who saw in it the picture of a modern proletariat. Echoing a central theme of *American Civilization,* James here offered a particularly penetrating analysis of the characters of the narrator, Ishmael, and the ship's three officers, Starbuck, Stubb, and Flask. They were the intellectuals, the educated, the possessors of technical knowledge, those trained to be "leaders;" and yet, when the *Pequod* neared its destiny, they wavered hopelessly, as did their twentieth-century counterparts, between submission to the monomaniacal power of Ahab and an affirmation of the crew's humanity. They could not decide.

Moving beyond *Moby Dick* to explore the relationship between the writer and the world around him, James developed this theme, the crisis of the intellectuals or what he called "the revulsion of modern man from an intolerable world."[19] But he was interested, too, in the process by which "strange stuff," the raw material of the imagination, was moulded and refined to make something new, an Ahab, ". . . that rarest of achievements – the creation of a character that will sum up a whole epoch of human history."[20] In *Mariners, Renegades and Castaways,* James located the novelist in the movement of history, placing him at the moment of transition from one world to another. At the same time, he celebrated Melville's ability to "see," to create a masterpiece out of the uniqueness of his artistic personality. This was at once highly individual and rooted in society, expressive of its fundamental dynamic.

In his critical study of Melville's work, James demonstrated the maturity of his dialectical method. Its foundations had been laid during his boyhood years of cricket watching and later developed self-consciously through political activity and the study of revolutionary leaders such as Toussaint L'Ouverture. Although James's investigation was of a major literary figure, it was closely tied to other theoretical and political work in which he had been engaged while living in America – work which by 1950 had brought about fundamental changes in his thinking. For this reason *Mariners, Renegades and Castaways* was more than a penetrating exercise in literary criticism; it was also a chapter of an autobiography, revealing aspects of the life of James himself. This was exemplified in the finale to the Melville study, where he described his experiences as an internee among the "renegades and castaways" of Ellis Island.

America had irrevocably altered James's perspective on the world and his fifteen-year stay there had enabled him to develop an original conception of political life. His vision was now founded on recognition that the fate of humanity lay in the hands of ordinary men and women, that intellectuals would play no decisive role in the working out of society's future. This was no fanciful notion or mystical belief, but a conception rooted in James's understanding of history and his many years of political activism.

In a sense, then, both *Mariners, Renegades and Castaways* and the longer, unfinished work, *American Civilization,* can be understood as the first stage in James's attempt to place himself in history, an autobiographical project which occupied him intermittently in his final years. This was so not just because together they contain the fullest statement of his political position as he reached the peak of his creative powers; but also because they have at their heart the excavation of the intellectual tradition to which James himself was so closely bound. Writing them cleared the way for a more explicitly autobiographical volume exploring the formative conditions of James's Caribbean upbringing, through an interpretation of the world of cricket. It appeared a decade later as *Beyond a Boundary*.

The period following his departure from the United States in 1953 was a difficult one for James. He had broken with the Trotskyist movement in which he had worked for two decades; and, although he remained in active communication with his own American organization and colleagues, he found himself separated from the vitality and expansiveness of the New World. Returning to a Europe changed by the experience of war, he found its intellectuals isolated and demoralized. In Britain the great socialist ideals of the 1930s had been transformed by the Labour Government into the palliative institutions of the welfare state; but emancipation struggles in the colonies had set in motion the disintegration of the British Empire.

James's dislocation, coupled with the pressing need to earn a living, left him struggling to continue the work inspired by the political struggles and popular arts of the United States. But the experience of America was something very specific, as he revealed in a letter written to his friends in New York shortly after his arrival in England: "It is most remarkable, but at the present moment the feeling that I have and the memory of life in the United States are expressed most concretely in gramophone records, jazz records in particular, and movies."[21]

The original 1950 manuscript of *American Civilization* languished, unrevised, among James's papers. At first, he tried to interest his old London publisher, Frederick Warburg, in his book; but it was no easy matter to revise the work for a European audience, a very different one from that which he had had originally in mind. Several sketches for a new version that he planned to write jointly with James can be found among his papers for the years 1953–5. By the beginning of 1956, the American civilization project became a focus for renewed discussion between James and his political associates in the United States, now organized as the Correspondence group. An incomplete draft, dealing mainly with American workers and women, was the only outcome of this collaborative exercise; and it was again put aside when the pressing issues raised by the 1956 Hungarian revolution and the independence of Ghana in early 1957 diverted the energies of James and his associates. Parts of this second document were later incorporated into a book, entitled *Facing Reality*, animated by the Hungarian question.[22]

Nevertheless, throughout the 1950s, James was actively exploring ideas concerning democracy and the arts which he had first articulated in his late American writings. He was seeking to develop a critical method by means of which the work of great artists could be approached, both to open up the individual creative process itself and to assess its place in social life. His critical approach was fused with his political perspective, for he believed that it was through artistic work that one could gain original insight into the central questions of society and human experience. This led James eventually to pose the question of the relationship between creativity and the popular movement for democracy. His discussion of the relationship drew heavily upon his developed sense of history and a keen sensitivity to contemporary artistic forms.

Beyond a Boundary, a highly original study of the development of the game of cricket, became the focus for these ideas; but James's analysis was already advanced, having evolved and crystalized in his mind during his lengthy sojourn in the United States. Although James had not seen a single cricket match between 1938 and 1953, *Beyond a Boundary* was made possible only by the work of his American years. In the context of the New World, James's extensive work on problems of philosophy and historical method had established the foundations of all his subsequent political activity. At the end of this labor he had transcended the divisions built into the European tradition – the separation of politics and culture, art and entertainment, intellectuals and the common people. *Beyond a Boundary*, in its broad imaginative sweep, gave expression to this newly found freedom. The heart of the book (and its alternative title) was contained in the question : "What do they know of cricket who only cricket know?" It stands as a brilliant analysis of the game itself, but it is also much more.

Here James forged a creative synthesis from the disparate elements of understanding. He integrated the individual and the social, the unique player with the conditions which produced him. He brought together the team and the spectators in an active, evolving relationship. He placed cricket firmly within the dialectical movement of history, as a manifestation of social and political change, at any one time embodying the fundamental forces of society. What distinguished James's approach in this book was the careful attention he paid to strictly technical matters, using his knowledge of style and method in cricket to push his interpretation of the game into new, unknown regions – into politics, aesthetics, and popular culture.

With the writing of *Beyond a Boundary* substantially completed, James returned to the Caribbean. He accepted an invitation from Dr Eric Williams, a former pupil, to edit the party newspaper of the People's National Movement. James arrived in Trinidad in 1958 at a time when the Caribbean was alive with political debate and when unresolved tensions, released by changes in postwar society, found expression on and around the cricket field. James was at once the same and a different man from the young, educated, colonial intellectual who, twenty six years earlier, had left Trinidad in search of a literary career abroad. This was the island of his formation and *Beyond a Boundary* was securely rooted there; but the quality of his analysis drew on the decades of intensive political work in Europe and America.

The book was autobiographical to a significant degree because, for the first time, James self-consciously examined the conditions of his childhood and youth through the lens of a mature method and understanding. But *Beyond a Boundary* was autobiographical for reasons more profound. In James's mind the completion of his book and the imminence of Caribbean independence were intimately connected. He sought through cricket to integrate history with personal biography, to "see" himself; and in this way he merged his unique vision of humanity with the historical movement which had brought forth a new political order.

James never retreated from this vision, from his belief in the creativity and capacity of the Caribbean people; but all around him political and economic conditions thwarted its realization. He left Trinidad on the eve of its independence; and *Beyond a Boundary* was published a year later, in 1963, to great critical acclaim. It was his last major work, representing as it did the completion of a personal journey which had carried him from a tiny outpost of the British Empire into the very heart of world politics and culture.

III. THE TEXT

When the founders of America posed the question of "the right to life, liberty and the pursuit of happiness," these goals were then little more than abstract ideas in Europe. But in the twentieth century the whole world has come to expect for itself that freedom, equality, and well-being which many continue to see as symbolized by the United States.

James's argument, throughout *American Civilization*, is conducted in the conventional language of liberal democracy – freedom, equality, individuality, happiness. The use of this language enabled James to engage his subject and audience directly; for, as he recognized, these ideas, born with America itself, retained the power to bridge the gap between intellectual discourse and popular understanding. Clearly, political language identifying the author with the opposite side in the Cold War would have left James addressing an isolated and tiny audience. James also took care to avoid terms which rooted his arguments in the specificities of immediate political controversy. To this end, he chose a vocabulary which he felt, despite its appropriation and debasement as propaganda, was yet capable of reaching to a deeper level of social analysis. Having avoided the terms "socialism" and "capitalism," James built his study around two oppositions: "civilization" vs "barbarism" and "democracy" vs "totalitarianism." However familiar these terms might seem, James used them both to convey the movement of modern history and to probe into the heart of the world crisis.

Although he attempted no formal definition in the text, James meant by "civilization" the progressive tendency of world history as a whole. Its core was the drive to integrate the individual and society; and its creed was a humanist desire for universal freedom and happiness. Its antithesis, "barbarism," sacrificed the individual to a limited version of society and was based on inhuman mores, coercion, and division. The social practices of the ruling segments of most historical civilizations, in contrast to their achievements in art and religion, were highly unequal, even barbaric. As James noted, Wendell Phillips, the nineteenth-century abolitionist, had described the American Civil War as a struggle between civilization and barbarism inside America itself.

Within the history of civilization, "democracy" represented for James a specific stage of politics – people power or rule from below. Its principles were self-organization, freedom of association, individual freedom, and equality. James contrasted the restricted form of parliamentary democracy with the direct participatory form of ancient Athenian democracy. For him the antithesis of democracy was "totalitarianism" – control from above, the fusion of party and state, the destruction of the individual in the name of totality. In the twentieth century this form of government was epitomized by the Stalinist regime. James held that the completion of the civilization process was socialism; and by this he meant the extension of democratic principles into the sphere of production. When the mass of ordinary working people controlled their own labor processes, the consequences for the organization of all aspects of society would be fundamental. Although the name "socialism" was largely absent, the idea permeated all of James's text; the daily evidence of the struggle for such a society in America was what he called "the thing itself."

James sought to capture this historical movement of society in the organization of the manuscript. Through the use of America as his example, he aimed to distill the universal progress of civilization into a specific contrast between the nineteenth and twentieth centuries. In essence, a high culture for the few was giving way to a society where common people now occupied center stage. Thus the first part of *American Civilization*, dealing mainly with the past, draws heavily upon literary sources in which the presence of ordinary men and women can only be guessed at; whereas in the second part, based largely on James's own observations, the people make themselves known directly in the fullness of their lives.

James made it clear that he had in mind both an intellectual and a popular audience; and he stated that later drafts would entail a movement from one to the other. In his attempt to integrate two levels of analysis, the abstract and the concrete, James's manuscript was reminiscent of the work of his great predecessor, Alexis de Tocqueville. Indeed, James explicitly placed himself in the tradition established by de Tocqueville's classic *Democracy in America* published a century earlier; and it is not difficult to find many parallels in the scope and method of their writing.

The dialectic of ideas and life, of form and content was also reproduced at the heart of James's critical theory. The principles of his method were exemplified by what he found best in Melville's writing, particularly in *Moby Dick* – a creative synthesis of the real and the symbolic. For James the distinctiveness of Melville lay in his great sympathy with the common man; he anchored his story of the *Pequod* in a precise description of various individuals at work and in their relations with others, bringing a sharp realism to the task. At the same time, by means of symbolism, he reached beyond the actual to the deepest stirrings of his age, finding "indications and points of support by which the innermost essence and widest reaches of the universal may be grasped."[23]

James's method was given its most serious test in his long, central chapter on the popular arts, the bridge between the two parts of his argument. He regarded this chapter as one of "unusual difficulty." Here he explored the relationship between different levels of human experience – the actual and the possible, the past and the future in the present. James believed that art (and in twentieth-century America that meant above all the movies) was the principal means through which people sought to make connections between real life and the world of the imagination. With this in mind, he identified the essential ingredient of great art as simplicity. The scope of the artistic medium was always widened, he felt, by a process of simplification, with a view to appealing to the widest audience possible. But once a new artistic form had become simplified, James added, there was a substantial increase in the complexity of relations which could be built up from it.

James illustrated his thesis by pointing to the finest example of modern art, the elemental quality of Chaplin's films before the watershed of 1929. James understood the appeal and greatness of Chaplin's pantomime to derive from the primitive connection it made with the visceral emotions of the people; but the simplicity of Chaplin's principal character – "the little man" – opened out, touching the universal, drawing the audience into the complexities of the modern world and linking its everyday experiences to the general movement of society. If the movement of the manuscript of *American Civilization* represents the shift from historical abstraction and literary ideas to direct personal observations of contemporary life, this chapter on the popular arts achieves a methodological synthesis.

James derived from his analysis of the contemporary popular arts a vision of the political movement of American society which he tried to realize in the second part of the text through an account of the actual lives of the people. What he saw in art, he also identified as being present in politics, namely that the American people, symbolic of modern people everywhere, were already beginning to shape the forms and content of political life. As a result twentieth-century politicians had to address popular needs with a specificity and concreteness that was lacking in the nineteenth century. More profoundly, the needs of the people were reflected in the increasing dominance of economic considerations in politics, something which had always been a fundamental concern of Marxists. At one level this simplification may be said to be reductionist; but, as James interpreted it, the economy touched directly the complexity of everyday life. In this way, his aesthetic found resonance in the historical movement of civilization from art and culture, through politics, to that projected reorganization of economic life which would be the foundation of the most profound of twentieth-century social transformations.

The remarkable power of *American Civilization* stemmed from the author's ability to trace the complexities of modern life from a unified base of simple ideas, ideas which contained in their form and substance the movement of our own age. But James knew, too, that it was impossible for a single individual or intellectual to achieve a unity of vision and method appropriate to the size of the transformation required, if the mass of ordinary people were to make a new society suited to their own needs. In some ways James, with his artistic vision, his fascination with the intricate details of everyday life, and his commitment to serving the genuinely popular forces of emancipation, was a kind of Melville and Wendell Phillips rolled into one. Yet he lived in a different age. It was one which they anticipated in their creative work; and one which James, in turn, seeing the struggle between the elements of the old and the new society at a time of transition, penetrated deeply.

American Civilization was drafted under difficult circumstances. At the beginning of 1950, James was living in New York. He had married Constance Webb not long before and their son was born in the spring of 1949. These new family responsibilities exacerbated his longstanding financial anxieties; moreover, he was being pursued by the FBI which was seeking his deportation because of his unresolved immigrant status. These pressing considerations were conveyed starkly in a letter James wrote to Daniel Guérin, a French colleague, on January 17, 1950. Here he revealed that for some years he had been planning to write a book on the civilization of the United States; indeed, a good part of the draft had already been written. He had received comments on his manuscript from Eugene Raskin, a member of James's circle of literary friends which included Richard Wright and Ralph Ellison; and, as he explained to Guérin, he was writing at great speed to complete a first draft of the work which he could show to a publisher. He hoped to raise an advance to alleviate his straitened circumstances; but he felt, too, that the work itself was assuming a new importance.

The haste with which James completed his manuscript is indicated by references within the text to articles in the *New York Times* from December 1949 to February 1950. It would appear that at this stage he was working mainly alone, intending to circulate the draft among his friends and collaborators before incorporating their comments into a final, publishable version.

James's correspondence about his project on American civilization conveyed an atmosphere of secrecy. There were a number of reasons for this. First of all, James did not wish his vulnerable personal situation (illness and shortage of money) to be known to his opponents, including the Federal Government. Furthermore, there was a potential conflict between publishing a highly personal document and the discipline required of him as an official member of the leadership of the SWP. Under the pressing circumstances in which James found himself, the 1950 manuscript never reached completion; and it subsequently languished among his unpublished papers.

In 1987, each of the editors arrived independently at the judgment that the 1950 manuscript was a coherent and original piece of work which shed new light on James's established corpus of writing. Moreover, although it was a document of the mid-twentieth century, it seemed to provide a unique insight into the contemporary crisis of the late twentieth century. *American Civilization* is important because it is by far the most substantial manuscript in James's corpus to remain unpublished and because it deals at length with America. Its availability makes possible a new assessment of James's contribution to the twentieth century.

With James's enthusiastic support the editors agreed to share the task of bringing the manuscript to publication. Over a period of two years he discussed points of substantive interpretation with us and offered comment on an early draft of our introduction. An extended excerpt from the larger manuscript was published in the *Times Higher Education Supplement* shortly before his death.[24] James felt that the publication of his American work, along with preparations for a *C.L.R. James Reader*, constituted a new phase in the public reception of his work. He approved our initial editorial decision to retitle his 1950 text *The Struggle For Happiness*, drawing on a chapter heading from the original work.

Since James's death this title has become the symbol of a wide-ranging dispute over the status of the text as a whole. We contend that James, like Saint-Just in France in 1794, brought to the world from America the idea of happiness as a revolutionary goal to be added to the European legacy of freedom (bourgeoisie) and equality (peasantry/workers). Happiness became a word which appeared repeatedly in James's later writing, from his assertion that Marx and Hegel "believed that man is destined for freedom and happiness,"[25] to his lengthy exposition, in a letter to the literary critic, Maxwell Geismar, on the centrality of happiness to American society and culture, in contrast to Europe with its sense of the tragic.[26] The notion of happiness lay, too, at the heart of his volume *Modern Politics*, but there James called it "the good life."[27]

Conventionally, "happiness" has been understood as a trivial thing, as a moment of pleasure which is necessarily fleeting. As James himself recognized, the notion was often reduced to mean simply material satisfaction. He took his lead, however, from the conceptions of the eighteenth century, where the pursuit of happiness in this life was contrasted with religious passivity in the face of earthly suffering.

Although he nowhere defined the concept closely, the idea permeated *American Civilization;* for he held happiness to be as essential to the human experience as the desire for freedom and equality. It was the desire of the modern age, "what the people want," expressive of complex and deeply rooted needs of human beings, for integration, to become whole, to live in harmony with society.

For James, then, happiness had two facets, the freedom to be a fully developed, creative individual personality and to be part of a community based upon principles conducive to that aim. This was the unity of private interest and public spirit which de Tocqueville had found in the early American democracy and which James believed was still the palpable goal of the American people in the twentieth century. It is significant in this respect that James used "The Struggle for Happiness" as the title for his chapter on the industrial workers. As he makes clear in the text, the integration of individuals in modern society would require a fundamental reorganization of the way people experience work.

America contributed the idea of happiness to our understanding of civilization itself. Today it has become a universal goal; and with the emergence of the people of Eastern Europe, Asia, and Africa as the potent symbols of the collective force of humanity in its opposition to the forces of oppression, we are reminded again that happiness is inseparable from the active struggle for its attainment.

IV. THE PRESENT VOLUME

It remains to give an account of some of the decisions which have led to this edition of *American Civilization* taking its present form. Although we intended at first to tidy up a manuscript which its author regarded only as a preliminary draft, we later agreed to publish the text as it was originally written, with the exception only of a few typographical corrections and the insertion of some chapter headings where none existed before. We believe that the benefits of an accurate historical record outweigh any that our tinkering might have contributed.

The text depends heavily on extensive quotation from sources identified only by author and title, without reference to page numbers. It was James's practice in lectures to read long excerpts from selected texts, thereby allowing the content and language of the original a full measure of expression. Although the habit of scholarship was deeply ingrained since his youth, he did not usually inflict his learning on his audience. We felt that adding page numbers to the quotations in *American Civilization*, as well as being an intervention on our part, would lend a spurious air of academic precision to James's freewheeling enterprise. We have, however, added a bibliography of references made in the text.

This Introduction was begun while James was alive and it has undergone significant revision since his death in response to criticisms made by the literary executor, Robert A. Hill. We have tried to keep its style consistent with the accompanying text, as well as with the expectations of a general readership. We were not able to take into account the literary executor's "Afterword" which concludes this volume. On the suggestion of Robert Hill, we have also added as an Appendix a piece written by James in 1944, "The Americanization of Bolshevism."

Anna Grimshaw and Keith Hart
Cambridge

Preface

The following is an attempt not to outline but to give a preliminary view of an essay I propose to write for the general public. Essay because it is a statement of a position. It will be 75,000 words, no more. This Ms. is neither an outline or an abridgement. It seeks only the best way to convey certain ideas. The person who has this copy, No.   , is asked to make marginal notes or make comments in any other way, preferably in writing.

This document is absolutely confidential. This means that it should not be talked about to anyone, should not be seen by anyone. Any exception made to this will be looked upon as a breach of trust.

Introductory

The American civilization is identified in the consciousness of the world with
two phases of the development of world history.

The first is the Declaration of Independence.

The second is mass production.

Washington and Henry Ford are the symbols of American civilization.
And on the whole this instinctive judgment is correct.

The corollaries to these two embodiments of the American civilization
express the past and the future.

The Declaration of Independence enshrines life, liberty and the pursuit
of happiness. To this day nowhere in the world is there such a struggle to
grasp at all the elements of life and liberty. Nowhere has happiness been
pursued with such uninhibited energy and zest.

Mass production and the economic power it brings represent the summation of the impact of the United States upon the modern world. Napoleon's
army, the German army, made the dominating impression upon their
opponents, and other contemporaries in the days when they forged the
national destiny. It is American production which was decisive in the last
war and recognized as such.

It is upon the strength or instability of the American economic system that
the modern world looks for indications as to the future. Russian Communism
bases its tactical perspectives and strategic plans for the victory of its system
in the struggle for world domination upon its estimate of the same alternatives – the continuing strength or instability and crisis inherent in American
production.

In fact, life, liberty, the pursuit of happiness and mass production are
today not distinguishable. They form an entity. For the spokesmen of
American civilization this entity is the basis of all the benefits and possibilities
which they propose to maintain and extend to a disintegrating world as the

only hope of its salvation.

In food and shelter, clothes, in physical transport and mental communication, railroads, automobiles, planes, telephones, radios, newspapers and periodicals, the American people enjoy not only an immense preponderance over the rest of the world. In historical terms the last generation has seen an accumulation of wealth in proportion to population which exceeds all previous estimates and when compared with the achievements of past ages removes the United States qualitatively from all previous civilizations. To this can be added a freedom of social intercourse and a sense of equality also unparalleled in any previous or contemporary society.

Yet the fact remains that this civilization is ridden with conflicts over economic, social, political, racial, over elementary human relationships, love and marriage, which create a sense of social chaos and fear for the future.

In 1929, with the Depression, the country entered upon a period of doubt of its traditional values, ideas and standards which has steadily increased to this day. If the root of the fear is not atomic war, it is not fear of the Russian rivalry in the ordinary sense of those words. The fear, the doubts are rooted in doubt and fear of the American system itself, fear and doubt of the ever-new conflicts and exacerbation of old ones that it ceaselessly breeds, and fear and doubt because both Western Europe and the millions in the Far East maintain a stiff and very often an aggressive hostility to taking the achievements and traditions of America as a model. Great masses of workers in Western Europe, hundreds of millions in Asia and impressive numbers in Latin America seem to prefer the Russian brand of communism. Thus the greatest power in Western civilization no longer knows what to believe about itself. From the incessant questioning in all sections of the press for years now of the lack of any clear perspective, I select only two recent examples. *Life* in its review of fifty years wrote as follows of America in 1900:

Its vigor and its vastness somehow typified a new spirit that was spreading across the country in the years between 1900 and the Great War; a cocksure confidence that Americans had the power to do anything in the world and do it better than the rest of the world. It was an adolescent spirit, boiling with the conflict between youthful naivety and mature sophistication that always marks adolescence in a man or a country. Looking back on that far-away and almost forgotten era, it takes on a soft, golden haze; as a nation we were at peace, the world loved us, and if there was evil among us at least some of our leaders recognized it and fought it. God was in his Heaven, the Devil in his Hell. It was probably the last time when people could be sure of things, when the world was in order and everybody knew where he stood in it. The scene was being set for the most surprising and adventurous half-century in the memory of man.

In the *New York Times Book Review* of January 15, Lewis Mumford wrote:

Before the First World War the greater part of Western civilization was still inflated by the profound optimism that had buoyed up the nineteenth century, the Century of Progress. Under the influence of the new ideology that had grown up with capitalism and mechanical invention, the leading minds of the period thought that mankind had found the secret of happiness by turning its attention to the quantitative solution of all its problems.

Absolute bankruptcy of perspective permeates the whole article. Today, as I write the above I see in the *New York Times*, January 17, 1950 one of the most remarkable manifestations of the day. R. L. Duffus is an editorial writer for the *New York Times* and that is as good a position as any from which to observe the world. He writes novels and his latest is reviewed by Orville Prescott. Here are some abstracts from the review.
   On the world in general:

Considering the nature of the world he has been writing about, it is interesting to note that Bob Duffus has never let its unhappy state sour his serene disposition.

   The hopelessness and misery of modern man in general:

It is also a moving one in its quiet way. It is moving because it seems true, true to the life we hectored and flustered citizens of the twentieth century know. The men and women on board Mr. Duffus' doomed plane are portrayed with a sure touch and deep understanding. And most of them are afraid. Their fears are different. Some lie in a past which won't be buried. Some concern a future without faith or hope. Some are vague and metaphysical and some are sharp and sadly personal. These people, young honeymooners and elderly vacationers alike, are people of sorrows acquainted with grief. Guilt and self-doubts gnaw at their vitals and the shadow of the world's sickness darkens their sky.

   The special hopelessness of youth:

Spark Crawford, the former bomber pilot on his honeymoon, was the most desperately afraid of them all. He was afraid of a world which had no secure place in which to preserve the idealism of youth.
   "That pilot up there," Spark said to his bride, "has got what they call a flight plan. He knows where he's going and what weather he can expect. I don't. I wish I did. I want to have some purpose – the way I did before. I want to think that I'm working with a lot of other people on a job that has to be done." It is one of life's tragedies that people like Spark can't feel sure of such a purpose.

Here this confession of universal hopelessness appears in a great newspaper and it is certain that no one will protest, no one will comment as upon

anything unusual. Everyone accepts this as normal. This hopelessness is
infinitely deeper than it was in Europe in the years preceding World War II.
In fact it is a question if in any of the great critical periods of human history
that we know, the decline and fall of the Roman Empire and the transition
from the religious to the secular age (Puritan Revolution, founding of
America, Thirty Years War), it is a question if at any time mankind at large
has ever reached such a state of hopelessness and doubt of itself as now
characterizes Western Europe and above all, the United States.

I propose to deal with this contrast in the civilization of the United States,
between the possibilities and the realities. Others have dealt with this. What
I do *not* propose to do is to deal with it in terms of the trade cycle, the crisis
of capitalism, government spending, etc. As a stranger who has lived in the
United States for twelve crucial years, I propose to analyze the concepts of
liberty, freedom, individuality, the pursuit of happiness as I have observed
them and studied them in the past history and actual lives of the American
people.

What exactly do I propose to do that is new?

In a review of D. W. Brogan's *The American Character* Max Lerner writes
as follows:

Actually the book deals with a few American problems but not with *the* American
problem, which still needs someone to define it. Actually it deals not with *the*
American character (assuming you can discover one amid the pitfalls of national
psychology) but with some American traits.

Whoever it will be who will write an important book on America today, he will
have to face much tougher questions of economics and social theory, of national
psychology, of politics and metaphysics, than Mr. Brogan has set for himself. He
will have to ask how we came to build up such immense power-structures as our
corporations, our trade unions, our political parties, and why we continue to fear
power; why we have a way with machines and a knack for handling physical reality,
yet flee from some of the crucial psychic realities; why we are at once idealistic and
tough, moralists and pragmatists; why a people that is so optimistic has poured some
of its best literary energy into the tradition not of "literary pessimism" as Mr.
Brogan puts it, but of tragic and interior writing; why a people so afraid of being
made fools of nevertheless has a variety of cults and heroes.

The not impossible commentator on America would have to deal with the Big
Press, the Chain Radio and Mass Movies; with our fumbling economic strategies,
with the paranoid sense the conservatives have of being surrounded by dangers, with
our administrative revolution. He would have to deal with our genius for organization and our contempt for intellect. He would have to pose the question of the
historical parallelism between us and another great organizing people, the Romans.
And in place of Mr. Brogan's easy optimism about the American future, he would
have to ask what inner strength there is in Americans and their culture which will

prevent them from completing the historical trajectory of Rome. The problem of America is the key problem to the modern destiny. (*Nation*, November 6, 1944)

Some basic approach of this kind I have had in mind from the beginning and Lerner is correct in saying that no such book has been written about modern America.

Two famous books dominate the field in the analysis of the United States: de Tocqueville's *Democracy in America* and Bryce's *The American Commonwealth*. The rise of America to world-power and its dominating position over large areas of the world has resulted in a renewed attempt by foreign commentators to grasp the essence of the American civilization. In addition to the work of Brogan, there is a careful study by Gorer on the American character, a full study by Harold Laski, and another by Wyndham Lewis. In my opinion, all these books, serious as they are, with many admirable pages, are fundamentally unsatisfactory. One book, in method and matter, de Tocqueville's, written in 1835–40, still remains the finest study of the United States ever written.

I propose to write an essay closer to the spirit and aims of de Tocqueville than any of the writers who have followed him.

Any attempt to show what America is today which does not scrupulously define and delineate the unique origins of the country and the creation of the special ideas and ideals which distinguish it, any book on America which does not do these things, is doomed to failure. Liberty, freedom, pursuit of happiness, free individuality had an actuality and a meaning in America which they had nowhere else. The Europeans wrote and theorized about freedom in superb writings. Americans lived it. That tradition is the most vital tradition in the country today. Any idea that it is *merely* a tradition, used by unscrupulous July 4 politicians to deceive the people, destroys any possibility of understanding the crisis in America today. The essential conflict is between these ideals, hopes, aspirations, needs, which are still the essential part of the tradition, and the economic and social realities of present-day America.

To pose this problem demands that men be not treated or analyzed as economic statistics. One of the two chapters dealing with early concepts of freedom, individuality, etc. of America will be devoted exclusively to an analysis of the writings of Herman Melville and Walt Whitman, for it is my belief that it is in the writings of these two men that both the past of America and the indications of the future were given. We cannot begin to grapple with the basic realities of modern America without as serious an analysis as possible of what these men saw and wrote.

However, when I come to contemporary America, I deal as comprehensively not with the writers, but with the film, the radio, the comic strip. This needs some explanation even at this stage.

Complementary to the vast accumulation of wealth and the tradition of liberty is undoubtedly the history of the culture of the United States, a paradox without parallel. It is most sharply pointed if we compare the modern United States with Greece.

Ancient Athens was a state perhaps as big as Vermont, Athens at its best may have had 100,000 people. Its material achievements would be rightly scorned by any single modern department store. Yet within two or three generations it produced Socrates, Plato, Aristotle as philosophers; Aeschylus, Sophocles, Euripides and Aristophanes as dramatists; Pericles as a statesman; Demosthenes and Aeschines as orators; Pindar as poet; Praxiteles as a sculptor; Xenophon as a journalist, Thucydides and Herodotus as historians. These men have never been exceeded in their respective spheres. In any estimate of contemporary culture, studies of the past or speculations into the future, their work is indispensable.

In this sphere of human life the mighty civilization of the United States by universal agreement stands at the bottom of all great civilizations. Until the latest phase of American economic and political power forced unwilling and self-interested recognition upon them, the universities, intellectuals and organized culture of Europe paid no organized attention to American literature, art, history or civilization. Greece and Rome; Italian art; the politics of the Italian Republics; France of the XVIIth century; France of the XVIIIth; German Classical Philosophers; France of the XIXth century; Goethe and German Romanticism; the Russian novelists, German science, Scandinavian drama, Oriental literature and philosophy, primitive sculpture, every conceivable subject was studied for knowledge and recreation except the American civilization. In this there was perhaps one significant exception. To the period which saw the Declaration of Independence was added the study of the Civil War as a military conflict only. It was seen as the first great modern war. But its full implications as a social phenomenon have been realized only in recent years and very imperfectly. America was famous for its material achievements and democracy, individual freedom. If, on the one hand, the culture of Europe ignored American culture, it was not so with the plain people. The hungry and oppressed European masses fled by the millions to economic opportunity and personal freedom. But organized, official society in its actions, far more than in its words, expressed and still expresses an unmistakable disdain of American society. And in this division of appreciation both sides are correct. If the positive contributions to the culture of Western civilization by America are insignificant, the concrete democratic life was, for many years and to this day, traditionally a phenomenon unique in the history of modern society.

The inherent justice of the century-old opinions is proved by the fact that it was shared for generations by the Americans themselves. And despite the self-conscious efforts of more recent days, it is still shared by them. The serious students of philosophy, literature and culture today in America are far more familiar with and interested in Dostoyevsky and Kafka, Picasso and Matisse, Kierkegaard, Heidegger, Marx and Freud, the philosophy of Existentialism than they are in the literature, art and philosophy of the United States. Politics as a science is studied in European models. And in a real objective sense, these students are correct.

This has to be admitted before its inadequacy is exposed.

It is not merely that there is not one writer, not one poet, not one painter or sculptor, not one philosopher, not one political figure of international status with the exception of Washington–Jefferson who has caught the imagination of the world. It is that if you remove from history the school of French Impressionist painters, German classical philosophy, the Russian novelists, the drama of Ibsen and Strindberg, the Utopian Socialists, you leave a gaping hole. The historical connections and movement of the world development are destroyed. But there is, so far even as American students are concerned, no movement in the United States whose absence would cause a like disruption. This is still an opinion more or less widely held.

It is one of the purposes of this essay to prove that this view, widely held and legitimate on the premises upon which it has been built, is false. To demonstrate this, however, at this stage in this form, requires that we understand the old premises and the new.

It is one of the weaknesses of American culture not to recognize that gifted individuals could have arisen only as the representatives of various tendencies, classes, groups, expressing the aspirations of a truly national culture. The great Greeks were an expression of Greek civilization. In the same way Molière who in the XVIIth century began the modern social drama, Richardson and Fielding in England who began the modern novel, Ibsen who created the modern social drama, Proust and T. S. Eliot who portrayed the modern disintegration, were representatives of social needs, moods and aspirations which, though national in form, transcended the national limitations and appeared to the world at large as characteristic of a certain stage of international civilization. Hume, Kant, Ricardo and Dostoyevsky, Spengler, were Europeans of a concrete environment, and yet were recognized as signposts in the advance and retreats of the human race. That Washington and Jefferson did this is acknowledged. National independence, life, liberty and the pursuit of happiness, the creation of a republican state, the right of people to decide their own fate, this was a landmark in the history of civilization. The same with the writings of Voltaire and Rousseau; the religious and political achievements of Martin Luther, Calvin, Oliver Cromwell. The examples are innumerable. But in no field has American civilization produced any figure of that status since Washington and Jefferson. The attempt to make such a figure out of Lincoln has had and can have no success. His most famous statement betrays why, ". . . so that government of the people, by the people, for the people, may not perish from the earth." This was not new. Lincoln was defensive. When in 1794 at the height of the French Revolution, Saint-Just uttered the famous phrase: Happiness is a new idea in Europe, he sent a shock throughout Europe. America had already shown the idea to the world – in America. But when Lincoln spoke, the First International, pledged to international socialism, was already a force in existence and in fact came powerfully to the support of the Northern cause. The late President Roosevelt cut a great figure in the world. But to have sponsored collective bargaining and social security in the United States was to achieve nothing that the world did not know. His most striking statements: "There is nothing to fear except fear itself;" "Quarantine the aggressor;" "Four Freedoms" mean nothing in the history of the world today. Patrick Henry's "Give me liberty or give me death," Tom Paine's "The Age of Reason" remain, because they were said at a time when to say them cleared a new road. Today as a contribution to the contemporary crisis, they mean nothing, as little as the "Four Freedoms."

Yet so distinctive has been the historical development of the United States and its positive achievements, so characteristic is it of human society today, such is its power and influence, that to probe the source of this colossal failure increasingly becomes one of the great analytical needs of the crisis-ridden civilization of today. Why has the United States failed to produce men who planted flags in unexplored territory? It is not for lack of gifted individual men. Politically the late President Roosevelt had enormous gifts. If his political testament rose no higher than the Four Freedoms and the New Deal, it was not because he lacked capacity. But we can take a less controversial figure. Walt Whitman had all the elements of literary genius. His literary career is of much greater significance to the nineteenth century and the twentieth than the work of Anatole France. He was in every respect superior as a man of letters to a Matthew Arnold, both in his understanding of the world of literature and of his own country. But France and Arnold produced solid, consistent, coherent and finished bodies of work. It was precisely this that Whitman failed to do. In the crisis of world civilization and the extraordinary contradictions, the successes and failures of American civilization, the failures and successes of Whitman are today of infinitely more importance than that of many men, great writers who achieved coherence and concentration. Whitman attempted to solve the contradictions between the individual and universal society. Similarly with Poe, a figure slighter than Whitman, with very little substantial work to his credit. Yet he can be seen today as one who in his convulsive stabs at various types of literature was the epitome, far more than any European, of the most pronounced literary manifestation in the world today, from the insatiable needs of millions on the one hand, to the work of aesthetic coteries on the other. It is in the failures and the reasons for the failures that lie the significance of the American historical experiences.

I propose then to show how and why a re-evaluation is necessary of the American writers of the middle of the nineteenth century. For the first time in the history of modern literature they were grappling with problems that could not be seen clearly in the American democracy. They could not write with the consistency and sustained force of European writers for whom the problems were narrower. But today, when the full complexity of the relation between individual freedom, individual liberty and democracy, to society as a whole, faces us all in Europe as well as in America, men like Whitman and above all Melville, can better be understood, and Melville's *Moby Dick* stands out as a product of American civilization which could only have been produced in America and is unsurpassed in the whole literature of the nineteenth century. He is being recognized at last, but nowhere have I seen anything like justice done to him as an interpreter of the United States and a guide to contemporary society and contemporary art as a whole.

But Melville has left no serious descendants. In the chapters devoted to contemporary America, the space given to Whitman and Melville is given to the modern film, the radio and the comic strip, to Charles Chaplin, Rita Hayworth, Sam Spade, Louis Armstrong, Dick Tracy and Gasoline Alley. I propose to show that here is not mere shoddiness, vulgarity, entertainment. On the contrary. Here, after the writers of the middle of the nineteenth century, are the first genuine contributions of the United States to the art of the future and an international art of the modern world. But I go further. I say that there also are some of the most significant manifestations (to be found nowhere else) of the deepest feelings of the American people to American life. The questions and problems posed by Whitman, Melville and Poe are finding their answer not in T. S. Eliot and Hemingway but in the popular arts of the American people. The reasons for this can be briefly stated.

America has had its own independent American attempts at political and artistic creation that were separate from Europe and were American and American only. Even the first great success, the War of Independence, was European in the origin of its ideas and their expression. As Wendell Phillips recognized, the first great independent expression of the American genius is the Abolition Movement, the work of figures like Garrison, Phillips himself and Frederick Douglass. It culminated in the formation of the Republican Party whose history between 1856 and 1860 is unique in the history of political parties. Similarly with Populism and to a lesser degree the I.W.W. [Industrial Workers of the World]. There has not been anything like them in Europe, and the reasons underlying their failure to establish themselves are the same reasons why the literary and other artistic movements of their time failed to complete themselves.

The distinctive social and political movements in the United States have been mass movements, uprisings of the people and unofficial individuals in a sense rare in Europe. From the days of the Revolution itself, through Jacksonian democracy, to the organization of the C.I.O., these astonishing outbursts have astonished foreign observers as well as the participants themselves. The vigor of the outburst has been paralleled by the rapidity with which most of them have collapsed. They left little behind. Even today the second creative outburst of American literature which began after World War I has been of abstract theoretical interest to European writers. So far the premises and conclusions of previous investigators. These premises must be extended.

During the last thirty years, *mass production* has created a vast populace, literate, technically trained, conscious of itself and of its inherent right to enjoy all the possibilities of the society to the extent of its means. No such social force has existed in any society with such ideas and aspirations since the citizens of Athens and the farmers around trooped into the city to see the plays of Euripides, Sophocles, and Aeschylus and decide on the prize-winners by their votes. The modern populace decides not by votes but by the tickets it buys and the money it pays. The result has been a new extension of aesthetic premises. The popular film, the radio, the gramophone, the comic strip, the popular daily paper and far more the popular periodical constitute a form of art and media of social communication which through mass production and the type of audience produced in the United States constitute a departure in the twentieth century as new in civilization as the art of printing in the fifteenth. It has transformed the production of art. New content, new principles, new forms, new conventions are in process of creation with the masses of the people in the United States as first and decisive arbiter. The men who seek to supply this imperative social need as a rule, and rightly, do not consider themselves artists. They are business men. They find their performers where they can get them. They are careful to observe in matter and manner the limitations of the economic and financial powers upon whom their business depends. But they are as dependent upon the mass audience for their success as were Euripides and Sophocles for their prizes, a situation unique in the modern world. The result has been that along with ephemeral vulgarity on a colossal scale, particularly in the sphere of the popular film and popular music, there have been in every sphere creations such as have hitherto been unknown in the history of civilization. In this sphere the American people have taken the lead and dominated the world as surely as the great artistic and literary schools of Europe dominated the intellectual world of their time.

It is here, in the origin and development of these manifestations, the popular film, popular music, popular journalism, that lies the most significant artistic and social phenomenon of today. The moods, desires, aspirations, needs, strength and weakness of the nation, as much by what is included as what is omitted, are portrayed here as in the art of no other period. And the vast successes of these specifically national productions are truly universal for our age. It is in the study of these that it can be seen why American civilization failed to achieve distinctive quality in the past and why to this day the distinctive literary talents, Hemingway, Wolfe, Faulkner, Wright, to the extent that they continue in the traditions of Hawthorne, Melville and Poe, remain, as does all American art from the beginning to the present day, divorced from any significant current in modern life. Whence its profound alienation from the society, its inability to satisfy either itself or the national need, or contribute to the development of civilization on a world scale. To give but one example: take the famous phrase describing Hemingway, etc. "The lost generation." Which was this lost generation? A body of intellectuals, no more. The great mass of the nation between 1920 and 1929 was not a "lost generation." For them it was the "generation" of Charlie Chaplin and Douglas Fairbanks, not of *The Sun Also Rises* and *A Farewell to Arms*. It is necessary to break harshly with this kind of thinking or the realities of the twentieth century will continue to elude us.

I propose to go further. In observing the content and form of the popular arts in America today, with their international success, it is possible to deduce the social and political needs, sufferings, aspirations and rejections of modern civilization to an astonishing degree. Still further, the writings of the Americans in the middle of the nineteenth century, Poe, Melville, Hawthorne, Whitman, Emerson, in relation to the popular social and artistic movements of today assume a new significance. In the ability of Hawthorne, Poe and Melville to adapt themselves to their society, in the ways they sought escape and reconciliation, it was possible to see anticipations of many developments in the literature and social writing of the Europe of the late nineteenth century. Today, however, in examining the productions aimed at satisfying the artistic needs of the masses, it is possible to say that it is in the study of these and the outbursts of American social and political action in the same period that there can be seen the beginnings of tendencies which have now reappeared with tremendous concrete force both among intellectuals and in the artistic fare of the masses. The literary and social expression of the popular arts in the United States, with all their defects, assume therefore a symbolical significance which raises them far beyond the status they occupied in estimates based on other premises.

That is why I devote substantial space to the lives of the great masses of the people in factories, offices, and department stores, their home lives, and seek a co-relation in this with what is so lightly called the "entertainment industry," but what is in reality one of the most powerful social and psychological manifestations of the American life and character.

Finally, I find the American pattern to be the dominant social pattern of our time and in this conviction I give a fairly detailed treatment of totalitarianism in the world at large and totalitarian tendencies in the United States. Gorer, for example, in his book (and a very serious careful study it is) spends a great deal of precious space on the prevalent fear of homosexuality among men in the United States; on the significance of the woman culture, clubs, etc. Many writers ignore totalitarianism in the United States or simply equate it with monopoly capitalism, finance-capital, etc. In my opinion all this is unpardonably superficial. The great body of American people have a deep and terrible fear of totalitarianism, but by it they do not at all mean the same thing. Wealthy and conservative interests identify this with opposition to communism and a determination to defend private property. Many radicals refer to the "fascist tendencies" of the N.A.M. and periodically watch the progress of Gerald L. K. Smith. The rival politicians make political capital over welfare state, statism, regimentation, individual freedom, etc. There are, however, two aspects which are fundamental to any treatment of totalitarianism in the United States. The first is the astonishment at the rejection by so many powerful social groups abroad of the traditional and specifically American concepts of democracy. There is, on the one hand, the fantastic spectacle of Moscow trials, 99% election victories, the gross impostures, deceptions, cruelties and barbarisms of the totalitarian regimes, and their success. There is a doubt if some retrogression in human affairs is not taking place inseparably connected with the bureaucratization and centralization of social life – and/or perhaps some incurable recession in human nature.

Side by side with this there is an understanding by the American people as a whole of the violent impulses which exist in the society around them. The large majority are hostile to them but know that they exist. This I propose to treat fully. I trace as carefully as I can the forces making for totalitarianism in modern American life. I relate them very carefully to the degradation of human personality under Hitler and under Stalin. I aim at showing that the apparently irrational and stupefying behavior of people in totalitarian states is a product of modern civilization, not merely in terms of the preservation of property and privilege but as the result of deep social and psychological needs of man in modern life. I believe that the close study of the United States will explain most easily to the people of Western Europe why totalitarianism arises, the horrible degradation it represents, its terrible cost to society, the certainty of its overthrow.

Such then is the book I propose to write. I have, however, to give a warning. What is written here is not a rough draft of the book. It is not an outline. It is not an abridgement.

New things will be added. Much of this will be drastically cut.

The whole will be put together in one closely interconnected logical and historical exposition for the average reader, in 75,000 words, not a word more, and written so that it can be read on a Sunday or on two evenings.

The final draft will therefore be quite different from this. I use in this manuscript long quotations, repetitions, digressions, historical and literary references, etc. because for the limited circle before whom I am placing these ideas and this project, it is the most convenient form.

The finished book is something else. For one thing I propose an immense research in the actual lives and opinions of the people so that the ideas which are expressed here in quotations by authorities will emerge in an entirely different form, will emerge as expressions of the lives and activities of the people concerned. Again I shall deal, for example, with Melville on the whole, and not with *Moby Dick* alone. The reader of this manuscript must bear these warnings carefully in mind and look upon what he is reading as an attempt to place before him a body of ideas and a method.

NOTE

In this volume there is made an identification of the regimes of Hitlerism and Stalinism under the common name *totalitarian*. It must be understood that this implies no identity of the regimes. The characterization has been made merely to emphasize the ultimate social consequences of any kind of regime which does not develop along cooperative creative lines, developing the creative spirit of the mass. Politically speaking the differences between Stalinism and Fascism, particularly on a world scale, are of immense, in fact of decisive importance.

Very careful revision will be necessary of the specifically political formulations and it would be very wrong to attribute to them more than a role in the explanation of essentially social phenomena.

1

Individuality 1776–1876

Here I propose to give not an outline but an indication of how I see Chapter 1 at present. It is an account of the development of economic forces, social relations and their specific expression in the United States from 1776 to 1876. These are seen, however, in relation to developments in Europe and in relation to European commentators, in particular de Tocqueville.

The geographical and physical conditions are the immense size and resources of the country. Insofar as it is settled in 1776, it is divided into well-defined regions – New England; the South – where it is possible to produce a sub-tropical agricultural product like cotton; the expansive West. These divisions are fundamental to an understanding of all aspects of American life from 1776 to the present day.

Historically, the country in 1776 is without the political and ideological relations of feudalism and a landed aristocracy which form the concrete milieu of the development of European culture. These conditions, the geographical and the historical, are the conditions within which America develops.

The history of America as a nation falls within certain well-defined periods: 1776–1831; 1831–76; 1876–1914; 1914 to the present day. The first period begins with one of the great events in international political history. It is the Declaration of Independence, the expulsion of the British, the organization of a new state on lines hitherto unknown in the history of the world.

America at the time presents a spectacle of economic and social equality unknown in history. No one is very rich, no one is very poor. Opportunity is open to all. Thus in actual living conditions America is unique. The social conditions embody the *ideal* conditions for bourgeois *individualism*. All individuals start level, the race is to the energetic and the thrifty, the bold. Ideologically, however, the European past hangs over the country. Jefferson is the product of Locke. The great pamphleteer of the revolution is a European, Tom Paine, the embodiment of the revolutionary consciousness of Europe.

It is the peculiar historical development of the United States that allows the *ideals* of eighteenth-century Europe to be expressed in a manner so close (approximately) to reality. The ideas of European individualism thus find their clearest expression concretely in the United States, and very nearly their finest political expression. Chatham expressed his admiration for the declarations, state-papers, etc. of the first American statesmen of independence. And they were indeed miracles of sober, disciplined adjustment of political ideas and economic forces. They do not achieve complete, i.e. abstract purity because (1) government to be effective must represent certain substantial citizens and classes in the country. The organizers of the state and the framers of the Constitution knew this. Hence they earn the hostility of the broad masses of mechanics and farmers who see government as the pure association of the combined individual wills. The principles of authority and democracy face each other. (2) The slave-owners of the South insist that the Declaration of Independence and the Constitution compromise on the slavery question. The regional question inserts itself into the new nation. (It will never be resolved.)

We now take up an essential part of the method of this essay. What is the development in Europe in the corresponding period up to the French Revolution in 1789? In France Quesnay's *Tableau Economique* appeared in 1762. In Great Britain there appeared in 1776 Adam Smith's *Wealth of Nations*. In Germany in 1781 appeared Kant's *Critique of Pure Reason*. In France, also in 1762, appeared Rousseau's *Social Contract*. In the next decade appeared the complete works of Voltaire in 70 volumes. The brilliant European *theory* is counterposed to the American reality.

These are not mere books. Voltaire symbolized the preparation of the French Revolution and the destruction of the privileges of Church and aristocracy in a world which had outgrown feudalism. Rousseau signifies perhaps the most potent political, literary and psychological influence of the century and has never lost his significance. While in opposition to the monarchy and aristocracy with the Encyclopedists, he attacked them in behalf of democracy. He established never again to be ignored the rights of the individual as the individual. Despairing of seeing the individual integrate himself into any society he began the cult of the individual psyche and the escape to Nature or elsewhere, from the weight of society.

Kant altered completely the idea of the analysis of ideas and revolutionized the methods of intellectual speculation. Quesnay sketched the first drafts of the modern science of political economy, and Adam Smith established the science. His *Wealth of Nations* was no mere treatise. It settled accounts with mercantilism and feudalism and constituted a program, method and guide by which the British bourgeoisie, the greatest industrial class then known to history, was to live for over a hundred years.

Why were these developments in such contrast with the United States? It was not lack of a cultural tradition. No public man could be more cultured than Jefferson. Quesnay was a doctor with an interest in political economy. Franklin as an amateur showed exceptional abilities in various scientific directions. *The central reason is the absence of sharp social differentiation and conflict.*

America reaches its greatest creative height in the conflict with Great Britain. But the British are an alien force. Driven out of the country they leave no roots. But the great European landmarks in theoretical analysis and statement are the result of clearly defined conflicts, of classes, and aspirations for national leadership. Adam Smith speaks for the British industrial bourgeoisie against the solidly established mercantilists and their aristocratic and monarchical allies, who dominate the state, the economy and financial system. Quesnay and the Encyclopedists represent similar forces in France. Rousseau signifies the coming of age of a new section of society, the intelligentsia, the exponents of economic, social and political ideas, of educational theories and psychological analysis, of literary and artistic criticism. It is a social grouping without actual power, but it has more directly expressed the social conditions of expanding ages than any other class in history. Kant is the first in the desperate attempt of the German middle class to find some way of raising backward Germany to the level of the surrounding countries. And each school of thought, pursuing its special interests, lifts itself above them and charts new roads which surrounding nations recognize as new stages in the universal movement.

We have to see the interrelations between the European and the American development. Between 1783 and 1835 America shows the ideal conditions for which Europe struggled so hard; in the struggle producing some of its most remarkable contributions to social thought. America took an entirely different development. Its development was in industry and agriculture; in extending the frontier, in the practice of democracy and the creation of the free individual. Most of this is familiar and does not need repetition here. There are, however, certain aspects which must be brought sharply into focus. I shall use a few quotations as the most convenient means of expressing them. They express what is loosely called the American Spirit, and it must be defined before it can be analyzed and its place in the contemporary development established. Bear in mind the famous European discoverers, Columbus, Vasco da Gama, the Spanish Conquistadors, the Elizabethan voyagers, small groups of men who represent the carefully selected representatives of the nation and achieve world-famous feats with the eyes of the nation upon them. The American experience is entirely different. Listen to Burke, pleading the cause of the Americans before the British Parliament:

And pray Sir what in the world is equal to it? Pass by the other parts, and look at the manner in which the people of New England have of late carried on the whale fishery. Whilst we follow them among the tumbling mountains of ice, and behold them penetrating into the deepest frozen recesses of Hudson's Bay and Davis' Straits, whilst we are looking for them beneath the artic circle we hear that they have pierced into the opposite region of polar cold, that they are at the antipodee, and engaged under the frozen serpent of the South. Falkland Island, which seemed too remote and romantic an object for the grasp of national ambition, is but a stage and resting-place in the progress of their victorious industry. Nor is the equinoctial heat more discouraging to them than the accumulated winters of both the poles. We know that whilst some of them draw the line and strike the harpoon on the coast of Africa, others run the longitude and pursue their gigantic game along the coast of Brazil. No sea but what is vexed by their fisheries. No climate that is not witness to their toils. Neither the perseverence of Holland, nor the activity of France, nor the dexterous and firm sagacity of English enterprise, ever carried out this most perilous mode of hardy industry to the extent to which it has been pushed by this recent people; a people who are still, as it were, but in the gristle, and not yet hardened into the bone of manhood. When I contemplate these things; when I know that the colonies in general owe little or nothing to any care of ours, and that they are not squeezed into this happy form by the constraints of watchful and suspicious government, but that, through a wise and salutary neglect, a generous nature has been suffered to take her own way to perfection; when I reflect upon these effects, when I see how profitable they have been to us, I feel all the pride of power sink, and all the presumption in the wisdom of human contrivances melt and die away within me. My rigour relents. I pardon something to the spirit of liberty.

These men are for the most part nameless, unknown; like the hunters and trappers and farmers who boldly extend the frontiers of the country into unknown forests. They pursue these astonishing adventures in pursuit of goods to sell.

Let me add that I do not choose wholly to break the American spirit; because it is the spirit that has made the country.

De Tocqueville visited the United States in the early 1830s. He describes also the seafaring industry, over half a century after Burke.

The following comparison will illustrate my meaning. During the campaign of the Revolution, the French introduced a new system of tactics into the art of war, which perplexed the oldest generals and very nearly destroyed the most ancient monarchies of Europe. They first undertook to make shift without a number of things that had always been held to be indispensable in warfare; they required novel exertions of their troops which no civilized nations had ever thought of; they achieved great actions in an incredibly short time and risked human life without hesitation to obtain the object in view. The French had less money and fewer men than their enemies; their resources were infinitely inferior; nevertheless, they were constantly victorious until their adversaries chose to imitate their example.

The Americans have introduced a similar system into commerce; they do for cheapness what the French did for conquest. The European sailor navigates with prudence; he sets sail only when the weather is favorable; if an unforeseen accident befalls him, he puts into port; at night he furls a portion of his canvas; and when the whitening billows intimate the vicinity of land, he checks his course and takes an observation of the sun. The American neglects these precautions and braves these dangers. He weighs anchor before the tempest is over; by night and by day he spreads his sails to the wind; such damage as his vessel may have sustained from the storm, he repairs as he goes along; and when he at last approaches the end of his voyage, he darts onward to the shore as if he already descried a port. The Americans are often shipwrecked, but no trader crosses the seas so rapidly. And as they perform the same distance in a shorter time, they can perform it at a cheaper rate.

The European navigator touches at different ports in the course of a long voyage; he loses precious time in making the harbor or in waiting for a favorable wind to leave it; and he pays daily dues to be allowed to remain there. The American starts from Boston to purchase tea in China; he arrives at Canton, stays there for a few days and then returns. In less than two years he has sailed as far as the entire circumference of the globe and has seen land but once. It is true that during a voyage of eight or ten months he has drunk brackish water and lived on salt meat; that he has been in a continual contest with the sea, with disease, and with weariness; but upon his return he can sell a pound of his tea for a halfpenny less than the English merchant, and his purpose is accomplished.

I cannot explain my meaning better than by saying that the Americans show a sort of heroism in their manner of trading. The European merchant will always find it difficult to imitate his American competitor, who, in adopting the system that I have just described, does not follow calculation but an impulse of his nature.

There is nothing like this in European history for the centuries before, far less in 1776–1835. Freedom, initiative, adventure, self-expression, in pursuit of trade and industry. The foundations of the American character are being solidified. The original stocks are bold, adventurous, hardy to make the journey at all. The historical and geographical circumstances form an environment which develops these qualities to the full. De Tocqueville continues:

The inhabitants of the United States experience all the wants and all the desires that result from an advanced civilization; and as they are not surrounded, as in Europe, by a community skillfully organized to satisfy them, they are often obliged to procure for themselves the various articles that education and habit have rendered necessaries. In America it sometimes happens that the same person tills his field, builds his dwelling, fashions his tools, makes his shoes, and weaves the coarse stuff of which his clothes are composed. This is prejudicial to the excellence of the work, but it powerfully contributes to awaken the intelligence of the workman. Nothing tends to materialize man and to deprive his work of the faintest trace of mind more than the extreme division of labor. In a country like America, where men devoted to special occupations are rare, a long apprenticeship cannot be required from anyone who embraces a profession. The Americans therefore change their means of gaining a livelihood very readily and they suit their occupations to the exigencies of the moment. Men are to be met with who have successively been lawyers, farmers, merchants, ministers of the Gospel and physicians. If the American is less perfect in each craft than the European, at least there is scarcely any trade with which he is utterly unacquainted. His capacity is more general, and the circle of his intelligence is greater.

The inhabitants of the United States are never fettered by the axioms of their profession; they escape from all the prejudices of their present station; they are not more attached to one line of operation than to another; they are not more prone to employ an old method than a new one; they have no rooted habits, and they easily shake off the influence that the habits of other nations might exercise upon them, from a conviction that their country is unlike any other and that its situation is without a precedent in the world. America is a land of wonders, in which everything is in constant motion and every change seems an improvement. The idea of novelty is there indissolubly connected with the idea of amelioration. No natural boundary seems to be set to the effort of man; and in his eyes what is not yet done is only what he has not yet attempted to do.

This perpetual change which goes on in the United States, these frequent vicissitudes of fortune, these unforeseen fluctuations in private and public wealth, serve to keep the minds of the people in a perpetual feverish agitation, which admirably invigorates their exertions and keeps them, so to speak, above the ordinary level of humanity. The whole life of an American is passed like a game of chance, a revolutionary crisis, or a battle. As the same causes are continually in operation throughout the country, they ultimately impart an irresistible impulse to the national character. The American, taken as a chance specimen of his countrymen, must then be a man of singular warmth in his desires, enterprising, fond of adventure, above all, of novelty. The same bent is manifest in all that he does; he introduces it into his political laws, his religious doctrines; his theories of social economy and his domestic preoccupations; he bears it with him in the depths of the backwoods as well as in the business of the city.

The highest political expression of these qualities is not in any theory. It is in the movement known as Jacksonian democracy. To see this movement in its fullest significance, we must watch Europe of the period.

After the effort of the French Revolution, Europe sinks back into the long struggle against Napoleon. From 1815 to 1828 when Jackson becomes president, the reaction of the Holy Alliance reigns. The total result is an outpouring of such literary and philosophical genius as Europe was never to see again. It is necessary only to list them. Disappointed in the failure of the French Revolution to initiate democracy, European writers discovered the Middle Ages (practically unknown to Voltaire, Rousseau and the Encyclopedists in general), Keats, Shelley, Wordsworth, Byron, Coleridge, gave to poetry new content and new forms in the British Romantic Movement. Chateaubriand in France, in revulsion against the prosaic results of the revolution, did the same for prose and came to America to celebrate the Nature and the noble savage of Rousseau. When Napoleon had finally fallen the achievements came thick and fast. In and around 1819 came Beethoven's Ninth Symphony, Ricardo's *Principles of Political Economy*, Shelley's Prometheus, the Logic of Hegel, crown of the German classical philosophy, and Savigny's famous thesis that law was part of a national growth and could not be constructed from logical and a priori principles. In France Fourier and Saint-Simon, in Britain Robert Owen propounded ideas of a new organization of society. All these had been expressed by 1820 and from them were to be developed the theoretical expression of European life for the next three-quarters of a century.

There is nothing of the kind in the United States. Instead there is the turbulent disorderly movement which culminates in Jackson's victory. It wipes away all political privileges in state after state, establishing manhood suffrage. It reorganizes elections to the presidency in its own favor as it conceives it; it takes the political party out of the hands of the aristocratic leaders and gentlemen who traditionally led these organizations and sought to make them responsive to the popular masses. The working men, artisans and frontier farmers carried out to the best of their ability the democracy that was inherent in the uninhibited individualism that was the ideal in 1776 but from which the Founding Fathers fell short. Their misadventures with the Banks etc. do not concern us. What does concern us is this. In contrast with the tremendous intellectual speculations and achievements of Europe, we have in the United States a rough, untutored empirical achievement in actuality of the most advanced speculations of the Old World. Shelley, philosophical anarchist, was so embittered with the Europe he knew that he hailed America as the hope of the future. It is doubtful, however, if he understood that the real achievement was what both Burke and de Tocqueville described – the freedom, the energy, the heroic quality of the individual pursuing his daily vocation.

A later writer, Turner, believes that this was purely the product of the frontier – the expanding West. This is incorrect. It could be found in the seafaring trade; and it could be found in the capitalism of the small masters and lack of restriction which flourished in the seaboard states. Every line of Benjamin Franklin's writings and his whole career show this There is no need here to show the inevitable limitations of a competitive society. These *limitations* were not the outstanding feature of the early United States. Listen to words by Daniel Webster, the acknowledged representative of industry and property:

I have said, gentlemen, that our inheritance is an inheritance of American liberty. That liberty is characteristic, peculiar and altogether our own. Nothing like it existed in former times, nor was known in the most enlightened states of antiquity; while with us its principles have become interwoven into the minds of individual men, connected with our daily opinions, and our daily habits, until it is, if I may so say, an element of social as well as of political life; and the consequence is, that to whatever region an American citizen carries himself, he takes with him, fully developed in his own understanding and experience, our American principles and opinions, and become [sic] ready at once, in cooperation with others, to apply them to the formation of new governments.

What has Germany done, learned Germany, more full of ancient lore than all the world besides? What has Italy done? What have they done who dwell on the spot where Cicero lived? They have not the power of self-government which a common town meeting, with us, possesses. . . . Yes, I say, that those persons who have gone from our town meetings to dig gold in California are more fit to make a republican government than any body of men in Germany or Italy. . . .

Again he says:

We have a great, popular, constitutional government, guarded by law and by judicature, and defended by the affections of the whole people. No monarchical throne presses these States together, no iron chain of military power encircles them; they live and stand under a government popular in its form, representative in its character, founded upon principles of equity, and so constructed, we hope, as to last forever. In all its history it has been beneficent; it has trodden down no man's liberty; it has crushed no State. Its daily respiration is liberty and patriotism; its yet youthful veins are full of enterprise, courage and honorable love of glory and renown. Large before, the country has now, by recent events, become vastly larger. This Republic now extends, with a vast breadth, across the whole continent. The two great seas of the world wash the one and the other shore.

Webster believed that 5/6 of the property in the North was owned by the laboring people, workers and farmers. I give these quotations to show how genuinely and sincerely America believed in its principles, however it might fail in practice. Also essay though the finished work will be, I propose to put it together with material of this type, to show the actual growth from stage to stage. Webster shows what Americans thought. It received its highest, most complete, most finished expression in Lincoln after 1861.

But a dozen years before that the whole ideal had been challenged. The challenge was literary and political. Today, and in fact long before today, it has become perfectly clear that Poe, Melville, and Wendell Phillips saw far more deeply than Webster and Lincoln into the America of 1840–60.

The regional division of the United States is now far more powerful an opposition to the general development than in 1775. Its dominant economic structure is not the free individual, expressing himself fully in industry or in adventure on the seas seeking trade. Since cotton has become an important element of world production, the dominant economic pattern is that of aristocratic plantation-owner and Negro slave. The South fights the universal suffrage. In 1831 Calhoun threatened nullification, i.e. to disrupt the union, and Jackson had to threaten him with suppression by force.

De Tocqueville, the most remarkable social analyst, native or foreign, to examine personally the United States in the first century of its existence, saw the country in 1831. His observations of fundamental importance are three:

1 The individual thought primarily of himself as a unit, being unconnected with definitive social stratification as in Europe. De Tocqueville's expression here is very sharp and should be borne in mind; he says the individual thinks only of a very "puny" thing – himself. That is where he starts – in a democracy.

2 This individual, however, showed an altogether exceptional capacity for free association, in industry, in politics and for any other purpose. Individuality and universality achieve a fusion unknown elsewhere.

3 Another observation of de Tocqueville's was the domination of the rule of the majority, the advantages and dangers of which he described in detail and at length. What de Tocqueville thought was a general situation, however, was a special one. De Tocqueville believed that it was this domination which resulted in the ostracism of minorities, and the total lack of any free discussion in the United States. In no country, he says emphatically, is there such lack of free and independent discussion. (We shall come to this again.)

The reason for this was the fact that the basic regional division in the United States had now reached the stage where war to the death faced the country. The conflict over whether Missouri would be a slave state or free state had ended in the Compromise of 1820 but both sides had seen the danger. Cotton was the basic industry. On it depended the existence of the South, the trade of New York, the cotton industry of New England, and an increasing trade with the rapidly developing Northwest. By common consent all agreed to a conspiracy of silence on this subject. Thus, side by side, with the democracy of Jackson, developed this blight upon the free play of economic and political ideas. Thus the suppression of free discussion was not *primarily* a consequence of the rule of the majority in a democracy in general, but a special result of the social conflict based upon the regional division. Beginning therefore in 1776, this conflict by 1831 had already poisoned the democracy. The history of America not only up to 1876, but to the present day is impossible to grasp unless this division is firmly borne in mind and traced in all its complex but consistent development. The masses of artisans, mechanics and farmers who had leapt forward two generations in advance of their age were indifferent to slavery or jealous of the free Negro and the potential competition of millions of emancipated slaves. They therefore accepted the compromise.

In one part of the United States, New England, the stratification of society assumed a form comparable to that of Europe. There to the practice of the old democracy was added a wealthier class of men who had made money in shipping (the fishing business had been almost entirely theirs); and were now engaged in cotton manufacture. Labor in the cotton mills was becoming a distinct class and in the small states the independent farmer still continued to work his small farm. This social structure produced a layer of intellectuals, similar to that same social grouping in Europe with a long tradition of interest in letters and scholarship. Placed in a similar situation to their corresponding elements in Europe, they gave to the United States its first important literary political movement, characteristic of the special condition of the country. They expressed the peculiar problems of the United States at the time both as a nation and in its regional divisions. It was impossible to appreciate their work until the last twenty years. It is a body of work full of failures, and with one single exception, not one major masterpiece. Yet on the whole *as a totality*, it now begins to emerge as the most *significant* body of national literature of the XIXth century. Neither the British Romantics, the French Romantics, the Symbolists of the great Russian novels have so much relevance. But the literature must be taken as a whole, the writers and the political figures, such as Garrison and Wendell Phillips.

2

The American Intellectuals of the Nineteenth Century

What I am proposing to do here is to pose in arbitrary outline a certain conception of the intellectuals of 1840–76, the period of the Civil War. I do not propose a complete formal treatment here. I shall take: (1) Walt Whitman; (2) *Moby Dick* by Herman Melville; (3) the Abolitionist intellectuals. Again, to repeat, for the purpose of this outline, I shall make only the necessary connections of Emerson, Poe and Hawthorne with my main thesis which is as follows:

Because of the peculiarly free conditions of democracy in the United States, the American intellectuals as a social group were the first to face as a practical question the beginnings of a problem which has been fully recognized during the last twenty years – the relation of individualism to democracy as a whole; while in Europe the question was narrowed and at the same time concretized by all sorts of special conditions. Thus Dostoyevsky, Flaubert, Rimbaud had very precise problems to deal with and the universality of their work emerges from the concreteness of the conditions. Problems were posed for the American intellectuals in a very different way – hence the vagueness and the uncertainty of their work, its inability to achieve significant form or, where it did, as in Hawthorne, the narrowness and limitations it showed. But now as society faces its fundamental problems, the work of these writers and the Abolitionist politicians assumes a new significance. Carefully read they mean more to the twentieth century than, for example, the great French literature of the late nineteenth and early twentieth centuries. Their only rival is the Russian literature of the nineteenth century, and while it serves no purpose to make invidious comparisons, this much can be said, World War I made the writings of the Russians familiar to the general modern reader. World War II already seems to have lifted the American literature of the middle of the nineteenth century to a new level.

It is necessary to be precise in what is involved here. *Madame Bovary* is a great masterpiece. It was written by Flaubert as a protest against what he considered the evil consequences of certain aspects of Romanticism. But the great French novelist set Madame Bovary so firmly within the environment which produced her, and saw both sides of the problem so clearly that modern readers (and film directors) see her today as a woman more sinned against than sinning, and this without doing any violence to the novel as written; in fact, Baudelaire, the enemy of the social values of his day, saw the novel in this way from the very beginning. Classics in that sense in which European literature is so profuse are very few in American writing. Precisely what the American writers and intellectuals have to give will now be indicated.

(The quotations, the circumstances of this outline, the newness of what I have to say will make these particular notes lengthy. They will be much briefer, more concentrated in a book.)

WALT WHITMAN

Whitman is the most comprehensive of the American intellectuals of this period, one of the most unusual figures in the realm of literature and an American who is the opposite pole to Melville. Until the end of World War I he was a larger figure in literature, both at home and still more abroad. Like Melville he embodies American and international characteristics. Like Melville what he represents, what he expressed is clearer than ever today. But whereas Melville grows from year to year, Whitman shrinks. This poet with the reputation of having devoted his life and his work to the struggle for American and world democracy may yet end by being excoriated by the popular masses everywhere if they take any notice of him at all. He is, on the surface, an enigmatic figure. There is no enigma about him really. Here is a case where we have to ignore all the things Whitman said about himself and depend entirely upon the literature as literature. We shall have to watch *that* and by watching *that*, we shall be able to reconstruct the real Whitman.

As an artist Whitman is first, last and nothing else but a lyric poet, self-centered, individualistic, in the tradition of the great individualistic Romantic writers and poets, from Rousseau through Wordsworth, Keats and Shelley, to Lamartine, DeVigny and Debusset. And all this shouting, and real hoarse-voiced shouting it is, about democracy is only because of this.

European Romantic individualism everywhere was expressed as a revolt against the domination of industrial civilization. Industrial civilization created the need for individualism, *free* enterprise and *free* institutions, but at the same time created horrible conditions for the great masses of men, and subjected sensitive intellectuals to such wealth and power above and such misery below that they declared their own soul's sufferings, defiance, solace, to be the only reality worth cultivating. That was Rousseau, Keats, Shelley, Byron, and in various ways the succeeding generations of poets.

Whitman was the same. This must be firmly grasped, it must never be let go or he will be terribly misunderstood, and his real significance for us completely lost. But this individualistic Romantic was an American, and he could find *neither feudalism nor oppressive capital nor any striking combination of both to revolt against.* Furthermore, America in 1850 was traditionally and actually a land of equality and heroic individual achievement. Whitman accepted it. Individualism, Romanticism *in the United States.* That is Whitman.

Now for his poems. His most perfect poem, i.e., the one in which he is master of all his powers and his inspiration is *Out of the Cradle Endlessly Rocking.* I shall not quote from this but it is a purely romantic poem – his own personal loss of a dear friend, set in the memory of an incident of childhood where a bird lost its mate. The apotheosis is a glorification of death. No European poet has surpassed it. In fact, in one important sphere, style, he breaks new ground.

This is the kind of poem Whitman was always master of. It is not a literary fact. It is a social fact. *Undoubtedly the greatest of American poets, he had nothing more to say really than the retreat from society to the individual experience which has distinguished European poetry for one hundred and fifty years.*

We must have some more examples of this. Here is his *Once I Pass'd Through a Populous City:*

Once I pass'd through a populous city, imprinting my brain, for
     future use, with its shows, architecture, customs, and traditions;
Yet now of all that city, I remember only a woman I casually met
     there, who detained me for love of me;
Day by day and night by night we were together, – All else has long
     been forgotten by me;
I remember, I say, only that woman who passionately clung to
     me;
Again we wander – we love – we separate again;
Again she holds me by the hand – I must not go;
I see her close beside me, with silent lips, sad and tremulous.

That was in 1860. Hear him again in 1870 in *On the Beach at Night.*

1

On the beach, at night,
Stands a child, with her father,
Watching the east, the autumn sky.

Up through the darkness,

While ravening clouds, the burial clouds, in black masses spreading,
Lower, sullen and fast, athwart and down the sky,
Amid a transparent clear belt of ether yet left in the east,
Ascends large and calm the lord-star Jupiter;
And nigh at hand, only a very little above,
Swim the delicate brothers, the Pleiades.

2

From the beach, the child, holding the hand of her father,
Those burial-clouds that lower, victorious, soon to devour all,
Watching, silently weeps.

Weep not, child,
Weep not, my darling,
With these kisses let me remove your tears;
The ravening clouds shall not long be victorious,
They shall not long possess the sky – they devour the stars only
    in apparition,
Jupiter shall emerge – be patient, watch again another night –
    the Pleiades shall emerge,
They are immortal – all these stars, both silvery and golden,
    shall shine out again,
The great stars and the little ones shall shine out again – they
    endure;
The vast immortal suns, and the long-enduring pensive moons,
    shall again shine.

3

Then, dearest child, mournest thou only for Jupiter?
Considerest thou alone the burial of the stars?

Something there is,
(With my lips soothing thee, adding, I whisper,
I give thee the first suggestion, the problem and indirection,)
Something there is more immortal even than the stars,
(Many the burials, many the days and nights, passing away,)
Something that shall endure longer even than lustrous Jupiter,
Longer than sun, or any revolving satellite,
Or the radiant brothers, the Pleiades.

Note the superb first stanza in particular. The end has a trace of Longfellow and Pollyanna, which by this time it was difficult for Whitman to escape. But the mood and the particular romantic power are there, the romanticism of Arnold's *Dover Beach*. He can be bitter as only the Romantic can be bitter.

I sit and look out upon all the sorrows of the world, and upon
      all oppression and shame;
I hear secret convulsive sobs from young men, at anguish with
      themselves, remorseful after deeds done;
I see, in low life, the mother misused by her children, dying,
      neglected, gaunt, desperate;
I see the wife misused by her husband – I see the treacherous
      seducer of young women;
I mark the ranklings of jealousy and unrequited love, attempted
      to be hid, I see these sights on the earth;
I see the workings of battle, pestilence, tyranny – I see martyrs
      and prisoners;
I observe a famine at sea – I observe the sailors casting lots who
      shall be kill'd, to preserve the lives of the rest;
I observe the slights and degradations cast by arrogant persons
      upon laborers, the poor, and upon Negroes, and the like;
All these – all the meanness and agony without end, I sitting,
      look out upon,
See, hear, and am silent.

At the very end of his creative period he writes *Prayer of Columbus,* in which he speaks of *himself, his* work, *his* hopes, *his* resignation.

All my emprises have been fill'd with Thee,
My speculations, plans, begun and carried on in thoughts of Thee,
Sailing the deep, or journeying the land for Thee;
Intentions, purports, aspirations mine – leaving results to Thee.

Oh I am sure they really come from Thee:
The urge, the ardor, the unconquerable will,
The potent, felt, interior command, stronger than words,
A message from the Heavens, whispering to me even in sleep,
These sped me on.

And later:

Is it the prophet's thought I speak, or am I raving?
What do I know of life? what of myself?
I know not even my own work, past or present;

Dim, ever-shifting guesses of it spread before me,
Of newer, better worlds, their mighty parturition,
Mocking, perplexing me.

But take another masterpiece, *Crossing Brooklyn Ferry*, one of the greatest poems of the nineteenth century. The duality in Whitman which lifted him to his highest (and ultimately ruined him as a poet) is here at its best. There is a marvelous fusion of nature, people, present and future generations, and *himself*. But *himself* is not a part of it. *He wants to be, terribly wants to be*, and here this American separates himself from his European counterparts. He, and this is a fundamental part of the modern American character, product of the whole country, is an isolated individual. But he craves *free association* with his fellows. The old heroic individualist *activity* was going and Whitman, the intellectual, passionately wanted to be one with his fellow-men. I have emphasized a few words in some stanzas from this wonderful poem to show precisely the proof of this terrible sense of separatism and the need to fill the gap which so characterizes Whitman and his countrymen.

Others will enter the gates of the ferry and cross from shore to
      shore,
Others will watch the run of the flood-tide;
Others will see the shipping of Manhattan north and west, and
      the heights of Brooklyn to the south and east;
Others will see the islands large and small;
Fifty years hence, others will see them as they cross, the sun
      half an hour high;
A hundred years hence, or ever so many hundreds years hence,
      others will see them;
Will enjoy the sunset, the pouring-in of the flood-tide, the
      falling back to the sea of the ebb-tide.

It avails not, neither time or place – distance avails not;
I am with you, you men and women of a generation, or ever so
      many generations hence;
I project myself – also I return – I am with you, and know how it is.
Just as you feel when you look on the river and sky, so *I* felt;
Just as any of you is one of the living crowd, *I* was one of a crowd;
Just as you are refresh'd by the gladness of the river and the
      bright flow, *I* was refresh'd;
Just as you stand and lean on the rail, yet hurry with the swift
      current, *I* stood yet was hurried;
Just as you look on the numberless masts of ships, and the thick-
      stem'd pipes of steamboats, *I look'd.*

I too many and many a time cross'd the river, the sun half an
    hour high;
I watched the Twelfth-month gulls,*I saw them* high in the
    air, floating with motionless wings, oscillating their bodies,
I saw how the glistening yellow lit up parts of their bodies, and
    left the rest in strong shadow,
I saw the slow-wheeling circles and the gradual edging toward
    the south.

Whitman there managed the fusion. Again, when he came into contact
with life at some point where he felt himself at one with his fellows, his
personal lyricism, although still intensely personal, assumes concreteness
and a genuinely national note. Hence the complete success of his poems on
Lincoln, particularly *When Lilacs Last in the Door-Yard Bloom'd*. Similarly
there are some very fine poems in *Drum-Taps* when he writes of the Civil
War.

That is one part, so to speak, of Whitman's work, the lyrics and the form.
The other, is, as poetry valueless, but extraordinarily significant as a portrait
of the United States between 1850 and 1914; and with a very special
development of them between 1937, the date of Roosevelt's quarantine
speech, and today.

What are these ideas? Whitman tried to prove that, contrary to Europe,
in America all men were equal, that all men were knitted together by a
common bond of Democracy with a capital D, that not only all men in
America were equal, but all men all over the world were really equal, and in
time, one generation, fifty generations (it did not matter) would all be really
equal with the equality of equal Americans; he was for revolutions in Europe
which would make Europeans able to be equal as Americans were equal. He
developed special poetical methods of his own to overcome the potent fact
that men were not equal, and as time went on, he adopted every shibboleth
of the time to maintain, in his verse his fantastic thesis. Americans *"en-masse"*
did not read, and would not read Whitman. It was not that he was too deep
– he was too shallow. They believed this more or less and would accept it
from public orators, public-minded parsons, newspaper editorials, com-
mencement orators and the like. When it was presented as poetry, they would
have nothing of it.

Let us take two poems, *Carol of Occupations*, and another more famous
one *Salut au Monde* and with the latter link, in this connection, *Song of the
Broad-Axe*. In *Carol of Occupations* occurs a typical Whitman passage,
ridiculous as poetry but not to be ignored. Here is one line.

The ankle-chain of the slave, the bed of the bed-house, the cards of the gambler, the plates of the forger,

Two lines later:

What is learnt in the public school, spelling, reading, writing,
 ciphering, the black-board, the teacher's diagrams,

A dozen lines more of the same. Then:

Manufactures, commerce, engineering, the building of cities, every
 trade carried on there, and the implements of every trade,

Skip a dozen lines, we are still at it:

Every-day objects, house-chairs, carpets, bed, counter-pane of the bed,
 him or her sleeping at night, wind blowing, indefinite noises,

Skip a dozen lines. Still at it:

The etui of surgical instruments, the etui of oculist's or aurist's
 instruments, or dentist's instruments,

Skip again:

Iron-works, forge-fires in the mountains, or by river-banks, men around
 feeling the melt with huge crowbars – lumps of ore, the due
 combining of ore, limestone, coal, – the blast furnace and the
 pudding-furnace, the loup-lump at the bottom of the melt at
 last – the rolling-mill, the stumpy bars of pig-iron, the strong
 clean-shaped T-rail for railroads,

Twenty lines later:

The area of pens of live pork, the killing-hammer, the hog-hock, the
 scalder's tub, gutting, the cutter's cleaver, the packer's
 maul, and the plenteous winter-work of pork-packing, . . .

It is funny at first, then irritating, and then the full significance breaks in
on you, as you remember scores of such passages enumerating things; and
enumerating people. Here is a man desperately striving to make contact with
his fellow-men at their daily work and play. He mentions hundreds of them,
trying to show that he knows what they do, that whether they are thieves,
prostitutes, Negroes, bakers, cooks, workers, he is one with them. But one

who is one with everybody is one with nobody. Whitman is alone, he has no sense of belonging to any section of society, no class to which he belongs, no class which he is against. His catalogues and shouting are a tale told by an idiot full of sound and fury. But it does not signify nothing. Whitman showed the American individualistic passion and the craving to mingle with all *his* fellow-men, the American dream which had been a reasonable reality and which was going to become a universal reality. The greatness of the effort and the poverty of the result show equally the greatness of the need and the impossibility of its realization in the America Whitman knew. The greatest of American poets, he wrecked himself trying to achieve the impossible. That still remains the basic social need of the great majority of the American people.

And because Whitman knew his own isolation, the new isolation *of the intellectual,* and he had been a professional journalist, he sought ceaselessly in his verse to bridge the gap. He ran away to the whole world.

Look at a page of *Salut au Monde.* You will see Arab, Mexican, Cossack, Thames. . . . Look at the next page, Rocky Mountains, Pyrenees, Mount Hecla, Anabmacs, Madagascar; the next page has one hundred names, the next page another hundred, and so it goes. In between are sometimes fine passages, but with the whole world for the workingman, he struggles desperately to make some contact, a contact that eludes him.

There is a logic to such colossal efforts to achieve the unachievable. Whitman, baffled, but no rebel at heart, discovered Science and Industry (both with capital letters) as the means whereby his precious individuality would be attained. In his *Song of the Exposition* he writes:

Mightier than Egypt's tombs,
Fairer than Grecia's, Roma's temples,
Prouder than Milan's statued, spired Cathedral,
More picturesque than Rhonist castle-keeps,
We plan, even now, to raise, beyond them all,
Thy great cathedral, sacred Industry – no tomb
A keep for life for practical Invention.

Here are other stanzas:

Materials here, under your eye, shall change their shape, as if by
      magic;
The cotton shall be pick'd almost in the very field;
Shall be dried, clean'd, ginn'd, baled, spun into thread and
      cloth before you;
You shall see hands at work at all the old processes and all the
      new ones;

You shall see the various grains, and how flour is made and then
    bread baked by the bakers;
You shall see the crude ores of California and Nevada passing on
    and on until they become bullion;
You shall watch how the printer sets type, and learn what a composing
    stick is;
You shall mark, in amazement, the Hoe press whirling its cylinders,
    shedding the printed leaves steady and fast;
The photograph, model, watch, pin, nail, shall be created before
    you.

In large, calm halls, a stately Museum shall teach you the infinite,
    solemn lessons of Minerals;
In another, woods, plants, Vegetation shall be illustrated – in
    another Animals, animal life and development.

One stately house shall be the music house;
Others for other arts – Learning, the Sciences, shall all
    be here;
None shall be slighted – none but shall here be honor'd, help'd,
    exampled.

This, this, and these, America, shall be *your* Pyramids and Obelisks,
Your Alexandrian Pharos, gardens of Babylon,
Your temple at Olympia.

The male and female many laboring not,
Shall ever here confront the laboring many,
With precious benefits to both – glory to all,
To thee, America, – and thee, Eternal Muse.

    A captain of industry, a financier set out to make money, to create industry for profit. He never claimed to be making a nation of great individuals, or if he did, he was not serious about that. The politicians between 1865 and 1892, when Whitman died, are not remembered today by anybody; they contributed nothing to individualism, free or unfree. Yet this writing of Whitman's was exactly what a skillful publicist on their behalf would have written, visionary *ideals* of individual freedom and concrete subordination to the *reality* of the prevailing regime.
    Another of Whitman's revolutionary discoveries was sex, or as he called it, animality. But today Whitman's revolutionary attitude to sex is a damp squib. It is no use saying it was revolutionary *in its day*. Melville's homosexual episode between Ishmael and Queequeg is as fresh and far more significant

today than the day it was written. And it is because Melville was not exploiting individuality. He was describing fundamentally what he had observed among many men.

Whitman preached the equality of women. To the end of his days he believed that he had made the workingman and the working woman the center of his literary innovation.

What is the actuality? Science, industrial development, the recognition of sex, of the body beautiful, equality for women, the equality of the working-man, all led by Democracy with a capital D. What are these but the ideals by which "progressive" America lived during the period that Mark Twain called "The Gilded Age."

What is the reality? People view with terror the development of Science. As we shall see in succeeding chapters the growth of the Cathedral of Industry has resulted in problems undreamt of by Whitman. The social ideas of other poets become outmoded and unimportant. His have never sunk into oblivion. They have remained. But they have remained in a manner which shows us how much and how little Whitman represented. Today in the "cold war" the picture of America which is being presented to the world by the rulers of America is Whitman's picture. Free individuals, free enterprise, science, industry, Democracy – that is the Voice of America and this at a time when every thinking mind in America is pondering over the outcome of precisely what these terms signify for American and human civilization. The very attempt to represent these as ideals for the whole world is no more than an extension of Whitman's *Salut au Monde* and *Passage to India*. His "body beautiful" and "body electric" and "seminal wetness" are the reservoir from which advertisers of foods, toothpaste, vitamins, deodorants draw an unending source of inspirations by which to cheat and corrupt the American people.

As Cyril Connolly, the English critic, reports in his magazine *Horizon*, he found where one would least expect it, among the rulers of America, serious probing into the realities behind these slogans and doubts of their validity. They are all there in Whitman. He couldn't write poetry about them. Nobody could. But he set them down.

And individuality? It has disappeared. That is the history of America since Whitman. The disappearance of the individuality he celebrated and the need for it, greater than ever.

Now this attitude of Whitman's was not mere Philistinism. It was an *evasion* as is proved first and foremost by nothing else than the miserable poetic character of his work in this sphere. It was an evasion because Whitman knew the political world of his day. A few years before *Leaves of Grass* appeared in 1855, he had written in a pamphlet unpublished until 1928, the following appreciation of politics, and he was, we remember, a practicing journalist:

Whence then do these nominating dictators of America year after year start out? From lawyers' offices, secret lodges, backyards, bed-houses, and bar-rooms; from out of the custom-house, marshals' offices, post-offices, and gamblinghalls; From the President's house, the jail, the venereal hospital, the station-house; from un-named by-places where devilish disunion is hatched at midnight; from political hearses, and from the coffins inside, and from the shrouds inside the coffins; from the tumors and abscesses of the land; from the skeletons and skulls in the vaults of the federal almshouses; from the running sores of the great cities; thence to the national, state, city and district nominating conventions of these States, come the most numerous and controlling delegates.

Who are they personally? Office-holders, office-seekers, robbers, pimps, exclu-sives, malignants, conspirators, murderers, fancy-men, port-masters, custom-house clerks, contractors, kept-editors, Spaniels well-trained to carry and fetch, jobbers, infidels, disunionists, terrorists, mail-riflers, slave-catchers, pushers of Slavery, creatures of the President, creatures of would-be Presidents, spies, blowers, elec-tioneers, body-snatchers, bawlers, bribers, compromisers, runaways, lobbyers, sponges, ruined sports, expelled gamblers, policy backers, monte-dealers, duelists, carriers of concealed weapons, blind men, deaf men, pimpled men, scarred inside with the vile disorder, gaudy outside with god chains made from the people's money and harlot's money twisted together; crawling, serpentine men, the lonely combings and born freedom sellers of the earth.

Stript of padding and paint, who are Buchanan and Fillmore? What has this age to do with them? Two galvanized old men, close on the summons to depart this life, their early contemporaries long since gone, only they two left, relics and proofs of the little political bargains, chances, combinations, resentments of a past age, having nothing in common with this age, standing for the first crop of political graves and grave-stones planted in These States, but in no sort standing for the lusty young growth of the modern times of The States. It is clear from all these two men say and do, that their hearts have not been touched in the least by the flowing fire of the humanitarianism of the new world, its best glory yet, and a moral control stronger than all its governments. It is clear that neither of these nominees of the politicians have thus far reached an inkling of the real scope and character of the contest of the day, probably now only well begun to stretch through years, with varied temporary successes and reverses. Still the two old men live in little respectable spots with respectable little wants. Still their eyes stop at the edges of the tables of committees and cabinets, beholding not the great round world beyond. What has this age to do with them?

He was caught and swept away by the grandeur of the national awakening in 1860, and to this day Whitman achieved the heroic only in celebration of the Civil War and the victory of national union. But before 1860 Whitman had discovered the means whereby he could avoid the realities which pressed in upon him. He mastered the art of substituting the individual for anything that was too difficult for him to overcome in reality. He develops a trick whereby nothing is what it is, but means something else. He always had it. In 1856 in *As I Sat Alone by Blue Ontario's Shore,* he writes:

Have you thought there could be but a single Supreme?
There can be any number of Supremes – one does not counter-
        vail another, any more than one eyesight countervails
        another, or one life countervails another.

All is eligible to all,
All is for individuals – All is for you.
No condition is prohibited – not God's or any,
All comes by the body – only health puts you in rapport with the universe.

Produce great persons, the rest follows.

   Later in the same poem it is going full blast:

I swear I begin to see the meaning of these things!
It is not the earth, it is not America, who is so great,
It is I who am great, or to be great, it is you up there, or any one;
It is to walk rapidly through civilizations, governments, theories.
Through poems, pageants, shows, to form great individuals.

Underneath all, individuals!
I swear nothing is good to me now that ignores individuals,
The American compact is altogether with individuals,
The only government is that which makes minute of individuals,
The whole theory of the universe is directed to one single individual –
        namely, to You.

(Mother! with subtle sense severe with the naked sword in your hand,
I saw you at last refuse to treat but deal directly with individuals.)

   It has a certain glamour but the modern man cannot help distrusting it. It is too facile, too glib, and before long the doubt is proved.

O I see now, flashing, that this America is only you and me
Its power, weapons, testimony are you and me,
Its crimes, lies, thefts, defections, slavery are you and me,
Its Congress is you and me – the officers, capitols, armies, ships
        are you and me,
Its endless gestation of new States are you and me,

The war – the war so bloody and grim – the war I will henceforth forget –
  was you and me,
Natural and artificial are you and me,
Freedom, language, poems, employments, are you and me,
Past, present, future, are you and me.

This was a perpetual maneuver of Whitman. Constitutions, laws, institutions, things, none of *these* were real. The real things were individuals – you and me. Over and over again he does it.

This characteristic of Whitman's opens a broad road to another significant aspect of one of the most comprehensive and powerful personalities of the nineteenth century, and therefore to the nineteenth and twentieth centuries. The characteristic of Whitman just noted is a gigantic symbolism, but the symbolism of evasion. This refusal to face *things*, the mass of *things* which dominate modern life, has dominated the poetic literature of the last third of the nineteenth century and the twentieth century. Its technical roots may be in Poe, its literary and social base is in this practice of Whitman. It has been used by poetic individualists, men who have turned away from the world or expressed their rage against it in strictly individual terms, Verlaine, Rimbaud, T. S. Eliot, and even prose writers like Joyce. It has been degraded into the preoccupation with technique and special symbols which now distinguish the majority of modern poets who write for a coterie.

Now this turn of the individual into himself was inherent in Whitman from the beginning. (It *might* have appeared earlier and he *might* have pursued it to its conclusion anticipating Rimbaud and the others but for the national unity of the Civil War which solved his doubts and made him feel that here the fullness of individuality would be realized.) But in those early poems that tendency to turn into himself is present, linked closely with a sombre preoccupation with Death.[1]

His *Song of the Open Road* is a splendid poem, an early one, which has appealed to lovers of the full and free life everywhere. But in it Whitman has left his preoccupation with the mass. You only have to compare him with Shelley who was a genuine if frustrated democrat. (I omit the last purely revolutionary poems.) Listen to the last stanzas of *The West Wind Ode:*

A heavy weight of hours has chained and bowed
One too like thee; tameless, and swift, and proud.

Make me thy lyre, even as the forest is:
What if my leaves are falling like its own!
The tumult of thy mighty harmonies
Will take from both a deep, autumnal tone.
Sweet though in sadness. Be thou, Spirit fierce,

My spirit! Be thou me, impetuous one!

Drive my dead thoughts over the universe
Like withered leaves to quicken a new birth!
And, by the incantation of this verse,

Scatter, as from an unextinguished hearth
Ashes and sparks, my words among mankind!
Be through my lips to unawakened earth

The trumpet of a prophecy! O, Wind,
If Winter comes, can Spring be far behind?

He, too, is tameless, and swift, and proud. He is defeated, but the call, the deep desire is to speak to *all* men. You hear it again in the last verse of the *Skylark:*

Teach me half the gladness
        That my brain must know,
Such harmonious madness
        From my lips would flow
The world should listen then – as
        I am listening now.

But in all the exuberance of *Song of the Open Road* Whitman, the super-democrat, is calling to a select few:

You shall not heap up what is call'd riches,
You shall scatter with lavish hand all that you earn or achieve,
You but arrive at the city to which you were destined – you
        hardly settle yourself to satisfaction, before you are call'd
        by an irresistible call to depart,
You shall be treated to the ironical smiles and mockings of those
        who remain behind you;
What beckonings of love you receive, you shall only answer with
        passionate kisses of departing,
You shall not allow the hold of those who spread their reach'd
        hands toward you.

Later on in the same poem he says:

My call is the call of battle – I nourish active rebellion;

He nourished nothing of the kind. He shared to the full his countrymen's delusive belief, based on America's early history, that America in its mere existence, was a rebellion. His rebelliousness is a personal sentiment but, like his other songs, to European revolutionaries, Whitman's rebelliousness was an individualistic gesture and nothing more. He had no sense whatever of rebellion as a social movement. He, and all who thought as he, would leave the workingmen and go to follow the Open Road. There is contained in the Open Road and much of his writing an element of exclusiveness, of an elite, the few who would live their own lives, irrespective of the harsh reality.

Whitman as a historical figure has drunk to the dregs his failure to solve the contradiction contained in his own position. If you insist on individualism as he did and then seek it in industry, science, etc. in general, not only are you used by those who control science, industry, etc. Individualism elevated to this position and unable to find a road inevitably turns in upon itself and makes itself and its accumulated misery the norm of society. The end of this is Existentialism, the gloomy doctrine of modern Europe which has so many devotees among intellectuals in the United States. Still another expression of the tendencies in Whitman has received perhaps the strangest embodiment of all. By no modern social group is Whitman more admired than the American representatives of the totalitarian barbarism of Russia. The American Communist Party in their self-interested hypocritical use of American tradition has made him their own. That combination of frenzy in praise of Democracy (with the capital D) and the complete abstractness of Whitman's poetic treatment of it, Whitman's messianic conception of poets as the great individuals to lead the nation, all this finds in them a response which seems far more than merely political hypocrisy.

Was his poetical work for democracy then a total failure? No. He was in his way a genuine democrat, in that he began with a vision of what early America had in its way produced, a conviction of the worth of the individual as an individual in work and play and all aspects of life, and the recognition that this individual could only find his fullest expression with other individuals equal to himself. The roads to which his failure led are evidence of his passion in seeking his aim, a passion still held by his countrymen above all other people. He failed because he tried to embrace all, took Democracy in general as synonymous with the growth of America. But if he succeeded as a poet only where he spoke of himself and his sorrows, he left behind the impact of his passion for his fellow-men in the verse form he perfected.

For fine as these poems are, Whitman's chief claim to fame is not the poems themselves. This American writer felt in all his bones that America was different from Europe. He felt that America needed a poetry that was characteristic of America, a poetry of the people, written by a poet who in himself as an individual represented the people and thereby was fitted to write for them. His whole life showed that this above all moved him. The result is that there, expressing his strongest and finest emotion, he *did* succeed. He felt the need for a new medium, free verse, and he worked at it. He was no slap-dash writer who never blotted a line but a devoted conscientious artist, seeking to create a new democratic form. The paradox of his career is that though he had little that was really new to say, his passion to identify himself with his fellow countrymen did enable him to create a new social medium.

Whitman's form is his profoundest contribution to literature, and it is here again that American writers of the middle of the nineteenth century have struck chords whose significance can only be recognized today.

Hegel has drawn attention to the fact that the verse of the ancients did not rhyme, and was a verse which depended upon quantity pure and simple, giving a tremendous flexibility of the individual line. He claims that this type of verse represented the oneness of the individual Greek with the social phenomena of life and the objects that Greek life dealt with. The Greek was a part of his society. Greek society did not know the individual separate from it, hence the *plasticity* of the poetry, which while rhythmic in form, sought to shape itself to the object described.

The growth of individualism in European society destroyed this. The individual, conscious of his isolation, could not allow the verse to seek to follow the object. The recurrent rhythm and the rhymes at the end of the line characteristic of modern poetry were the concrete contact of the subjective individual with what otherwise would have escaped him. He had a need that the educated Greek or Roman did not have. In the first great revolutionary age of modern times when the individual felt himself representative of society, we have the formation of the national languages. Calvin, Luther and the early English translators of the Bible, religious leaders all, led this transformation.

At the moment when Britain was preparing to introduce secular society as opposed to feudal, Shakespeare and the Elizabethan dramatists broke with rhyme and introduced blank verse, which in the hands of its greatest masters, remains to this day unsurpassed as a poetic medium both for depth and flexibility. It was closer to the plasticity of the Greeks and Romans than anything we have seen before or since. With the end of the Elizabethans its greatest period was gone, and it has since known nothing but decline. The genuine passion of the isolated Whitman to get into contact with his fellow-men and the character of his fellow-men, produced another great stage in the development of poetic language.

Whitman's verse can express, as he expressed, the most intimate personal feelings, using as all new languages must do, the intimate nuances of the past. But it is also a chant, a chant to be sung by millions of men. It is popular, yet in the hands of a master, it can be subtle and intricate beyond the elaborate verse-forms that preceded it. If some day all men will be educated and feel the need of expression in verse, some such form as Whitman used will be the medium. It has been, as so much that he did, taken up and made into the most precious of verse forms by modern masters, but all the schoolchildren in the United States who write verse use it. His passion for identification did find some permanent expression, but not in the same sense that he intended.

HERMAN MELVILLE

Herman Melville is the exact opposite of Whitman, at least in his great book, *Moby Dick,* with which alone I propose to deal. Melville's greatness and superiority to Whitman is due to the fact that, stirred by the critical period, he did the very things that Whitman did not do. He described with absolute precision various individuals in their social setting, the work that they did, their relations with other men. This led him to see that individualism in certain sections of America had become one of the most dangerous vices of the age and would destroy society. Before we take up the book itself, however, we wish to place before the reader one page of Melville in which he describes an individual who is quite unnecessary to the organic structure of the book. It is a description of an old carpenter on board the ship. The extract is very long, but it is the easiest way to express at present the fact that in scores and scores of single pages of Melville you find more sympathy with the common ordinary man, and at the same time realism, than you will find in all of Whitman's poetry put together. Here it is:

A belaying-pin is found too large to be easily inserted into its hole; the carpenter claps it into one of his ever-ready vices, and straightway files it smaller. A lost land-bird of strange plumage strays on board and is made a captive; out of clean-shaved rods of right-whale bone, and cross-beams made of sperm-whale ivory, the carpenter makes a pagoda-looking cage for it. An oarsman sprains his wrist; the carpenter concocts a soothing lotion. Stubb longed for vermillion stars to be painted upon the blade of his every oar; screwing each oar in his big vice of wood, the carpenter symmetrically supplies the constellation. A sailor takes a fancy to wear shark-bone earrings; the carpenter drills his ears. Another has the toothache; the carpenter out pincers, and clapping one hand upon his bench bids him be seated there; but the poor fellow unmanageably winces under the concluded operation, whirling round the handle of his wooden vice, the carpenter signs him to clap his jaw in that, if he would have him draw the tooth.

Thus, this carpenter was prepared at all points, and alike indifferent and without respect in all. Teeth he accounted bits of ivory; heads he deemed but to-blocks; men themselves he lightly held for capstans. But while now upon so wide a field thus variously accomplished, and with much liveliness of expertness in him too; all this would seem to argue some uncommon vivacity of intelligence. But not precisely so.

For nothing was this man more remarkable, than for a certain impersonal stolidity as it were; impersonal, I say; for it shaded off into the surrounding infinite of things, that it seemed one with the general stolidity discernible in the whole visible world; which while pauselessly active in uncounted modes, still eternally holds its peace, and ignores you, though you dig foundations for cathedrals. Yet was this half-horrible stolidity in him, involving too, as it appeared, an all-ramifying heartlessness; yet it was oddly dashed at times, with an old crutch-like, antediluvian, wheezing humorousness, not unstreaked now and then with a certain grizzled wittiness; such as might have served to pass the time during the midnight watch on the bearded forecastle of Noah's ark. Was it that this old carpenter had been a life-long wanderer, whose much rolling, to and fro, not only had gathered no moss; but what is more, had rubbed off whatever small outward clingings might have originally pertained to him! He was a stript abstract; an unfractioned integral; uncompromised as a newborn babe; living without premeditated reference to this world or the next. You might almost say, that this strange uncompromisedness in him involved a sort of intelligence; for in his numerous trades, he did not seem to work so much by reason or instinct, or simply because he had been tutored to it, or by any intermixture of these, even or uneven; but merely by a kind of deaf and dumb, spontaneous literal process. He was a pure manipulator; his brain, if he ever had one, must have early oozed along the muscles of his fingers. He was like one of those unreasoning but still highly useful, multum in parvo, Sheffield contrivances, assuming the exterior – though a little swelled – of a common pocket knife; but containing, not only blades of various sizes, but also screw-drivers, cork-screws, tweezers, awls, pens, rulers, nail-filers, counter-sinkers. So, if his superiors wanted to use the carpenter for a screw-driver, all they had to do was to open that part of him, and the screw was fast; or if for tweezers, take him up by the legs, and there they were.

Yet, as previously hinted, this omni-tooled, open-and-shut carpenter was after all no mere machine or an automaton. If he did not have a common soul in him, he had a subtle something that somehow anomalously did its duty. What that was, whether essence of quicksilver; or a few drops of hartshorn, there is no telling. But there it was; and there it had abided now for some sixty years or more. And this it was, this same unaccountable, cunning life-principle in him; this, it was, that kept him a great part of time soliloquizing; but only like an unreasoning wheel, which also hummingly soliloquizes; or rather, his body was a sentry-box and this soliloquizer on guard there, and talking all the time to keep himself awake.

This was the way Melville saw America. He saw each man separately, concretely, but in all his individuality and all his relations. His insight came from the fact that he saw all men in this way and because of this saw them all in relation to Nature. In *Moby Dick* he was the counterpart of Whitman. He sought not the violent self-expression of individuality which is so peculiarly American but that conviction of the need for communication with all types of men which is also peculiarly American. Many European intellectuals write for common men, organize for them, and will readily die for them, do everything for them in fact except meet them as men. Melville described common men as they have been described in no modern literature. But he saw no way for them to form a harmonious society and drew a society which would crash to its doom by individuals.

Melville wrote *Moby Dick* in 1851. As is well known, it is a story of a whaling vessel led by a maniacal captain which pursues a white whale so intemperately that the ship is lost with all on board except one survivor. Melville was bitter in his protest that his book was not some miserable allegory, and the general tenor of his meaning is correct. As allegory it concretizes and imprisons the universal. Melville's book is symbolism – it gives indications and points of support by which the innermost essence and widest reaches of the universal may be grasped.

Melville painted a picture of the society of his day, not merely the society of America, but all of society. He indicated very clearly where he thought it was heading – at the end of the book the last sight of the ship shows an eagle, symbol of America, caught in an American flag and being nailed down without possibility of escape, to the mast by the blows of an American Indian. It is impossible to speak more clearly. The social perspectives, however, are *not* completely hopeless. The survivor is not saved merely for the purpose of relating the story. He is saved by a coffin, prepared by the request of another savage, and fitted for its ultimate purpose so deliberately by the author as to exclude any idea that this is accidental. Who the survivor is, who rescues him, etc., its symbolical significance will appear later. It is enough that while Melville sees no solution to the problem of society, he does not say that there is none. *He* can see none.

The mysticism of life which Melville deals with, and which some writers pay great attention to, is not the most important part of the work. Mysticism is an expression of inability to arrive at rational solutions of the problems of nature and society. Melville's whole book shows that this is what concerned him, man and his relation to Nature, and as a result, man in relation to his fellows, i.e., social man.

That is the significance of the white whale, Nature in relation to the active life of man. But the white whale must be seen as symbol, not as allegory, as Melville insists. For it is precisely symbol which offers the widest variety of reference and interpretation. Unlike Dostoyevsky, Melville places his symbolical characters in a very concrete environment, the environment of an industry, of men doing the daily business of the modern world. Melville is to this day unique in his portrait of an industry. Where else does anything like this appear in literature? Certainly not in the sprawling overemotional novels of Zola, nor in modern propagandist novels, nor in the romantic sea stories of Conrad. Not one great novelist even faintly approaches the realistic description of the process and personnel from the signing up of Ishmael and

Queequeg, the preparation of the *Pequod* by the owners, to the final catastrophe. Melville's sense of society was American, the opposite of the talkers, reasoners, arguers, of Dostoyevsky.

The *Pequod* was doing a legitimate business, one of the greatest industries of the middle of the nineteenth century. This cannot be overemphasized for it is of the essence of Melville. Furthermore, Melville takes care to show that there had been whales which had terrorized whalers, and there had been captains who in the way of business, had sought out and destroyed such whales. Thus Ahab's maniacal quest is merely the exaggeration, the intensification beyond reason, of the legitimate and in fact necessary pursuits of men. Which is precisely why it is so terrible and so dangerous.

This legitimate activity symbolizes the perpetual relation of civilized man with Nature. The whale was the most striking of living things which man had to subdue in order to have civilized lives. The whale is not a mere fish. The conquest of the air, the mastery of atomic energy, all these are symbolized by the whale. The symbol as such could appeal more easily to men in 1851 than to our own day when the contact with Nature is so much more mechanized, complicated and scientific. But Melville has that relation in mind. Man must perpetually seek to conquer Nature, to bend it to his will. And Nature is malevolent, making him pay a heavy toll, and creating such strains and stresses in his character as can turn him into a monomaniac.

Melville carries the symbolism further. He divided society as a whole into two spheres, the stable society of the land; and the society of the sea, the shifting boundaries of man's need to go further and ever further. *How* Melville does this, however, is characteristic and very important for understanding the particular method to be used in this book. Melville is not a social scientist. He is an artist, first, middle and last. A great artist is not a politician and his social and political ideas are to be deduced from his artistic work. Melville as a matter of fact, was not even an ardent Northerner in the pursuit of the war with the South. But no man had more sympathy for the great masses of slaves and primitive peoples than he. But this is to be seen in his work, not in such political views as he expressed.

Melville shows what the sea means for him in the strange and haunting episode of Bulkington. Bulkington appears first in chapter III, a sailor who has just landed, a superbly handsome man, a Southerner, a man reserved, with deep problems of his own but loved by his fellow-sailors. Then in chapter XXIII Bulkington reappears, in a brief chapter, wholly devoted to him. Ishmael sees him at the helm on a bitterly cold winter's night:

I looked with sympathetic awe and fearfulness upon the man, who in mid-winter just landed from a four years' dangerous voyage, could so unrelentingly push off again for still another tempestuous term. The land seemed scorching to his feet.

Then come three clauses which are in reality a brief poem in the elegaic style of the Greeks:

Wonderfullest things are ever the unmentionable; deep memories yield no epitaphs; this six-inch chapter is the stoneless grave of Bulkington.

No novelist anywhere can surpass Melville at such moments. The power of the poetry derives not only from the monumental weight of the words but the dramatic setting. Bulkington appears no more in the book. Melville then continues:

Let me say only that it fared with him as with the storm-tossed ship, that miserably drives along the leeward land. The port would fain give succor; the port is pitiful; in the port, all that's kind to our mortalities. But in the gale, the port, the land, is that ship's direct jeopardy; she must fly all hospitality; one touch of land, though it but graze the keel, would make her shudder through and through. With all her might she crowds all sail off shore; in so doing, fights 'gainst the very winds that fain would blow her homeward; seeks all the lashed sea, landlessness again; for refuge's sake forlornly rushing into peril; her only friend, her bitterest foe.

Then he states what for him man's life means:

Know ye now Bulkington? Glimpses do ye seem to see of that mortally intolerable truth; that all deep, earnest thinking is but the intrepid effort of the soul to keep the open independence of her sea; while the wildest winds of heaven and earth conspire to cast her on the treacherous slavish shore?

But as in landlessness alone resides the highest truth, shoreless, indefinite as God – so, better is it to perish in that howling infinite, than be ingloriously dashed upon the lee, even if that were safety! For worm-like, then, oh! who would craven crawl to land! Terrors of the terrible! is all this agony so vain? Take heart, take heart, O Bulkington! Bear thee grimly, demigod! Up from the spray of thy ocean-perishing – straight up, leaps thy apotheosis!

That is the sea for Melville, the unknown that man must continually seek to know. Death and destruction face him, but man, men who matter, cannot resist. Moby Dick is merely the active principle in the sea, Nature, the unknown, which is in constant conflict with man. *Moby Dick* is a baffled, defeated, but not a hopeless book. Ishmael, the writer of the story is an individualist intellectual who goes to sea because he is sick at heart. Ahab is the individualist whose individualism imperils all of society. Bulkington is an individual, a superb person, physically and in the effect of his personality; yet he is a Southern mountaineer, turned ordinary sailor and loved by his fellow-sailors. Melville has greater respect for no one in the book. He recognizes the significance of the type. It holds the future of man in its hands, the things that for Melville matter. But Melville can only describe him as from a distance and praise him. He can do nothing else with him. We shall appreciate the significance of this when we see later where Melville openly confesses his bafflement.

Melville, as is known, describes every detail of whale-fishing, the conversion of the ship into a factory at sea for the extraction and storage of oil – one of his profoundest and most far-reaching symbolical episodes is based upon this conversion of the ship into a factory. But his book is often misunderstood because critics take the tiresomeness of his endeavor, never lost sight of for a moment, to root the madness of Ahab *in the normal.* Thus whaling is described from the most ancient days, classical times, and the days before Columbus when Indians in canoes chased the great fish. Noble passages show how the discoveries of Australia, the trade with Latin America, the independence of those countries all came from the days of the whalemen. And all through Melville shows the world-wide scope of the industry. Again his style is at its most magnificent when he describes the course of the *Pequod* in its chase after Moby Dick.

The struggle then is the struggle between man and Nature, as old as historical time and as wide as the world. But though less obvious, Melville is equally concerned with the relations between man and man, relations which man must enter into, in order to pursue his destined task. Once more the ship symbolizes the whole world, in which are portrayed the most characteristic social types, with the most delicately shaded individual types of character to represent the organic types of Melville's day.

There is a crew of thirty men on board. In chapter XL, Melville lists them, 1st Nantucket sailor, 2nd ditto, a Dutchman, a Frenchman, one each from Iceland, Sicily, Long Island, the Azores, China, the Isle of Man, 3rd Nantucket sailor, a Lascar, a Tahitian, a Portuguese, a Dane, a 4th Nantucket sailor, an Englishman, a 5th Nantucket sailor, a Spaniard, and one from Belfast.

They are in their way skilled workmen. But Melville repeatedly calls them a heathen crew, renegades, castaways, the scum of the earth. Yet again in a manner unique to himself this American writer, invests them with dignity. They do their work splendidly, the ship is kept in fine shape, the whole crew does its daily work heroically, to recall de Tocqueville's phrase. Melville draws the reader's attention to it.

But this august dignity I treat of, is not the dignity of kings and robes, but that abounding dignity which has no robed investiture. Thou shalt see it shining in the arm that wields a pick or drives a spike; that democratic dignity which, on all hands, radiates without end from God! Himself! The great God absolute! The center and circumference of all democracy! His omnipresence, our divine equality.

If, then, to meanest mariners, and renegades and castaways, I shall hereafter ascribe high qualities, though dark; weave around them tragic graces; if even the most mournful, perchance the most abased, among them all, shall at times lift himself to the exalted mounts; if I shall touch that workman's arm with some ethereal light; if I shall spread a rainbow over his disastrous set of sun; then against all mortal critics bear me out in it, thou just Spirit of Equality, which has spread one royal mantle of humanity over all my kind!

But it is not only that he says so. The whole treatment shows an absolutely unique objectivity about ordinary labor without sentimentality which cannot be found in any other novelist.

Having laid his basis, so to speak, Melville then portrays a social stage higher, the picked men, the highly skilled harpooners, who represent the highly skilled craftsmen so characteristic of the economy of his time. There was no necessity whatever for Melville to do what he does. He gives this vastly important role to three savages, Queequeg, a cannibal from the South Seas, Tashtego, an American Indian, and Doggo, an African giant. They are the representatives of the three continents where primitive men were still found. Here again Melville's unbounded sympathy and admiration within a strictly realistic framework is unique in literature. The men are masters of their craft, brave and skillful as virtuosos. But over and over again they perform the bravest acts, far beyond the line of duty. Whenever anything remarkable is done, one of them does it. Queequeg at the very beginning saves a boat in danger and rescues a sailor given up for lost. To save Tashtego, he dives into the head of a dead whale, slashes a hole in it, grabs Tashtego first by the foot, recognizes that he cannot pull him out that way, spins him round inside the head to get him by the arm and then drags him out. When a whale is sighted, it is Tashtego who sees it and sings out in a marvelous chant. Doggo is an "imperial" Negro. These men have some scenes of truly Shakespearean humor while they eat in the captain's cabin.

As if that there were not enough, Melville makes Queequeg into one of the most carefully realized characters in the book. He is an admitted cannibal but he has left his country to learn from civilization to go back to teach his people. Ishmael, the narrator, the soul-sick intellectual, finds in Queequeg a friend and a brother, and the opening pages of the book describe a thinly disguised homosexual relationship between the two in a manner that is as plain and yet as inoffensive as it could possibly be. Here is Ishmael's description of Queequeg as he gets to know him:

I have noticed also that Queequeg never consorted at all, or but very little, with the other seamen in the inn. He made no advances whatever; appeared to have no desire to enlarge the circle of his acquaintances. All this struck me as mighty singular; yet, upon second thought, there was something almost sublime in it. Here was a man some twenty thousand miles from home, by the way of Cape Horn, that is – which was the only way he could get there – thrown among people as strange to him as though he were in the planet Jupiter; and yet he seemed entirely at his ease; preserving the utmost serenity; content with his own companionship; always equal to himself. Surely this was a touch of fine philosophy; though no doubt he had never heard there was such a thing as that. But, perhaps, to be true philosophers, we mortals should not be conscious of so living or so striving. So soon as I hear that such or such a man gives himself out like a philosopher, I conclude that, like the dyspeptic old woman, he must have "broken his digester."

The last shot is at Ishmael himself. Queequeg in fact is a remarkable individual.

Through all his unearthly tattooings, I thought I saw the traces of a simple honest heart; and in his large deep eyes, fiery black and bold, there seemed tokens of a spirit that would dare a thousand devils. And besides all this, there was a certain lofty bearing about the Pagan, which even his uncouthness could not altogether maim. He looked like a man who had never cringed and never had had a creditor. Whether it was, too, that his head being shaved, his forehead was drawn out in freer and brighter relief, and looked more expansive than it otherwise would, this I will not venture to decide; but certain it was his head was phrenologically an excellent one. It may seem ridiculous, but it reminded me of General Washington's head, as seen in the popular busts of him. It had the same long regularly graded retreating slope from above the brows, which were likewise very projecting, like two long promontories thickly wooded on top. Queequeg a George Washington cannibalistically developed.

In that strange crew, Bulkington and Queequeg are the men Ishmael admires.

Let us pause here for a while. It is obvious that these savages do key work in the whaling business, that Queequeg is a distinguished personality. But he is a savage, a cannibal. If in addition to his grand physique, his skillful work, and his noble character, he were a civilized human being, then there would be some hope for the world which Melville sends to its doom. But splendid as he is, the primitive Queequeg cannot save society. Melville in the person of the distraught Ishmael can admire and love. It is not difficult to see the significance of this for the world of today and the whole problem of world civilization.

Next in the hierarchy are three American mates, Starbuck, Flask and Stubb, capable men all, but differentiated with a marvelous skill and sureness. Starbuck is a conscientious man, Stubb a man of humor and Flask a devil-may-care who took everything as it came.

Now the question that Melville poses is: Why did this ship's crew not revolt, put Ahab in irons or kill him, and thus save the ship and crew? This problem, so pregnant for today, is handled by Melville with unique insight and mastery, and the subtlety of the relations between Ahab and the crew, and Ahab and the mates is a political study of rare discrimination. No generation but our own could have appreciated this. Melville himself poses the question, but says that crews had been known to revolt against captains and says that the men of the *Pequod* were perfectly capable of it. One of his most telling strokes is his statement that the crew were not only mongrel, renegades, castaways and savages, but that they were "morally enfeebled also by the incompetance of mere unaided virtue or rightmindedness in Starbuck, the invulnerable jollity of indifference and recklessness in Stubb, and the pervading mediocrity of Flask." The relations between Starbuck, a brave, honest conscientious man, and Ahab will be dealt with later – they are a most important part of the book. It will be useful to make clear here that Melville was deeply concerned with the inability of the crew to put an end to the mad captain by revolt.

In chapter LIV Melville breaks his narrative to introduce a story and goes to great length to give the impression that it is true. This story is the story of a revolt. A vessel with a crew manned almost entirely by Polynesians met the *Pequod* on its fateful journey. The white sailors on board took the story to Tashtego by whom it was made known to the men. But it never went further. The men kept it to themselves. The story briefly is as follows: On board was a magnificently handsome sailor from the Lakes called Steelkilt. He was hated by the mate and persecuted by him so that he led a mutiny. Betrayed by his fellow mutineers, Steelkilt nursed revenge. But he was allowed to work afterwards. The ship had to put in to an island. Steelkilt and some of the men deserted. The captain set out in a canoe to find a crew. Steelkilt and his fellows intercepted the captain's canoe, made him stay on an island until they made their escape, got a boat and reached home safely. There is no space to tell of the bravery, the resource, and the decision which characterized Steelkilt in this narrative which is superbly done. It could not have been accidental that Melville made this particular story known to Ahab's crew. Even more. The men on this ship after the mutiny had decided not to call when they saw whales so as to be sure to get the ship to port as soon as possible, and only one uncontrolled sailor shouted to call attention to a whale which the men in the look-out had seen for hours but had ignored in accordance with their plan. Thus Melville made Ahab's men get every possible indication of what they should do.

Why didn't they do it? And here Melville does a most extraordinary thing. He gives some reasons which we shall take up later. But he says frankly that he doesn't know. Ahab inspired his men with his hate of the white whale. The whale seemed to the men also "in some dim unsuspected way . . . the gliding great demon of the seas of life." But why should this be so "all this to explain would be to dive deeper than Ishmael can go." Melville cannot understand why. It should be obvious by now that behind this marvelous sea story, this writer was digging into problems of far greater social significance for us today than were Flaubert, Dostoyevsky and Rimbaud.

And yet the study of Ahab is a masterpiece, perhaps so far the only serious study in fiction of the type which has reached its climax in the modern totalitarian dictator.

Here we must pause a bit to get our literary and sociological points of reference clear. Melville was *not* writing a political tract for 1950 nor a political tract for the times he lived in. But he was looking at society as a whole, painting it in as comprehensive a series of relations as he could. He saw the characteristic social types of his day and because he lived at a turning point, *he saw also a characteristic social type of the age which was to follow.*

This, in fact, seems to be the condition of many of the greatest works of the genuinely creative writers. Dante summed up not only the Middle Ages but saw clearly the new secular age. Balzac, temperamentally and politically, admired the aristocracy. But although he disliked, he was fascinated by, the new bourgeoisie and his imagination was stimluated by the new men and their impact upon the old society. The greatest example of this is Shakespeare. He held all the ideas of the radical aristrocracy. But he came at the turning-point, just before the Puritan Revolution, the revolution of individualism. How great passions could shake men who had escaped the rigid roles of feudalism – this more than anything else was what interested Shakespeare. Hence the great tragedies and the tragedy above all of Hamlet, who could not decide. The very greatest writers seem to be those who come at the climax of one age, but this is because the new age has grown up inside the old and they are watching both.

This was the case with Melville. The old heroic individualist America he knew; but he could see as artists see that the old individualism was breeding a new individualism, an individualism which would destroy society. The prototype of this was Ahab. The modern dictator whose prototype he is, is best exemplified by Adolf Hitler.

Again it is necessary to stop and make clear what we are doing. Melville did not write a political treatise. The modern dictator arises from economic and social circumstances profoundly different from those of Melville's day. Nevertheless, the greatness of a writer is revealed by the fact that peering and probing until he finds what he considers the fundamental types of his own period, he portrays what we in later years can see are the ancestors of what exist in our own world. We are therefore entitled, in fact we have to, with the knowledge that we have gained through the development of history and our own experiences, examine earlier writers and see how much they saw that was permanent and enduring.

In this respect Ahab is an astonishing character in fiction. He is not only the individualism that Melville saw and feared, run mad. Contrary to Dostoyevsky, Melville places the individualism in opposition to a representative section of the society of his time. In addition, and here he touches Dostoyevsky, he shows the conflicts within Ahab himself. Before we attempt briefly to indicate some of the main facets of this character and activity, it must be remembered, first of all, that no historical character like Ahab has yet appeared on the American social and political scene. But he has appeared in Europe. Hitler is not only an individual. A man like Hitler could only appear when an essential number of people, representing the type, had become a social grouping, representing vast social forces. If there has been no outstanding social and political figure like Ahab in the United States, we shall show later that among large sections of the population, and particularly in the popular art and popular literature of the day, figures of this type, vulgarized but essentially the same, are more and more becoming the dominant type of hero in the United States.

First of all, Ahab's relations with his men and his employers. Ahab is an executive, he is a captain of a vessel and a very skillful and able whaling captain. His employers would not have countenanced for one moment, as Melville says, this mad chase of Ahab's. His mates were against him. Nothing is more pathetic than the relationship of Starbuck, the honest conscientious man, to Ahab. Starbuck is the only man who challenges Ahab and tries to turn him back, talks to him of the ease and comforts of life at home. Ahab dominates him by sheer force of personality. At a certain stage when Starbuck sees that Ahab is, as he says, going to ruin the lives of perhaps thirty men, he takes a gun and goes towards Ahab's cabin to shoot him. But he cannot do it. Inside he hears Ahab talking in his sleep about his quest and he gives way. When Ahab takes to the boat for the last fights against Moby Dick, he places Starbuck in charge of the ship and thereby places his life in Starbuck's hands. The other mate, Stubb, is told by Ahab to get out of his cabin. Ahab threatens to kick him down. But Stubb, who admits that he has never been treated in this way before, accepts it, dominated also by the overpowering personality and will of Ahab.

Profound, far-reaching and subtle are the relations between Ahab and the men. It is impossible here to go through stage by stage the maneuvers of Ahab with the crew. Sufficient to say that very early he recognized the danger. To use Melville's own words:

Ahab was now entirely conscious that . . . he had indirectly laid himself open to the unanswerable charge of usurpation; and with perfect impunity, both moral and legal, his crew if so disposed, and to that end competent, could refuse any further obedience to him, and even violently wrest from him the command. From even the barely hinted imputation of usurpation and the possible consequences of such a suppressed impression, gaining ground, Ahab must of course have been most anxious to protect himself. That protection could only consist in his own predominating brain and heart and hand, backed by a heedful, closely calculating attention to every minute atmospheric influence which it was possible for his crew to be subjected to.

This occurs as early as chapter XLV, when there are still two-thirds of the book to go and the reader of this outline must accept for the time being that the rest of the book is a manual of political practice between a dominant political figure and the officers and ranks whom he must dominate. Every change of atmosphere in the men, every doubt, every enthusiasm is used by Ahab in order to maintain control. At a certain stage the men are doubtful and suspicious, but so certain, so domineering, so overwhelming is Ahab's concentration on his purpose that they dare not raise the question with him and his mates move around unable to look at him. At a certain stage, when Starbuck is considering arresting Ahab, he trembles at the idea of having to stand the wrath and hatred of the old man, as he would be even when confined and chained as a prisoner of the crew.

There is no need so far as this is concerned of any special interpretation. Melville knows and says repeatedly that the conflict is between man and Nature, the demonism that is in Nature. Melville knows also, however, that the struggle with the demonism in Nature involves a certain relation between men and men. And he himself states:

To accomplish his object, Ahab must use tools and of all tools used in the shadow of the moon, men are most apt to get out of order.

Perhaps it would be easiest by means of a long quotation to show how important is the manipulation by Ahab in the book, to show how carefully Melville distinguishes between the relationships of Ahab to Starbuck and Ahab's relationships to the men.

He knew, for example, that however magnetic his ascendancy in some respects was over Starbuck, yet that ascendancy did not cover the complete spiritual man any more than mere corporal superiority involves intellectual mastership; for to the purely spiritual, the intellectual but stands in a sort of corporal relation. Starbuck's body and Starbuck's coerced will were Ahab's, so long as Ahab kept his magnet at Starbuck's brain; still he knew that for all this the chief mate, in his soul, abhorred his captain's quest, and could he, would joyfully disintegrate himself from it, or even frustrate it. It might be that a long interval would elapse ere the white whale was seen. During that long interval Starbuck would ever be apt to fall into open relapses of rebellion against his captain's leadership, unless some ordinary prudential circumstantial influences were brought to bear upon him. Not only that, but the subtle insanity of Ahab respecting Moby Dick was noways more significantly manifested than in his superlative sense and shrewdness in foreseeing that, for the present, the hunt should in some way be stripped of that strange imaginative impiousness which naturally invested it; that the full terror of the voyage must be kept withdrawn into the obscure background (for few men's courage is proof against protracted meditation unrelieved by action); that when they stood their long night watches, his officers and men must have some nearer things to think of than Moby Dick. For however eagerly and impetuously the savage crew had hailed the announcement of his quest; yet all sailors of all sorts are more or less capricious and unreliable – they live in the varying outer weather and they all inhale its fickleness – and when retained for any object remote and blank in the pursuit, however promissory of life and passion in the end, it is above all things requisite that temporary interests and employments should intervene and hold them healthily suspended for the final dash.

Nor was Ahab unmindful of another thing. In times of strong emotion, mankind disdain all base considerations; but such times are evanescent. The permanent constitutional condition of the manufactured man, thought Ahab, sordidness. Granting that the White Whale fully incites the hearts of this my savage crew, and playing round their savageness even breeds a certain generous knight-errantism in them, they must also have food for their more common daily appetites. For even the high lifted and chivalric Crusaders of old times were not content to traverse the two thousand miles of land to fight for their holy sepulchre, without committing burglarism, picking pockets, and gaining other pious perquisites by the way. Had they been held strictly to their one final and romantic object – that final and romantic object, too many would have turned from in disgust. I will not strip these men, thought Ahab, of all hopes of cash – aye, cash. They may scorn cash now; but let some months go by, and no perspective promise of it to them, and then this same quiescent cash all at once mutinying in them, this same cash would soon cashier Ahab.

The captain then is a leader of men; and all aspects of the leadership of men by a dominating individual are present in the book. It is necessary here in an outline of this kind to repeat once more the limitations, to point out another aspect of the study of a book like *Moby Dick*. The main purpose of Melville's book in his own mind was the struggle between men and Nature. That must be admitted. But with his vast experience of the world and his immense insight and a certain comprehensiveness, which distinguish the selectivity of a great artist, Melville attempted to paint a rounded picture, to symbolize the world as he knew it in this whaling story. That accounts for the great attention that he paid to the social, and what I am calling, the political structure of his symbolical presentation. Now after a hundred years, as repeatedly happens with great books, the book, so to speak, can be seen by us in a manner which amounts to a reversal of the particular emphasis which Melville may have had in mind when he wrote. We cannot attempt to see the book precisely as Melville wrote it. The greatness of the writing is due to the fact that, while his original purpose is not in any way diminished (we today, for instance in the conquest of atomic energy and the accomplishments of science and the deadly destruction that they seem to hold for society, can appreciate more than ever what Melville calls the demonism in the world), nevertheless the accuracy and insight of the social structure which he built, and the social and political significance of his characters assume for us a significance which perhaps they did not have for him. They are a testimony to the depth and accuracy of his observation and the profundity of his imagination.

Melville then understands the manner in which a dominating will and an immense concentration can overpower men who do not resist it with an equal will and force. He thereby has penetrated to the heart of the secret of the mechanism by which political power is grasped and wielded today in a period of revolutionary changes. To repeat once more, Ahab exemplifies this capacity to the various sections of society who are represented on his ship. How intricate all this can be and the immense opportunities for examination can only be indicated here by one remarkable fact. All persons on board are affected by Ahab one way or another, except the magnificent harpooners who, with complete indifference, do exactly what Ahab says without seeming in the slightest degree affected by him. Melville does not only see this but says it precisely. But it is impossible for us to stop here to examine all the various avenues of exploration which are opened up by the particular approach we are making.

And finally, there is the character of Ahab himself. It is extremely difficult, if not impossible, to give the symbolical significance of Ahab in himself and in relation to modern man. However, I shall try to give some indications here. I believe that sufficient has been said to enable the reader to understand much that will have to be implied.

Ahab's madness is effective, because, as must be insisted upon, it is a madness which is just one stage beyond the normal activities of man. The crew, as Melville points out again and again, shared some of his aspirations and to some degree sympathized with his aims. Even Ishmael, the educated intellectual, feels the demonism in Nature as represented by the White Whale and feels also the spell of Ahab's personality, so that even he for a time is captivated and shouted with the rest of the crew. Melville insists that Ahab's individualism is just a part of what every man feels but which has been allowed to run away with itself and hence is so dangerous. Ahab further attempts to convey the impression that his hatred of the White Whale is due to the fact that Moby Dick ate off his leg. Melville knows that that is not so. He shows quite clearly that Ahab with his enormous will and instinct to dominate is merely the result of an exasperation with the insoluble moral and intellectual problems with which the society of his day faced him. It is necessary to get this clear. For nearly seventy years after *Moby Dick*, individualism in the shape of captains of industry ran wild in the United

States. We shall see in the next chapter its economic achievements and the social and political problems which it has brought. But *Moby Dick* has begun to come into its popularity only since World War I. Ahab represents far more the new individualism which captured America after the Civil War. With an almost mathematical logic, Melville took individualism to the extreme limit of what it could accomplish and then faced it with the crisis which he inevitably foresaw would face it. He could see that as in every age society presented serious men with profound problems. There was ahead a tremendous crisis and it would be the type of Ahab (that was all he saw). Quite early Melville makes us aware of what Ahab represents and what the White Whale represents to Ahab:

In his frantic morbidness he at last came to identify with him, not only all his bodily woes, but all his intellectual and spiritual exasperations. The White Whale swam before him as the monomaniac incarnation of all those malicious agencies which some deep men feel eating in them, till they are left living on with half a heart and half a lung. That intangible malignity which has been from the beginning; to whose domination even the modern Christians ascribe one-half of the worlds; which the ancient Ophites of the east reverenced in their statue devil; – Ahab did not fall down and worship it like them; but deliriously transferring its ideas to the abhorred white whale, he pitted himself, all mutilated, against it. All that most maddens and torments; all that stirs up the less of things; all truth with malice in it; all that cracks the sinews and cakes the brain; all the subtle demonisms of life and thought; all evil, to crazy Ahab, were visibly personified and made practically assailable in Moby Dick. He piled upon the whale's white hump the sum of all the general rage and hate felt by his whole race from Adam down; and then, as if his chest had been a mortar, he burst his hot heart's shell upon it.

Ahab represents not merely man in general, but the individualistic man of the nineteenth century at a stage where he faces the insoluble nature of his problems both with Nature and society. That is where modern man has reached today. And if in Ahab's day, Ahab felt it more than all the others and thereby gained the domination through his will, Bulkington felt it also and Ishmael, the intellectual. So in their various ways did many of the crew. Today we have reached a stage where this consuming rage with the social and psychological problems of society is eating away at the whole of humanity. However, society is not the same. Where Ahab, the dominating executive felt it most, today it is in the great masses of the people in whom it stirs. All this we shall come to later. It is sufficient that Melville saw it, understood it, and painted it with what we can see today was a marvelous clarity.

The final aspect of Ahab's character is the fact that he is a human being. We do not live far enough removed from a man like Hitler to be able to understand the real secrets of the power which he wielded over men. For politics, although the sum total of economic and social forces, is made by individual men. Ahab gains Starbuck's sympathy because he confessed to him that he did not understand why he was so torn and driven. For forty years he had been a whale man, forty years he tells Starbuck of suffering and privation. What is the cause of it? Much of the passage is too long to be quoted. It is sufficient, however, to say that it is precisely the need of man to live, to work, to struggle for his existence, constantly to go on further, which is the basis of Ahab's madness. And finally Ahab comes to the conclusion that it is fate, it is the destiny of man so to act, and he, Ahab, is merely fulfilling destiny. It is impossible to understand the modern social and political world without real and genuine insight into this aspect of modern society. As Ahab says:

What is it, what nameless, inscrutable, unearthly thing is it; what cozzening hidden lord and master, and cruel, remorseless emperor commands me; that against all natural lovings and longings I so keep pushing and crowding and jamming on myself the time; recklessly, making me ready to do what in my own proper, natural heart, I durst not so much as dare? Is Ahab, Ahab? Is it I, God, or who, that lifts this arm? But if the great sun move not of himself; but is as an errand-boy in heaven; nor one single star can revolve, but by some invisible power; how then can this one small heart beat; this one small brain think thoughts; unless God does that beating, does that thinking, does that living, and not I. By heaven, man, we are turned around and round in this world, like yonder windlass, and Fate is the hand-spike. And all the time, lo! that smiling sky, and this unsounded sea! Look! See you Albicore! who put it into him to chase and fang that flying-fish? Where do murderers go, man! Who's to doom, when the judge himself is dragged to the bar?

In the end, however, as inevitably happens to these men, beginning upon the basis of the ordinary needs of mankind, driven by the dominating will to positions of authority, feeling in time that the immense catastrophes and social upheavals are merely the result of inevitable destiny, they reach the stage where they see themselves as chosen instruments and ungoverned by any law. Ahab tells Starbuck near the end:

Ye two are the opposite poles of one thing; Starbuck is Stubb reversed, and Stubb is Starbuck; and ye two are all mankind; and Ahab stands alone among the millions of the peopled earth, nor gods nor men his neighbors!

Ahab's final word is fate:

This whole act's immutably decreed. 'Twas rehearsed by thee and me a billion years before this ocean rolled. Fool! I am the Fates' lieutenant; I act under orders. Look thou underling! that thou obeyest me.

No attempt has been made here to compare the bold strokes by which Melville draws the complete picture of Ahab's psychology with, for example, the more intimate and deeper psychology of Dostoyevsky. It is sufficient, however, that Melville draws the picture of modern tormented man driven by the inevitable desire to solve his problem, bringing the whole world down with him, and all this with a combination of realism and symbolism unmatched in the works of any author of the nineteenth or twentieth centuries.

The last word, so far as the social significance of the book is concerned, must be with Ishmael in which is perhaps the most remarkable page. The *Pequod* has been converted into a factory at sea – the try-works. The factory is aglow, the oil is boiling. It is night, and Ishmael, the intellectual, suddenly feels that the whole spectacle is not within the bounds of reason. "The burning ship drove on, as if remorselessly commissioned to some vengeful deed." See now what can easily pass for a picture of the more primitive type of industry but which was characteristic of much of the unskilled industry of Melville's time. Note particularly the role played by the men in this astonishing bit of symbolism.

The hatch, removed from the top of the works, now afforded a wide hearth in front of them. Standing on this were the Tartarean shapes of the pagan harpooners, always the whaleship's stokers. With huge pronged poles they pitched hissing masses of blubber into the scalding pots, or stirred by the fires beneath, till the snaky flames darted, curling, out of the doors to catch them by the feet. The smoke rolled away in sullen heaps. To every pitch of the ship there was a pitch of boiling oil, which seemed all eagerness to leap into their faces. Opposite the mouth of the works, on the further side of the wide wooden hearth, was the windlass. This served for a sea-sofa. Here lounged the watch when not otherwise employed, looking into the red heat of the fire, till their eyes felt scorched in their heads. Their tawny features, now all begrimed with smoke and sweat, their matted beards, and the contrasting barbaric brilliancy of their teeth, all these were strangely revealed in the capricious emblazonings of the works. As they narrated to each other their unholy adventures, their tales of terror told in words of mirth; as their uncivilized laughter forked upwards out of them, like the flames from the furnaces; as to and fro, in their front, the harpooners wildly gesticulated with their huge pronged forks and dippers; as the wind howled on, and the sea leaped, and the ship groaned and dived, and yet steadfastly shot her red hell further and further into the blackness of the sea, and the night, and scornfully champed the white bone in her mouth, and viciously spat round her on all sides; then the rushing *Pequod,* freighted with savages, and laden with fire, and burning a corpse, and plunging into that blackness of darkness, seemed the material counterpart of her monomaniac commander's soul.

It is impossible to say more clearly that modern industrial society was going to its doom and that Ahab's madness was the result of this society.

Finally in this very chapter Melville brings out clearly the character of Ishmael the intellectual. He is the exact opposite of both. He is the man without will. He is the man who sees Ahab's madness, is swept up by it, is intelligent enough to oppose it but like Melville himself has no substitute, no force with which to oppose the mad captain. That night he is at the helm. He can see nothing ahead but disaster.

Nothing seemed before me but a jet gloom, now and then made ghastly by flashes of redness. Uppermost was the impression, that whatever swift rushing thing I stood on was not so much bound to any haven ahead as rushing from all havens astern.

Melville saw, and indeed on the basis of his experiences, could see no solution whatever, but it is noticeable that this American, this product of the heroic individualism of 1776 to 1850 had no sympathy whatever with intellectualism or escapism of any kind. The society was doomed, and he sent it to its doom. Ahab knew what he wanted and Melville not only admires Ahab but has nothing but scorn for the intellectual without will. The book begins with Ishmael stating that when he has reached a stage where he could no longer stand the world, then he goes to sea. But in a remarkable chapter called "The Masthead," Melville deals once and for all with the soul-sick. Ishmael climbs up the mast to do his share but up there he keeps a "sorry guard," "the problem of the universe is revolving in him." He is up there deep in thought and reveling in his sorrow, so to speak, reveling in his intellectual problems. But Melville, with that sarcastic yet genially Shakespearean humor which he uses so often, soon puts him in his place, making him say of anyone so loftily perched:

There is no life in thee, now, except that rocking life imparted by a gently rolling ship; by her, borrowed from the sea; by the sea, from the inscrutable tides of God. But while this sleep, this dream is on ye, move your foot or hand an inch, slip your hold at all; and your identity comes back in horror. Over Descartian vortices, you hover. And perhaps, at mid-day, in the fairest weather, with one half throttled shriek you drop through that transparent air into the summer sea, no more to rise for ever. Heed it well, ye Panthesis.

Melville had no use for the ivory tower, nor would he have had for those for whom the problems of the universe revolve in their own insides. The point is that he knew the type.

There must be a final point on his style. Buffon says that the style is the man. And that is true. But the really great man is the society. And therefore, through remote refractions, the style is more than the man. It is the society too.

It has been noted that Melville is very strongly influenced by, among other writers, Shakespeare and Sir Thomas Browne. Melville's *Moby Dick*, as I have indicated above, is truly Shakespearean in the geniality and breadth of its humor. But Shakespeare's influence on Melville is, in my opinion, a social matter. Shakespeare came on the eve of a great change in the society of his country.

He expressed the immense vitality of an age which was finishing and another which was about to begin. He felt the individualism and its ramifications which were to distinguish European society for hundreds of years. It is clear that Melville felt the same about the America of his time, clear that he viewed the new man with the same interest, insight and at the same time, fearful admiration with which Shakespeare feared Macbeth, Othello and Lear. At the same time, the influence of Sir Thomas Browne is very strong. Browne in his *Urn Burial* expressed a learned historical scepticism of the very vitality which so attracted Shakespeare. Browne seemed to say that history in the end worked out only to dead bones and a tomb. I do not think it at all surprising that both these authors influenced Melville to the extraordinary extent that they did. He was conscious of the immense vitality and dangers of the individualism which he now saw about to rise to a new and unprecedented stage. But he was conscious also as Browne was conscious of the inevitable end of all things:

. . . all collapsed and the great shroud of the sea rolled on as it rolled five thousand years ago.

THE ABOLITIONISTS

Whitman and Melville were intellectuals, and their work must be treated as the work of such. With the Abolitionist intellectuals, we touch a new dimension, intellectuals whose whole intellectual, social and political creativity was the expression of precise social forces. They were the means by which a direct social movement expressed itself, the movement of the slaves and free Negroes for freedom. Any kind of analysis of the Abolitionist intellectuals must therefore begin with the slaves.

The decade 1820–30 in the United States marked the birth of capitalist America. The transition from colonial America did not take place tranquilly. The election of Jackson in 1828 marked a great political uprising of the people, believing that by their votes they had overthrown a corrupt and aristocratic administration. In 1824 Denmark Vesey had led a major slave revolt.

After the failure of the Denmark Vesey revolt, the Negro slaves had to find other means to gain their liberty. The Underground Railroad began to function around 1825. In 1826 the free Negroes organized the Massachusetts

General Colored Peoples Association. Terrified by the emergence of a political leadership among the Negroes themselves, the slave-owners concentrated their efforts on persistent persecution of the free Negroes, particularly through the propaganda of the American Society for the Colonization of the Negroes in Africa. In the middle states, through which the Underground Railroad passed, there were eighty branches of this society. Against this persecution the Negroes mobilized to publish *Freedom's Journal*, the first Negro newspaper in the United States.

Such was the condition of the slavery issue when, in 1829, a Negro named David Walker wrote, printed and scattered over the South a pamphlet entitled Walker's Appeal. It was addressed to the free blacks who were urged to make the cause of the slave their own; it censured that meekness and non-resistance of the blacks; and in a third edition, published in 1830, it went so far as to touch on the superiority in numbers and bravery of the blacks over the white, and to advise an insurrection when the time was ripe. The effect was immediate. Copies found in the hands of Negroes in Richmond (Virginia), in New Orleans, in Savannah, in Tarborough (North Carolina), were seized and formally transmitted by the governors of Virginia, Louisiana, Georgia and North Carolina to their respective legislatures; and sharp laws against the free blacks were enacted by Georgia and Louisiana.

The excitement produced by Walker's Appeal had not subsided when the danger of writings of this sort was brought home to the slave-owners by a rising of slaves in Virginia – an outbreak known as "Nat Turner's Insurrection." It was quickly put down; and every Negro concerned in it, together with many who were not, was hanged, shot, mutilated or beheaded.

Thus the *Cambridge Modern History* describes this period.

The free Negroes continued to organize. The *Rights of All* appeared at this time, and the first National Negro Convention was called in September 1830. It was in 1831 that Garrison's *Liberator* appeared. At first a supporter of the Colonization Society, Garrison had been converted by the political organizations and publications of the free Negroes to recognize that colonization was merely a euphemism for the slave-owner's persecution of the free Negroes. At first obscure and isolated, Garrison's *Liberator* became after the Nat Turner Insurrection nationally famous. Thus continues the *Cambridge Modern History* account:

The insurrection was at once attributed to Negro preachers and "incendiary publications" such as Walker's pamphlet and the *Liberator*. . . . To attack the *Liberator* now became habitual in all slaveholding states. The corporation of one city forbade any free Negro to take a copy of it from the post office. A vigilance committee in another offered $1500 for the detection and conviction of any white person found circulating copies. The governors of Georgia and Virginia called on the Mayor of

Boston to suppress it; and the legislature of Georgia offered $5000 to any person who should secure the arrest and conviction of Garrison under the laws of the state. Undeterred by these attacks, Garrison gathered about him a little band of Abolitionists, and towards the close of 1831, founded at Boston the New England Anti-slavery Society, and in 1833 at Philadelphia, the American Anti-slavery Society. The mission of the society was to labour for the abolition of slavery and the immediate emancipation of the slaves, and to carry on this work by organizing societies, sending out orators, and enlisting the pulpit and the press, and by the circulation of anti-slavery books, pamphlets, newspapers, and pictures.

From that beginning there was no turning back. It is sufficient to say here that the Underground Railroad with its constant stream of Negro slaves and the free Negroes were the driving force of Abolition from which it drew its most effective policy and most effective personnel. Without this constant contact with the mass, Abolitionism would have been nothing, and none knew this and admitted it more freely than the Abolitionists themselves. They had found what both Whitman and Melville had failed to find.

A finished book will have to relate Emerson, Thoreau and the Transcendentalists to Whitman, Melville and the Abolitionists. It cannot be done here. Sufficient to say that even Parrington says that the soil which produced Emerson also produced Garrison – they were complementary parts of the same movement. What we have to show is that if Whitman anticipated the new loneliness of the American character, its passion for the old free association which it was losing, the powerful but false ideals which it tried to substitute and did substitute for many years; if Melville brushed aside the slaves and painted a picture of impending catastrophe for America and the whole world, whose significance we are only today able to see; then the Abolitionist intellectuals in their political action showed a solution or rather a method of solution that corresponded in range and intensity to the inspired vision of Melville. If Melville saw the totalitarian dictator as the ultimate end, the Abolitionist intellectual embodied an American anticipation of the most radical political action that the nineteenth and twentieth centuries have known. To show this could best be done here under the following headings:

The social situation from which the Abolitionists sprang
The actual characteristics of the movement
Its foreshadowing of the future.

The situation from which Abolitionism sprang:

Earlier we have referred to the blight which had descended upon the nation in regard to the discussion of slavery. New York commercial houses, New England cotton manufacturers led the powerful interests in the North;

their spokesman was Daniel Webster. Henry Clay spoke for the West. The clash which ended with the Missouri Compromise had frightened the nation. By common consent slavery was declared unfit for discussion. Says John Jay Chapman:

The years between 1820 and 1830 were the most pitiable through which this country has ever passed. The conscience of the North was pledged to the Missouri Compromise, and that Compromise neither slumbered nor slept. In New England, where the old theocratical oligarchy of the colonies had survived the Revolution and kept under its own water-locks the new flood of trade, the conservatism of politics reinforced the conservatism of religion; and as if these two inquisitions were not enough to stifle the soul of man, the conservatism of business self-interest was super-imposed. The history of the conflict which followed has been written by the radicals who negligently charge up to self-interest all the resistance which establishments offer to change. But it was not solely self-interest, it was conscience that backed the Missouri Compromise, nowhere else, naturally so strongly as in New England. It was conscience that made cowards of us all. The white-lipped generation of Edward Everett were victims, one might say, even martyrs, to conscience. They suffered the most terrible martyrdom that can fall to man, a martyrdom which injured their immortal volition and dried up the spirit of life. If it were not that our poets have too seldom deigned to dig into real life, I do not know what more awful subject for a poem could have been found than that of the New England judge enforcing the Fugitive Slave Law. For lack of such a poem the heroism of these men has been forgotten, the losing heroism of conservatism. It was this spiritual power of a committed conscience which met the new forces as they arose, and it deserves a better name than these new forces afterwards gave it. In 1830 the social fruits of these heavy conditions could be seen in the life of the people. Free speech was lost.

"I know of no country," says Tocqueville, who was here in 1831, "in which there is so little independence of mind and freedom of discussion as in America." Tocqueville recurs to the point again and again. He cannot disguise his surprise at it, and it tinged his whole philosophy and his book. The timidity of the Americans in this era was a thing which intelligent foreigners could not understand.

Chapman also says of the Transcendentalists:

The transcendentalists were sure of only one thing – that society as constituted was all wrong. In this their main belief they were right. They were men and women whose fundamental need was activity, contact with real life, and the opportunity for social expansion; and they keenly felt the chill and fictitious character of the reigning conventionalities.

Boston was particularly difficult, but Melville and Whitman as well as the New England intellectuals felt the stifling bonds.

But there was an immediate problem. Let us take Garrison's biographer:

The slavery question had shaken men's faith in the durability of the republic. It was therefore adjudged a highly dangerous subject. The political physicians with one accord prescribed on the ounce-of-prevention principle, quiet, SILENCE and OBLIVION, to be administered in large and increasing doses to both sections. Mum was the word, and mum the country solemnly and suddenly became from Maine to Georgia.

We must get that atmosphere well. Everything seemed at stake.

The characteristics of the organization:

It is necessary here to *abstract*. Any rounded portrayal of the Abolitionists is out of the question. But as we look back at them in the light of modern history, we can extract and tabulate from their concrete activity certain characteristics:

(1) They proposed immediate and unconditional emancipation of the slave on the soil.

This meant to tear up by the roots the foundation of the Southern economy and society, wreck Northern commerce, and disrupt the union irretrievably. Washington, Jefferson and the others had challenged a *foreign* Europe. There had been a long train of usurpations, they had been pricked and goaded by revolutionary elements at home, they went to the goal by stages.

Garrison took a stand on fundamental principle and principled the movement remained to the end. They renounced all traditional politics, denouncing all political parties of the day as corrupt. After thirty years, they supported Lincoln's government only when they saw it would lead a war against the South.

(2) The movement was pacifist, and Garrison depended on what he called moral suasion. But it was a strange pacifism which had as its avowed aim to "startle the South to madness." In fact the violence of the polemic, the attack without bounds upon everything that stood in the way, the unceasing denunciations of slave property, the government, the constitution, the laws, the church, was in itself a repudiation of pacifism and before the Civil War began, Garrison was almost alone in his pacifism.

(3) In time they denied the authority of the Constitution, calling it a pro-slavery document. They called upon the government to break the tie with the South, and as late as 1860, welcoming [sic] the secession of Georgia, etc. This principled denial of the very authority of government was and is a very feature of mass politics and they carried it out in their day-to-day

policies.

(4) Yet Garrison's party aimed at being a mass party. It aimed at convincing the masses of the people and by this means overturning the deeper foundations of the evil which had corrupted society, politics and the church.

(5) The movement was an international one. From the very beginning the Garrisonians covered Europe, carrying on an incessant unbridled polemic against slavery, among monarchs, statesmen, organizations and common people. One Negro alone brought home a million signatures from Germany. In the minds of most Americans they were the bitterest traducers of their country not only at home but abroad.

(6) They took this attitude to a logical conclusion and openly hoped for the defeat of their country in the Mexican War which they claimed was for the purpose of extending slavery.

(7) They were interracial. They preached and practiced Negro equality. They endorsed and fought for the equality of women.

(8) They were intolerant. They hated and mercilessly excoriated all who had the slightest touch with slavery. Hale, the head of the Free Soil Movement, was denounced for putting his name to a petition to raise a monument for Henry Clay.

They respected nothing but their cause and denounced equally those leaders of the Free Soil Party who walked in the funeral procession of Daniel Webster. Phillips explains their principles:

When we think of such a man as Henry Clay, his long life, his mighty influence cast always into the scale against the slave – of that irresistable fascination with which he moulded every one to his will; when we remember that, his conscience acknowledging the justice of our cause, and his heart open on every other side to the gentlest impulses, he could sacrifice so remorselessly his convictions and the welfare of millions to his low ambitions; when we think how the slave trembled at the sound of his voice, and that, from a multitude of breaking hearts, there went up nothing but gratitude to God when it pleased him to call that great sinner from this world – we cannot find it in our hearts, we could not shape our lips to ask any man to do him honor. (Great sensation.) No amount of eloquence, no sheen of official position, no loud grief of partisan friends, would ever lead us to ask monuments or walk in fine processions for pirates; and the sectarian zeal or selfish ambition which gives up, deliberately and in full knowledge of the facts, three millions of human beings to hopeless ignorance, daily robbery, systematic prostitution and murder, which the law is neither able nor undertakes to prevent or avenge, is more monstrous in our eyes, than the love of gold which takes a score of lives with merciful quickness on the high seas. Haynau on the Danube is no more hateful to us than Haynau on the Potomac. Why give mobs to one, and monuments to the other?

Phillips generalized the policy:

We do not *play* politics; antislavery is no half-jest with us; it is a terrible earnest, with life or death, worse than life or death as the issue. It is no law-suit, where it matters not to the good feeling of opposing counsels which way the verdict goes, and where advocates can shake hands after the decision as pleasantly as before.

And again:

We will gibbet the name of every apostate so black and high that his children's children shall blush to bear it.

And by apostate they meant anyone who was not with them. If he was not with them, then he as good as supported slavery.

(9) The Abolitionists among themselves showed another startling characteristic. They argued over every comma of their doctrine with the utmost pertinacity and unyieldingness. "Sincerity," says Phillips, "is no shield for any man from the criticism of his fellow-laborers," and he attacked a man so devoted to the cause as Senator Sumner. Correct policy was what mattered. Nothing else. So much so, that one well-wisher after hearing an acrimonious debate uttered a sentiment general at the time: to listen to the Abolitionists abuse each other was a sure way to become an anti-Abolitionist. Yet despite the innumerable splits and the venomous controversies, a radical Abolitionist was a man apart, and recognized as such by his colleagues as well as by the rest of the population. Despite the acrimonious and recriminating character of their discussions and denunciations, they never at any time showed the faintest trace of that totalitarianism and degrading uniformity which characterizes the Communist Parties of today.

(10) They sought no rewards, fighting for the pure idea. But they faced the hostility of the state, the local police, and the best citizens. They were beaten, stoned and mobbed. Some of them were killed. Garrison had the narrowest of escapes. Douglass was beaten and left for dead. Pacifist though they were in theory, they took part in the rescues of fugitive slaves, not only by underground methods but in open defiance of all authority.

That Garrison was opposed to the labor movement as such, that these Abolitionists would have failed had it not been for fundamental social forces working in their favor, (which they knew and counted on) all these things and many others are true. Any full study would have to show them in their concrete environment, would show their many weaknesses, contradictions, and even many absurdities. But one thing emerges. Out of America, with no assistance from any alien tradition but from the very genius of the country emerged this clearly recognizable replica of the early Christians, the Puritans, and later the early Bolsheviks, types which have appeared only when fundamental changes are shaking a society to its depths.

Like Whitman and Melville, the Abolitionist intellectuals were only anticipations, an eruption in a crisis whose full significance would only be seen later. By 1855 when the Republican Party was formed, their work was historically over, that is to say, if they had disappeared, the course of history would have been little altered. But before they disappeared in 1865, they were able to take their ideas to their logical conclusions and leave the clearest anticipation of the modern world that was to come out of this upheaval. In the last decade before the Civil War, the Abolitionist intellectuals reached their furthest point in Frederick Douglass who in himself represented the forces of the nation opposed to the South to a degree more than any other single individual of the time. But as the war approached, Wendell Phillips developed a political policy for Abolitionism which to this day remains ignored and almost forgotten. Yet seen in its context, it is perhaps the highest peak reached by the United States intellectuals in the foreshadowing of the future of the world of today and in indicating how deeply all great world currents are integral to the United States as a nation.

Phillips in the past had openly preached and practiced disregard of law:

I admit the right and duty of minorities to disregard immoral or unconstitutional law.

Now after John Brown's raid he said:

The Lesson of the Hour! I think the lesson of the hour is insurrection (Sensation). Insurrection of thought always preceded the insurrection of arms.

He developed fully the thesis of a slave insurrection. From the beginning of the Civil War he preached that the Negro slaves were the key to America's future. He opened his speech on Lincoln's election by saying that for the first time the *slave* had elected a President of the United States.

The Negro for fifty, or thirty, years has been the basis of our commerce, the root of our politics, the pivot in our pulpit, the inspiration of almost all that is destined to live in our literature.

The Negro was the key:

The papers are accumulating statistics to prove that the Negro will work, and asking whether he will fight. If he will not fight, we are gone, that is all! If he will not work without the leash, the Union is over.

As early as February 1861 he came clearly out for an insurrection among the Negroes:

Strictly speaking, I repudiate the term "insurrection." The slaves are not a herd of vassals. They are a nation, four million strong; having the same right of revolution that Hungary and Florence have. I acknowledge the right of two million and a half of white people in the seven seceding states to organize their government as they choose. Just as freely I acknowledge the right of four million of black people to organize *their* government, and to vindicate that right by arms.

The Negroes began to come early over to the North:

The blacks are with us, and not with the South. At present they are the only Unionists.

That was the force which would win the war:

McClellan may drill a better army – more perfect soldiers. He will never marshal a stronger force than those grateful thousands. That is the way to save insurrection. He is an enemy to civil liberty, the worst enemy to his own land, who asks for such delay or perversion of government policy as is sure to result in an insurrection. Our duty is to save these four millions of blacks from their own passions, from their own confusion, and eight millions of whites from the consequences of it.

I maintain therefore the power of the government itself to inaugurate such a policy; and I say, in order to save the Union, do justice to the black.

Some men, say, begin it [the new Union] by exporting the blacks.

For him the freed Negroes with land were the very basis of democracy in the South.

If you do, you export the very fulcrum of the lever, you export the very best material to begin with. Something has been said about the Alleghanies moving toward the ocean as the symbol of colonization. Let me change it. The nation that would shovel down the Alleghanies, and then build it up again, would be a wise nation compared with the one that should export four million blacks and then import four millions of Chinese to take their place. To dig a hole, and then fill it up again, would be Shakespearean wisdom compared with such an undertaking. I want the blacks as the very basis of the effort to regenerate the South.

They were the allies of Northern democracy.

We are to take military possession of the territory, and we are to work out the great problem of unfolding a nation's life. We want the four millions of blacks – a people instinctively on our side, ready and skilled to work; the only element the South has which belongs to the nineteenth century.

What then of the South? He preached the complete destruction of the old South. He was ready then to advocate subsidies to the loyal slaveholders but land to the blacks.

That sum which the North gives the loyal slave-holder, not as acknowledging his property in the slave, but a measure of conciliation – perhaps an acknowledgement of its share of the guilt – will call mills, ships, agriculture into being. The free Negro will redeem to us lands never touched, whose fertility laughs Illinois to scorn, and finds no rival but Egypt. And remember besides, as Montesquieu says, "the yield of land depends less on its fertility than on the freedom of its inhabitants." Such a measure binds the Negro to us by the indissoluble tie of gratitude; the loyal slaveholder, by strong self-interest – our bonds are all his property; the other whites, by prosperity, – they are lifted in the scale of civilization and activity, educated and enriched. Our institutions are then homogeneous. We grapple the Union together with hooks of steel, – make it as lasting as the granite which underlies the continent.

He attacked the South with a violence matched only by the attacks of the South upon the North. The South was "one large brothel." By the South, he said, he meant a principle:

And by the South, I mean likewise a principle, and not a locality, an element of civil life, in fourteen rebellious States. I mean an element which, like the days of Queen Mary and the Inquisition, can not tolerate free speech, and punishes it with the stake. I mean the aristocracy of the skin, which considers the Declaration of Independence a sham, and democracy a snare, – which believes that one-third of the race is born booted and spurred, and the other two-thirds ready saddled for that third to ride. I mean a civilization which prohibits the Bible by statute to every sixth man of its community, and puts a matron in a felon's cell for teaching a black sister to read. I mean the intellectual, social, aristocratic, South – the thing that manifests itself by barbarism and the bowie-knife, by bullying and lynch-law, by ignorance and idleness, by the claims of one man to own his brother, by statutes making it penal for the State of Massachusetts to bring an action in her courts, by statutes, standing on the books of Georgia today, offering five thousand dollars for the head of William Lloyd Garrison. That South is to be annihilated. [Loud applause.] The totality of my common sense – or whatever you may call it – is this, all summed up in one word: This country will never know peace nor union until the South (using the words in the sense I have described) is annihilated, and the North is spread over it.

Our struggle, therefore, is between barbarism and civilization – such can only be settled by arms.

This was no matter of vengeance or mere subjective hatred of evil. Phillips understood sooner and more clearly than any in the North what was involved. He claimed that any compromise with the South would mean an agreement on the South's terms and these terms would inevitably mean the nationalization of slavery, and the subjugation of free speech and democracy in the North to aristocratic tyranny. Hence the ruthlessness of his conclusion:

I am for conciliation but not for conciliating the slave-holder. Death to the system and death or exile to the master is the only motto.

But Phillips' revolutionism did not stop there. In pursuit of this policy Phillips was ready to overthrow the government. He denounced the President and his Commander-in-Chief as traitors:

I do not say that McClellan is a traitor, but I say this, that if he had been a traitor from the crown of his head to the sole of his foot, he could not have served the South better than he has done since he was Commander-in-Chief. [Applause.] He could not have carried on the war in more exact deference to the politics of that side of the Union. And almost the same thing may be said of Mr. Lincoln – that if he had been a traitor, he could not have worked better to strengthen one side, and hazard the success of the other. There is more danger today that Washington will be taken than Richmond. Washington is beseiged more truly than Richmond is. After fifteen months of war, such is the position of the strongest nation on the globe; for the nineteen Northern states, led by a government which served their ideas, are the strongest nation on the face of the globe. Now, I think, and if I were in the Senate I should have said to the government, that every man who under the present policy loses his life in the swamps of the South, and every dollar sent there to be wasted, only prolongs a murderous and wasteful war, waged for no purpose whatever. This is my meaning. In this war, mere victory on a battle-field amounts to nothing; contributes little or nothing toward ending the war. If our present policy led to decisive victories, therefore (which it does not), it would be worth little. The war can only be ended by annihilating that oligarchy which formed and rules the South and makes war – by annihilating a state of society. No social state is really annihilated, except when it is replaced by another. Our present policy neither aims to annihilate that state of things we call the "South," made up of pride, idleness, ignorance, barbarism, theft, and murder, nor to replace it with a substitute. But an aimless war I call wasteful and murderous.

He developed what he believed with extraordinary clarity. He believed and said that only *defeat* would stir the government.

If we are ever called upon to see another President of the United States on horseback flying from his Capitol, waste no tears! He will return to that Capitol on the arms of a million of adult Negroes, the sure basis of a Union which will never be broken. [Applause.]

He was prepared to purge the government not only during the war but after:

I believe in events, I believe in the inevitable tendency of these coming ten years towards liberty and Union. But it is to be done as England did it in 1640, by getting rid gradually, man by man, of those who don't believe in progress, but live and mean to live in the past. And as man by man of that class retires, and we bring to the front men who are earnest in the present, victory, strength and peace are to be the result.

The reference to the year 1640 is significant. All his life he was a student of the Civil War in England and in 1640 began the conflict which ended in the government of Cromwell in 1649.

He claimed that Lincoln's government had the characteristic Whig ignorance and distrust of the people. Properly led, the North could have defeated the South in a few months. He insisted that the people were ready, and he spoke as one who had worked among them for thirty years. We can only briefly indicate his tactical proposals which were as ruthless as his politics. He was no abstract anarchistic democrat. Lincoln's government, like any war government, was correct in assuming dictatorial powers. But the only justification for this was a policy based upon the people. He refused to cease his criticism. He said that if he were a member of the Senate he would not have voted one soldier or one penny until his policy had been adopted. This was not mere talk. He made some of these statements surrounded by hostile crowds and in those days his life was more than ever in danger. He was by now the virtual leader of the Abolitionist movement. To conclude this brief sketch, the policy of seizure of the land by the Negroes was known in the South among the Negroes as a Wendell Phillips. Phillips at one time was organizing a party to challenge Lincoln's government but by degrees the power of the North asserted itself, and for the same reasons that the Republican party superseded the Abolitionists, Lincoln's government was never challenged from the Left.

But one thing is clear. The great national crises in social upheavals are caused by challenges to revolutionary governments, not to established ones. It was the challenge of Lilburne and the Levellers to Cromwell; of the Paris Commune to the Committee of Public Safety and Robespierre which marked the most desperate crises of the revolutionary regime. It never came to this in the Civil War. But the Abolitionists and Phillips in particular show that in the United States, such an embryo, such an anticipation of extreme revolutionism had developed. Phillips in his context and in his political programs showed the same breadth of view, the revolutionary conception of democracy, and political ruthlessness which are associated with what is loosely called Bolshevism. His ideas for America, and he was prepared to go through blood and fire for them, should be indicated.

There is a party for whom I have ever the right hand of conciliation, and whenever the foot of military despotism is lifted from that party, I believe that in the South itself we shall be surprised by the weight, strength and number of the men who still love the Union. There is a party for whom I have conciliation and this [taking by the hand a beautiful little girl of five years old, with a fair complexion and light auburn ringlets] is its representative. In the veins that beat now in my right hand runs the best blood in Virginia's white races and the better blood of the black race of the Old Dominion [applause] – a united race, to whom, in its virtue, belongs in the future a country, which the toil and labor of its ancestors redeemed from nature and gave to civilization and the nineteenth century. [Applause.] For that class I have ever an open door of conciliation – the labor, the toil, the muscle, the virtue, the strength, the democracy, of the Southern States. This blood represents them all, – the poor white, a non-slaveholder, deluded into rebellion for a system which crushes him – some equally deluded and some timid and gagged masters – the slave restored to his rights, when, now, at last, for the first time in her history, Virginia has a government and is not a horde of pirates masquerading as a state. So, the South has not yet felt the first symptoms of exhaustation. Get no delusive hope that our success is to come from any such source.

He ends another speech:

Never until we welcome the Negro, the foreigner, all races as equal, and melted together in a common nationality hurl them all at despotism, will the North deserve triumph or earn it at the hands of a just God. [Applause.] But the North will triumph. I hear it. Do you remember in that disastrous siege in India, when the Scotch girl raised her head from the pallet of the hospital, and said to the sickening hearts of the English, "I hear the bagpipes, the Campbells are coming," and they said, "Jessie, it is delirium," "No, I know it; I heard it far off." And in an hour a pibroch burst upon their glad ears, and the banners of England floated in triumph over their heads. So I hear in the dim distance the first notes of the jubilee rising from the hearts of the millions. Soon, very soon, you shall hear it at the gates of the Citadel, and the Stars and Stripes shall guarantee liberty forever from the Lakes to the Gulf. [Continued Applause.]

The simplicity and sincerity of his whole life show that he was one of those rare politicians who say such things and *act upon them*. The attempt of the American Communist Party to appropriate Phillips as one of their national heroes is not very successful. It cannot be – reshaped though he is – and this will not continue long. The great orator and inflexible politician cannot *in America* be manipulated for any other purpose than those he professed.

It is possible now with extreme brevity to sum up a lengthy chapter:

(1) Whitman: a singer of loneliness and Democracy with a capital D.

3

1876–1919: The New Individualism

1876 marked the end of the attempt of the South to establish a democracy upon the traditional pattern. Northern capital, in the full tide of its strength, unrecognized before 1865, now organized the West upon a pattern entirely different from the old equalitarian democracy. Except for the Populist outburst at the end of the century, which we shall take up later, the South seemed to become a backward part of the United States, content to work out its Negro problems along its own lines. The expansion westward dominates the development. In this period it is precisely here that the clash between the traditional America and the modern America first represents itself most sharply.

After de Tocqueville, the writer on America who has earned for himself both in the United States and abroad the greatest reputation as an analyst of the United States is Viscount Bryce, author of the *American Commonwealth*. Bryce was ambassador to the United States, a highly educated and trained example of the British politician of the late XIXth century. He had all its limitations, the chief of which was a fascinated interest in details, especially in political details which showed the difference between the British system and the American; conversely, he was deficient in analytical power. His mistakes are important.

In 1888, the year the first edition of his book appeared, he wrote as follows: (I propose here to use quotations heavily. The positive choice and gathering of material, its organization, is precisely what constitutes the actual writing of a book. Similarly, the using of Turner's work as a medium of controversy is for the present purpose and the present purpose only. The *probable* method in the book would be gathering the material from independent and preferably original sources and then posing the problem in terms of the conflicting views of well-known American politicians, writers, thinkers, etc. and the programs and actions of organizations).

There are no struggles between privileged and unprivileged orders, not even that perpetual strife of rich and poor which is the oldest disease of civilized states. One must not pronounce broadly that there are no classes, for in parts of the country social distinctions have begun to grow up. But for political purposes classes scarcely exist. No one of the questions which now agitate the nation is a question of rich and poor. Instead of suspicion, jealousy and arrogance, embittering the relations of classes, good feeling and kindliness reign. Everything that government, as the Americans have hitherto understood the term, can give them, the poorer class have already, political power, equal civil rights, a career open to all citizens alike, not to speak of that gratuitous higher as well as elementary education which on their own economic principles the United States might have abstained from giving, but which political reasons have led them to provide with so unstinting a hand. Hence the poorer have had nothing to fight for, no grounds for disliking the well-to-do, no complaint to make against them. The agitation of the last few years has been directed, not against the richer sort generally, but against incorporated companies, and a few wealthy capitalists, who are deemed to have abused the powers which the privilege of incorporation conferred upon them, or employed their wealth to procure legislation unfair to the public. Where violent language has been used like that with which France and Germany are familiar, it has been used, not by native Americans, but by newcomers, who bring their Old World passions with them. Property is safe, because those who hold it are far more numerous than those who do not; the usual motives for revolution vanish; universal suffrage, even when vested in ignorant newcomers, can do comparatively little harm, because the masses have obtained everything which they could hope to attain except by a general pillage. And the native Americans, though the same cannot be said of some of the recent immigrants, are shrewd enough to see that the poor would suffer from such pillage no less than the rich.

Six years later, in 1894, in revising his book, he added an observation:

Revising this chapter in 1894, I leave these words, which were written in 1888, to stand as they were. They then expressed, as I believe, the view which the most judicious Americans themselves took of their country. Looking at the labour troubles of the last three years, and especially at the great railroad strike riots of July 1894, that view may seem too roseate. It is, however, to be remembered that those riots were mainly the work of recent immigrants, whom American institutions have not had time to educate, though the folly of abstract theory has confided votes to them; and it must also be noted that the opinion of the native Americans, with little distinction of class, approved the boldness with which the Federal Executive went to the extreme limits of its constitutional powers in repressing them. In any case, it seems better to await the teachings of the next few years rather than let matured conclusions be suddenly modified by passing events.

Bryce was a very able man. And his blindness is of importance because it exemplifies the blindness which distinguishes so many foreign commentators.

It is important also because it expresses an opinion which is still widely spread in Europe and Asia; it formed the prevailing ideology of an important section of the American people until less than twenty years ago.

In 1893, however, a very acute observer and scholar, Professor Turner had already seen and stated the *new* problem of American civilization. Turner saw a great deal clearly. At the same time his very mistakes illumined the problem to an extraordinary degree. He saw the actuality and the future in a manner impossible to the limited vision of Bryce. Turner saw clearly the heroic quality of American individualism in the early days. It is worthwhile to repeat this:

The result is that to the frontier the American intellect owes its striking characteristics. That coarseness and strength combined with acuteness and inquisitiveness; that practical inventive turn of mind, quick to find expedients; that masterful grasp of material things, lacking in the artistic but powerful to affect great ends; that restless, nervous energy; that dominant individualism, working for good and for evil, and withal that buoyancy and exuberance which comes with freedom – these are traits of the frontier, or traits called out elsewhere because of the existence of the frontier.

Turner fails to understand that the very conditions of early capitalism in a country without feudal remains developed these same qualities among its most active elements. He does not understand clearly enough that the frontier by itself would have been the home of nothing but wild animals and wild men but for the drive of *capital* constantly reaching out for further expansion. But he sees the change that took place after the middle of the century. Writing in 1901 he says:

But the most striking development in the industrial history of the Middle West in recent years has been due to the opening of the iron mines of Lake Superior. Even in 1873 the Lake Superior ores furnished a quarter of the total production of American blast furnaces. The opening of the Gogebic mines in 1884, and the development of the Vermillion and Mesabi mines adjacent to the head of the lake, in the early nineties, completed the transfer of iron ore production to the Lake Superior region. Michigan, Minnesota, and Wisconsin together now produce the ore for eighty per cent of the pig-iron of the United States. Four-fifths of this great product moves to the ports on Lake Erie and the rest to the manufactories at Chicago and Milwaukee. The vast steel and iron industry that centers at Pittsburgh and Cleveland, with important outposts like Chicago and Milwaukee, is the outcome of the meeting of the coal of the eastern and southern borders of the province and of Pennsylvania with the iron ores of the north. The industry has been systematized and consolidated by a few captains of industry. Steam shovels dig the ore from many of the Mesabi mines; gravity roads carry it to the docks and to the ships, and huge hoisting and carrying devices, built especially for the traffic, unload it for the railroad and the furnace. Iron and coal mines, transportation fleets, railroad systems, and iron manufactures are concentrated in a few corporations, principally the United States Steel Corporation.

He adds and rightly:

The world has never seen such a consolidation of capital and so complete a systematization of economic processes.

The last sentence is the key to the new West. In the cooperative and social nature of the productive process is the complete repudiation of the old individualistic America. But Turner, like so many Americans to this day, could not recognize that the emphasis had passed from individual to social. He does say:

But when the arid lands and the mineral resources of the Far West were reached, no conquest was possible by the old individual pioneer methods. Here expensive irrigation works must be constructed, cooperative activity was demanded in utilization of the water-supply, capital beyond the reach of the small farmer was required. In a word, the physiographic province itself decreed that the destiny of this new frontier should be social rather than individual.

But he adds:

Magnitude of social achievement is the watchword of the democracy since the Civil War. From petty towns built in the marshes, cities arose whose greatness and industrial power are the wonder of our time. The conditions were ideal for the production of captains of industry. The old democratic admiration for the self-made man, its old deference to the rights of competitive individual development, together with the stupendous natural resources that opened to the conquest of the keenest and the strongest, gave such conditions of mobility as enabled the development of the large corporate industries which in our own decade have marked the West.

Turner is not unaware of the dangers, but it is noticeable that his chief emphasis is still on de Tocqueville's (1) *Freedom of the Individual* – in this case the great captains of industry (2) *Freedom of Association* – the lack of obstacles in the way of free association of the great corporations which built these vast industries. It is perhaps the most astonishing thing about the way modern America thinks of itself – the need to believe that the individual industrialists and financiers who organized the vast industries of the West were merely new forms of the individualism of 1776–1861. Even by such a man as Turner things absolutely opposite are called the same.

The persistence of these ideas (we ignore the content with which Turner endows them) testifies to the undying vitality of the American ideal, a fundamental factor in all aspects of the life of the country today. Turner recognizes that immigrants who have come here have been attracted not by mere material conditions but by the needs of freedom.

The democracy of the newer West is deeply affected by the ideals brought by these immigrants from the Old World. To them America was not simply a new home; it was a land of opportunity, of freedom, of democracy. It meant to them, as to the American pioneer that preceded them, the opportunity to destroy the bonds of social caste that bound them in their older home, to hew out for themselves in a new country a destiny proportioned to the powers that God had given them, a chance to place their families under better conditions and to win a larger life than the life that they had left behind. He who believes that even the hordes of recent immigrants from southern Italy are drawn to these shores by nothing more than a dull and blind materialism has not penetrated into the heart of the problem. The idealism and expectation of these children of the Old World, the hopes which they have formed for a newer and freer life across the seas, are almost pathetic when one considers how far they are from the possibility of fruition. He who would take stock of American democracy must not forget the accumulation of human purposes and ideals which immigration has added to the American populace.

Thus, far from lessening the tradition and the needs of heroic individualism the immigrant millions have fortified it. Turner realizes the historic social consequences of this transformation:

Never before in the history of the world has a democracy existed on so vast an area and handled things in the gross with such success, with such largeness of design, and such grasp upon the means of execution. In short, democracy has learned in the West of the United States how to deal with the problem of magnitude. The old historic democracies were but little states with primitive economic conditions.

It is at this stage that Turner asks the fundamental question:

The question is imperative, then. What ideals persist from this democratic experience of the West; and have they acquired sufficient momentum to sustain themselves under conditions so radically unlike those in the days of their origin? In other words, the question put at the beginning of this discussion becomes pertinent. Under the forms of the American democracy is there in reality evolving such a concentration of economic and social power in the hands of a comparatively few men as may make political democracy an appearance rather than a reality? The free lands are gone. The material forces that gave vitality to Western democracy are passing away.

His answer is a pattern for the actual development which has taken place today and its complete futility.

It is to the realm of the spirit, to the domain of ideals and legislation that we must look for Western influence upon democracy in our own days.

It is a historic moment in American thought and practice, and in the thought and practice of Western civilization. That is precisely the dominant form that American social and political life has taken for fifty years and which it seeks to impose upon the world. The realm of the spirit, ideals, legislation. To which must be added institutions:

The problem of the United States is not to create democracy but to conserve democratic institutions and ideals . . . public schools . . .

The break with the past is complete. For it was the material conditions and social relations which created the individuality and freedom of early America which with all its defects was unprecedented in history and exceeded the best that the most advanced theorists of Europe could hope to see realized in their own day.

The very phrasing of Turner shows his realization of the fact that by 1901, an end had been reached. For half a century the United States has sought by legislation and institutions and the propagation of ideals to create what Turner calls a new democracy. The names of the political slogans tell the story. The Square Deal of Theodore Roosevelt was succeeded by the New Freedom of Woodrow Wilson. Franklin Roosevelt made new combinations. He proposed the New Deal and he specified the freedoms as four. President Truman continues the sequence with the Fair Deal. The result is democracy by state or as its enemies call it "statism." And pathetically, both sides argue for and against "statism" on behalf of our traditional freedom. What has happened to this freedom within the last fifty years?

It is idle to pretend that between 1876 and 1920 there appeared a development of American literature from the heights reached in 1840–65. Whitman continued his career, the foundation of which had been laid in 1855–65. A new figure emerges, however, Mark Twain. That both he and Whitman before they died repudiated the America of their day is not too important for us. What is remarkable is that two of Twain's books, *Tom Sawyer* and *Huckleberry Finn* have earned a secure place in the hearts of European intellectuals. In fact, as finished complete works, many European critics would give them a very high place in the American contribution to world literature. Thus the most popular writer of the advancing industrial age achieved his most finished expression in writing of the old democratic America – in this case the America of the frontier. That old America produced not only the greater writers of the middle of the century, it produced Lincoln and was the source, if only through nostalgia, of the two acknowledged masterpieces of the fifty years which followed the Civil War. Still more. Hemingway has gone so far as to say that the specific prose of America begins with the prose of Huck's journey down the river and modern critics have traced the "flat declarative" sentence which Hemingway used and popularized among so many modern writers as the specific speech of the frontier. It is altogether remarkable, and its significance will be appreciated later, how not only during the period of industrial growth but far more, in the contemporary period, whatever is socially significant in literature and the arts takes its roots from the United States which came to an end in the Civil War.

4

Freedom Today

(1) The official opinions of a very substantial organized body in the United States revolve around the thesis of the freedom of the individual, in business enterprises but elsewhere also, and free association. To sneer at this means to misunderstand the past of the United States and the tremendous power of this idea which is and will always remain a part of the national tradition. It cannot be abstracted from the nation. It is the peculiar, the special contribution of the United States to international civilization. It is reinforced by the national and international propaganda of those who rule, guide and instruct the United States and the people of the world about the United States. It is the axis of United States propaganda in the "cold war." In the minds of the American people, it is inextricably allied to the growth of productive power of the United States, both as cause and effect.

(2) At the same time, however, the economic and social structure of the United States has created so huge an apparatus of economic, social and political institutions that the freedom of the individual except in the most abstract terms does not exist. This is expressed in absolute terms by the phrase "welfare state."

(3) Caught in this contradiction and under the pressure of the labor organizations, the state actually proposes now no longer freedom but security; security for children; against sickness; better housing; for the rural areas technical education and fixed prices; for full employment; for vacations and pensions for the infirm and aged. There can be no more striking contrast to the heroic frontiersman, trader, sailor and artisan striving to be a capitalist, of the early days.

This is the perspective of some of the most liberal elements in the United States. It is the social and political perspective of the labor leaders. Center, left of center, progressive, reactionary, revolves around this program as the axis. In Europe it is claimed that this can be done only by nationalization of industry. America prepares to do it by free enterprise. But the aim is the same.

The *feasibility* of this program is not in question here, by which I mean that it is not germane to the argument. The decisive question is this. The great body of the American people have sufficiently demonstrated though so far chiefly in a negative fashion, that this program is not at all their idea of individual freedom and democracy. What exactly is individual freedom, freedom of association in the world of today, that they do not know. But their rejection of the present perspective is in our opinion sufficiently established.

In any essay of this kind it is necessary to take great leaps. We are faced now with the question of what has happened to individual freedom and freedom of association. The simplest way is to state (1) that freedom has been lost in modern industrial production (2) that the outstanding social fact of the United States is that the population has gone a long way on the road to recognizing that freedom has been lost.

This is the most important stage reached in the history of the United States since the Civil War. The real situation in the country is far more thoroughly understood than it was in the decades preceding the Civil War. The plain fact of the matter is that the leading industrialists in the country realize that the workers in the United States do not wish to work in the factories under the best conditions that industry is able to offer them. This must be established without a shadow of doubt for this explains the gaps between programs and the reality.

In 1932 Elton Mayo published his book *The Human Problems of an Industrial Civilization.* The result of careful experiments and investigations conducted over many years, the book seriously tackled for the first time the question: What are the conditions, wages, incentives, social aspirations of the average worker in industry? Mayo demonstrated the divorce that existed between the worker's conception of his relation to industry, what he thought of his work, his own relation to it, the incentives that evoked satisfactory work. He painted a picture of a working force in deep but baffled hostility with the conditions of labor as they existed in contemporary industry. The book was in sharp contrast with the methods of improving productivity associated with the names of Bedaux and Taylor. Mayo's proposals do not concern us here. Sufficient to say that his work can be adequately summed up in the need for individual freedom and free association of the modern worker. It was during the war and immediately after that the problems assumed the proportions of a fundamental crisis in the very bowels of the productive system. Burleigh B. Gardiner of the University of Chicago published in 1945 his *Human Relations in Industry.* In his introduction he quotes Elton Mayo that the "result of his studies is that while material efficiency has been increasing for two hundred years, the human capacity for working together has in the same period continually diminished. Of late the pace of this deterioration seems to have accelerated." And later: "Discussions about 'collective bargaining as a means of preventing industrial disputes' merely serve to mask the fact that the human capacity for spontaneous cooperation has greatly diminished or, at least, has not kept pace with other developments."

Collective bargaining has shown not the slightest ability to solve this problem. Yet the problem is fundamental because it involves:

(1) The question of productivity.

(2) The sleepless antagonism between the workers and supervising personnel, from which arises an abnormal tension, continuous disruption of production and an atmosphere which periodically explodes in labor conflicts of great violence over apparently secondary questions. Journalists never tire of pointing out the vast sums lost by workers in strikes, in comparison with the best they can gain. If money pure and simple was involved, such strikes would be far fewer in number and would be infinitely easier to settle. Within recent years the industrial capitalists of the country have recognized this as their most difficult problem because it is the problem which admits of no solution they can readily see.

Here are some extracts from the by now innumerable studies, pamphlets, articles, leaflets, circulars, etc. issued by the organizations of industrial capital or research institutions with which they cooperate closely.

Research Division, California Personnel Management Association – "The Break-Even Point in Employee Relations."

We have come a long way in the socialistic type of thinking in our relationship with our employees. We have assumed many of the responsibilities for the ultimate welfare of the individual that at one time was considered the worker's individual responsibility. I know that many people on our side of the table have arrived at the conclusion that there is an obligation on the part of industry to 'look after' its employees, to safeguard them from the hardships and other vicissitudes of life. Intelligent handling of the manpower on our payroll is the real answer of how to keep the break-even point in industrial relations low enough so we may perpetuate our individual businesses and our national economy. If our workers can be made to understand that there is nothing magic about success in business, if the workers can be made to believe that they as individuals have an obligation to bring to their work stations all the energy and all the ability which they possess, then and only then will the break-even point in business maintain itself at a place where everybody profits.

We know that the worker can do a better job. The job which men do in case of emergencies, is evidence of what they can do if they have the right attitude.

This organization has published up to 1949 forty-eight reports. I give a few titles:

No. 3: Future of Industrial Relations in the United States
No. 4: What Should We Tell Employees
No. 17: What Facts Need Facing in Industrial Relations
No. 19: Labor Relations and Hindrances to Full Production
No. 34: New Demands on Management
No. 47: Management's Uncertain Position in Union Relations

I quote from No. 47:

In the capitalistic and mechanistic economy we had, in promoting efficiency, we somehow or other went a little too far in treating employees as units of production, and not enough as members of the team. I know this is preaching and you have heard it time and time again, but this matter of winning back the primary allegiance of the employee seems to me to be the key business.

The social and political implications of the conflict are always present to these men:

I don't believe men join unions for better wages, shorter hours or things like that. They join unions because they want to belong to something that is "on their side."

How did these workers get the idea that a union with headquarters three thousands of miles away is more on their side than the employer who gives them the job?

I cannot avoid the conclusion that somehow or other managers, their bosses, and owners, missed an enormous opportunity at the turn of the century in not taking some steps to see that did not occur.

Fifteen million employees, rightfully or wrongfully, have come to the conclusion that they have more in common with unions controlled from distant places, with interests of which they know nothing whatsoever, than they have in common with the fellow who gave them a job. And let's not say that is not so. Simply look at the votes.

I quote again from No. 45:

The coming years may well represent our final chance to create the constructive relationship between management and employees which the public of our nation demands. For unless industry and business as a whole succeed in winning the loyalty and support and the confidence of the workers, the bell may toll not only for a free industry, but for the American form of government as we know it now, as well.

Again from No. 30:

To be satisfied with one's job people need more than high earnings, pay for overtime, financial incentives, benefit programs, bonuses, holidays and vacations with pay. These are the financial satisfactions in every job and they *are* important . . . but not *all* important. Employees, including presidents and vice presidents *also* desire the non-financial incentives in their jobs. They want security, opportunity, free treatment and social recognition.

I will grant that many "managers of men" do not believe these non-financial incentives are important. They say, "Employees are only interested in their pay." The record does not bear out this contention. Actually, it seems that we have failed in our attempts to buy-off employees with monetary "tid bits." Meanwhile *unions* have done quite well in winning the confidence of our people. It will pay us to look into the methods unions use to win confidence.

The speaker repeated his points:

There is even added proof that employees desire more than money from their jobs. Many surveys have been made to determine what employees want. In none of these has the pay check been the number one satisfaction. Security always comes before money. Opportunity and fair treatment usually have occupied a higher place on the list than the monetary factors. Social recognition invariably runs a close second in the other non-financial satisfactions. The nationwide studies by the Opinion Research Corporation bring out these facts. Our own employee opinion surveys from California to North Carolina prove this contention over and over again.

The speaker in every case is a highly placed executive speaking to other executives of the same status.

No. 40 of the same series is by Leo M. Cherne, Executive Secretary of the Research Institute of America, speaking to this body of West Coast executives:

I was particularly impressed with a few things Sumner Schlichter said about a year ago. Sumner Schlichter is accepted by management and he is permitted to say things which might prove irritating for someone else to say. If you will recall at a meeting of top executives at the Harvard Club in New York, Sumner Schlichter said quite clearly that the major reason unions are in existence in the United States today are these:

1　You have failed to provide the workers in your plant with any sense of identity or belonging.

2　There is no way by which the employee can or believes he can communicate with you.

3　You have failed to convey to your people that there is any importance in what they are doing or any importance in themselves.

Examine unionization and the protestations it makes to its own membership in terms of those three basic psychological factors and I think you have a new slant on what is too readily assumed to be a solely economic phenomenon. There are fewer union members among those who belong to YMHA, YMCA or YWCA than among non-belongers. Why? Because those organizations are opposed to unions? No! But because the people already belong to an organization. They already have a book, they already have an identity. Secondly, communications: communication has become a very common word in recent months. It is part of the post war human fever . . . the fever of human relations which has moved quite rapidly through industry.

In "How Industrial Relations Men are Planning for Period Ahead," a survey made among Pacific Coast Industrial Relations and Personnel Executives, the following occurs:

One top corporate official declared in his return that his company has been seeking for years to find some basis for measuring worker effort. He believes if personnel executives will undertake some form of research on this problem that a new basis might be found for more fairly and adequately compensating personal effort at all levels of work. This gentleman could get no comfort from the explanation that a good job evaluation program is intended to get the same result.

Let us now turn to Detroit.

C. K. Wilson of General Motors is the most indefatigable crusader on behalf of the benefits and advantages of working in American industry. In articles, in reprints, in pamphlets, addressed to his employees he combats precisely this antagonism of the workers to the very work itself.

In an address by Henry Ford II to the Economic Club of New York, he says:

It is worth remembering that output per man hour in this country has increased on average about 2 per cent a year. Mere continuation of this trend would mean a future full of better things for more people. But it is my own feeling that the tremendous gains which have been achieved by machine techniques may be substantially matched when we learn to make better use of ourselves as people.

There is significant evidence on this point. We have seen many instances of greatly increased productivity on the part of men under certain favorable conditions – increases which were achieved very often with less individual physical effort and greater individual satisfaction than the same men experienced under different conditions. Men have not yet learned to work at anything like their easy capacity. Instead, they have often been persuaded that they ought to do far less than they are able to do – that they should mark themselves down – that they should be second-rate when they can be first rate.

I am impressed also by the fact that no one – in industry, labor or government has spent a fraction of 1 per cent of the time and effort on research into the problems of the human factor that has been spent on pure and applied research in the field of the physical sciences. We need to find out how to do the same continuous difficult, experimental and research work in the field of human science which we have done in the field of the physical sciences. I think we can then expect to get comparable results.

These are the industrialists themselves.

I now give a statement from *Industrial Counselling* by two workers in education and research.

The uncertainty of the future of industrial counseling is covered by the long shadow which cloaks in doubt the entire future relationship of labor and management. Man has advanced technologically with gigantic steps, but socially and politically he has fallen far behind. The worker lives in a society today where there is little pride or understanding of the worth of one's job – there is a keen and cutting sense of personal futility. Employees and employers understand neither themselves nor each other, and the sense of belonging, of having an established and solid niche in the social group is rapidly disappearing, if indeed it exists at all. Those who plan counseling programs cannot ignore this trembling social structure, in which the place of the digger of the ditch is of no less importance than that of the big desk executive.

The end of the war saw the end of certain counseling problems, and certain new ones have been added, but the greatest changes may yet lie ahead.

There is no need to continue with this. From one end of the country to the other the university schools dealing with business or industrial administration, Harvard, Princeton, Massachusetts Institute of Technology, University of Pennsylvania, are occupied with the problem in close collaboration with industrial capital. The problem has by now reached the general public. The spate of books increases daily. I list a few with some extracts:

"The Social System of the Modern Factory by W. Lloyd Warner *et al.*:

The introduction of the machine into all parts of the production processes of the shoe factory in Yankee City has destroyed the skill hierarchy so that workers have become interchangeable cogs in a machine . . . and come to feel that the only security for the individual lies in belonging to an organization of fellow workers.

Understanding Labor by Bernard H. Fitzpatrick:

The labor problem is not strictly an economic problem . . . basically it is a problem which is human – a problem of adjusting men to men, men to themselves, and men to matter.

Beyond Collective Bargaining by Alexander R. Heron
Union Management Co-operation by Kurt Braun
Foundations for Constructive Industrial Relations by R. C. Hyman
Human Leadership in Industry, The Challenge of Tomorrow by Sam A. Lewisohn
Management Can Be Human by Harvey Stowers:

Industry today is faced with human problems that may hold greater dangers than the Second World War. . . . Human understanding and the building of men are the greatest need of the world. The author is convinced that *management can be human* only when we realize that our workers are human. We must realize that our workers possess more brains and more good ideas collectively than could possibly be possessed by the most gifted supervisor.

Psychology in Industry by Norman R. F. Maier
Employee Counseling by Nathaniel Cantor
Management and the Worker by F. J. Roethlisberger and Wm. J. Dickson
Together – or Forfeit Freedom by Robert Wood Johnson:

As a human being no worker can thrive and give good service in the void of loneliness. He must feel that he "belongs," that he is a responsible and respected person who counts for something in his group. With this must go dignity and satisfaction in the job beyond the pay for doing it. Each employee must understand his work, not merely as a set of movements, but as a part of the operation of his plant, office or store.

Industry and Society by the Committee on Human Relations in Industry, and including articles by Warner, Harbison, Whyte *et al.:*

As science and technology have advanced the capacity of the industrial organization to elicit the cooperation of its members has undergone a serious deterioration.

It has been commonly assumed that the working man is motivated primarily if not exclusively by a desire for material rewards. . . . The Western Electric research, along with unnumerable studies of primitive and civilized societies, has shown that human motivation is an exceedingly complex thing, with economic rewards being only one factor.

While economic incentives are still given primary emphasis in industry their limitations are coming to be more recognized. However, in many cases this has led management off in vain pursuit of some other simple factors that will solve the problem. Industry has gone in for insurance plans, employee recreation, plant libraries, recorded music, free vitamin pills, inspirational posters and various other supposed morale builders . . . but none of them touch the heart of the problem; the relations of the individuals to one another in the social system.

In the popular press surprisingly far-reaching and thoughtful articles appear, notably two by Peter Drucker in *Colliers* for April 18, 1946. What is most striking is the unanimity of all industrialists, journalists, professional investigators, university professors, on the simple fact that the workers, not merely in coal-mines but throughout industry have reached a definitive stage in relation to industry. The whole may be summed up in the following extracts from an article in *Fortune*, October, 1949. The importance of the article is that it rather flamboyantly sums up the sober anxious preoccupations of industrialists and social students of industry all over the country:

One of the most difficult problems management has to face in a large industrial plant is that of the human being. And the failure to solve this problem has had as much to do with the weakening of the enterprise system, here and throughout the world as any other single factor. As Elton Mayo has said: "While material efficiency has been increasing for two hundred years, the human capacity for working together has in the same period continually diminished."

A man's work is of necessity a commodity that he sells on a market. The problem is, how to buy it without taking over the man too – that is to say, without making him the slave of the machines that he is supposed to command . . .

The worker needs not only a power to bargain but a sense of *belonging*. He wants to be treated like a human being – not just a number on a payroll. In a big plant this is not easy . . .

The humanization of industry is something that has to be undertaken with the utmost earnestness, and it must have the personal attention and enthusiasm of the topmost executive. Loudspeaker systems, plant newspapers, suggestion boxes, depth interviewing and similar devices are perfectly sound so long as their limitations are understood. It is obviously necessary to develop adequate forms of communication between employer and employees. But the communications must have integrity. Management must really respect the workers' ideas . . .

That which has hitherto been lacking in this field, however, is precisely the theme of this article, namely, the recognition by the employer that his employee is possessed of certain rights, the implementation of which is the joint concern of the boss and the worker. From this principle the humanizing of the shop will inevitably follow.

The last paragraphs are typical in the realization that here in the factory is the denial of all human individuality and freedom of association. We can sum up the preceding:

1 The *employers* know that there is among American workers an antagonism to the circumstances of their labor which goes far beyond mere wages.
2 The *employers* recognize that there in the factory is the problem which must be resolved before they can have any serious hope of restoring any stability and successful harmony in the future of production.

3 This conflict affects all relations in society, not only the strictly political, but the very attitude with which the worker contemplates his whole relation to society.

4 The employers and their advisers are completely at a loss what to do.

At the purely economic root the problem has been sufficiently diagnosed not only by industrial psychologists, but the diagnosis has been accepted by writers like Margaret Mead and Gorer. The specific feature of American heavy industry is the transference from man to machinery of the bodily and mental activities which formerly distinguished the craftsman or skilled laborer. The modern worker is a cog in a machine. All progress in industry consists of making him more and more of a cog and less and less of a human being. The process has now reached a breaking point.

I do not propose here to go into all the details by which I shall establish the profound actuality and ramifications of this central social problem in the United States. I wish here to indicate a few points:

(1) White collar workers have testified to the not dissimilar monotony of their daily lives.

(2) Doctors and junior executives have testified to the enormous strains and tensions to which their increasingly routinized activities subject them and the pressures upon them as individuals of the organizations to which they belong.

(3) It is not merely the daily grind of assembly-line workers. It is that the whole of productive life is tuned to this pattern. I take as example not the millions of sub-standard migrant laborers whose miserable conditions are well known, but a worker on a modern well-appurtenanced ranch in the West (owned by a famous popular singer). The worker has a good clean room and bed. He has a good breakfast at a fixed time, all the men together. He is taken to work in the fields. His mechanized work occupies him, with an interval for lunch. After dinner he has an hour or two to spare. But he is forbidden to drink, he is forbidden to go to town so that he will be fit for work next day. Saturday nights the men are free. They go into town and get drunk. Sunday night the routine begins again. The whole week, except for the weekend, is organized around fitness for the work. Conditions and pay are not bad as such things go. But on this ranch as on so many others, wherever they are good, they are so organized as to squeeze the last ounce out of the laborer.

I have taken an agricultural worker to establish the first consequence from the central industrial problem posed above. The whole week is just one round of work and sleep, eating, etc. *to prepare for work*. The worker no longer works an eight-hour day. It is one long week of forty hours. On Saturdays he recovers slowly. By Sunday night he is just beginning to feel relaxed when he must be ready for another forty-hour stretch.

I have purposely emphasized the evidence of the opinion of employers, journalists, etc. Strangely enough, the attitude of the workers themselves has received little attention and documentation except insofar as the employers themselves and their investigators have made them known. I am, however, in the position where I shall be able to match the documentation with material that I can gather which will place before the reader the attitude of experienced workers who have for many years studied the effects of modern industry upon themselves and upon their fellow-workers.

The results of the above would be far-reaching enough if they were limited to their immediate consequences. But within the limits of an essay it would not be difficult to show that the stage of industrial production to which we have arrived has placed its stamp upon the whole civilization. Let us just sketch the main outlines.

The waiter or waitress who serves the food, the grocer who sells the articles, the bus driver who is in charge of transport, the whole civilization takes tempo and method from the basic economic structure and the relations it brings with it. And finally the whole social arrangement of life bears the stamp of this mechanization.

In city after city, street after street, are the two or three rooms, kitchen and bath, the same breakfast cereal, however disguised, the same ride to work, the work itself, the same evening paper, the same radio commentator, the packaged foods, the neighborhood movie. However different, they all combine to a deadly uniformity and monotony.

There is no necessity here to trace the relation of de Tocqueville's comments through Bryce to the more acute observers of the present day. De Tocqueville praised the individual American because he had accepted the stultifying effects of division of labor. The uniformity of American life was the basis of equality. Bryce noted the uniformity of American life. Turner saw only the individual activity and freedom of capital to associate which built the gigantic economic structure of the West. Now these various trends in a development have arrived at an impasse. We can sum up this chapter.

Upon a people bursting with energy, untroubled by feudal remains or a feudal past, soaked to the marrow in a tradition of individual freedom, individual security, free association, a tradition which is constantly held before them as the basis of their civilization, upon this people more than all others has been imposed a mechanized way of life at work, mechanized forms of living, a mechanized totality which from morning till night, week after week, day after day, crushed the very individuality which tradition nourishes and the abundance of mass-produced goods encourages. The average American citizen is baffled by it, has always been. He cannot grasp the process by which a genuine democracy escapes him. With the crash of the economic system in 1929 and now the perpetual crisis of world war threatening world-wide destruction, all the tensions are arising, confusedly but remarkably to the surface.

These tensions have been the driving force in the extraordinary scope and manifestations of what is loosely called in the United States the entertainment industry. Far from being entertainment it is so far the most striking expression of the tensions and deep crises of American society, occupying a similar relation to the developing society as the writers of 1840–60 occupied in relation to the America of Webster and Lincoln.

5

Popular Arts and Modern Society

At every stage in a book there is reached a certain climax. We approach it in the sketch for this chapter. The chapter will embrace so much that it is necessary here to place the main points already made briefly before the reader.

1 There is today an immense concentration on freedom, individuality, the individual and the state; the one-party state, the welfare state, planning versus free enterprise, etc.
2 The concepts of individuality, liberty, etc. had a meaning and a great historic meaning in the years of the foundation of America.

There has developed a type of economy and society where individuality, freedom, etc. are in essence lost. The industrialists of America consciously see and understand this more clearly than any other section of the population.

We laid stress on Whitman, Melville and the Abolitionists because they expressed, as was the way, the inescapable way of the nineteenth century, the great individual writer expressed in his artistic reactions the deepest and most enduring social and ideological currents of his age. These writers were not introduced for purely historical reasons, or for reasons of elucidation or to point out the contrasts and similarities between then and now, important as these are. They were introduced for all these reasons but also because, representing America at its coming of age as a modern nation, what they stood for endures. But the fundamental ideas are now placed in an entirely different setting. To state it crudely, where formerly we had to look at the economic relations of society, the political and social movements and the great artistic expressions to get a whole, complete and dynamic view of the society, while as far as the great mass was concerned, we had to guess; today it is not so. The modern popular film, the modern newspaper (the *Daily*

News, not the *Times),* the comic strip, the evolution of jazz, a popular periodical like *Life,* these mirror from year to year the deep social responses and evolution of the American people in relation to the fate which has overtaken the original concepts of freedom, free individuality, free association, etc. To put it more harshly still, it is in the serious study of, above all, Charles Chaplin, Dick Tracy, Gasoline Alley, James Cagney, Edward G. Robinson, Rita Hayworth, Humphrey Bogart, genuinely popular novels like those of Frank Yerby (*Foxes of Harrow, The Golden Hawk, The Vixen, Pride's Castle*), men like David Selsnick, Cecil deMille, and Henry Luce, that you find the clearest ideological expression of the sentiments and deepest feelings of the American people and a great window into the future of America and the modern world. This insight is *not* to be found in the works of T. S. Eliot, of Hemingway, of Joyce, of famous directors like John Ford or Rene Clair.

I have to stop here and make myself perfectly clear. I believe that the novels of Frank Yerby, particularly the last one, are as bad, as writing, as they can possibly be. *Pride's Castle* (the latest) in fact sets a landmark for illiteracy. I believe also that in *Dubliners, A Portrait of the Artist as a Young Man* and *Ulysses* James Joyce expressed one of the greatest literary temperaments and genius of the modern world; I have never been to see *The Informer* without being tied up in knots inside for days afterwards. But this recognition of the greatness of these men has nothing to do with the issue, despite the fact that men like Joyce and Eliot express so much of the modern world – one-half of it. On the other hand, Cecil deMille with his mighty historical spectacles represents something else. And precisely this, what it is and what it is *not* expresses the American people today. We shall have to take the problem from many angles and bit by bit they will create a composite picture of the tremendous social manifestation hidden behind what is called "entertainment."

We shall see also an equally valuable picture of new, entirely new conditions of the relation between art and society which are unfolding before us. In addition, this relation will give us deep insight into modern political psychology and help us to knit together various currents in what is a world movement towards the creation of man as an integral human being, a full and complete individuality with the circumstances and conditions of that fully integrated individuality.

We shall have to take:

1 A general historical sketch of the modern popular arts as they have developed since 1929 and before 1929.
2 The critical analysis of the specific features of modern popular art in relation to social and political phenomena of the day and in particular the star system.
3 The outline of integrated man with specific reference to:

(a) the permanent mass needs of the future as outlined in the present;
(b) war and the popular arts;
(c) Greek drama and the popular arts.

The whole concept is of unusual (though not insuperable) difficulty, especially as this is the first tentative statement. There will be some overlapping and repetition. It cannot be as easy to grasp as after it has been rewritten half a dozen times and thoroughly discussed. But even as it is, there is absolutely no reason why the general ideas cannot be grasped at one careful reading.

First of all, let us take the film and the comic strip together, and observe the most obvious fact about their history. The film began about 1900 (roughly), the comic strip a few years later. Their history can be divided into two parts: (1) before the Depression of 1929; (2) after the Depression. Al Capp, the famous comic strip artist, has written for the *Encyclopedia Britannica* on strips. When he began as an artist in 1934, strips were about 40 years old. Early comics were simple straightforward pictures with gags. But by the Thirties they had changed entirely. Says Capp:

The clowns had been pushed off the comic page by the misery-vendors, the horror-vendors, the blood merchants. The hilarious "Pam!!!" or "Zowie!!!!" ending of the comic simpleton overcome by the brutality, misunderstanding, avariciousness, or bad temper of his fellow-men had been supplanted by the "Help!! The rattlesnake is strangling me, Mother dear!!!" – or – "Take dat, you copper – right t'roo the head!!!" type of ending wherein the comic simpleton was supplanted by a pathetic golden-haired little girl simpleton whose perils never ended – in fact, increased each day in violence and intricacy. . . . The comic strips, with a few die-hard hard-fighting exceptions were no longer comic . . . The word went out from circulation department that anxiety about the fate of Orphan Annie's dog sold far more papers than did joy over the foolishness of Boob McNutt.

In fact, we know that the author of Dick Tracy, Chester Gould, had spent years trying to interest various editors in his work and failed. It was in 1931 (note the date) that Patterson of the New York *Daily News* accepted the idea of Dick Tracy. This Patterson had a reputation with cartoonists, because, according to a recent article, he always seemed "to know exactly what would be popular." Where previous editors had turned down the idea of a detective strip as "preposterous" Patterson (in 1931) accepted it with the following words, some of which I have emphasized:

People call detectives "dicks." "Dick Tracy" – that sounds all right. But *he's not a cop to start with. He's an ordinary guy.* Have him going with a girl; call her Tess. Her old man runs a little store of some kind, and every night he takes the cash upstairs –

they live over the store. There's a stick-up and the gunmen kill the old man. *Show the bullets going right into him.* Tracy chases the hold-up men but *they slug him.* He sees them escape *in a black sedan.* He clenches his hands, looks to heaven and says he'll avenge the old man. *"To this I'll dedicate my life."* (*Saturday Evening Post,* December 17, 1949)

1 "Show the bullets going right into him."
2 He is "not a cop to start with, he's an ordinary guy."
3 "To this I'll dedicate my life."

The bitterness, the violence, the brutality, the sadism simmering in the population, the desire to revenge themselves with their own hands, to get some release for what society had done to them since 1929 – Patterson understood it perfectly. He understood also that the people did not want this avenger to be a cop – the law, authority, the state. He had to be an ordinary guy – *one who went out and did the job himself.* But Patterson was no artist. He was a man of business in a society with principles and ethics which had to be protected. He launches Tracy on his career as a dedication to the preservation of order. When salesmen went out with the strip they had to point out that "Tracy was the Law and therefore entitled to use weapons." Patterson no doubt thought that thereby society was protected, but we believe him to have been mistaken. The strip began on October 12, 1931, and this was the *first* murder in comic strip history.

The same year saw the appearance of *Public Enemy* with James Cagney, and in this period began the exploits of Cagney, Edward G. Robinson, Paul Muni and George Raft as gangsters. In these films these men were the best actors, the most striking personalities, the whole film revolved around them. They were its "heroes." Of that there was no question. In one film where he played a Chinaman of Chinatown, the "Hatchet-man," Edward G. Robinson killed three men with his hatchet and as a heroic character walked off with the girl in the end. In two of the murders he had taken the law into his own hands. Where this sort of thing would have ended but for the Hays office is anybody's guess. A recent commentator has pointed out:

In the good old days of Rudolph Valentino and John Gilbert, a woman found that the movies gave her emotions an enjoyable vicarious workout. But "post-war picture advertising" is plastered with maniacal killers, rapists, thugs of all varieties. . . . The typical woman gets more than she wants of that in the news columns. She is not disposed to go to the movies for the same.

That is to some degree true but the argument is superficial. More to the point is the fact that the critic noted that:

Many a student of the cinema thinks it was that shattering 1931 scene in which James Cagney pushed a grape-fruit into Mae Clarke's face. From that day on, the old-time chick romantic screen lover began going into eclipse.

Enough has been said. The whole popular so-called entertainment world began its turn to violence, sadism, cruelty, the release of aggression immediately after the consciousness of the Depression had seized hold of the country. 1932 was the year of Burnett's gangster story, *Little Caesar*, and in the years that followed, Dashiell Hammett and James M. Cain poured out book after book of the same genre. The detective story had a long history by this time. It is a product of our age and space forbids the analysis of the work of Poe, its anticipation of every major development in popular art and the reasons for this. The detective story as such was no novelty, both in typical novels and for years before in dime novels (Nick Carter). But this kind of gangster-detective fiction, this was new.

Why did the reaction to the Depression take this particular form? We have first to consider the conditions (unique for over two thousand years) in which these films, strips, etc. are produced. The producer of the film or the newspaper publisher of a strip aims at *millions of people*, practically the whole population, and *must satisfy them*. Dick Tracy appears today in newspapers with a circulation of 43 millions. Of every four books that appear today one is a detective story.

If even for the sake of argument, it is agreed that the publishers, the movie magnates, the newspaper proprietors and the banks which directly or indirectly control them, are interested in distracting the masses of the people from serious problems or elevated art, then the question still remains, why, at this particular time, this particular method of distraction should have arisen and met with such continuous success. To believe that the great masses of the people are merely passive recipients of what the purveyors of popular art give to them is in reality to see people as dumb slaves. It is a conception totally unhistorical and it is far more reasonable to believe that when Patterson planned the first murder and wanted the bullets shown going into the victim, he had sensed that mood in the population, a mood which had not existed before.

No, we have to examine more closely the conditions in which these new arts, the film, and with it the comic strip, the radio and jazz have arisen, in order to see exactly why they become an expression of mass response to society, crises, and *the nature and limitations of that response*.

It is one of the most astonishing things about the modern American film which as many as 95 million people per week look at in the United States, that it does not treat of the Great Depression, the pervading fear of another economic collapse, the birth and development of the union movement, the fear of war, the fundamental social and political questions of the day. In novels and plays, yes; on the radio in carefully organized speeches and reports, yes; in radio drama, no. It might seem that this is deliberate sabotage by those who control the economic life of the country. That is quite false. The industrial magnates, a movie producer so anti-union as DeMille, and great numbers of people in authority would wish nothing better than to employ the finest available talent in order to impose *their* view of the great political and social questions of the day upon the mass. *They dare not do it.* The general public accepts, or to be more precise, appears to accept the general political ideas, standards, social ethics, etc. of the society which is the natural framework of the films as they are produced today. Whenever possible a piece of direct propaganda is injected, but the C.I.O., the great strikes, capital and labor, war and peace, these are left out by mutual understanding, a sort of armed neutrality. If those who control films dared, in ordinary times, to give their view of these problems in films, for instance, they would empty the movie houses. The large masses of the people would not stand for any employer view of unions in films. In totalitarian states the state does exactly the opposite. It uses the film, the popular film, to the limit. In fact the film is merely an arm of the government. In the early days of the Russian Revolution the remarkable films that came from Russia were highly political films, openly revolutionary. The films, comic strips, etc. of the United States are what they are because of the specific stage of the relations between the classes. Each agrees to leave these dangerous topics alone.

This is the fundamental determinant of the artistic content and form of these productions. The mass is not merely passive. It decides what it will see. It will pay to see that. The makers of movies, the publishers of comic strips are in violent competition with each other for the mass to approve what they produce. Any success tends to be repeated and squeezed dry, for these people are engaged primarily in making money. *Huge and consistent successes are an indication of mass demand.* An enormous amount of energy, thought and intelligence are spent to probe and profit by this mass demand. The idea that movie-makers spend their time thinking about how to use movies in order to maintain capitalist society is nonsense. In fact, if a movie-maker could get the money from the banks and (most important) was sure of distribution, many of them, dyed-in-the-wool supporters of free enterprise, would not hesitate to make films of a pro-worker political and social charac-ter, if only they were sure they would make profit. The films, therefore, if only negatively, represent some of the deepest feelings of the masses, but represent them within the common agreement – no serious political or social questions which would cause explosions.

That is the first point to be borne in mind. If, as in Greece, in the days when the drama was written for the mass, for the *whole population* (except the slaves), and the national question was such that the basic problems could be tackled, then this specific response we have noted would be different. *If* on the films, the problems of the Depression, of the relation of the individual to a collectivized social environment, his relation to the state, the tremendous story of the growth of the C.I.O., free enterprise versus socialism, lynching, race prejudice, *if* these were the *common* stuff of the films, not as propaganda merely, but different points of view dramatized in individual figures or as social symbols, attacks and counter-attacks such as, for example, Aristophanes used to make in his plays for the Greek *populace*, then the gangster film or detective film or strip as such, would just be one of many others and could not possibly play the dominating role that it does.

Radio has followed the films and the strips and expresses the violence and anger which the modern crisis generates among the American people. Every night on the radio half-a-dozen people are killed and a succession of private detectives go out on their own and fight these criminals. Law and order must be preserved – and the gangster has been transformed into a private detective. But this detective is in reality the same character as the gangster. He uses what methods he can, he is as ready with his gun-butt or a bullet as the gangster. *Both have a similar scorn for the police as the representative of official society.* As a matter of fact, the number, the variety, the constant employment of these detectives says as plain as day that for preserving order against the real criminals the police are not needed. The District Attorney and such are merely an attempt to save face for the police. In *The Maltese Falcon* Dashiell Hammett makes his detective Sam Spade give a summary of his social ethics to a woman whom he loves, but is going to send to prison. It sums up what the private detective represents by a master of his craft:

"Why must you do this, Sam? Surely Mr Archer wasn't as much to you as . . ."

"Miles," Spade said hoarsely, "was a louse. I found that out the first week we were in business together and I meant to kick him out as soon as this year was up. You didn't do me a damned bit of harm by killing him."

"Then what?"

Spade pulled his hand out of hers. He no longer either smiled or grimaced. His wet yellow face was set hard and deeply lined. His eyes burned madly. He said, "Listen. This isn't a damned bit of good. You'll never understand me, but I'll try once more and then we'll give it up. Listen. When a man's partner is killed, he's supposed to do something about it. It doesn't make any difference what you thought of him. He was your partner and you're supposed to do something about it. Then it happens we were in the detective business. Well, when one of your organization gets killed, it's bad business to let the killer get away with it. It's bad all around – bad for that one organization, bad for every detective everywhere. Third, I'm a detective and expecting me to run criminals down and then let them go free is like asking a dog to catch a rabbit and let it go. It can be done, all right, and sometimes it is done, but it's not the natural thing. The only way I could have let you go was by letting Gutman and Cairo and the kid go. That's . . ."

"You're not serious," she said. "You don't expect me to think that these things that you're saying are sufficient reason for sending me to the . . .!"

"Wait till I'm through and then you can talk. Fourth, no matter what I wanted to do now, it would be absolutely impossible for me to let you go without having myself dragged to the gallows with the others. Next, I've no reason in God's world to think I can trust you and if I did this and got away with it, you'd have something on me that you could use whenever you happened to want to. That's five of them. The sixth would be that, since I've also got something on you, I couldn't be sure that you wouldn't decide to shoot a hole in *me* some day. Seventh, I don't even like the idea of thinking that there might be one chance in a hundred that you'd played me for a sucker. And eighth – but that's enough. All those on one side. Maybe some of them are unimportant. I won't argue about that. But look at the number of them. Now on the other side we've got what? All we've got is the fact that maybe you love me and maybe I love you."

This man lives in a world of his own according to ethics of his own. He is a gangster who, however, has chosen the side of the law because it is safer that way. He, Philip Marlowe, the detective creation of Raymond Chandler, Perry Mason, and others, are in constant warfare with the police, sometimes in danger of arrest, imprisonment and the chair.

It is out of the question here and now to make any precise analysis of all the basic implications of the world that these writers create. But it will help to look for a few minutes at Dashiell Hammett. Hammett published his first, or one of his first stories in October 1923. It is a story of robbery, but it is a brief psychological study of what takes place in a man's mind. Robbery and soul-searching. But Hammett moved rapidly and Sam Spade appeared in 1929. As *Ellery Queen's Mystery Magazine* notes: "the psychological probing . . . was apparently a passing phase in Hammett's creative development, to be replaced later by his psychological preoccupation with violence and brutality, and still later, with nonchalant cynicism." His writing is not a factory production. His work develops in relation to his environment; and like many more profound writers he seems to sense in advance the period ahead.

Again, one of his earlier creations was a typical detective of the new school, the Continental Op, a nameless detective. Hammett, who once worked as a detective in the Pinkerton Agency, claims that he based the character on a real-life detective whom he knew, giving his name. This question of the relation of this fiction to life is a subtle and complicated one. Men like Hammett and Chandler who are in their way very serious writers know what they are doing. They would probably deny that their stories represent real life; and if even many big city gangster episodes are no more incredible than episodes in these stories, no serious person could for a moment take these stories as representative of modern life in America as a whole.

But that is only on the surface. First of all, these stories have tension. And that is what is characteristic of modern American life – an enormous tension. The millions of modern readers feel it in these novels and in well-made gangster films. Secondly, on the question of the effects aimed at. André Gide says of Hammett's *Red Harvest* that it is a "remarkable achievement, the last word in atrocity, cynicism and horror." That is precisely what the millions of readers want, and what Hammett is giving them. (Gide at the same time makes it clear that he is quite aware of Hammett's subordinate place as a creative writer.)

More difficult is the relation between this fiction and reality. In 1931 the first full-length study of the detective story was published in England. The writer claimed that Sam Spade is an "honest-to-goodness, 100% American detective." This is extremely doubtful as fact. But Ellery Queen, no mean practitioner of the form, says that no one could really quarrel with this judgment. Whether there are people like Spade is irrelevant. Here, known to millions and millions of readers is a carefully delineated *type* of character who is looked upon at home and abroad as a 100% American type. If it is pure fiction, that makes it not less but more remarkable. Obviously it is a sociological fact of the first importance.

Finally, Hammett is a very careful writer whose method will repay more serious and detailed examination later in relation to the fantastic sales of his books, radio programs, movies, etc. Hammett is not merely careful in style. He knows the effects he is trying to get and pursues them in story after story until he gets them as he wants them. Thus Sam Spade's credo, quoted above, was tried in an earlier story. Hammett did not get it as he wanted it, and tried again in *The Maltese Falcon.*

Let us now take a concrete example of how this process works as an expression of the feeling and desires of the mass, from their point of view and not from the point of view of a writer. In the late Thirties Humphrey Bogart was a competent but rather unknown actor, one of a thousand others. Then he appeared in a film, *High Sierra*, by W. H. Burnett, the author of *Little Caesar,* in which he played a gangster hurt by society who fought back and, trapped in the end, went up and up and up among the sierras, going to his death, but defying the police below. Ida Lupino, his girl friend, was led off at the end, asking: Why should this be? From this moment Bogart was made. But he was made as a *detective*, not as a gangster. He is an ordinary guy; that is his chief attraction, his ordinariness; tough, going his own way, as sick of the pretences of the world as is Hemingway but he has to intervene. That he has to intervene is not merely the necessity of official law and order. It is a necessity of the mass which looks on. Society would fall entirely to pieces if the gangster were to triumph. But gangster and private detective are one character, each being absolutely necessary to the other.

Nor is this gangster-private detective type at all accidental as a symbol of a frustrated population. The gangster did not fall from the sky nor does he represent Chicago and the underworld. He is the persistent symbol of the national past which now has no meaning – the past in which energy, determination, bravery were certain to get a man somewhere in the line of opportunity. Now the man on the assembly line, the farmer, know that they are there for life; and the gangster who displays all the old heroic qualities in the only way he can display them, is the derisive symbol of the contrast between ideals and reality.

Finally, we can sum up this phase. The film, strip, radio-drama are a form of art which must satisfy the mass, the individual seeking individuality in a mechanized, socialized society, where his life is ordered and restricted at every turn, where there is no certainty of employment, far less of being able to rise by energy and ability or going West as in the old days. In such a society, the individual demands an esthetic compensation in the contemplation of free individuals who go out into the world and settle their problems by free activity and individualistic methods. In these perpetual isolated wars free individuals are pitted against free individuals, live grandly and boldy. What they want, they go for. Gangsters get what they want, trying it for a while, then are killed. In the end "crime does not pay" but for an hour and a half highly skilled actors and a huge organization of production and distribution have given to many millions a sense of active living, and in the bloodshed, the violence, the freedom from restraint to allow pent-up feelings free play, they have released the bitterness, hate, fear and sadism which simmer just below the surface.

The gangster and detective film, the strip and the radio-drama are the product of the peculiar conditions in the United States. But they represent a universal. Not only do the masses abroad respond to them. Cyril Connolly, one of the most original and sensitive of the traditional British critics, a man very familiar with literature and life in Britain, France and America, writes as recently as December 18, 1949, in the *New York Times* on the influence of American on British literature in recent years. He says:

Meanwhile, the American film and the American thriller infiltrate into our popular culture and the American film meant the gangster film. Between-war Europe was gangster crazy because the gangster represented the anarchic adolescent conception of liberty which civilization in time of peace had perforce to stifle, because the police-and-gangster relationship reflects the decay of society, and because the trapped gangster who aimlessly butchers friend and foe alike is a symbol of the cruelty and lack of meaning of life itself.

This is on the surface reasonably close to what is being said here. But a little later Connolly writes:

"When necessity is associated with horror and freedom with boredom," Auden opens *The Age of Anxiety*, "then it looks good to the bar business."

This is completely false, it is a nineteenth-century intellectual speaking about another nineteenth-century intellectual in the nineteenth-century manner. The boredom is not the boredom of freedom at all. Intellectuals are bored. The masses are not. They have no freedom and they resent it. They cannot drink their problems away.

Connolly wavers in one section of the truth. He says:

Gangster and Prohibition, Violence and Drink and the consequent self-examination to which they lead, these formed undoubted the American contribution – and still do.

But he says almost immediately:

American humor has had an ever more devastating influence than American despair, probably because it is, through the sense of the absurd, so close to despair.

Another half-truth. There may be despair in these intellectuals; it permeates the greatest writers of the last thirty years. There is no despair in the art the masses accept. There was great laughter and sadness in early Hollywood; now the mass response is a consuming anger and rage.

Again Connolly continues:

In France the bracing and pessimistic existentialist philosophy supplies a perfect ideological background to American fiction. Faulkner, Caldwell, and Steinbeck are household words. Sartre is a kind of Franco-American figure; the American novel, supreme expression of the American attitude to life, moves instantly into the fabric of the French philosophical anecdotal essay which is the espression of their outlook, like an ostrich egg descending the gullet of a python. The German occupation made the French "mad" in the American sense and brought them nearer to the American "madness" than to the British good-tempered fortitude.

Here are his limitations complete. Connolly is a gifted man with real knowledge and insight. But he still thinks that Faulkner and the rest express America. Whitman and Melville expressed America in the nineteenth century, they were intellectuals, writing for intellectuals. These will be taken up in the finished study. It is an important link in the chain. Serious research will have to be done to find out how the real mass expressed itself in any literary or artistic way. But the absence of this powerful mass impact upon them shaped the art of these writers. But today we have something else. The mass is vocal and articulate in its art. It does not sense underlying currents as the great writers we have analyzed did. Being the social organism that it is – its responses are immediate almost from year to year. "America" today is to be found far more in these responses than in the writings of the artists. In fact you cannot understand the artists unless you bear in mind the mass responses and the social conditions which make these possible. And it is my opinion that a real insight into Melville and Whitman can only be had by recognizing what the society of their time lacked. To take an example, I am convinced that, and I will be able to show without difficulty *Moby Dick* is in essence a scenario for a film and such a film as is the closest to the spirit of the tragedy of Aeschylus as anything written in the nineteenth and twentieth centuries.

Film, strip and radio have certain limitations. Published fiction has very few. The relations between these forms and how each treats murder, violence, atrocity, etc. will be an important part of this study. At the moment, however, we take them separately. The success of Frank Yerby's novels completes the general picture of the "entertainment" world. Thirty years ago, novelists like Hall Caine, Gene Stratton Porter *(A Girl of the Limberlost)*, Marie Corelli, Florence Barclay *(The Rosary)* satisfied the emotional needs of the fiction-reading mass that did not take its reading too seriously. A generation before that, Augusta Evans Wilson (*Beulah, St Elmo, Vashte, At the Mercy of Tiberius*) satisfied the needs of a vast public. But these books need and will be given a special analysis which cannot be made here. But they were more or less in harmony with the ideas of the society. They were adventurous perhaps in love (one of Hall Caine's women did sleep with a married man) but for them character was stable. They knew the difference between right and wrong, good and evil, their world was an ideal world based on a real society. Yerby is characteristic of something entirely new in fiction sold to the millions. His characters break every accepted rule of society. They are out for what they want and get it how they can. They cheat, lie, scheme, plot, are brutal, cruel, lustful, expressing their free individuality. They are also successful. It is true that there are powerful elements of sentimentality and society is not in the end destroyed. But the difference between these and previous popular novels of the same genre is immense. The novels are eagerly read by millions who find in them the same satisfaction that is found in the gangster film. The passionate individualistic American temperament that Melville knew so well and saw only as a danger to the organizers of society, is now stirring in tens of millions of individuals, the masses of the people, thwarted in their daily lives, hemmed in on all sides. Yerby's books are a primitive elemental response to some of the deepest needs of the American people in their reaction against society. That is not aesthetics; or some kind of social "interpretation." It is as clear as day that the great mass of the nation no longer accepts, or takes for granted, the traditional ethics, social ideas, social aspirations, etc. by which the great masses live at any given time in a given society. The great success of the main characters in Margaret Mitchell's *Gone with the Wind* shows the same response to characters who let nothing stand in their way. The same with Kathleen Winsor (*Forever Amber*). The jackets of many recent popular novels show pictures of lustful women with their breasts almost uncovered, indications of the violent, uninhibited characters inside.

Society has obviously reached that stage where formal concepts of social living are in such direct opposition to what the people so obviously feel that it is ripe for drastic social transformations. It was precisely this kind of bewilderment at society and resentment at the differences between what was preached and what the people really thought, that formed the psychological basis for the acceptance by such millions of people in Germany of Hitler's irrationalism, mysticism and nonsense. Faith in the traditional rationalism, modes of thought, ideas of progress, etc. had been undermined and destroyed long before Hitler became a force, and this has been traced in the critical study of the fiction of Germany following World War I. It is clearly shown that in America, particularly, and in the contemporary world in general, the place to look is in the popular arts.

It is obvious that there are many more types of film, strip and radio-drama than the gangster-detective theme. The reader of a sketch like this will understand that we concentrate upon what is now, outstanding. The Depression obviously marks a turning point. There was an interlude during the war, precisely during that period of the actual shedding of seas of blood: violence and gangsterism of the type described disappeared. But with the end of the war, blood, violence and crime have achieved heights undreamt of in 1931. How much this trend has intensified since the war is usefully expressed in the March 10, 1947 issue of *Life* which says:

Homicide, always popular, became an obsession with the movies in 1946, and thrillers that racked up less than four or five murders before the final fade-out seemed almost sissified. Movie killers were *no longer drawn exclusively from the ranks of gangsters*, however. Hollywood's sudden discovery of psychology late in 1945 meant that *any character* in a film might turn out to be an undiscovered murderer. Regular movie-goers were confronted by a procession of minds warped enough to confuse old Freud himself.[1] (I have emphasized a few words.)

They stamp on his face, they crush his jaw, when he is knocked out, they hold him up and beat him, they revel in violence. A succession of evil women has appeared, as cruel and as ruthless as cobras. Here is a quotation from the *New York Times* dealing with the latest film of that distinguished actress, Bette Davis:

Playing a thoroughly no-good woman, married to a humble doctor in a small

Wisconsin town and lusting for the attentions of a Chicago sportsman millionaire she is called upon by a crass script and Director King Vidor to perform some of the most offensive and ridiculous rascality that we have ever seen an actress play. She must flaunt herself in tight dresses and a mop of unruly black hair, she must sneer and rail at her poor husband (Joseph Cotten) and she must shoot a guy named Moose. And in the end, she must drag herself grimly out of a bed of feverish pain, smear her hot face with make-up and wobble to her death in a dusty road.

Here is the unhappy climax of Miss Davis' eighteen-year career at the studio which really launched her and which gave her some mighty fine roles. Here is the ultimate portrait in her long gallery of evil dames.

This steady increase in the portrayal of evil women, their characteristics, etc. we cannot go into here, though it is of the first importance, with a history of its own. Bette Davis' evil women were women of psychological difficulties. In this latest picture of hers she was attempting to portray a new development which with astonishing rapidity has lifted Lizabeth Scott to stardom. Joan Crawford who had built an international reputation as the healthy, active American girl, came back to build a new reputation as a woman who lived entirely in scenes of blood, murder, suicide, and physical and psychiatric violence of all kinds. Barbara Stanwyck's career is recent years has been built on the portrayal of this type of gangster woman; and one of the most amazing phenomena of recent "entertainment" is the course of a radio script called "Sorry, Wrong Number." It is remarkable because here, what happens very rarely took place; a woman overhears on the telephone by chance that she is to be murdered by gangsters, tries frantically to prevent it but fails and is murdered, the murderers going free. Here for once was a gangster murder in which the gangsters did not pay the price demanded by society, etc., etc. The response was in every way unparalleled. Aided by a superb performance by that gifted actress Agnes Moorhead, the radio drama had to be performed at least four times, owing to repeated public demand. Barbara Stanwyck played the part in the film. On January 9 she played the film role on the radio. This actress who is just one more or less of the more competent stars, turned in a performance which curdled the blood and is undoubtedly the most effective piece of work I have ever heard on the radio. Which brings us to another question which can only be raised here: the vigor, tension, artistic force which seem to inspire directors, script-writers and performers when they have to do a really serious murder film. The writer is informed by one sensitive and very well-read observer that she prefers murder and gangster films and radio-dramas to all others because they are the only performances that seem to be *real*. There for the time being, but only for the time being, we shall have to leave this.

James Cagney has once again had a startling success as a maniacal killer who dies in a blaze of glory by firing into a chemical tank, and perishing in the flames. One after the other, these films pour out, vying with each other in bloodshed and violence, cruelty, sadism and disregard for all established standards. It has continued and increased for twenty years.

BEFORE 1929

This twenty-year period has little artistic innovations to its credit. Except for some work by Orson Welles, from which little came in the end. Exactly the opposite is the history of the previous period. The artistic achievements of the film up to 1932 are the most remarkable of our age. Consider. The early producers, actors, directors, etc. worked on their own for the simple public, despised by intellectuals, critics, and all the educated members of society. Yet by themselves, pioneers and commonplace public between them, they produced the greatest artist of modern times, Charles Chaplin, and in him they produced something that was *new* and contains in it the elements of the future. By new I mean what Greta Garbo is not. In Garbo there was or is undoubtedly a tragic actress with the physical qualifications for transference to the screen. But there was nothing "new" about her. Chaplin was new. Bogart, Edward G. Robinson, Gable and the rest are interludes – they and what they stand for will disappear. But Chaplin goes very deep into the social needs of today and tomorrow.

Let us see first where he originated. He was a product of the Mack Sennett comedies, and it seems that at last people are beginning to understand and appreciate what they represented. Repeatedly a new popular art, or a new stage of development of a traditional art appeals to wider strata of the population. It is the belief of some that this means a lowering of standards. This is (with all necessary qualifications) utterly false. When Wordsworth broke with the diction of the eighteenth century and wrote his famous preface in 1798, stating that he would use the language of the people, he widened immeasurably the scope of poetry by the simplification of the medium. The Romantic movement at its best did precisely this. Pascal in the *Provincial Letters* made modern French prose. He took the theological disputes from out of the churches and the monasteries into the general public. Calvin did the same, in fact he crystallized the modern French language. The popularization which Shakespeare introduced into drama and his care to satisfy the groundlings drew bitter comment from the scholarly men who preceded him. The history of literature, to which for the time being, I confine myself, is filled with these examples.

In their crude mercurial manner, but having a new medium to play with and very sensitive to their audience (if they were not, they would go broke) the early makers of these comedies simplified the medium – they went for the viscera. In the multitudinous confusions, collisions, accidents, pie-throwing, etc. in which they worked, they aimed not at wit but at finding the most primitive, elemental source of humor and human discomfiture. This much is certain. Aristophanes, the greatest of all comic dramatists and a deadly serious social critic of his time, would have reveled in their type of work. His was full of it. Molière also with his undying interest in farces would have appreciated what they were doing; and it is not improbable that Shakespeare also, with his clowns and broad buffoonery would have understood what they were after and used the medium much as they did; though for other purposes. They sought their humor in the very bellies of the audience where Aristophanes sought his. Modern critics who now realize how completely their work is gone, say that they rocked their audiences with laughter, achieved form and made many of the discoveries which are still used by modern film directors. Yet in all this primitive film-making they were social critics. They had an enemy – the pretensions and hypocrisies of Romanticism in its decay. They belabored the fantastic furniture which still filled middle-class houses, they belabored the conventions of Victorian romantic drama; and they were in perpetual conflict (though friendly) with the policeman, the representative of the modern state, the man of law and order. They collapsed in 1929, not because of the talkies as so many still seem to believe, but because of the Depression.

It was out of these that Chaplin came, and the vulgar directors and the common public between them had settled the line of his art long before any intervention by the critical elements in society. Chaplin has been called the one universal man of modern times, appealing to all, intellectuals and populace alike. He is new because of the primitiveness, the elemental quality of his medium – pantomime. He strikes deeper than mere wit or dramatic situation. Yet from this primitive element he has created some of the most subtle and complicated constructions of our time, and the care he lavishes on every inch of his films is known.

It is impossible to write on Chaplin here more than the elemental. First of all, as a social figure, for this is the most important thing about him. *The tramp was an individual.* He defied the growing mechanization and socialization of life. He was an individual to the point of *extreme idiosyncracy*. With his flopping shoes, baggy pants and derby he invaded every scene and sought to make himself at home. This, seen in retrospect, is an astonishing blow at what the film has become since 1929. The great masses accepted this truly audacious symbolism instinctively. If the tramp had walked into a session of Congress declaring war, *he* could not have been out of place in the eyes of his audience. This symbolism with far-reaching implications in aesthetics and its relation to society came very early in the film. Since the Thirties, it has been entirely lost.

Secondly, Chaplin represented the ideals of the society in their constant conflict with reality. Life (then) was supposed to be gracious, elegant, delicate in responses, full of human sympathy, etc. The tramp persistently tried to be all these things; as persistently the result was his grotesque contact with reality. But he never gave up. He picked himself up, brushed off his derby, settled his cane and went off again. Few today would deny that the twentieth century so far shows that either a new society is on the way or the old society is headed for complete catastrophe. Chaplin is best understood if we compare him to another character of three centuries ago – Don Quixote. Then, too, a new society, bourgeois society, was on the way. The ideals of the old society still held sway. Cervantes used the new form, the modern novel, and launched his fantastic knight on horseback who went forth colliding with the world around him as the tramp collided with the modern world.

Chaplin in those days could laugh at the world, and the world could laugh with him. But the Depression killed him as it killed all genuine creativity in the cinema.

After 1929 the banks got a grip on the film, but Chaplin has had enough money to make his own films. He is therefore a particularly instructive example of what the Depression did. The influence of a society is far more powerful than the actual financial control. *City Lights* (1931) was his last masterpiece, a bitter response to the Depression. But then Chaplin, a man of deep social sensibility, was finished. *Modern Times* tackled labor and machinery, a conflict which that very year was due to explode in the formation of the C.I.O. Chaplin attempted to laugh at it, to deride it. *It could not be done*. Chaplin was not merely a comic man. The finest comedy is possible only where the author is comic because if he were not, the environment would become tragic or collapse altogether. This destruction of humanity by machinery could not be laughed out of existence. It was no passing evil which laughter could cure. It was there, a monster growing. René Clair had tackled it in *A Nous la Liberté*. His hero left the factory and went out into the forest and listened to the birds, a romantic and dishonest evasion. Chaplin made a gallant attempt but failed. Then came the war. No man could laugh at this. Chaplin could deride Hitler and Mussolini but in the end he had to speak *in his own person*, to deliver the message. The symbolism was completely gone. The modern world was too harsh for the traditional tramp. This harshness and not talking-pictures killed him. In the last picture, *M. Verdoux*, the tramp has disappeared. *M. Verdoux* is a very interesting sensitive film, with a "progressive" content and some fine moments. Chaplin had enough money and reputation to make his protest. But there is nothing "new" in the film. It is the film of an intellectual who has translated these ideas into personages. Good or bad, it is the nineteenth-century individualism over again. The masses did not recognize the artist they knew. And they were correct.

Now it is by no means inevitable that Chaplin was bound to go the way he has gone. Those who know his latest work can see that emotionally he feels powerfully about unemployment, war, the jungle morals of industry, etc. His friends report that as a pantomimist in *every field* he is superb and can do what he pleases. It is not to be excluded that in a different society the tramp *might* have made his protest against war as Aristophanes made his. He might have gone into a Congress engaged in declaring war. The present writer believes that Chaplin would have been able to do even this and emerge triumphant. But for this he needed what he had in the early days, the warm sympathy of many millions who could see what he pointed out and laugh at it. He might even have reached heights of tragedy and of majestic indignation and wrath. But all this for him was impossible. His decline was rooted in his social environment and the definitive change which had taken place in 1929.

But that creative outburst, which he more than all others signalized, was part of the happy, carefree attitude of the United States up to 1929 (with its undercurrent of frustration and tragedy but not yet strong enough to dominate the emotions). Those were the great days of comedy. Harold Lloyd showed how an active energetic American could try and fail, and sometimes succeed, and more often fail and keep on trying again, starting from the beginning. He was Horatio Alger who wasn't doing very well but it was still far enough away from reality for people to enjoy it. The Depression put an end to his popularity. The last of the great film comedians was W. C. Fields. He was too a man of elegance, in language and style, but he was a rogue and querulous, annoyed constantly by all sorts of mishaps. As a recent biographer says, he was eternally suspicious and he appealed to the streak of pessimism in human nature, to which we add particularly contemporary human nature. With him the old tradition was dying. Today it is completely dead. There are no comedians in the grand manner in film. Today there is nothing but the perpetual gagging of Bob Hope, Jack Benny and the rest, all hammering wise-cracks at the jaded appetite of the listener to which is added a direct and crude appeal to his sense of superiority by constant references to Benny's baldness, reputed stinginess, etc. All that Hope does on the radio, he does on the film.

Yet the powerful creative tradition of the comic film did not collapse altogether. It had two remarkable outbursts before it finally disappeared. These were Walt Disney and the Marx Brothers. They have a great importance. First, they continued the creative tradition of boldly defying reality, and secondly, they were in very close relation to modern society. Chaplin had achieved the ultimate. His creation was himself and from this he had an infinite range in facing reality. Disney was on a lower level. He transformed reality. In an age when machinery was crushing man, he gave life to machinery, successions of fantastic brooms, teapots, staircases, etc. became alive and tormented innocent bystanders. Donald Duck voiced a perpetual exasperation with the never-ending irritations of modern existence. The last of the creative tradition appeared in the Marx Brothers and not for long. At their best, however, they showed a surrealist tendency to transcend reality. They did what they pleased in defiance of all restraint, tradition, and the multitudinous difficulties of modern society. And when they got into serious difficulties reality itself became fantasy to help them out. It was a bold attempt at escape by wish-fulfillment. That was why it could not last. But for a brief period it rounded off that astonishing cycle which had begun with the Mack Sennett comedies.

Such then is the dividing line of the films – the Depression, the great economic and social fact which forever separates the old confident America from the America of today. Before that, the film, for example, had its stars, its gay adventurous conqueror, Douglas Fairbanks, symbolical of the time; it rapidly ran through various types of women, the vampire, the corrupted men, Mary Pickford the timid shrinking Puritanical sweetheart and wife, now going out for good in a burst of laughter in *Life with Father*, the "It" girl, and Mae West's healthy and very human "Come up and see me sometime." It experimented with drama, etc. It even in those early days produced not only a man of technical imagination but found in him an eye for masses of men in landscape, a historical sense and a gift for dramatic characterization within that framework (D. W. Griffith) such as it has never seen again. To repeat: the great creative days died in 1929. With all allowance made, the dividing line stands clear. In its first contact with the masses and aiming solely to make money by pleasing them, there emerged the most remarkable artistic heritage of the times. It was killed by the Depression. The social conditions in general and the special conditions under which movies were now produced and distributed prevented the mass from giving that direct impulse which it exercised in the early days. The brilliant beginning stopped. But instead we have a complete inversion, the mass exposing its rage, anger and hostility, its desire to smash the impasse in which it finds itself, and making this the outstanding new characteristic.

All through the above we have made it clear that particularly for the period after 1929, owing to the very limitations the social situation imposed upon the film, the gangster in particular was essentially an individualist response to what was essentially a social problem. It is sufficient for the time being to point out that where millions of individuals make a common response to a social problem, they thereby give proof of a *common collectivized social attitude* to that problem. The writer will not turn aside from the important social task of delimiting with all precision possible, in a finished book, the different social classes and their special responses and responsibilities here. But it is enough to point out the differences between audiences of the traditional drama and the audiences of the film. The film is essentially the art of the masses, the working classes, the dwellers in remote agricultural areas and small towns, the lower middle classes. Those are the ones we mean by the masses, the vast majority of the nation. For the time being, if only for the time being, that is enough.

It is obviously impossible here to take up all the popular arts. But the history of jazz follows the same pattern. In the early days it was a genuinely popular music. To America being whipped into a remorseless discipline by mechanization, its strong recurrent rhythm and its abandon within that rhythm offered a relief that matched the strains of modern life. But early jazz was essentially music for the *new dancing*. One of the old band leaders speaking recently compares the modern bands and listeners to the old. "We," he said, "played for folks to dance to. And how they danced in the old days." And then he added what in the writer's opinion is the most remarkable statement ever made about modern jazz. In a big hall, he said, a sensitive leader *caught the rhythm for the evening from the dancers*. And when he had caught it, he told his band to hold it. The crowd of dancers therefore expressed their particular feeling for that evening and it was transferred to the musicians. Today, with the commercialization of jazz, that is gone. In a more complete rounded finished presentation, I shall pile up the evidence to show that the great popular tunes, the famous blues, were all the work of composers who did their best work before the Depression. Recently *Life* in its tracing of fifty years writes that the song and dance musical, a peculiarly American form, reached its climax in 1931. It isn't that Hollywood, for example, does not attempt to work over the old field and that the public fails to respond. It tries but simply is unable to do what it did thirty years ago. Says a *Life* critic about *Mr Peabody and the Mermaid*:

Mermaids belong to that world of the unreal and fantastic which was where Hollywood began.

This is extremely profound and is another testimony to the genuine creativeness of early Hollywood. He continues:

But in this film the sum total of fantasy consists of putting a tail on Ann Blyth. . . .

Hollywood today cannot do it. And we shall have to go seriously into the question of the organic relation between the creative imagination of an artist, the receptivity of a public and the connection between them. And in the same connection we should note the underlying similarity between Chaplin and Jackie Coogan in *The Kid* and the modern *The Bicycle Thief* which comes from Italy where the society is in such disorder that artists have some freedom. In 1919 Chaplin and his audience had some freedom of thought, the freedom of confidence and a lack of a sense of responsibility. Yet there is the same sense of mankind lost in a world beyond his understanding and this is emphasized by childhood as the new Italian directors understand so well. Hollywood could do this once upon a time. It cannot do it now.

We can conclude with a quotation from James Thurber, a practicing humorist with both pen and pencil, a man of talent and great experience with the public and with fellow-artists.

The most alarming thing about today is that all the kids are worried about the world situation. They didn't when I was young. Then the greatest menace was Halley's comet. And my Cousin Earl's motorcycle. They have things to worry about now.

In the year 1930 Perelman published his first stories and Ogden Nash his first poems. All the rest of the humorists got started in the Twenties. The Depression had a much more shattering effect on people than the first war. When a kid saw his father come home in uniform it seemed a natural thing. When a kid heard his father say he was wiped out and saw his mother burst into tears, it was a shattering thing. There is a grim turn to the stories today, even to humor. There were so many writers in the Twenties without this sense of doom.

The sense of doom that they (the "lost generation" writers – Fitzgerald, Hemingway, Dos Passos) had was more legendary than real. They were the lost generation, but they were lost in Paris, and having a pretty good time. All of them had a good twenty or thirty years to look ahead to. There just wasn't the sense of another war to look forward to then, as there is now.

Thurber in one sense is mistaken. It is not merely a question of "war." Men are not so afraid of the chances of death. The blight (and the turn to murder and violence) which has descended upon the American people since 1929 expresses the fact that the bottom has fallen out of the civilization, men have no confidence in it any longer, and are brought sharply up against the contradiction between the theories, principles, ideas, etc. by which they live and the realities which they actually face.

SOME POSITIVE ASPECTS IN POPULAR ART

Al Capp claims, or it is claimed for him, that since 1932, he is one of the few who is opposing the comic strip tendency to blood, murder, cruelty and sadism. This is not true. For years before him and side by side with the murders there has appeared another powerful tendency which holds its own. It is represented by the enduring popularity of Gasoline Alley and Blondie, to take only two and it is continued in the much-abused soap operas.

It is the need of the great modern population of the United States to have the daily incidents of its life, the everyday commonplace inconsequential actions of life dramatically represented. There is no need here to give examples from Gasoline Alley, the most remarkable perhaps of them all in this respect. Incidents, ideas, conversations, hopes, fears, that take place ten million times a day or could take place in any one of ten million families are presented and followed by millions with a passionate interest every day. This is something entirely new. During the war the writer followed for months during 1944 one particularly interesting soap-opera. The characters were an attractive woman whose husband had gone to war. She got a job as secretary to a businessman who fell in love with her. Day by day, the relations between them in business and then inevitably out of business, were developed, not without skill. The girl had a younger sister who fell victim to war hysteria and the general loosening of morals, took up with loose characters and had to be rescued. At the same time as this was being shown, the course of the husband in France was also portrayed. He was wounded, was taken care of by a beautiful French girl. Again there were complications. Letters passed between husband and wife constantly. The whole was kept within two or three days at most of the actual historical events in Europe, as for instance, celebrations of July 4 (or some such holiday) were constantly being participated in by the hero and heroine within a few days of their actual occurrence.

It is possible to laugh at the simplicity, the naivete and the simple conventions within which this radio serial was written and produced. As art it did not make history. But it represented the situation of many millions of wives in the United States out working, a younger sister who had gone astray, a husband abroad who was in danger from enemy bullets and foreign women. There were millions who day after day could identify a tense personal situation with these symbolical figures. And investigation has already shown that these serials, ridiculous as they are, mean more than mere idle passing-the-time to the women who listen, overburdened with domestic work, the care of children, illnesses. They should be listened to and examined in the light of the fact that art has now assumed a very intimate relation to the daily lives of the great masses of the people. It is not difficult to imagine a social situation in which by means of fine artists and gifted performers, there will be an almost day-to-day correspondence between the ordinary experiences of many millions of human beings and their transmutation into aesthetic form. There enters into the field of art a closeness to life unknown in past periods of human history which will not fail to have far-reaching effects on both. The same trend can be seen in magazines like *True Confessions*, etc. There, especially some years ago, the attempt was made to tell "true" stories. The language was high-flown, the sentiments commonplace. But there was this wish to get away from romanticism and deal with "actual" life, the things that "really" happen to people. Looking through recent issues I have seen at least two stories dealing with the problems of an ordinary kid of seventeen, weighing the chances as to whether she should go to bed with her boyfriend or not. Gasoline Alley and its prototypes, the soap-operas, the "realist" stories of the old *True Confessions* can be abused on the score of vulgarity, triviality, exploitation by manufacturers, etc. But when all of that type that can be said, has been said, there remains an immense social and artistic movement – which points a broad arrow to the future and the integration of the social and aesthetic aspects of life.

The war, as always with any great war, also brought into concrete form, in very distorted form, powerful tendencies in modern social life and a similar integration. An important part of this work will be to show how during the Civil War there appeared with great apparent suddenness many of the economic and social tendencies which had been germinating almost unperceived in the pre-war period and the same has to be done for World War II.

Popular art in World War II saw an orgy of propaganda and boosting of all aspects of the cause of the United Nations. The best that can be said of it was that it served its purpose. Nevertheless it symbolized infinitely more than the actual purposes it served. *Politics invaded and dominated the popular arts of screen and radio.* Democracy, the coming "new society" repeatedly referred to in film after film, directly political films such as *Mission to Moscow*, underground movements abroad, revolution and counter-revolution, heroism and self-sacrifice, for a cause, denunciation of wealthy collaborators, war departments, military headquarters, intelligence services, suddenly under the stress of events it was possible to see representations of the actual concrete events which were shaking the world. Here again to look woodenly at the actual performances is to make a serious analytical error. It is inevitable that in the future not merely the daily simple experiences of the population will undergo rapid transformation; the great social and political events of the day, war or no war, will find themselves artistically on the screen and radio, with the result of a still further integration of all aspects of the life of modern man.

Perhaps the most important aspect of the war films was the attention given to the actual life of the common man. True the film did not dare to touch except very gingerly on the work of the people in the factories. But every service, the air force, infantry, navy, merchant marine, coastguard, was made the subject of special pictures, revolving around the day to day activity of the servicemen, all ranks included. Here again it is clear that sooner or later we shall see as subjects of modern popular art the workers in the great industries. It is inevitable. Already some union papers have comic strips which show the problems and conflicts and triumphs of workers in the factory over scabs, stooges, and the intrigues and injustices of the employer.

THE CHARACTER OF THE MEDICINE

Earlier we gave a brief (and very much over-generalized) idea of a certain movement in literature – a simplification of the medium due to great social changes and an increase in the total complexity of the relations which can be built up from it. This is a difficult idea to make clear in the kind of statement this is. Yet it is essential. We stated that Chaplin's method was new, elemental. It was pantomime raised to the greatest possible degree of universality and its use by him is rooted in the changed social conditions and the mechanical possibility which are an integral part of them. This movement is characteristic of our age. It can best be explained by a series of examples. To begin with Freud. His psychology is a reduction of the complicated personality of modern man to a primitive elemental urge and two checks upon it. All men are psychologically reduced to the simplest of common denominators. From this immense simplification can be raised structures infinitely more complicated than in the old psychology, as can be seen nowhere more clearly than in some of the writings of Freud himself, who had nothing in common with the crude interpretations that pass popularly for psychoanalysis today.

It can be seen in the work of Joyce – particularly *Ulysses* – the highly organized and complex sophisticated analysis deals with certain very primitive needs and expressions of man's nature. D. H. Lawrence is another who reduced the whole modern problem to the creation of a *whole* personality living in instinctive harmony with its deepest instincts which he identified with a sexually satisfactory life, life of the blood, etc.

The Russian film directors of their great period achieved their effects by simplifying their symbols, the elements of the medium. They went for the viscera, and their greatest scenes tore at the insides of intellectuals and peasants alike. Tolstoy had put his finger on the question long ago in *What is Art?* What is this art, he asked, which only a small section of rich and cultivated people can appreciate. He talked much nonsense, and his own attempts to make a popular art by writing parables were doomed to failure. But he saw that in the modern world this division of serious art into art for the few and rubbish for the mass could not continue. It was *wrong* somehow, suitable for a slave society or a feudal society, but wrong in the modern world.

In as fundamental a matter as "politics" this simplification and complexity is taking place all around us. The contemporary crisis is recognized among vast sections of the world as an economic crisis; and the old conception of politics that reigned in America for example during the nineteenth century is gone. Politics today comprises *all* aspects of life, and more than ever, wages, conditions of labor, employment, etc., and the political party must deal with these elemental necessities primarily or promise to deal with them. In 1871 when someone in his cabinet mentioned unemployment to Gladstone, he replied quickly and definitively that his government had nothing to do with that problem. In a complicated way that will need strenuous analysis to explain, the modern world now faces in every sphere basic realities. The Russian regime appeals to its followers in terms of a future higher stage of Communism in which *all* the basic problems of life will be solved. The Fascist regime made war for "living space" and its attempt to appeal to the profoundest instincts raised questions of "blood," "soil," "race," "the folk-community." That was its way of evading the basic elemental issues which had transformed the parliamentary games of the nineteenth century and the diplomatic maneuvers which preceded wars into a recognition of the real relations which constitute contemporary society.

In their way Chaplin and Walt Disney are examples of this. The film has given them the opportunity of dealing with the most elementary symbols and relating them to very complicated social structures. It is the medium itself which enables them to make the universal appeal *to all classes*. Nor is language any serious barrier; the American film is the most popular film *in every modern country*. This was particularly striking in the creative period with its bold symbolical characters, the tramp, the gifted men who formed the foundation of the comedies, Buster Keaton, Fatty Arbuckle, Mickey Mouse and the other Disney characters. The audiences accepted these without any difficulty.

For twenty years no new characters have appeared. That type of imagination and the readiness to respond to it (they are by and large intimately united) are gone. What we get instead is a new type of symbolism, a symbolism that goes to the very heart of the modern age, its denial of personality to the mass and the determination of the mass to realize some form of individuality in however vicarious a form.

The great characters of 1910–30 were individuals but individuals that boldly defied reality. At the same time we had the star system, the heavy dramas, the light comedies, etc. which must form the stock-in-trade of the film. For the last twenty years, however, along with a surface realism, technical discoveries, etc. the most outstanding feature of the American movie is the complete domination of the star system. What has happened is that side by side with the representation of murder, violence, atrocity, evil, the masses have fostered a system whereby a certain selected few individuals symbolize in their film existence *and their private and public existence* the revolt against the general conditions. If the great body of the public did not need stars, there would be no stars.

Let us get first of all the elements of the phenomenon. In *Life* a year or two ago Winthrop Sergeant wrote an article on Rita Hayworth. I quote somewhat at length:

She was born in 1918. By 1941 the dark-haired baby had blossomed into a red-haired girl whose undulant figure and speculative smile were already becoming as familiar to Americans as those of the Madonna were to the Italians of the Renaissance. By 1945 at least 6000 Americans a week were busy writing her poems and prayers, and the armed forces of the most powerful nation on earth were carrying her enshrined image with them into war-battered cities, jungles and typhoons. In 1946, during

Operation Crossroads at Bikini Atoll, her picture was reverently and symbolically pasted to an atomic bomb while the world's scientific and military minds anxiously awaited one of the greatest destructive explosions mankind had yet contrived. A few months later an expedition into the wilderness of Canada's unexplored Headless Valley came across an abandoned trapper's shack. In it the expedition found three things: a candle, a can of beans and her picture. Soon an expedition to the South American jungle will plant a print of her latest movie *Down to Earth*, in a time capsule at the base of the Andes Mountains, where it will no doubt some day be unearthed by historians piecing together the archaeology of ancient 20th century civilization.

Sergeant's attitude is absolutely correct. This is indeed a phenomenon. And such a mass of feeling, good will and international emotion was aroused by her marriage and the birth of her baby as probably was never seen in the world before. To point out the great limitations as an actress of this from all accounts simple unassuming young woman in the typical fashion of intellectuals is to cut oneself from recognizing the tremendous social significance of what she represents. Sergeant continues:

To these historians it will be obvious that Rita Hayworth, as Margarita Carmen Cansino was known in her cinematically transfigured form, was only incidentally a movie actress and a dancer and that her place in ancient American civilization was actually that of an important religious institution. For comparisons they will inevitably turn to the goddess Aphrodite, who was worshipped by the still more ancient Greeks. As to the significance of the movie *Down to Earth*, they will be under no misapprehensions. Ostensibly *Down to Earth* is a drama which, as several critics have pointed out, is one of the shoddier, duller and more heavy-handed examples of a type produced with relentless regularity by the Hollywood studios. The idea that it is really a drama and hence subject to the laws of aesthetic criticism exists, however, only in the minds of movie critics. The American public, less hampered by academic theories, knows and accepts it for what it is: a ritual . . .

The legend itself, endlessly repeated in 90% of the movies present-day Americans see, is not unique or remarkable, but its peculiar position in American folk-lore undoubtedly ranks it as one of the curiosities of anthropolgoy. Its supernatural or purely mythological character is attested by the fact that it has nothing whatever to do with real life. The goddess, endowed by a vast priesthood of make-up men, costumers, cameramen and hair-dressers with a concentrated allure no real woman could approach, moves through the ritual as its center and goal; minor variations of plot are unimportant. She is pursued by the hero who overcomes various obstacles in the process and is finally rewarded with a sacramental kiss or a walk with the goddess, arm in arm, into the illusory future. Despite the fact that sex is presented here as a sugar-frosted dream of romance rather than a procreative reality, no doubt is left as to its all-pervading power.

The writer does not follow Sergeant in his interpretation of the Rita Hayworth cult as a modern version of the Greek worship of Aphrodite or the cult of the love-goddess. There is not the slightest doubt that what she represents – and we have been able to get its full impact solely in the modern film for the mass – is very closely associated with the mass cults of more primitive peoples and can throw a great deal of light on them. The important thing is that she is in no sense a mere creation of predatory industrialists for stupid masses but is a product of the age. She and Lana Turner and the rest symbolize women, love, Aphrodite, what you will. What is important is that unlike the tramp, Mickey Mouse, Harold Lloyd, etc., she, as a concrete human being, without a trace of genius, talent or even remarkable personality, has become such a symbol. These stars do not exist to interpret plays, to express emotions, ideas, etc. Plays, scripts, etc. are written to give them an opportunity to display the personality. It is realism at its lowest, a complete denial of any serious creative effort on the part of the artist or the audience. It is purely primitive. Sergeant says and rightly:

Rita Hayworth in her role as the goddess is more intimately known to many Americans than their wives or sisters. They have watched her gravely sensuous face with its curious flat-topped forehead and amber-colored eyes, register the whole gamut of emotion from petulant fury to little-girlish glee. They have watched the wind rustling through the freshly shampooed masses of her famous red hair. They have heard whispered words of love from her full voluptuous lips. They know every detail of the proud assured, feminine Hayworth walk. They have gloated over the Hayworth personality – that ideal mixture of American girlish health with just a teasing trace of Latin dignity and feline exoticism. They have noted how the Hayworth look contains subtle traces of the goddess' other standard impersonators – slight suggestions of the kittenish predatoriness of Lucille Ball, the healthy sensuality of Ann Sheridan and Esther Williams, the wide-eyed virginal innocence of Loretta Young. They have followed the vicissitudes of her private life, her marriages and divorce, the birth of her child, the adventures of those fortunate few males who occasionally take her dancing or play tennis with her.

How true this is has now been demonstrated by the outburst of feeling which has followed her recent marriage.

Rita Hayworth is but a single one. The great mass that in the last analysis decides these things, for no publicity in the world can create a great star, the mass chooses its major stars with remarkable judgment. From 1920–30 it worshipped Douglas Fairbanks and Rudolph Valentino; from 1930–40 its great star was Clark Gable; 1940–50 Gregory Peck was the most striking. Each is in a curious way representative of his decade, and when taken with their particular colleagues, this is even more clear. Equally notable is the manner in which the mass selects international types. There never was such an English type as Ronald Colman; Boyer was accepted, the courteous Romantic Latin lover as different from Valentino as Peck is from Douglas Fairbanks; they would not accept Jean Gabin. From Germany the public accepted Emil Jannings, Eric von Stroheim, and to a lesser degree Conrad Veidt. Cary Grant is a new and very important symbol. He is an Englishman but far removed from Ronald Colman and Leslie Howard, representative of a new type of Englishman on whom the influence of American civilization has been very strong. He has the freedom, natural grace, simplicity and directness which characterize such different American types as Jimmy Stewart and Ronald Reagan. But behind it all there is the British reserve. He anticipates, so to speak, the emergence of a new social type, the inevitable result of increasingly close relations between Britain and America.

The femme fatale was from the Continent, Garbo or Dietrich. It is not difficult to recognize in the special feeling for Ingrid Bergman a recognition of Protestant Western European dignity and charm, with that grace which the English and the Dutch so conspicuously do not show. Hence the violent shock at her recent actions. She complains that so many other actresses have done so much more than she. The apparent unfairness of the public is due essentially to the fact that she violated not morals in general but what she stood for. Some of these people can act, some cannot – that is not their function. The public turned its back on Bogart in a supposedly serious picture – *Sierra Madre*. The reason was diagnosed accurately. They did not want to see Bogart acting. They wanted plain Humphrey Bogart. The critics who hail "good" pictures and "good acting," etc. are howling in a wilderness of their own creation. If they and their critical and artistic friends were given the opportunity to make movies, they would in all probability empty the theaters.

In a recent discussion held by *Life* attended by movie-makers, critics, journalists, etc. it was noticeable how over and over again, Dore Schary of MGM showed his clear if empirical grasp of the conditions of modern movies and the exceptional abstractness and downright silliness of the "progressive" intellectuals and liberals who took part. Schary was dealing with realities, millions of dollars and millions of people. The intellectuals dealt with neither, having only a vague if verbose dissatisfaction with the mass "which needed better films" and the producers who were exhorted to satisfy that need.

The characters portrayed are part public and part personal. A vast army of journalists, magazine writers, publicity men, etc. keep every detail of the lives of the great stars before an avid public. Particularly interesting are the movie magazines which sell in millions every month. The vulgarities and absurdities of these magazines, the way in which they show a loving couple who, owing to the exigencies of mass printing, are not infrequently divorced before the article comes out, all this is diverting and in a sense demoralizing.

But these articles are not mere nonsense. They follow a method. If a star is dull, gloomy, stupid, the magazine writers build a portrait of a serious deep-thinking student of modern life. If the star is superficial or giddy, the portrait is touched in to represent a gay Mercutio laughing at the troubles of life. The aim is to give standard patterns of modern character and these patterns, together with the physical film personality, comprise the character whom the genuine film fans go to see. That the plot is good or bad, the characters consistent, all this is beside the point. Sometimes they are, more often they are not. But it is totally irrelevant to consider these things when watching Marlene Dietrich in her hey-day in the Thirties and Lana Turner today.

It should be said that the general level of acting ability is higher than can be imagined. When, for example, Ray Milland in *The Lost Weekend* turned in a serious performance, there was a general comment, "He can act." The statement shows that his popularity did not rest on that. Also, during the post-war period, for the first time in the history of the film, we are seeing a body of young players, chiefly actresses, who get good parts without fanfare, ballyhoo or glamour. Their claim to attention is primarily that they can act. Some of these are Barbara Bel Geddes, Colleen Gray, the little girl who played opposite John Derek in *Knock On Any Door* (Arlene Roberts), Betsy Drake. Here we have the absolute reverse of the star system as we have described it. The tendency is not to be exaggerated. But it gives an indication of the possibilities of the future.

It would seem that deprived of any serious treatment of the problems which overwhelm it since 1929 the modern masses have reacted in two main ways. They have fostered on the one hand an individualistic response to violence, murder, atrocities, crime, sadism; and on the other they have pertinaciously fostered and encouraged by their money and interest this creation of synthetic characters.[2] Through them they live vicariously, see in them examples of that free individuality which is the dominant need of the vast mass today. Not only in their artistic but in their public lives these stars are the real aristocracy of the country and they perform one essential function of any genuine aristocracy. They fill a psychological need of the vast masses of people who live limited lives. The whole vast creation of early Christianity with its hierarchy of saints and its precise descriptions of Heaven were a similar complement. The 400 of American society with its wealth and extravagance draw from a confident America, with the traditions of liberty, equality and freedom, nothing but derision and irreverent laughter. The aristocracy of the films is something else. So great is the consideration that they enjoy that during the war the government found that these stars were the ones from whom it got the most results when it wished to make important announcements. The generals, politicians, etc. were glad to get a few minutes on the radio programs. The great sporting figures are the same. In the daily press there is the same rush to read columnists – anything to get away from the routine mechanized existence.

These synthetic film characters are a far more serious social phenomenon than the detectives who reappear in book after book and radio-drama after radio-drama. They are limited to elementary conceptions of human character by which the existing deadness of life is made more tolerable. Yet within these limitations a spark can burst into flame. When John Garfield defied social workers, do-gooders and in his gloomy uncooperating personality claimed that the Depression had ruined his chances of life, and he would get what he wanted how he could, the public made no immediate and powerful response. But Garfield was soon tailored to fit the framework within which the synthetic characters operate.

There is another connected aspect to this question of personality and the modern mass. Take the case of Tom Brennan, the originator of the "Breakfast Club," who died recently. He was neither a dramatic personality in the commonly accepted sense of the term, nor could the present writer discover any trace of what can be described as wit, humor, excitement, energy or any of the qualities by which one human personality is able to express itself and draw a common response from many others. Yet this man was able to discover among middle-aged and elderly women a streak of cheated romanticism, a readiness to express it and at the same to laugh at it, which drew him millions of followers on the radio, to whom he became a dearly-loved symbol of some gap or need in their lives. Thousands wept and mourned when he died. The Townsend Plan gives one indication of the attitude of the middle-aged and the old to society. Brennan's "Breakfast Club" is another. There is the case of Arthur Godfrey with his fantastic following; as also Mary Margaret McBride who can sell vast quantities of some food by merely mentioning it, just as when Clark Gable discarded his undershirt in a picture, sales of undershirts fell by fifty per cent. But great as is the power exercised, it is a very irrational thing. Mary McBride took one look at herself on television and fled from it. One glimpse of her might destroy her hold over the millions who listen.

It is clear that in the modern mechanized collectivized world, with its building up on the one hand of all sorts of possibilities and vistas for the individual personality, and on the other its confinement of the personality to a narrow routinized existence with the mechanical means, there arises the need to realize the thwarted possibilities or certain parts of them through some symbolic personality. Yet the narrow basis on which it rests shows how unreal, how unsatisfactory it is as a reality, and how much it is a substitute for some profound inner need. For a brief period Father Coughlin showed the political possibilities that slumber behind these manifestations of our time. Other countries in the modern world have shown not only the possibilities but the realities.

We have stressed all through that in the immediate sense the violent bloody reactions and the acceptance of synthetic individuals who on the screen and off live freely, the reaction of the public is of each person as an individual. But if fifty million people react as individuals in a common way, they become or rather they are expressing a profound communal social force. This violence on the one hand, the absense of any creativity and the decline to accepting a few individuals as the raw material of the functions art must fulfill is a sign of a profound dislocation in society, as profound as it can possibly be, a dislocation in the deepest, most intimate, most instinctive elemental life-process of the modern human being. Between them they are the psychological preparation on a vast social scale of the most striking social and political actuality of our time – the emergence of the totalitarian state. Blood, violence, atrocities, cruelties beyond all record of human history or human expectation; and a relation between a totally mechanized mass and a few individuals; a complete conscious reversal of all standards and ideals of human conduct slowly built up over hundreds of years. The inhabitants of these countries are not made. "Human nature" is not subject to relapses. Every basic feature of the totalitarian state is the product of social development and the psychological responses it generates. The educated, the intellectuals, express themselves and their social ideas, their intimate personal lives in innumerable ways, witness for example, Joyce's novels. But the great masses are for the most part only statistics, voters, wage-earners, unionists, white-collar workers, etc. But in the modern world as soon as they had the choice of what they should choose as "entertainment," they have expressed themselves in negative and concealed form, but clearly enough within the limitations allowed to them.

So far it has not been possible to differentiate within what I have designated as the mass more than to say what I have already said – it is the vast new audience which the film has brought into existence. To what extent are the violent murderous rejection and the adoration of individuals characteristic of the mass in general? They are inherent in society but only in a society in which the actual deepest desires of the mass cannot find expression. They are essentially a perversion. It is to grasp this that we have to consider the drama of ancient Greece. It is the only example that we have in all the centuries of Western civilization of a dramatic art which served all the citizens of a state, an art which was designed for them and which the populace loved far more than the modern mass loves the film. There is no other feasible comparison; in addition to which this ancient art, written for the masses, produced a series of masterpieces which have never been surpassed to this day.

THE DRAMA OF GREECE

Why is this a means of illuminating the modern American film and the future of modern art and society? The average reader who has not studied this subject knows that scholars and students believe and have for hundreds of years believed that the writings of these Greeks are some of the greatest plays ever written. And he is content to leave it at that. If he is interested in the modern film, and modern popular art, democracy and modern society, he would be very wrong. Let me give you some immediate reasons which have nothing whatever to do with the literary quality of the plays as art.

(1) The Greek poet in the great days of the Athenian drama was the spiritual and social leader of the state of Athens, the most influential intellectual force among all classes of society and not only among the cultivated and educated. There is nothing in the world today to compare with the position he held. As W. H. Auden, the British poet, says in a recent study:

Athenian drama, while being definitively works of art, whose value can be judged by rote, became the dominant religious exercise of greater importance than sacrifices or prayers. In the nineteenth century and in our own the individual artistic genius has sometimes claimed a supreme importance and even persuaded a minority of aesthetes to agree with him; but only in Athens was this a universal social fact, so that the genius was not a lonely figure, claiming exceptional rights for himself but the acclaimed spiritual leader of society.

The nearest modern equivalent is not any work of the theatre, but a ball game or a bull-fight.

(2) I have been emphasizing the fact that the *great mass* of the modern population now is the object of modern popular art. It will astonish the ordinary critic of the poverty of modern films and also those who excuse them on the score that they are intended for the mass, it will astonish such to be reminded that practically the whole of the able-bodied population of the free citizens of Athens went to the theater to see the plays *and decide by their votes* who was the prize-winner. Generals, statesmen, artists, tanners, sausage-sellers, workers, peasants, who lived in the countryside near and belonged to the city-state, these were the audience and the judges. It was for this mass that Aeschylus and Sophocles and Aristophanes wrote. We should not be deceived by the word "religion." Going to the plays was a sort of national holiday. Auden says that the nearest modern equivalent is not any work of the theater but a ballgame or a bullfight. The idea that he is trying to convey is correct. The Greek masses went to the theater as if they were going to the World Series, Independence Day and a film festival all com-

bined.

To believe that this Athenian multitude was better "educated" or more "intelligent" than the modern film audience is to use words without any discoverable sense. The *society* was different and we shall have to see why and in what way. The reader will have to imagine the population of New York listening in on the radio on a public holiday to a play in which a dramatist brings Bernard Shaw and Eugene O'Neill on the stage and makes them argue why they write their plays as they do, why they use the different styles, what was the benefit to the citizens; all this with quotations from the plays thrown in and analyzed as if in a class on literary analysis at a university, with the audience recognizing the quotations and rocking with laughter as today they laugh at Jack Benny or Bob Hope.

(3) There is much talk today about "democracy" and the privileges of "democracy." Many democratic ideas and practices that we have, the Greeks knew nothing about; but they had a conception of democracy that we know nothing about. The Greek dramatist could take up any subject, *any subject* he pleased at these public festivals and treat them how he liked. Imagine a public festival coming on and the dramatists rehearsing their plays in secret. Meanwhile a national election of great importance has taken place and John L. Lewis succeeds Truman as President. Imagine too that Lewis has been carrying on political negotiations with the State of Persia, the British Prime Minister and the President of Brazil. They are in New York, and naturally the President takes them to the festival, along with all the people. The play begins and a modern Aristophanes is seen to have launched a bitter merciless direct attack, with the most violent language (but with marvelous satire and poetry) against Lewis. He criticizes Lewis, compares him adversely to Truman, makes a sausage-seller of the utmost vulgarity drive Lewis out of power on the score that it takes a bigger and more illiterate scoundrel to defeat a big illiterate scoundrel. In the play before the very rulers of foreign states, the dramatist criticizes the way Lewis has negotiated with them. This fantastic episode is more or less what Aristophanes, a boy of nineteen, did to Cleon, the new ruler of Athens. This was going rather far, but all Cleon could do was to prosecute Aristophanes before the courts; Aristophanes escaped.

It is the writer's belief that in modern popular art, film, radio, television, comic strip, we are headed for some such artistic comprehensive integration of modern life, that the spiritual, intellectual, ideological life of modern peoples will express itself in the closest and most rapid, most complex, absolutely free relation to the actual life of the citizens tomorrow. In fact it cannot be escaped. It is being done in the totalitarian states already. But whereas among the Greeks free expression was the basis of intellectual life, the integrated expression of the totalitarian states is the result of the suppression of free expression. In the one case, therefore, we have perhaps the greatest intellectual civilization known to history; in the other case, we have barbarism. It is important to get a clear concept of integration. This perhaps can best be done with another quotation from W. H. Auden:

It is impossible to say, for example, of a harvest dance of a primitive tribe, whether it is aesthetic play, undertaken for the pleasure it gives the participants in performing it well, or religious ritual, an outward expression of an inward piety towards the powers who control the harvest, or a scientific technique for securing the practical effect of a better harvest; it is indeed foolish to think in such terms at all, since the dancers have not learned to make such distinctions and cannot understand what they mean.

In a society like our own, on the other hand, when a man goes to the ballet, he goes simply to enjoy himself and all he demands is that the choreography and performance shall be aesthetically satisfying; when he goes to Mass, he knows that it is irrelevant whether the Mass be well or badly sung, for what matters is the attitude of his will towards God and his neighbor; when he plows a field, he knows that whether the tractor be beautiful or ugly or whether he is a repentant or a defiant sinner is irrelevant to his success or failure. His problem is quite different from that of the savage; the danger for him is that, instead of being a complete person at every moment, he will be split into three unrelated fragments which are always competing for dominance; the aesthetic fragment which goes to the ballet, the religious which goes to Mass, and the practical which earns his living.

If a civilization be judged by this double standard, the degree of diversity attained and the degree of unity retained, then it is hardly too much to say that the Athenians of the fifth century B.C. were the most civilized people who have so far existed. The fact that nearly all the words we use to define activities and branches of knowledge, e.g. chemistry, physics, economics, politics, ethics, aesthetics, theology, tragedy, comedy, etc. are of Greek origin is proof of conscious differentiation; their literature and their history are evidence of their ability to maintain a sense of common inter-relation, a sense which we have in great measure lost as they themselves lost it in a comparatively short time.

We have now reached a state in modern society where this integration must take place or the complexity and antagonisms of society will destroy the personality. Society is already on the road to ruin through its inability to resolve the contradictions which are preventing this integration.

To get a rough, a very rough picture of the historical circumstances, we must take a look at the Greek democracy. The founders of the American nation knew quite well what was the difference between a democracy and a republic. Classical scholars as many of them were, they discussed and agreed that a democracy in America was impossible. By democracy they meant the democracy of Athens. They, in common with Montesquieu, Rousseau and other great thinkers of the eighteenth century believed that this was possible only in the small city-state, one city. For a large country, it could not work. But in the eighteenth century they discussed the question. The argument may have had some validity in 1776 (and Colonel McCormick of Chicago still uses it). It has none in the age of the railway, the auto, the plane, the radio, the telephone and the modern newspaper.

The city-state of Athens in its great period had a population of no more than 90,000 with 200,000 slaves. It is not unlikely that all their material possessions could have been housed in the warehouses of one modern department store – perhaps of two department stores. Yet in the great century, from the sixth century B.C. to the fifth, this insignificant collection of poorly equipped human beings produced more in the sphere of ideas and great men, men great for the future of civilization, than the United States has produced in the nearly two hundred years of its existence. I shall repeat some of these achievements.

There are to this day no greater tragic dramatists than Aeschylus, Sophocles, Euripedes; no greater comic dramatist than Aristophanes; no greater creative statesman than Solon; no greater orator than Demosthenes; Pindar remains unexcelled in elegiac poetry in the grand style; Aristotle and Plato still stand at the head of philosophers; Praxiteles as a sculptor, Socrates as a publicist, Thucydides and Herodotus as historians are to this day in the first rank. It is not merely that they were great men as Cervantes or Dostoyevsky or Melville or George Washington were great men. These men and their associates laid the intellectual foundations of modern civilization. If today we distinguish between epic poetry, comedy, drama, rhetoric, logic, being, essence, appearance, dialectic, democracy, mathematics, science, etc. with all their manifold divisions and subdivisions and connections, if we do these things in a certain way, it is because the Greeks (for the most part) of the sixth and fifth centuries B.C. worked them out. They were not merely great practitioners in the arts and sciences, politics and philosophy. It is true to say that they discovered them, worked them out, organized them. And it is true to say also that to this day, the moment you begin a scientific study of any of the purely intellectual practices of mankind, you are at once faced with the necessity of reckoning with the Greek originator. Except in science they have not been superseded to this day. You cannot live by Aristotle's philosophy today, but if you wish to understand philosophy, you have to understand Aristotle.

In the sixth century B.C. Athens reached the most advanced stage of any city-state, the characteristic political form of ancient society. Briefly, the old aristocratic class was defeated, and a new democracy was established, a democracy based on the substitution of commerce, exchange, trade and money for the old domination of landed property. Except for the slaves, the artisans, merchants, etc. were free citizens as were the peasants who lived on the countryside near. At about this very period Athens was in mortal danger from the Persians. At the famous battles of Marathon and Salamis, the Persians were defeated and the great period of Athens began.

The new democracy had no bureaucracy, it had no organized priesthood, every citizen took part in the government, took part in debates, voted, served on the various assemblies. A man was supposed to take part in *everything*. Politics did *not* mean what we used to mean by it. Used to mean, because now we are beginning to recognize that *everything* is political. For the Greek in the great period this was an axiom. An *idiot* in the Greek sense was a man who was not interested in politics, and politics was what concerned the polis, i.e., the state. Everything concerned the state, and thus everything concerned the individual man. As Auden puts it: an Athenian of the fifth century looking at the world today would say: "Yes I can see all the works of a great civilization; but why cannot I meet any civilized persons? I only encounter specialists, artists who know nothing of science, scientists who know nothing of art, philosophers who have no interest in God, priests who are unconcerned with politics, politicians who know only other politicians.

With this idea of universal man, the Greek citizen had a peculiar attitude to the state. Religion was the belief which the state taught to strengthen morals and the city-state. The state was all-powerful, controlling everything, but *he* was the state. The state, for example, organized the dramatic festivals. But unlike Stalin who decides on music and Hitler who decided on art, the populace went down, listened to the dramas and voted who was the winner. This, roughly, very roughly, is some idea of the Greek city-state.

Out of this state sprang the drama. It came and developed as suddenly as the film. Before the great period there was no drama – absolutely none. At the religious festivals there used to be choruses and a speaker who recited a ritual of chants, old historical tales with a moral, etc., and a chorus which answered. At certain of these religious festivals there was a good deal of drunkenness and horse-play. But when Athens won the great victory over the Persians and after years of struggle had established the new democracy, suddenly overnight as it were, Aeschylus created practically single-handed the Athenian drama. All people who talk about centuries of education, etc. before the public is able to rise to the height of intellectuals, etc. simply have no conception of the historical dynamic, the way that history moves.

Aeschylus added another speaker to the man who led the chorus at the religious festivals and then added another; and the Greek drama was born, to last for a century and then to collapse with the collapse of the democracy. Aeschylus passionately loved the new democracy as did the great body of the people. Somehow Aeschylus understood the new society well enough to know that it wanted, it terribly wanted a new way to express the new moral, social and political process which had been created by the new democracy and which alone could make it work. He introduced these new speakers and transformed the religious ritual into *political* plays, political plays in the highest sense, the Greek sense of that word. The chorus he kept to act as commentator on the drama, representing the people.

What was the essential problem? Life was uncertain, justice did not reign among men; sometimes evil prospered, the just failed to prosper. Why did men suffer? Was there some interior harmony and meaning to life? The new democracy felt that it had to have guidance and new insights in these questions. It found them in the tragedy begun by Aeschylus. Aeschylus took as his heroes great men, men of status. They did not commit ordinary crimes. In the most famous of his dramas, Orestes commits the crime of marrying his mother. But Orestes did not know she was his mother when he married her. Here we come up sharply against the modern conception of tragedy. For Aeschylus and the Greeks Orestes had broken the laws and the laws by which men live in society must not be broken. The Greeks, author and audience, believed in their society. They were not, like contemporary democrats, perpetually questioning the values of democracy, wondering whether it will work, if it will be superseded, etc. Therefore the hero of their tragedy was not a gangster or a plain and simple bad man. The Greeks would have been bored at seeing him punished by fate. He was a man who somehow by no obvious fault of his own found himself in conflict with the principles by which men lived. And the tragedy consisted in watching what the consequences were and how they worked out. This is a tremendously bold conception. It is not mere good and evil, but the conflict between the individual, a good individual if you will, and society.

But there was much more to it. The tragic hero was a distinguished man. He usually suffered from some weakness – a kind of personal pride to which the Greeks gave a special name – *hubris*. And any man who sought too much power, too much distinction, to remove himself from the normal, then the tragic destiny was likely to fall upon him. It was a warning to the democracy to maintain a certain balance, a certain sense of proportion.

The gods who play such a role in these dramas were not gods as we understand them. They were the transformation into individual personalities of the ideas and principles by which the society lived. (Note where the characteristic individualization takes place – where it matters most to the audience – in the sphere of ethical and social principles.) Sometimes there was a conflict between these principles, which appears as a conflict between the gods. The unfortunate hero is torn and rent until there is some sort of reconciliation among the gods, *among the contending principles*. Hanging over all is the sense of doom, the certainty that when a man and an important man is out of line, however it happened, there is no stopping until the power and righteousness of God and law are justified.

To put this into drama, plays, was something entirely new. The Greeks of Athens understood Aeschylus for they gave him the prize many times and worshipped him. They could not fail to understand, for Aeschylus from the very start wrote for the people. On the stage, the chorus acted as the representative of the ordinary citizen, the great masses of the people. And Hegel has pointed out how as the democracy declined, the chorus began to be left out, and with the collapse of democracy came the almost complete collapse of the Athenian drama. From start to finish, the people, the mass were an integral part of it. This is very hard for us to grasp. Werner Jaeger in his famous book on Greek culture writes:

As the spectators shared in the agony of the tragic characters and chorus beneath the thunderstrokes of fate . . . they felt their highest spiritual energies called out to resist the storm, and were driven by pity and terror, the immediate psychological effects of their experience, to fall back on their last defense – their faith in the ultimate meaning of life itself.

Jaeger is here explaining the meaning of the statement by Aristotle (who was a contemporary of Athenian tragedy) that its function was to purge the citizens by pity and terror. Jaeger interprets it as a completely social experience. The masses of people *had* to pity the hero, *had* to feel terror at the doom which stalked him. But because they believed in their society, felt that so to speak God was with them, they could stand the apparent injustices which were taking place on the stage and in fact could accept them only because they believed. Jaeger continues:

The specifically religious effect on the audience of sharing in the terrors of human destiny, which Aeschylus' tragedies succeeded in producing as an integral part of the action is the essentially tragic element in his drama.

It is impossible to say more sharply what the present writer has in mind as inherent in modern popular art. Jaeger ends:

To appreciate them, we must abandon all modern conceptions of the essence of drama or the essence of tragedy and direct our attention to that element alone.

Here I agree with Jaeger only to part company with him. What I am trying to say about modern popular art is that, in the modern world, we have in our hands, the means, and a social situation in which once more, in an infinitely more complicated manner, great drama will be written, about the great problems which confront men today, by men conscious of the mass audience as Aeschylus was conscious, with an audience ready to participate to the full, its participation an integral part in the drama.

Yet despite the limitations of his age, one modern writer did manage to achieve the genuine Aeschylean approach. The character of Ahab and the whole novel is as near an approach to the Greek concept as a modern writer has got. When Melville finished he wrote to Hawthorne that he had just finished an evil book but he felt very happy. Something of the Aristotelian spirit of purgation by pity and terror is there, for Melville believed in democracy. One must imagine an America worried about democracy and individualism as America was worried at that time. One must imagine a Melville aware of the fact that the whole nation would gather on a certain day of national festival to listen to *Moby Dick* as a play or a film. Imagine too that Melville's writing would be profoundly affected by this. Then think of the character Ahab and the others, and Melville's profound thesis presented to the people and a tremendous response by the whole nation to the dramatic presentation of fundamental problems. We then have some idea, however rough, of what the Greek drama was, and the failure of popular art today. So concrete and yet so profound were Melville's conceptions that his imagination in attempting to encompass all that he saw fell almost naturally into what can easily be read as a scenario for a type of film which modern film-makers have not as yet even dreamt of.[3] We shall take this up in time.

To get the idea of participation, we must go back to Auden's image of the ball game but even that is not enough. Perhaps a mass-revival meeting of Negroes just relieved from slavery would give another avenue to understanding. A realistic sermon on the sufferings of Christ or the saints would elicit from the audience a tremendous response for they too had suffered and were suffering; but at least they were now free, and the bitterness of the exposition could serve only to call forth and strengthen their fundamental faith.

Aeschylus wrote about 90 plays. We have only seven. I have neglected here the disputed problems as to what exactly was his attitude to the democracy, whether he sought to restrict it, thought it had gone far enough, etc. I have summarized with great brutality. But the thing to remember is that a body of dramatists took up the great problems year after year, wrote with the highest seriousness, gave an integrated view of the various problems facing the country and held the attention of the masses to the end. They gave with the consciousness and intensity of great art an insight into the relations of the great problems that troubled the universality-minded Greeks. They became in the end intellectual leaders of the people, stage after stage, they gave a spiritual meaning to the underlying problems. This art was inextricably tied to the realities of the day.

Now I believe, and it will be the function of a finished study to show, that we are headed for such a relation. Art, film, radio, television, offer arts of the mass, for the mass, offer the means whereby great artists in the infinite complexity of modern life, in the way great artists always have done, will simplify and dramatize and attack the emotions as well as the intellect with dramatizations of the great problems. The old forms of art as Shakespeare and Melville practiced them are exhausted. The new forms are under social conditions and in a tradition which prohibit their being developed as Aeschylus developed drama. But an art for the mass openly and directly must come. This whole chapter has tried to show its inevitability by analyzing existing tendencies. A modern society *must* do this in the manner of the totalitarians or in the manner of the Greeks.

A word about Greek comedy. Side by side with the tragic treatment the comic dramatists developed. What did they write about? To quote Jaeger again, they wrote about:

the polar oppositions between the individual and the community, the mob and the intellectual, the poor and the rich, liberty and oppression, tradition and progress.

The Greeks could not have understood it if a serious comic artist did *not* write about these things. Aristophanes in particular took up religion, education, democracy, philosophy, the art of writing tragedy, every conceivable subject which affected the city was a fit topic for his merciless satiric drama. And, to repeat for the last time, they were not written for the educated or the cultured. They were written for the mass, the same mass that today goes to the films, reads the comic strips and listens to the radio. Does anyone who knows the American people doubt that if today the social environment were such that it was possible, understood in the deep consciousness, that such things could be freely treated for the millions to see and listen to, does anyone who knows the American doubt that along with the inevitable rubbish and routine stuff, great masterpieces would appear as in Greece and shake the nation to its soul. It is fairly certain that the modern mass has a far better formal education than the Greek though comparisons here face historical difficulties.

If Aristophanes came back today and were given a free hand, he would scorn the limited audience in the theaters. Being a Greek dramatist of the fifth century, he would naturally consider it his business to write for the films to which 95 million people go every week. He would arrange for a great film festival for the coming July 4 as a natural part of the celebrations. Then in the presence of the Chief Executive, the Judiciary, Congress and all the notables, in one theater in Washington, the whole population on the same day at the same time would see his film. It would have in it slapstick, a great deal of plain indecency, but precisely because of the present political situation of democracy, the film would contain the most unbridled blows at American democracy, calling things by their names and naming names as well. He would probably put in the film characters easily reconizable as great personages of the day. He would call corruption corruption, and graft graft. He would not imply that though some were corrupt, on the whole everything was not so bad. He would be bitter beyond belief. He would do all this, however, from the standpoint of a lover of his country (he would not use this as a means of praising some other country); the Greeks would accept all this, for in their great period, free discussion meant precisely free discussion of fundamental problems. Without it they could have never achieved in any sphere the marvelous things that they did, drama included. When the modern film, comic strip and radio can take up capital and labor, housing, the union question, religion, the Negro question, Russian communism and dramatize them with the freedom of sixth- and fifth-century Greece, we would open out just such possibilities as Aeschylus saw when he added extra characters to the leader of the chorus. Until then gangster films and Rita Hayworth.

Imagine now the Philistinism which would profess to believe that the American masses could not understand it inasmuch as they were not "educated" enough as yet. They would understand it only too well. That is why such things are not written for the film. A comic strip which dealt realistically with the life of a Negro family, living in various parts of the United States, and traveling abroad, could easily wreck great chains of newspapers if they dared to print it and could result in violence, bloodshed and riots in a dozen cities from one end of America to the other, yet even Hollywood is quick to sense a change in public opinion and has shown recently how instinctively it can play with the Negro question without touching it seriously. But when modern popular art is free, free in the consciousness of the artist that a vast public is ready to assemble together to listen to him, a whole new phase of art will begin. It has no connection with "intelligence" and "education."

The Greeks of the fifth century aimed at universality. They accomplished the miracles that they did but they failed because they did not, they could not, take into account one particular aspect of universality – how a man labored. The slave did the hard work. Labor as such became degraded. We cannot go into that here. But it was slavery which killed the democracy. Today we are once more at an age when universality is on the order of the day. But today universality *begins* with man in the labor process. That we have shown fully enough in the previous chapter. The totalitarian states do not alter this. In fact the most important function of the totalitarian regime is to chain the worker more tightly than ever to working as a slave in the factory.

Impotent rage, anger and frustration which can find expression only in a popular art of blood, destruction, torture, sadism; and an outlet for cheated, defrauded personality in vicarious living through a few striking personalities, these are the basic results in the only field where the masses are not free but at least have some choice in deciding.

But these are precisely the dominant aspects of the totalitarian state. It is only another way of showing, another very important proof that these states are states not of release but of repression, repression of the same basic needs of the great mass in the most democratic of democracies. Violence, cruelty, terror and sadism are and must be characteristic of the totalitarian states. These regimes are the most cruel, the most barbarous history has known. There is not and there could not be anything in previous ages to equal them. We must make a preliminary examination of this.

We have seen the tremendous antagonisms which are eating away at the core of the personalities of the great masses in the free democratic society of the United States. We emphasized the basic fundamental antagonism in the day-to-day existence; whether there is peace or war, whether wages are good or bad. We want to separate ourselves entirely from those who see "low wages" or "insecurity" or "fear of war" as the root. We have drawn attention only to the Depression as the primary event which made Americans begin to realize that the ground under their feet was unsure. We have omitted such features of our age as inflation, bad housing, seasonal unemployment (as opposed to the Depression which undermined confidence in the whole economy), racial prejudice, the dislocations of war, the struggles in the factories, struggle over civil liberties, etc. We shall treat these later, but they all have their peculiarly acute impact upon the society because they affect a population which is fundamentally as antagonistic to its mode of life as the early Americans, for example, were not.

The totalitarian states do not change this. They change neither the fundamental antagonism nor their subordinate manifestations. But they do not merely replace the old regime. The possibility of totalitarian power arises only when the suppressed hatreds, antagonisms, frustrations, burst irrepressibly into the open. At this period, it is clear that the social, political ideas of the old regime are exhausted and recognized as such by the vast majority. The function of the totalitarian state is to substitute a new state organization and a new ideology for the old. But not only is it unable to solve the old social conflicts. It must deal with them now that they are in the open, now that the old veneer has been discarded, and the hopes of decades are seeking realization.

The necessity to suppress unrealized instinctive needs for a new way of living, but the *actual* demands, wishes, deep hopes of a new universality for the individual, this can be done only by violence, brutality, terror and sadism which must correspond in depth to the hopes aroused and now in the open.

It is curious but quite in harmony with contemporary thought that the actual social life of individuals occupies so little attention among the abstractions of economists, political philosophers, etc., that few pay serious attention to the unheard-of cruelty, terror, brutalization of millions of people which form the essence of totalitarianism. Unable to analyze the deep social roots of this monstrous apparition in modern society, people are apt to fall back upon the weaknesses of human nature in general and feel a general hopelessness about human progress. Characteristic of this is the statement in the recent best-seller by Vannever Bush that mankind today shows such cupidity and barbarism and cruelty as never at any time in its history. He makes the statement and leaves it at that, just as if the whole point of any historical analysis is not to show why man at this stage in civilized society shows more cupidity and cruelty and barbarism than at any time in human society. Innumerable similar statements permeate both the intellectual and the popular press. In reality, this violence, brutality, and sadism are the only means by which a modern population, seeking free expression for individuality – a broadened and deepened conception of democracy, a modern universality – it is only by a previously undreamt of organization of oppression that such a population can be suppressed.

The strength of the needs which could find expression (but such powerful expression) in the popular arts are a social force of immeasurable magnitude. Once it is out in the open, how is it possible for society to continue at all but by the organization of repression such as no previous societies had need to organize. In the slave society of classical antiquity no one told the slave that he was a free individual and that the whole society existed for him to organize his free individuality. He was told exactly the opposite.

The totalitarian regimes therefore are not proof of the depravity of human nature. They are proof of exactly the opposite – the tremendous hopes, desires, wishes for a truly human existence and the consciousness that it is possible to achieve this. Czarism needed only a moderate regime of oppression to suppress the backward Russian people; once they had broken out in revolution, cleared away the old feudal rubbish and sought to realize the vision of a modern existence, it takes the most monstrous state known to history to keep them in subjection.

We emphasized the suppressed antagonisms, the suppressed rages, the violence which a careful study of the popular arts would show. The totalitarian state is built upon this. Violence, terror, intimidation, cruelty is the cement of its social engineering. Such organizations as the Gestapo and the GPU are the essence of the new state. Goering once told Sir Neville Henderson the British ambassador, that the British did not cultivate brutality. Brutality and terror are cultivated by such regimes. They must have at their disposal millions of men not only armed but psychologically ready for the constant application of violence, cruelty, torture and intimidation. The social necessity attracts the types of the population who can best carry out these harsh requirements; the types are trained; the authoritarian, the sadist, the killer, the man who is as ready to kill as be killed, the gangster and the private detective become the ideal of the social regime. The most obvious proof of this is to be found not so much in the relations between the rulers and the ruled, but between the rulers themselves. Not a soul among the ruling strata in Russia except Stalin is reasonably sure that he will not be dead, in prison, in exile or in disgrace a year from today. When Molotov (the second man in the state) dropped out of public view some months ago, no one could say for certain that he had not been liquidated. If he had been liquidated, no one, least of all in Russia, would have been surprised. It is the rule of the gang elevated to a gigantic scale. We repeat once more, the violence, the blood, the cruelty of what is called the "entertainment world" is the projection of the obverse side of our civilization. The process whereby it becomes reality is not at all complicated. The reader is also asked to reflect for a moment on the outstanding character in that brilliant, profound and *best-selling novel* of the war, *The Naked and the Dead*, by Norman Mailer. The book recognizes the miserable, physical and spiritual poverty of the lives of the great masses of the people, how little democracy as they know it means to them; it discusses socialism, fascism, Marxism, etc. It is a book written with great humanity and a sense of actuality in social relations which show it to be lineal descendant of *Moby Dick*. But the outstanding character, the man of force, resolution, will, power to command, and in his own way, of imaginative vision is the sergeant, Croft, a ruthless, brutal, sadistic killer.

Such is the social and psychological basis of the otherwise inexplicable transformation of modern man which takes place in the totalitarian regime. By carefully observing the trends in modern popular art, and the responses of the people, we can see the tendencies which explode into the monstrous caricatures of human existence which appear under totalitarianism and closely intertwined with the blood and violence and cruelty, now elevated into social forces, is the social substitution of the individual for the mass. It is the need for free and full expression of individuality which is shaking a modern world. The totalitarian state first suppresses this completely from top to bottom. Party members, generals-in-command, heads of institutions, all are but cogs in a vast wheel. General Eisenhower testifies to the incapacity of Marshal Zhukov to make a single decision just so long as it was possible for him to communicate with his superiors, and so on to the most miserable petty bureaucrat. We have seen how, deprived of individuality, millions of modern citizens live vicariously, through identification with brilliant notably effective, famous or glamorous individuals. The totalitarian state, having crushed all freedom, carries this substitution to its last ultimate. The idol worship of Stalin is not mere "human nature" or a "mere" imposition by the totalitarian bureaucracy upon the population for purposes of authority and prestige. It is inherent in the modern situation. The Russian or German pregnant woman who bore her baby "for Stalin" or "for Hitler," the abasement of a whole population before the all-wise, the good, the genial, the philosopher, the great general, the great critic of music, the protector, the little father, Stalin, is the totalitarian use of the now universal tendency to atone for the felt deprivations of existence by transferring the need to some concrete reality, however remote and unreal.

The practice is carried right down the hierarchy. Every little leader bows his head before the leader above him, and accepts the unqualified obedience and homage of the leader below. In the advanced countries of Western Europe, there can be found tens of thousands and many intellectuals among them who, without the pressures of violence, police-terror and fear to which the populations of the totalitarian state are subjected, are ready to pay this homage to Thorez, to Togliatti, to Browder today and to Dennis the day after, and if necessary to Browder once more. In the section on the popular arts and the worship of "stars" we did not go into the fact that in national politics, in the union movement such figures as Roosevelt, John L. Lewis, etc. were or become the personal embodiment of what ideas they represent in a manner unknown to previous generations.

Within these two poles the totalitarian state directs the lives of its citizens. Universality is the aim, the need to exercise the will, the intelligence, the judgment, the faculty of decision, to take action in regard to the problems which today decide the fate of tens of millions. Totalitarianism solves this problem by depriving its citizens of any volition whatever in any sphere. There is no subject, war and peace, foreign policy, production and consumption, art, literature, music, chess-playing, on which the citizen in a totalitarian state is not informed what his opinion must be and from which he departs at peril of his life. Isn't it obvious that the necessity for this can arise only in a world in which free discussion and free action has become an imperative necessity for the great mass of the population?

Integration was the source of the miraculous outpouring of creative genius which distinguished the Greeks, integration of all aspects of life, above all in the state, because in the world as he knew it, every man (who was not a slave) felt that the state, composed of free assemblies of free citizens, was the embodiment of the city-state and that his personal individuality could only be expressed through it. This is the great need of modern man for under those circumstances the state is not a state at all, in the modern sense of the word. The totalitarian state integrates every aspect of life, production, politics, entertainment, aesthetics, sport into a single whole and imposes these with the utmost ruthlessness upon the mass of the nation.

Modern man's quest for universality needs a new sense of belonging, the community. "My" country, democracy as voting, etc. are insufficient. This is universal. There is a genuine terror expressed openly in papers like the *New York Times* that all the billions spent on the Marshall Plan and on the rearming of Western Europe will mean nothing if the average citizen in these countries does not feel any compelling necessity to defend them against the Russian army. Such a conception was unthinkable a generation ago. The totalitarian states offer a new identification for the individual with the community, "blood," "race," "soil," "the folk-community" of Nazi Germany, and in Russia (a regime of different historical origin) an adaptation of the social perspectives of Marxism for a unified world and a society free of conflict and exploitation. But in reality the population does not accept these fraudulent gestures and both regimes fall back upon a frantic refurbishing of the old nationalism which has meaning in colonial countries but little in Western Europe as the fears of the *Times* show. Here again the totalitarian state betrays its real function – to substitute a new ideological system for the ruthless enforcement of traditional values whose inadequacy is recognized in various degrees by the masses in all parts of the world.

Behind the inflated language and hypocritical "ideology" the whole regime sinks to a primitive level commensurate to the destruction of free individuality and its concentration by violence and terror upon a few individuals. The party becomes the sphere of personal safety, material privilege and power to oppress. It is the overseer, the rest are the slaves. The nation moves between such concepts as the leader, the mass and the perpetual enemy – in Hitlerite Germany, the Jews; in Russia, the Trotskyists. The antagonisms and frustrations which find manifestation in the popular arts of the United States are given an official enemy in totalitarian states.

The urge to expression of the modern intelligence, stimulated and fed on all sides by the vast scientific organization of modern society and its innumerable means of communication and dissemination of information, this the totalitarian state must crush and keep on stamping on. Hence, a ceaseless barrage of propaganda, visual and auditory, refusing to allow it to have one single opinion of its own, to think, to exercise itself in any way. Precisely because only a free and powerful activity can satisfy it, passivity unknown in history must be imposed upon it.

Thus every fundamental aspect of the totalitarian state is an adaptation by tyranny to the deepest social needs of the modern age, to needs which can be clearly discerned in the democratic countries and nowhere more than in the United States.

We shall examine only two other phenomena to show the relation we are seeking to establish. Both deal with psychological phenomena. The first is the mass trial. Neither the organizers of these trials nor the people for whom they are intended are in any way outside of the main streams of modern civilization, understanding, intelligence, faculty of judgment. Examination of the evidence, exposure of the absurdities, the grossness of the frame-ups is a political necessity but can easily give the impression that the people concerned have lost elemental faculties of intelligence and judgment. It is the opinion of the writer that these trials are a type of public social drama, a representation before the nation of whatever political ideas the totalitarian bureaucracy wishes for the moment to impose upon the country. Do the people believe in them? The people are not supposed to exercise any judgment. This is the fact, this is the crime, this is the enemy, exposed before the whole nation. The mass is supposed to absorb the primitive elemental representation. True or not true, this is what is to be believed today.

Tomorrow the accusers become the accused and vice versa. Then that is what is to be believed.

But that is not all. The trials indicate not merely the tyranny, the shamelessness of the organizers of these trials. It indicates something very different – that the modern community is ripe once more for great tragedies and comedies in the Greek manner, in which the whole population will assist and see the great social and political issues of the day placed before them for their judgment, response and participation. If they were merely the concoction of stupid and cheating bureaucrats, they would long ago have lost whatever political value they had and would have been discarded. Barbarous and degrading spectacles as they are, they represent something of new political and aesthetic needs which are stirring throughout the civilized world.

Of a similar character are the great spectacles which the Nazis above all carried to such a pitch at Nuremburg and which are celebrated every May 1st in Moscow. The mass spectacle in which free citizens participate is a product of the French Revolution. There for the first time in modern history vast assemblages of citizens expressed their new status and their joint participation in these festivals. The greatest painters, musicians, engineers, etc. in the country took part. They were a demonstration of force and historians like Michelet and Jaures date the founding of the modern French nation from the great fetes of the Federations. But they were far more than a demonstration of strength. They were festivals of joy, of social celebration, of preparation, of participation of individuals in community life, for great moral and spiritual exertions – they were very close to what the Greeks expressed in the drama festivals. They have almost disappeared from modern life. Modern festivals are routine, flags are hung out, notables drive past and make conventional speeches; at military parades, the people watch. The totalitarians know these needs. The Nazis understood thoroughly that modern man is aching for a sense of participation in great community festivals. The Russian totalitarians strive to achieve a similar result. But mass participation – that is beyond them.

Now it is necessary to stop. The general line of the ideas is clear. The totalitarian states represent a perversion, a cruel, barbarous but *necessary* perversion of the instincts and desires for high civilization characteristic of modern man.

In the next chapter we shall deal more precisely with politics in the United States, the political manifestations of the needs and desires we have traced. But two things must be said at once. The totalitarian barbarism unless overthrown signalizes the destruction of the nation which it conquers. Twelve years of Hitlerism finished Germany and brought Europe down with it. And secondly, the force which will be needed to impose a totalitarian regime upon the American people does not exist and cannot be constructed. The great masses of Americans are backward in "culture" in the European sense; but in the essential needs of modern civilized men as we have described him, they are the most advanced people upon the face of the globe. We must now examine the nation from the way this has been concretely shown in the last twenty years.

6

The Struggle for Happiness

The question must now be faced, and faced at once. What is it that the people want?

We shall make the attempt to answer this now, for without an answer to this, most of the analysis of politics in the United States is not worth the paper it is written on. That "full employment," "better working conditions," "more leisure," "security" is what the people want – this is a doctrine which reduces mankind to the level of horses and cows with an instinct for exercise. It would astonish the proponents of these doctrines if they really were able to give every one "full employment," "security," etc. It is then that social crisis in the United States would assume the outline and proportions of a gigantic nightmare.

For the purposes of this rough sketch I propose to say in my own words very simply and directly what the great body of the people want. After I have done this, I shall give the evidence, some of the evidence. Only then will it be possible to take up some of the actual social and political struggles for only then will it be possible to begin to understand the apparent irrationality and illogical behavior of millions.

First, the industrial workers. Because, simplifying it, putting it simply and crudely, and forgetting for the moment such terms as free enterprise, socialism, communism, etc. the industrial workers and their future are the basis of the whole edifice.

The industrial workers, automobile workers, miners, railway-men, marine-workers, rubber-workers, and in addition the millions who are not organized, want to manage and arrange the work they are doing without any interference or supervision by anybody. I am a little nervous here because even the few readers of this may rush to the conclusion that I believe the majority of workers in the United States are at heart anarchists, communists or socialists. Let me say at once that millions of these workers accept the traditional principles of American democracy, not only vote for Truman, but get out the vote for him and would sincerely and rightly repudiate any idea that they are communists or socialists. In fact, a not insignificant number of them have been and still are Republicans. But careful investigation by trained observers and experience in the plant by competent workers show that the political ideas of workers are one thing, the deep responses to their work, the thing by which they live is something else. *That* is the worker's life, that determines his existence, and that he knows. Therefore, over and over again, the same workers who express as far as general politics are concerned, conservative and even reactionary sentiments, will immediately turn around and express with regard to their daily work sentiments with the most revolutionary implications conceivable. To those who do not grasp this duality, the real relations and forces at work in the great mass of people in the United States will remain a mystery.

To continue with this in the plainest and simplest language, the immense majority of the American workers want to work and love handling the intricate scientific masses of machinery more than anything else in the world. A worker who has been on strike, fought the speed of the assembly line, denounced scientific improvements which give him more work and has behaved for a whole year like a convinced anarchist, this same worker takes a delight in seeing the finished Buick, Dodge or whatever it is, and as he walks or drives about the street observes the cars from this plant with immense satisfaction and an almost personal pride.

Another type of worker works at a machine which he handles himself. Listen to him: "I *know* this machine. The engineers don't know it, and as for the boss, he knows nothing. I can give instructions to the makers to make certain changes which will increase production fifty per cent, for I have worked on this damn thing ten years and I know all about it." So far so good. He not only knows what is to be done, but he would love to see it done and handle the new machine himself. Anyone who knows the American people at all knows the absolute fascination which all mechanical appliances have for them. But this worker then adds: "Why the hell should I? All it means is more work for me and more money for the boss. I will get nothing out of it, nothing but a speed-up for me and all who are working with me. Let the thing stay as it is."

This is the fundamental conflict. There is on the one hand the need, the desire, created in him by the whole mighty mechanism of American industry, to work, to learn, to master the machine, to cooperate with others, in building glittering miracles that would achieve wonders, to work out ways and means to do in two hours what ordinarily takes four, to organize the plant as only workers know how. And on the other hand, the endless frustration of being merely a cog in a great machine, a piece of production as is a bolt of steel, a pot of paint or a mule which drags a load of corn.

This conflict is staggering in its scope and implications. It goes on all day and every hour of the day. No one can measure the hatred the workers have for this. Every age has two facets – the one on the surface, the framework within which everybody or nearly everybody works, thinks, writes and lives in general; below it is another intimately related to it but sometimes for generations unrecognized. Sometimes it is not seen at all except by a few until it bursts out. No one in the world dreamt that underneath the France of 1789 had developed the passion for equality which was to burst forth in the French Revolution (to take one example) and help tear down the age-old structure of monarchy, aristocracy and clergy. Yet historians after the event could go back and trace the stages by which this growing passion was developed, established itself below and in the interstices of the old regime, its advances and retreats, the disguises it assumed, and how and why it became so much a constituent part of the nation that finally it burst forth as it did.

Generations to come will trace the fundamental history of the modern United States in the contrasts between workers and employers. It is in these, what the workers demand, what they get, the millions of conflicts over grievances, large and small, the interminable friction and jockeying for position, it is here that in the eight hours where the worker expends his life, his blood, his energy, it is here that the basic forces of modern life are in action. A man eats and drinks and sleeps and procreates and in this respect is no more than a highly specialized animal. But it is in his work that he is a specifically human being, and it is the circumstances and conditions of his work that shape his deepest responses to life, and his whole outlook upon the world. This, as we have shown, and will show further, is pretty well recognized today. But such is the habit ingrained in men through countless generations, that in all the multitude of books poured out every year on the conditions of the people, the writer has not seen one that seriously analyzes the contract, the charter by which the worker lives.

To continue this highly simplified rendering.

As we showed in an earlier chapter, the industrialist who deals with the worker every day is aware in some measure of what is wrong. But both to him and to the worker, the conflict seems insoluble. The industrialist does not run a modern plant. It is truer to say that the plant runs him. That vast and intricate machinery which is modern industry is worked out by scientific men who deal with such entities as production plant, the assembly line, raw material, half-finished products, the finished product, unskilled labor, semi-skilled labor, etc. It seems to them – and very genuinely – that there is no other way in which industrial production can be organized. When the production plans are worked out, men, labor, have to fit themselves to these plans. But these men are not automatons or ancient slaves. They are literate, educated, highly sensitive human beings who are educated not only in schools but by the immense educative process which is modern life. (We shall take this up later.) The industrial machine must discipline these workers. Therefore a whole apparatus of supervision arises. The men organize to fight it. Thus is engendered the conflicts over how long to eat, how long to go to the toilet, whether smoking is permitted, whether talking is permitted or how much, what will be the speed of the line, how much work is to be done on a very hot day, should a worker walk the twenty steps to his material or should he have an assistant. . . . Day after day the conflict goes on, it may subside but it is always there, present in the mind of every worker, the struggle to prevent himself being converted entirely into a mere part of the machine. There is no end to it. The worker during the last twenty years no longer has any illusions that by energy and ability and thrift or any of the virtues of Horatio Alger, he can rise to anything. That is his life, will be his life for ever and ever.

A finished document will show this in concrete terms. I shall here give only a few incidents. One worker, for example, in a rather small plant who told his employer: "Tell us what you want every day and we shall give it to you, but you go out of here, go and sit on a chair on that piece of grass there and leave us alone." At the other end of the scale are the mass walk-outs, the continous wild-cat strikes and the great strikes apparently over wages in which workers will strike for three months and lose millions upon millions of dollars over whether the increase should be eleven cents or fourteen cents. The bitterness, the frustration, the accumulated anger at times reach such a stage that the particular issue on which the strike is called is an issue and no more than an issue. Far deeper social forces are coming into action. And the frustration is as deep a frustration as can affect any modern man, for as I insisted at the beginning, it is a frustration, and one that seems absolutely hopeless, of the desire to know, to learn, to master the processes and to make them work beautifully and efficiently. This is the modern individuality, but it is an individuality which can express itself only in common with thousands of others. Meanwhile higher wages and security and welfare state and more education and more leisure are the only things the masses of industrial workers can put their hands on. The truth is that this which we have described is not articulated at all by the great masses of workers. Perhaps the strangest thing about it is that it has become known through the work of industrialists and the organizations they employ. One important reason for this is that the labor leaders have not a single word to say about this. They dare not touch it at all. This is a world problem, but it is at its most extreme in the United States. Nowhere in the world are the battles between the industrial machine and the protesting worker so continuous, so relentless, and so fierce. But as always, America only shows the pattern for Europe.

In Britain, the workers support the Labour Government, the nationalization, social security, etc. But *the* problem in Britain is the attitude of the workers in the plant or in the mine. They are more hostile than ever to the conditions which they thought that somehow they would begin to leave behind. The miners in particular with increased pay and special privileges say point-blank that nationalization has changed nothing for them in their work, and while on the one hand, they vote for all sorts of high-sounding resolutions, in their actual work (they) are little changed from their previous attitudes. And behind this is the spectre of what is called "real planning" in which the organizers demand the power to move workers where they are wanted, from one place to another, from one industry to another. The British have not dared to do it. But this too is involved in any scientific planning. The workers in the democracies watch the workers in totalitarian states in horror and revulsion and wonder if these workers gain anything by the total loss of liberty.

Let it be said at once that there is no easy solution to these problems, none cut and dried, nothing in any book, nothing to be worked out at any conference of men, however wise, honest, sincere, learned. Many observers, not only industrialists and reactionary politicians but many serious intellectuals show open or sometimes conceal a deep contempt for parliamentary democracy. They know that the basic problems of modern life are not to be solved by voting or free speech. To many industrialists in the United States the idea of socialism is no more than the substitution for themselves of a corps of labor leaders as managers of industry. They believe that this will be worse for the workers and for society as a whole. This does not mean that they hold on to what they have for these idealistic reasons. But it means that they and many who live in their orbit cannot see the world as changing in any serious way from the world as they know it. Labor leaders, as we shall show, see full employment, more wages, more leisure, security, price-control, etc. as things to fight for. If they cannot get these, then they perhaps may be forced to follow Britain. That is as far as they go. It is not that these things are not spoken about. Later we shall report in detail a recent meeting of the U.A.W. in which Reuther, trying to put over the pension plan, told the U.A.W.: "It is either this or workers control, anarchism. Make your choice." The workers, hostile and bitter, accepted what seemed to be the only reasonable alternative.

To reinforce the depth and scope of the dilemma it must be said that Lenin who knew what communism meant, in the early days of the Russian Revolution, wrote quite frankly that he could not say what form the new relations of labor would take in a socialist society; no one could work them out but the workers themselves, millions by trial and error; there relations would be "subtle and intricate," a phrase worth pondering. He trusted to the historical creative energies of the masses; the tactics and shifts which he adopted with a frank realization of the backwardness of a huge peasant country.

So that anyone who expects from this book a recipe had better stop reading at once. We face a problem that goes to the very roots of our civilization, of the intimate and at the same time social lives of the great majority of the population. In the ultimate analysis, it was slavery which wrecked the civilization of the classical world; feudal society reached a stage where its peasants and artisans and guilds could no longer function. The totalitarian states end by having soldiers in the factories. This that we have put here so roughly, so unambiguously, is not everything but everything springs from there. It took 100 years before French historians recognized plainly that the French Revolution was a social revolution springing from depths that affected the ultimate social lives of the great majority of the population. The Roman Empire collapsed and for centuries men did not know why. Gibbon's *Decline and Fall,* and this is a very great book, as late as 1800, thought that the fall was due to Christianity. And so it was but only because the masses who were rejecting slavery found a banner in Christianity. Gibbon never knew this. An immense number of concrete everyday things seem to press upon us, but the root cause eludes us.

Is there a solution? In the most abstract terms the solution is that somehow the creative energies of modern man, the sense of personality of hundreds of millions of modern men must be made to function in their daily work. Utopian maybe. But if not, then the fate of Rome and of medieval Europe will be our fate. Just turn again and read the opening quotation from *Life*'s review of fifty years, Lewis Mumford in the *New York Times* and Orville Prescott's review of Duffus's book; bear these things in mind and look at popular films, gangster and detective stories, the new millions of fantastic scientific tales that are sweeping the country, and the co-relation will begin to become clear.

Now we are in a position to take some evidence, some material which illustrates the above, but which could only be understood in the light of the above. It will have to be highly selective and, as usual, for the purposes of this sketch, it is easier to use quotations. This, however, must be said, I do not claim here to have discovered what no one else has discovered. In 1927 Andre Siegfried, a very intelligent European, published his book *America Comes of Age.* He says in the last pages:

If the aim of society is to produce the greatest amount of comfort and luxury for the greatest number of people, then the United States of America is in a fair way to succeed. And yet a house, a bath, and a car for every workman – so much luxury within the reach of all – can only be obtained at a tragic price, no less than the transformation of millions of workmen into automatons. "Fordism," which is the essence of American industry, results in the standardization of the workman himself. Artisanship, now out of date, has no place in the New World, but with it have disappeared certain conceptions of mankind which we in Europe consider the very basis of civilization. To express his own personality through his creative efforts is the ambition of every Frenchman, but it is incompatible with mass production.

We must not imagine that thoughtful Americans are unaware of the peril which is threatening their manhood, but it is too much to expect them to sacrifice their machines; for they give production priority over everything else. Having refused to save the individuality of the factory worker, they shift their defense to other grounds. During the day the worker may be only a cog in the machine, they say; but in the evening at any rate he becomes a man once more. His leisure, his money, the very things which mass production puts at his disposal, these will restore to him the manhood and intellectual independence of which his highly organized work has deprived him. This change in the center of gravity of the life of the individual marks an absolute revolution in the ideas on which society in Western Europe has been built up. Can it be possible that the personality of the individual can recover itself in consumption after being so crippled and weakened in production? Have not the very products in the form in which they are turned out by the modern factory, lost their individuality as well?

It is a remarkable passage, written in 1927. But its defects are as great as its merits. Siegfried poses the whole thing in terms of an aristocratic conception of self-expression. He says a little later:

Thus they are advancing in one direction and retrogressing in another. The material advance is immeasurable in comparison with the Old World, but from the point of view of individual refinement and art, the sacrifice is real indeed. Even the humblest European sees in art an aristocratic symbol of his own personality, and modern America has no national art and does not even feel the need of one.

He had not and I doubt if he has the faintest conception that this was not a matter of art and self-expression but a question of the essential day-to-day lives of civilized men, wearing them down and against which they are revolting.

Without this there is no understanding of American politics. The first and most fundamental illusion to be shattered is that the C.I.O. was formed as an instrument of "collective bargaining," to negotiate about wages, to protect the "interests" of workers, to ensure higher wages in order to prevent the economy from collapsing, to help in redistribution of income, etc. All this is as about as true as the ideas taught for many decades in the United States in the North that the Civil Was was a war "to free the slaves" and in the South that the war was a war for states' rights. Today we know that, as Beard called it, the war was "the second American revolution," that one system, industrial capitalism, was threatened by another, chattel slavery, and that for decades the great clashes were merely this conflict expressing itself. But although the men of that time knew that, they did not see it that way. And Beard writes that only after the war was long over did men begin to see it as it was. He says:

It was then that the economist and lawyer, looking more calmly on the scene, discovered that the armed conflict had been only one phase of the cataclysm, a transitory phase; that at bottom the so-called Civil War, or the War between the States, in the light of Roman analogy, was a social war, ending in the unquestioned establishment of a new power in the government, making vast changes in the arrangement of classes, in the accumulation and distribution of wealth, in the course of industrial development and in the Constitution inherited from the Fathers. Merely by the accident of climate, soil and geography was it a sectional struggle.

I seem to labor the point. Perhaps I do. But it is the only way to make clear that the C.I.O. was not originally what so many people seem to think it is today. It was no instrument for collective bargaining and getting out the vote for the Democratic Party. It was the first attempt of a section of the American workers to change the system as they saw it into something which would solve what they considered to be their rights, their interests and their human needs. As is characteristic of a society like ours, little attention has been paid to this by writers and publicists who prefer to spend their time accumulating piles of books on an abstraction they call the "economic system." Workers also are neither creators of theoretical systems nor writers. The books written on this momentous movement are pitifully few. Some of the material is hidden away in little known newspapers, pamphlets, etc.; most of it is in the recollections of the men who led these struggles and today are not even union officials. But some little work has been done, and for the time being we shall use it.

The best book is the result of some ten years of research by Keith Sward on the Ford plant and Henry Ford. Few books are as revealing of America as this, particularly because the writer has no clear social or political views; he seems to be some kind of vague pro-labor liberal. The book is nearly 500 pages long and therefore the reader must see these extracts as only indications. Many things which the author just hints at are things which we would have wished to be developed fully. But for the time being it will serve.

Here is what the Ford workers thought of production:

What had loaded the wage and seniority question with a terrific emotional charge in all automotive plants, however, was a third pre-union condition of unemployment – the speed or "pressure" of the line. On this primary issue – as to what constitutes a rate of production that is tolerable as well as efficient – automobile labor had developed its deepest rancor and its strongest antagonisms toward management.

This is not to say that the typical factory hand of Detroit was dead set against speed-up in any form, or that he was bothered by the feeling that he was "above" his work. It was clear to him, as to anyone, that if the machine is to be given a chance to do the work of the world, someone – in fact, millions of someones – must do the minute, routine, mechanical chores of line production; the endless, repetitive, high-speed sorting and bolting and screwing and assembling. At Ford's or at similar shops the average worker was probably content and even anxious, to submit to a fast-moving line and to the necessary discipline of mass production – under certain conditions. All he asked (and nothing else could give meaning and dignity to his ant-like tasks) was that he should share, with others, the fruits of the machine economy, that his efforts be related to a common purpose. Up to a certain point, the man on the automobile assembly line could identify his own welfare with the great social gains of the machine order. He took pride in the fact that he was a part – if never a very secure one – of the workshop whose technology is the admiration of the world. Like most other members of society, he unquestionably believed in the machine system; he knew that only the miracles of line assembly could bring the automobile and other goods within reach of the common man.

The writer here touches on the key question. It was not the speed of the line in the abstract that exhausted the men. The soldiers of the French army during the revolution increased the traditional number of steps per minute by some forty per cent. Where the former commanders dared not advance their line except in solid order because once they were separated from each other, the men seized every opportunity to lag behind or desert, for "liberty, equality and fraternity," the army could be hurled at cannon in massed thousands or deployed with wide spaces between them over the countryside. This is central. Sward, in company with most writers, thinks that the "fruits of the machine" are higher wages, more leisure, etc. This is false in every sense. False, because before all these "goods" and "leisure" (for leisure is a result of production) can be produced at reasonable cost, the producer, the worker, must devote his best energies to his work and not in an exhausting, stultifying conflict with supervision over what constitutes work. The conditions for a new stage in production are far beyond what Sward seems to think. Scientific knowledge, technical mastery of industrial processes, equality, consciousness of productive effort in harmony with the general will, i.e. the aims and purposes of society as a whole, these and these alone can create a new stage in industrial production. This will result in reorganization of the productive process and incredible speeds of machines, assembly-lines, etc. where these are required. The alternative is the policeman and the soldier in the factory. To continue with Sward:

Rebellion against the speed-up hit the industry like a tidal wave at the point where the man in the shop was convinced that the machine had failed to live up to its promise insofar as it affected him. The success of high-speed technology, in enriching its owners and managers, and more particularly in widening the mass market for his own product, added to his feelings of resentment. Against these partial successes of the machine, he coud contrast the hard fact of what factory speed-up had meant to him in twenty-five years' time; it had pushed him on production in most shops beyond the limits of human endurance; but it had not made his station in life proportionately better off or more secure. On the contrary, the pressure of the line had become, in a personal sense, the chief threat to his security and well-being.

However, these processes, and this is very important, do not take place in logical sequence. These things existed. But:

The revolt against factory speed-up did not crystallize . . . until the Depression. It came, finally as a result of management's rigorous effort to retrench at a time when it was no longer possible to cut corners or to achieve great, new economies merely by rearranging the machinery of production. It came after all the major efficiencies of line production and all the revolutionary mechanical arts of the trade had been worked out to perfection, and after the machine as such had lost its cost-cutting magic of the '20s. By 1930, therefore, the only way to run this remarkable and almost perfect apparatus cheaper was to run it faster, just as it stood. On the line this meant additional pure man speed-up, or in the language of the shop, lowering costs by "taking it out of the men."

This is the way. Men can stand a great deal as long as the society in which they live is stable. They protest, they are dissatisfied, they strike, they make political changes, etc. But when, as happened in 1929, the whole society seems to go to pieces, then the fundamental social forces, needs, antagonisms come to the surface.

In the two succeeding paragraphs Sward shows the way the incidental provoked the fundamental:

In depression speed-up the man on the line saw, first of all, a threat to his earnings. It was as logical for him to call the effect of the stretch-out a "disguised wage cut" as it was for the management to describe the same process as a means of "lowering costs." Earnings had withered; the trade was operating on a short year and with limited schedules of production. Under such circumstances it was a worker's natural, if selfish, reaction to feel that the faster he labored the sooner he would "work himself out of a job" and the chance of earning any income at all.

Now, however, note the following:

In addition, when operated at abnormal rates of speed, the automotive belt was a man-killer. Its Depression toll in accidents alone will never be known because many, if not the majority, of the lesser mill injuries of the period went unreported. A stiffer price for the speed-up was paid in terms of nervous and mental tensions that left no record of any kind. But the fact remains that the men who tended the lines at the time considered the pace more than their bodies could stand. They could feel the speed-up in their bones. They were convinced that standing up to such a pace was aging and debilitating.

How long men can stand this "in addition" is indicated by the following paragraph:

When Ford speed-up, uncurbed for twenty-five years, finally produced a protest movement of major dimensions, the verdict of "the men" was borne out in Detroit both by members of the medical profession and by attorneys who were recognized authorities in compensation law. According to a substantial number of reputable local physicians who were engaged in the practice of industrial medicine, it was a common occurrence to find fatigue states and neurotic symptoms of every description in patients who had long been exposed to the "Ford pressure." In diagnosing what ailed innumerable Ford men, at least some of these medical experts put their finger on the sheer wear-and-tear of the Ford line, aggravated in its debilitating effect by perennial feelings of insecurity and a so-called Serviceman phobia. Perhaps the weightiest evidence on this point came from leading compensation specialists whose experience was state-wide, covering all the shops of the industry. In the opinion of a number of such observers, no assembly line in the history of the trade had ever devitalized men or aged them prematurely more quickly than Ford's. One of Detroit's leading figures in this branch of the law reported in 1939 that nothing was more characteristic of his "Ford clients" than the person who looked sixty-five at fifty or the worker who at thirty-five looked like a man of forty-five or fifty.

In this outline and in the finished book, we devote important space to totalitarianism, and in the introduction we warned that it seemed somewhat superficial to us "merely" to denounce the anti-labor N.A.M., the activities of Gerald L. K. Smith, etc. Totalitarianism is much more serious than these. And there has been no more serious manifestation of totalitarianism in the United States than the efforts of Ford to maintain the men in a position of subjection to the machine and to crush them when they sought to organize to put an end to it. I shall merely string some of the more important passages together.

According to payroll records which the NLRB introduced in evidence, the Fords were maintaining at various plants from 1937–1939 a ratio of one Serviceman to every thirty production workers. In one instance, the proportion was much higher. At the assembly plant in Kansas City which employed more than a thousand men in 1937, there was one Serviceman on the job for every fourteen workers. Ford Service reached its peak in manpower by the summer of 1937. It was then that the organization was designated by the *New York Times* as the largest privately owned secret service force in existence.

Who were the men Ford recruited?

The prisons and the police courts of the nation had their day as recruiting centers for a certain personnel in which Bennet had an interest. From this source came many an operative or auxiliary of Ford Service, as well as large numbers of regular Ford factory workers.

Among the law-breakers who began to honeycomb Bennett's immediate staff and the general working force of the Ford Motor Co. could be found perpetrators of nearly every crime listed on the statute books. The gamut of their police records ran from rape and gross indecency to leaving the scene of an accident, carrying concealed weapons, forgery, embezzlement, burglary, robbery, violation of the Drug Act, felonious assault, murder and manslaughter.

The hiring of former criminals was indeed a Ford custom that antedated Bennett. But the practice seems to have attained large-scale proportions only after Bennet's accession to power and during the lush years of the Service Department. In 1928, when Bennett was a relative newcomer, still bearing the title of chief of Ford's private police, the *New York Times* reported that the company was employing 2600 ex-convicts. Six years later, after Ford Service had reached maturity, Henry Ford was quoted by the *Detroit Times* as saying that the number of former prison inmates on his payroll had risen to 8000. Such a number would have represented anywhere from 10 to 20% of the total force working at the Rouge.

Ford's recruitment of former penitentiary inmates was all the easier both because most business establishments are somewhat wary of hiring men with criminal records and because Bennett proceeded to exert his influence with the office of prison parole in the state of Michigan. In 1935 the "Little Fellow" was appointed by a Republican Governor to serve on the Michigan Prison Commission. The *Detroit News* acclaimed the appointment by remarking editorially that "Mr Bennett has an intimate knowledge of convicts. He has handled hundreds of them, perhaps thousands." While rounding out his two-year term on the commission, Bennett introduced a resolution which enabled prisoners to shorten their sentences by receiving credit for "extra good time." At this juncture convicts discharged from the state's penal institutions were being paroled to the Ford Motor Co. at the rate of approximately five per week.

Innumerable former policemen and countless professional athletes, active or retired, have wended their way to Dearborn along still another route. These additions to Ford Service were, as a rule, men who had fallen from grace or who had been discredited in their previous callings, sometimes without ever having been legally convicted for the commission of any wrong.

On Bennett's payroll were any number of castaways from Detroit's police department. Such was the history of three city detectives – Stephen Merritt, John Colon and Hugh Turney – on whose guilt a Detroit jury, in convicting the leader of an automobile theft ring, could not agree in 1936. Under a cloud of suspicion, however, these officers were suspended from the force. Bennett promptly hired all three.

The least reputable of the retainers at Dearborn were not mere unfortunates who ran afoul of the law unwittingly, or on only one occasion. They were case-hardened criminals. These recipients of Ford patronage ranged from small fry to some of the most desperate characters of the American underworld. They included thugs and gunmen just emerged from jail, as well as criminal racketeers at large.

One such gangster was Joseph ("Legs") Laman, a former rum-runner and kidnapper. A creature of the prohibition era, Laman acquired the name "Legs" in connection with the kidnapping of David Cass, an abducted child whose body was retrieved from a gully along the Flint River. This gangster was caught by the police with $400 in ransom money on his person. One of the officers who made the arrest later reported than Laman sprinted so furiously to escape apprehension that he seemed to be all "legs." The leader of a ring implicated in at least thirty kidnappings, Laman earned still another nickname by turning state's witness after he had been sentenced to prison for a term of thirty to forty years. Because of his revelations, six other prisoners received long prison sentences. Laman was rewarded by having his own prison term commuted to six years. The Michigan underworld rechristened him, meanwhile, "Legs the Squealer." Once more at large, Laman was aparoled to the Ford Motor Co.

At least two renowned racketeers have enjoyed the double privilege of holding a lucrative business concession from the Ford corporation, and of continuing their careers of crime simultaneously. One such character was the former boss of the Brooklyn underworld.

The biggest name in crime ever associated with the Ford business was that of Chester (Chet) LaMare, a gangster who at one time was the "Al Capone" of Detroit. During the prohibition era, LaMare came closer than any of his rivals to wielding absolute control over the down-river, Sicilian gangs which infested Detroit's 70-mile waterfront. The bootlegging enterprise which his men dominated was ranked by federal agents as the state's largest industry in 1928. It was said to be collecting a gross revenue of $215,000,000 a year. At the apex of his career in 1931, LaMare was depositing money in the bank at the rate of $3500 a day.

The leader of this organization was, of course, the infamous Bennett. At the basis of the organization were these thugs. But Bennett *incorporated other classes in society.*

In the choice of his immediate co-workers, while coming into his own at Ford's, Bennett leaned to athletes of every caste, from smooth clean-cut amateurs to the shoddiest of cast-off professionals. In the first category were former college football stars. His personal secretary, for several years, was Stanley E. Fay, captain of the University of Michigan's championship football team of 1933. Also admitted to the inner circle was Harry Newman, a former all-American quarterback at Ann Arbor – and one of the few Jews ever employed at Dearborn. Until drafted for army duty in 1941, the Negro Willis Ward filled one of the key posts in Bennett's office. Ward had distinguished himself on the college gridiron. More than that, he was probably the greatest track star ever produced by the University of Michigan.

It was Bennett's further policy for many years to give preference in summer jobs to football players who were still listed as undergraduates at one or another of the neighboring universities. This practice was particularly in evidence when coach Harry Kipke was producing brilliant football teams at Ann Arbor. Bennett and Kipke became fast friends at the time. Finally, in the summer of 1937, Bennett hired en masse a good proportion of the men who would make up the University of Michigan football squad in the season just ahead. They were paid the regular Ford wage for an eight-hour day. Nearly one-half of their working time, however, was devoted to the practice of football. For this side activity, the squad was assigned locker space in the Dearborn police station. Freshly laundered uniforms were provided three times a week. Coach Kipke never put in an appearance on the practice field, but the football drills subsidized by the Ford Motor Co. were attended by the team's captain. Inasmuch as the rules of the Big Ten Conference forbid organized practice sessions up to September 1st, the legality or propriety of Bennett's arrangement was taken to task by the *Chicago Tribune*.

There, in the greatest industrial plant in the world, in one of the greatest industrial cities in the world, one of the centers of our civilization, the forces faced each other and fought it out; the workers on the one hand; on the other, the industrialists, the gangster storm-trooper element, athletic middle class elements. We cannot tell here how Ford and Bennett branched out to control the political life of Detroit and Michigan, corrupting politicians, police, public officials and press; of the way in which the workers drew to their side many of the middle class, of the final defeat of Ford in this, the first engagement. *The whole community of Michigan was involved.* It is the fundamental social clash of our times. Ford was the sharpest expression of it, but it runs through the whole nation in an infinite variety of forms. There was a compromise settlement in the United States. The C.I.O. won acceptance. But it solved nothing fundamental. The great strikes of 1946 showed that. By this time it had become clearer what was involved.

Some observers were astonished by the violence of the employers' reactions – the full page advertisements claiming that "socialism" and "totalitarian regimentation" were the aims of these strikes. The apparently wild full-page advertisements have continued. Those who did this in 1946 and continue with it are not in the slightest sense wild or exaggerating. They are perfectly aware from harsh experience of the torrent of rebelliousness and the unplumbed depths of resentment at the whole process of production which is contained in their workers. They do not know where this will lead, once it is unloosed. At the present time their chief hope is the labor leaders. Meanwhile, as we showed in Chapter 4, they work assiduously at it.

I now propose to do three things. (1) I want to state very carefully and as precisely as possible the stage of development which the workers have reached. It sums up what we have done so far and explains what we shall do in the rest of the chapter. This is a very difficult thing to do. (2) and (3) I shall then take two commentators of great importance. One of them is Elton Mayo and the other is Peter Drucker. I take them as symbolic of currents in the United States.

I have to keep referring to what the workers want and to try to get as clear as possible the difference between the essential question, i.e. the force which underlies the whole, and the concrete stage which the development has reached. So far the workers in the United States have not been articulate at all as to their basic needs. What they want is said for the most part and only by implication in discussions in unions, and by implication again, in their opposition to what exists.

There is a unionist walking about in a Midwestern city today who carries around with him in his wallet a typewritten copy of the first contract between the U.A.W. and a famous industrial plant. It is a very brief document, and his analysis of it is as follows. This is the best contract that we ever had. At the present time the contract has hundreds of clauses and these clauses are for the most part precise statements of what the workers may not do. They need to be interpreted by workers' leaders who sit with employers and at courts of arbitration, lawyers and trained investigators intervening. The worker is absolutely lost before all of this. The original idea at the formation of the C.I.O. and as exemplified in this carefully preserved piece of paper, was that the workers in the plants should decide what they wanted and then deal with the employers directly. Immediately after the formation of the U.A.W. and for some years afterwards the relationship between the men in the plant and the industrial management was simple and direct. The men met together, decided what they wanted and took it immediately to the employer. If they were not satisfied, they struck. The plants were closed down, departments were closed down, sections of departments were closed down, and this went on continuously over the whole industry. This is what one important union of the C.I.O. was formed for, direct control of the process of production by the men.

Now if this observation were allowed to stay there, it looks like anarchy. However, the work that has been done over the last dozen years and not by workers or workers' leaders, has established for good and all that the workers are not opposed to work, they wish to work, they need the sense of belonging and purpose, etc. which every serious commentator brings out as the most decisive part of his investigations. From these investigations and the attitude of the workers at the beginning of the C.I.O., the legitimate conclusion can be drawn and has been drawn by certain writers that it is only when the workers are able themselves to run the plant completely that there will be any assuagement of the conflict which handicaps industry at every turn and increases daily the bitterness and frustration of the masses of the workers. It must be understood that the workers as such and their leaders have had little to say about this. The workers usually speak by action.

What has happened is that the unions which were created by the workers for the purposes which we have described have now become instruments of the management for the purpose of maintaining production. The labor leadership has been forced into this position because, except for the alternative, utopian as it may seem to the ordinary mind, of the workers themselves controlling production, there is nothing else for them to do but to attempt to preserve the interests of the workers as they see them; but this they can do only on the condition that they satisfy not only the industrial leaders but the country at large that they are performing an essential social function. Thus the very unions which the workers built up for controlling the system of production have now turned out to be the means whereby they are maintained in the subordination to which they are fundamentally opposed. Caught in this situation the union leaders have sought for support in those elements of politics and government sympathetic to them. Hence the alliance with the Democratic Party. But this alliance has resulted in a huge organization of government investigators, NLRBs, etc., the total result of which is to pile upon the workers an immense bureaucracy in which the state bureaucracy and union bureaucracy are closely allied. In conflicts over wages, social security, pensions, etc. this dual bureaucracy, in accordance with the political fortunes of the last few years, balances between the workers, the employers, the consumers and the country as a whole. The relative merits of its championship of the workers and the extent to which they benefit is not of importance here. What is important is that the worker in the plant can gain no support whatever in the matters which concern him most, the daily struggle. The contrast to be emphasized is the contrast between the little slip of paper which was a charter of the worker when the C.I.O. was formed, and the interminable routine and the mighty bureaucratic system which now faces him when these vital and immediate matters have to be settled. An important part of the present contract is the regulations and rules by which the worker is prevented from striking except with the consent of the union after a lengthy procedure, cooling off periods of ninety days, etc. In addition to which the union leaders have agreed with the industrialists upon severe penalties for those who carry out unauthorized strikes. All questions of wages, social security, pensions, etc. must be swept aside if this question is to be understood. *The worker like the management is interested in production.* But production from his point of view. And after a dozen years of the C.I.O., although it is impossible to return to what took place under Bennett, he is almost as far from controlling production as he was at the beginning. Certainly he has infinitely more difficulty than he had in the days of the C.I.O.

The name of Elton Mayo stands at the head of those who are concerned with this problem, both as an originator and in his contributions. Exactly how does this very representative and very serious thinker conceive the problem and a solution. We use him and shall quote from his most famous book, published in 1933, *The Human Problem of an Industrial Civilization*, because:

1 Mayo saw that the problem was worldwide and went to the roots of modern civilization.
2 Mayo saw as the serious industrialists and investigators see today that this is a problem far beyond voting, free speech, democracy, etc.
3 The general trend in his thinking is characteristically American, and would represent more or less the ideas of practical industrialists and many American liberal intellectuals.

We shall take up each briefly and then show the obvious fallacies and the abyss in America above all places that yawns at the end of this type of thinking.

In *The Human Problems of an Industrial Civilization*, Mayo says in his concluding chapter:

The first problem is that of the failure of collaborative effort within the nation. This failure, considered as a symptom of social disorganization, is far more significant than the emergence of black spots of crime or suicide upon the social geography. It is illustrated in the developed misunderstanding between employers and workers in every civilized country; this has persisted for a century without any sign of amelioration. It is, however, only the name of the problem which has persisted; the problem itself has, I think, completely changed its form since, for example, the England of 1832. At that time, as the Hammonds show, it was essentially a problem of wages and working conditons; long hours of work and low wages were the rule. Since then wages have risen considerably, the conditions of work have much improved; the worker's standards of consumption are higher, he has established for his children a right to education and to freedom from the worse forms of exploitation. Communist Russia has not yet been able to establish, in respect of real wages and satisfactory working conditions, an equivalence with the countries she calls 'capitalist'. This is not a fair criticism, but merely passing comment; the new Russia is too newly born for her achievements to be assessed. The idea that Russia will necessarily do better by her workers in the future, immediate or remote, than we do by ours is, however, equally unwarranted. For the moment she is obsessed, as we are, with the need of developing better methods for the discovery of an administrative elite, better methods of maintaining working morale. If the actualities of the situation be considered, and mere words such as capitalism and Bolshevism for the moment set aside, then it must be admitted that the present problems of Russia, on her own confession, are remarkably like the present problems of Detroit.

Better methods for the discovery of an administrative elite, better methods of maintaining working morale. The country that first solves these problems will infallibly outstrip the others in the race for stability, security, and development.

It is not the whole truth, but the core of the truth is here. The new regime in China, *every* regime in the world, the British Labour Government all know that here is their central problem. It is clear also that when Mayo removed this question from types of government, although he simplified it enormously, it was a necessary and in fact indispensable simplification.

But his solution of 1933 immediately awakens terrifying reverberations in minds which have fully experienced the seventeen years between 1933 and 1950. Mayo is a believer in democracy. Yet his proposal is for an elite. It appears in the passage quoted. Here are others:

It is no longer possible for an administrator to concern himself narrowly with his special function and to assume that the controls established by a vigorous social code will continue to operate in other areas of human life and action. All social controls of this type have weakened or disappeared – this being symptomatic of the diminished integrity of the social organism. The existing situation, both within the national boundaries and as between nations, demands therefore that special attention be given to restatement of the problem of administration as the most urgent issue of the present.

Again:

Pareto, the eminent Italian author of the only treatise on general sociology, discusses the importance of high quality in the administrative group in relation to the maintenance of social equilibrium. He observes that leadership in any society rests in two types of elite – the governmental and the non-governmental, the latter including the direction of all industrial and economic activities.

Once more:

We are suffering from what McDougall has described as "lopsidedness" in the development of an elite. We have developed scientific research and the training of scientists admirably; we have failed utterly to promote any equivalent educational development directed to the discovery and training of administrators of exceptional capacity. These considerations led Brooke Adams to infer that "the extreme complexity" of the administrative problems presented by modern industrial civilization was "beyond the compass" of the mentality of the administrators of his time. "If this be so," he adds, "American society as at present organized . . . can concentrate no further and, as nothing in the universe is at rest, if it does not concentrate, it must probably begin to disintegrate. Indeed we may perceive incipient signs of disintegration all about us." . . . Who shall say that this prophecy, made twenty years ago, has not found some fulfillment in the present crisis?

This was in 1933 in reference to the previous twenty years. Nearly twenty years more have passed. The results on a world-wide scale are before us.

What is so startling about Mayo's ideas is that as far as they are *possible*, *they have been tried*. The Hitler regime, the Stalinist regime, Ford, proposed to discipline the workers. Hitler called his administrators and rulers an elite; they are enshrined in the Russian constitution as the intelligentsia. Mayo's idea of intelligent, kind, sympathetic administrators, and he now demands that they be equipped with the very latest knowledge in psychology, this is a Utopia if ever there was one. There is no way of gently, peacefully, quietly, kindly disciplining millions of modern men to the constantly increasing mechanization of modern production. For every scientific progress results in the mechanization of men. The elite administers with armed soldiers in the factory.

Mayo, in what to him seemed a moment of fantasy, turned his head in another direction. He writes:

Indeed, if the predictions of engineers have any value, we are about to enter upon an era in which our material production will be accomplished by machines directed by engineers, and the worker, as we at present conceive him, no longer needed by industry. If this is to be, then history will record not the triumph but the extinction of the proletariat. And communist theories of revolution will be superseded by the profoundest revolution mankind has ever contemplated – the development of a society in which there will be no place for the illiterate or the ignorant.

But these ideas are fantastic.

Between the idea of an elite and the idea of a society in which there will be no place for the illiterate or the ignorant, Mayo chooses the first as reality and the second as fantasy. This much is certain: the America I have seen and studied in a dozen years will never accept an elite. If by any chance an elite should establish itself after what will be one of the bloodiest civil wars in history, the human, social and economic forces it will need to maintain itself will assuredly result in the collapse of civilization. We have written in vain if we have not established that the peculiar politics of the United States, the maneuvers of lobbyists, the making and breaking of election promises, the frantic laudation of free enterprise, the very hatred of totalitarianism, all these are actual concrete phenomena which must not for a moment disguise or obscure the profound passionate instinctive attachment to liberty and freedom, and full self-expression of the American people as a whole. The crisis in America is a crisis of tens of millions who have only an instinctive conception of life, liberty and the pursuit of happiness. They would interpret this as a society in which there are no longer illiterate or ignorant people, but not in general; each individual American sees no reason why he should be illiterate or ignorant. But what to do, how to achieve this, that they do not know. Conceptual thinking is not the practice in America, and that is why observers like Sartre who sees with the eyes of an artist notes the doubts, the fears, the uncertainty, the terror of the future that are so obvious everywhere. Roosevelt understood many aspects of America very well, and his famous statement in 1933, that all we have to fear is fear itself put a finger on the deep sentiment which has only grown with the years.

The American employers for the time being depend upon the labor leaders. They try to hold the balance between employers and the workers. The "public" looks on deeply disturbed at the constant crises in the labor movement. The industrialists periodically try out the union as was admitted on all sides in the late steel strike, but they find that the unions cannot be broken. The workers will not stand for that at all. Therefore the only solution is towards some sort of elite, some sort of highly skilled and trained administration which will somehow or other manage to assuage the conflict and develop productivity to the degree which is now required. But as far as this book is concerned, all attempts at the establishment of an elite must inevitably involve totalitarianism and will never be accepted not only by the workers but by the great masses of the American people. There is no solution that way.

We now take up the analysis of Peter Drucker. Drucker is a university professor and acts as a consultant to General Motors. He has a theoretical knowledge of the labor and union movement. It is obvious in every line of his writings. But Drucker is important for another reason. He forms part of a protest which is growing in the United States against the rationalist and democratic tradition. It is powerfully established at the University of Chicago which occupies a key position in the Middle West. It is now making its way at Columbia University. Its theoretical roots are a hostility to the rationalism which began with the French Revolution and has now ended in the crisis that we face. Its own theoretical basis is Catholic Humanism. It is to be noted that whereas the great masses of the Protestant peoples in the United States are some of the most militant of the protesters against the curtailment of civil liberties, the growth of militarism in the state, etc., they are unable to put forward any kind of theoretical analysis or open out any perspective except some of the traditions of democracy which served so well during the nineteenth century. There is an immense interest in the ideas of education put forward by Robert Hutchins and they are gaining ground in American universities as the inadequacies of the liberal sociology of Dewey, Beard and Parrington for the post-Depression world become increasingly clear. What has happened in Europe, in France, and in Italy, makes the position of Drucker and the Catholic Humanists' revival very significant.

The point is that they have an analysis of modern society and offer a wholesale rejection of its philosophical premises. They attack the evils of capitalism in the process of production itself more powerfully than any section of American society. But it is equally certain that their solution in the last analysis is no different from Mayo's. And therefore, as has been shown by the experiences of a similar grouping in pre-Hitler Germany, revealed in the memoirs of Herman Rauschning (we shall take this up later), the very roundedness of their attack on the atomization of the human being in modern society can assist in the crystallization of certain academic and educated strata for an alliance with totalitarianism.

I propose to give first a series of extracts from Drucker's book *The Future of Industrial Man*, published in 1943, to show how far he has reached in his criticism. It must be remembered that this is no journalist but a man very familiar with industry and industrial processes. After that I shall show his development in an article which was published in 1946. I just put down the extracts from his book in 1943 without comment.

When we call the new system "automatic" or "mechanized," we do not mean that the machines have become automatic or mechanical. What has become automatic or mechanical is the worker. . . . Today, however, the automatic mechanized worker is the most efficient worker, producing the most per unit of labor.

Denial of the existence of an individual with social status and function is really the essence of the new approach; in mass production technology the worker is only one sloppily designed machine. To bring this human machine to the full mechanical and automatic efficiency which its Maker apparently failed to achieve is the main aim of the new science of "human engineering." That means, however, that the individual must cease to exist. The new technique demands standardized, freely interchangeable atomic labor without status, without function, without individuality. It demands graded tools. But there is no relationship between the worker's function as part of a precision machine which the present-day industrial system assigns to him and any individual purpose. From the point of view of the system the individual worker functions only, makes sense only, is rational only, when he ceases to be a member of society. From the point of view of the individual worker, the society of the mass production age does not and cannot make sense at all.

Unionism also fails to provide the other prerequisite of a functioning society, the social integration of the individual. For what is the status and function of the member of a unionist society? What social purpose does this life have? And what individual purpose does a unionist society fulfill? A union must of necessity enforce equal conditions in all comparable plants in the same industry. Hence it cannot allow one plant to become a community of its own with a functional integration of the worker and his work. It can only protect the worker politically and economically against exploitation. But what is its purpose when it dominates and when the union of the exploited workers has become the top dog? There are no answers to these questions;

they are unanswerable.

The central fact in the social crisis of our time is that the industrial plant has become the basic social unit, but that it is not yet a social institution. Power in and over the plant is the basis of social rule and power in an industrial world.

At this stage it is necessary to stop a bit in order to appreciate the last sentence:

Industrial society can function only if the plant gives social status and function to its members. And only if the power in the plant is based on the responsibility and decision of the members can industrial society be free. The answer today is neither total planning or the restoration of nineteenth century laissez-faire but the organization of industry on the basis of local and decentralized self-government.

So far we have had the most devastating criticism of modern industrial production and what is undoubtedly some step towards a solution. Then with his final sentence Drucker blows the whole thing sky-high. He writes:

And the time to start this is now when workers and management, producers and consumers, are united in the one purpose of winning the war.

It does not seem possible for a man who has written about the workers as he has written above to be putting forward precisely the idea that the vast task which is the total reorganization of society can be started during a war by decentralization because management and workers and consumers are united. Who is to begin it? And who is to begin what? The absolute foolishness of this conclusion is to be measured against the seriousness of the indictment which comes from Drucker's pen.

To appreciate the significance of Drucker, we have now to turn to an article which he wrote in 1946 during the great strikes. Again we give merely some quotations:

A spate of labor laws and union regulations today would probably not prevent a single strike because they would not be dealing with the basic cause. And the basic cause is the discontent of the worker himself.

The men on the machines are afflicted today by a deep, though vague discontent, by tensions and pressures. Even the best labor laws would be futile so long as this discontent persists. And the rising cost of living is only one, perhaps even a minor, cause of the trouble.

A Communist system such as Russia has been as little immune as Socialist Britain or capitalist America.

Yet there is a deep disturbance, almost panicky fear and violent resentment among our workers. It is the worker rather than the union leader who has been clamoring to strike and to stay on strike.

In the five major strikes of the first post-war winter, 1945–6, the General Motors strike, the meat packers strike, the steel strike, the electrical workers' strike and the railway strike, it was on the whole not the leadership which forced the workers into a strike but worker pressure that forced a strike upon the reluctant leadership; most of the leaders knew very well that they could have gained as much by negotiation as they finally gained by striking. And again and again the rank and file of the union membership refused to go back to work even though management conceded all their demands.

Drucker then tells of the terrible crisis of unemployment in the conscious-ness of all the workers, and there he is absolutely correct, and a finished study will give evidence of what the Depression means to the great mass of the American people. Drucker realizes what the unions meant:

In the strike all the old excitement and fervor, the old unity of purpose and action are restored again. On the picket line the worker finds again the satisfaction of citizenship and participation, of a common cause and of a common enemy which the routine of day-to-day union life no longer gives. "In the old days," a veteran steelworker said to me, "we went on strike after every other means had failed; today we strike first, then we figure out what we strike for, and then we negotiate."

And then comes a collapse equally as striking as in 1943:

It is quite possible that time by itself will bring the cure and that, in a few more years, the American worker will accept the kind of union England has had for many decades; a strong and respectable but basically a bureaucratic and most unexciting routine organization, interested mainly in defending what it has. But it is equally possible that the American worker will continue to demand from his union a satisfaction that goes beyond wages, working conditions and job security; the satisfaction of community life, of a cause and of the fulfillment of individual ambition such as he had in the great union drives.

He says that unions can do the job and that has been shown by the New York garment workers union which went in for a large-scale educational program, organized community recreation, etc. This as a solution to the problems he has analyzed with such insight and power in the extracts which we have quoted from his book of 1943.

So that we have here the attempt once more to dodge the problems of the work in the plant by substitutes of union activity, democratic ideals, social legislation, etc. It is perfectly clear to any reader of this article that Drucker sees what it is that drives the workers to what recalls the unity of purpose and action on the picket line as against this activity. He says so, though not in so many words. He says:

But no union can survive, especially not a national union covering an entire basic industry, if it makes the strike its normal way of life rather than an extreme remedy.

He ends:

The job is up to management and union leaders.

So that the Catholic Humanists in the last analysis have no solution whatever, but state the problem only to run away from it, state that strikes are no solution, hope for a bureaucratic regime of the labor movement, play about with democratic ideals and legislation, social education, etc. and end by placing the problems right back in the hands of management and union leaders. So far on the surface. But it is absolutely certain and history has shown that this type of mentality which goes to the lengths that it does in pointing out the evils but at the same time has no solution to offer is one of the surest ways of preparing those who listen to it and follow it for a drastic solution of the totalitarian kind.

The labor leaders do better than that. They do not analyze nor do they attack the concrete basic conditions of modern industrial production. That they keep away from, because from their point of view there is absolutely nothing that they can do about it.

We now have to take the labor leadership itself and we shall deal with two of them only, (Walter) Reuther and John. L. Lewis.

Reuther is an extremely able energetic labor leader who is head of the most powerful union in the United States – the U.A.W. In 1940 he made history by challenging the capacity of the automobile manufacturers to convert the industry to war purposes and made it clear that he thought the union could do it better. This was startling enough in the United States, but in 1945–6 during the great strikes and after, he put forward the slogan among others of "Open the Books." The general public never got the full significance of this. Reuther did *not* mean profits. The yearly accounts of the corporations are matters of legal record, easily accessible. The industrialist and the worker knew what was meant. Reuther was proposing that the *production schedules* of the company be thrown open to union representatives before they were put into operation, and the union men would inspect these, observe changes, increased productivity, etc. and make their demands. This explains the incredibly violent reaction of the manufacturers.

Reuther did not go on with it. He modified the demand, soon dropped it and has never raised it since. Instead he has become one of the most active proponents of the welfare state. We say *instead*. Here is one proof.

In 1949, the American working class, in the opinion of the public at home and abroad, added another buttress to the welfare state by gaining the principle and practice of free pensions. This is what happened in the U.A.W. over the 1949 contract which ended with the gain by the workers of the pension plan. Here we shall take the opportunity of going into more detail and using some of the concrete material of which the finished book will contain far more than the quotations we have used here, and which are more convenient at the present time to indicate the general line.

The union contract was due to expire in July 1949. At the beginning of the year, the union leadership announced its economic demands. The workers were indifferent. They expected nothing. By March the workers began to show some interest. A survey taken among 200 workers, representative of a plant of 7000 workers, showed 58 per cent were for changes in the contract, 27 per cent for the pension scheme, 12 per cent for a wage increase. Of the 58 per cent who wanted a change in the contract, 98 per cent wanted the right to strike restored. The second demand, dealing with production standards, had 75 per cent of the 58 per cent.

Two opinions were represented here. Behind this demand for the right to strike is the intention to control production. For as we described above, this right to strike means that *at any time* a group of men in a department can bring production to a stop immediately, and refuse to work until their demands are met.

The reader to whom this is new and repulsive should keep his temper. "This ought not to be." "This is going too far," is an evasion of the question. Serious industrialists do not evade it. They know the millions of men whom they have to deal with, and they know that these men are serious ordinary American workers, not Communists or anarchists, but men who have become that way by all the circumstances of their lives and work.

These votes show what the majority of the men want. And most of those who voted for pension or wages would go along with the 58 per cent if these showed any sign of being able to achieve control of production.

However, when a strike vote was taken, only half the men in the union voted, and half were against the strike. The reasons for this were very clear. (1) A strike by the 75,000 men River Rouge plant led by Reuther had failed. (2) Reuther was pushing for pensions and the men in this plant had no interest in pensions. (3) There was a distrust of the union leadership. This leadership not only sponsors the clause in the contract forbidding strikes, but would be repudiated by the company and the government if they gave way to the men on this.

Then the state entered and conducted an official poll as is prescribed by law. At the same time Ford carried on an immense propaganda among the men on the following grounds:

1 the union leadership was inadequate;

2 the company was ready to give social and political leadership to the men;
3 a long strike was dangerous;
4 the demands harmed the nation;
5 all the trouble was due to internal union politics.

Thus the government and the company had entered the fray openly. The result? 98 per cent of the men voted and voted 15-1 for a strike.

There is the situation complete. The men want to control production. They distrust the union leadership. But as soon as the government and the company want to take the slightest steps against the union, they turn out en masse and say "Hands off." This is the tight-rope that the union leaders walk. The union leaders now use the militant mobilization for the pension demands, but the men were not militantly for pensions except as these became a symbol of the permanent struggle as to who will rule production.

The negotiations continue, the men become embittered, there is threatening and counter-threatening at the bargaining table. Then the great success of the pensions scheme, new addition to the welfare state, etc. is announced with great headlines and photographs in the press. But the men are overwhelmingly hostile to the whole business; for as always the company has seized the opportunity to tighten its control over production and Reuther has agreed.

Reuther now faced the most critical moment of his career. He had to get the men to accept. The temper of the men is shown by this one fact – in the plant which we discussed earlier, 7000 men walked out (a wild-cat) over some trivial issue.

Now let us follow the meetings at which Reuther tried to get the men to accept. At a nationwide meeting of the Ford Council, with all the delegates supporters of Reuther and members of his caucus (a very tight bond) 1/3 voted to refuse the settlement. Owing to the statistics of the union voting this 1/3 represented far more than a third of the men. Opposition was based on the terms of the contract (production) irrespective of pensions. The arguments against acceptance were based upon (1) the right to strike; (2) the work standards. Reuther's speech took the following line. It is the best contract possible under the circumstances. If you doubt it, look at the other unions, the steel, coal, electrical workers, etc. The question as posed is insoluble. What the men want is no contract at all. Reuther knows this and told them so.

In this discussion and the ones that followed, Reuther's main opponent was a worker, an enemy of the Communist Party but a revolutionary socialist. He is widely known in Detroit as a revolutionary and militant unionist and is a committeeman in his plant. Except as a good union man his influence is very small, although Reuther and the powerful union bureaucracy know him well. He now became the leader of the opposition. Reuther told the men and these are almost his exact words:

I am for a disciplined union. X is for wildcats. I am for the company setting standards with the union having the right to challenge. X wants the men to set the standards. X is for workers councils. I am not for that *yet*.

Workers councils mean complete control of the plant by the workers. This was the program of the Industrial Workers of the World, the semi-anarchist union of the early twentieth century. Reuther referred to it sympathetically. Then:

X is for that type of union. *They are doomed to failure*. They do not believe in compromising the class struggle, they do not believe in any restriction on the worker.

X on the other hand saw:

The heart of the contract is production standards, the right to strike and the company's right to disciplinary measures. The company would concede anything and everything but this. It is a waste of time to talk about anything but this.

X had no organization to speak of. He was practically a lone figure, but he and Reuther were the leading figures as the debate continued in various meetings including a meeting where the huge River Rouge plant discussed the terms. Here are parts of the speeches. Every sentence should be closely studied:
Reuther:

This is the best possible settlement in conditions, there are two points of view, mine and X's. Mine involves an orderly settlement of work standards disputes and X's involves class conflict. I am for authorized strikes and X is for using the strike weapon recklessly.

X:

Reuther tries to improve time-study in workers' interests whereas workers are opposed to time-study as such. He wants to set production. The worker wants some leisure time to himself. In all of society the production worker has the hardest, the most monotonous, the lowest paid, etc. job. He sees everyone around him with the opportunity to sit down and chat, etc., yet the company wants him to work all the time. I'm a committeeman and I have a good job. I enjoy my job, yet I want to be able once in a while to go into the lunchroom and sit down and smoke, etc.

X at another meeting:

The history of the union shows this. In the beginning you take the right to strike, etc. into your own hands. Gradually the leadership assumes this right, saying it can get more for you. You cede it. The facts show that they have done poorly. Now in order to solve the basic questions, etc., it is necessary to retrieve this right.

X at another meeting:

I agree with Reuther. We'll never be satisfied with conditions under capitalism. That's why I'm against capitalism and am a revolutionary. We want the right to strike and we also want the right to set standards and to take the men out of the iron grip of discipline that the company has them in. Reuther preaches the theory of gradual improvement whereas in reality living standards and working conditions have worsened under this philosophy and the trend will continue. The problems in the shop can't be solved by the contract, it can only be solved by the men in the shops themselves. Reuther's way is helping the boss to put us in chains.

Reuther was forced to admit that the contract was no good, but that the only alternative was a long strike. All through the discussions he never dared to call X a red. The president of one big local, a Reutherite, told X: "If he dares to red-bait you, I'll call him down." Reuther's proposals were finally accepted (1) because the bureaucracy and its supporters knew that it would precipitate what all are trying to avoid if Reuther had been forced to go back to the company and call off the settlement. (2) The men had no confidence that this leadership fighting so hard for the proposals would lead what would inevitably have been a terrific struggle. Furthermore they were caught before the public with company proposals for a pension which was being trumpeted everywhere as a great gain for American workers, triumph of democracy, etc. But there was not a plant in the whole country where the majority of workers of the rank and file did not know what was involved and that the fundamental conflict had been sharpened, not assuaged. It is common talk all over the country among the automobile workers that Reuther's prestige had received the most damaging blow it had ever had at the very moment when the press and the country as a whole are full of news of the great pensions victory.

The *political result* will be a burst of frantic activity by Reuther on behalf of better housing, higher social security, more civil rights, denunciation of reactionaries, conferences with friends of labor, warnings to reactionaries in the Truman government, intense activity to get out the vote in 1950 to assure repudiation of Taft–Hartley, etc.

That is the central fulcrum of United States politics – serious politics. The big industrialists are for the most part Republicans but they too understand the situation perfectly. Periodically as in the last steel strike, they will have a test of strength with the union. Can they weaken it or even break it? But as they push at it a certain distance, the union, more or less indifferent on the specific proposals, pulls itself together and rallies to its defense. The industrialists cannot afford to push Murray too far. Some say openly: What would we do without him? Once they feel the resisting strength of the union, they retreat. But how long is this to continue? There is obviously gathering among the workers a tornado of anger and determination to bend production to their will which will put the formation of the C.I.O. to shame.

This explains the maneuvering around the Taft–Hartley Act. Industrialists, union bureaucracy and government, workers, all are aware of the unstable relationship. No one wishes to push these to an extreme. Hence in the United States we have a great deal of talk about the traditional American system, etc. while this is in reality only a facade below which the basic realities of modern politics as they have been expressed in Western Europe exist, and in certain ways more acutely and with more explosive force than anywhere else in the world. The motive force which will explode this extremely unstable equilibrium is the working class itself. But the American workers will not play at politics. In 1932 they made the switch from the Republican Party to the Roosevelt Government. That was a political move in the European sense. Their real independent move was the C.I.O. in 1936. It seems apparent over the past years and particularly with the election in 1948 that the industrial workers have made in their minds the kind of decision which excludes for the future any voting for the Republican Party. Win or lose, as labor movements in Europe, they are going to support the Democratic Party as against the Republican Party. And to the astonishment of the whole world they ignored the barrage of suggestive propaganda which filled the press and the radio and turned out to give victory to President Truman. But as their vote in 1932 was merely a preliminary to their attempt to settle their own industrial problems by the organization of the C.I.O., so at present it is the grossest illusion to believe that the vote for Truman in 1948 or maybe again in 1952 is their final word. The whole history, particularly of the postwar period, shows that forces are gathering below the surface, and if we can judge at all by the past, forces of a power of which we have had so far only indications. That is why John L. Lewis and his miners are of such great importance in the United States today.

This extraordinary man is the exact opposite of the new type of labor leader whom Walter Reuther represents. But the first thing that is to be said of him is that his activities over the years and their recent climax in the 3-day week, the 5-day week, the no day week, are concerned with control over the industry. Thus the *New York Times* as recently as January 22, 1950, writes as follows:

Thus far the union is standing pat in the belief that it must "stabilize" the industry to save it from itself. If the union relinquishes its ability to enforce a share-the-work program through the "able and willing" clause, many mines will work only one or two days a week while others put in five or six days, the union maintains.

How far a union can go in regulating an industry is the big question before the courts. The ruling on the Benham injunction plea may have a significant effect on the whole economic history of our time.

We trust that it is clear by now that important as this control of the industry is, it is not the type of control that we have been discussing so extensively above. Lewis has shown that he accepts the fact that modern industry in America must grind up the flesh and bones of millions of men to accomplish its purposes. All that he proposes to do is to see to it that the workers are adequately paid and get regular work. To that extent he is, as the above quotation shows, determined to control industry as far as he can against the will of the mine-owners. And limited as this is, limited in relation to what we have shown above, it is clear that this too is a constituent part of the movement of the workers in the United States. Lewis, however, is at the exact opposite of Reuther, Carey, Emil Rieve, and the other labor leaders who are tied up with the Democratic Party and the government. He is an old type labor leader who detests the idea of the government in industry. His conception is that the workers and the industrialists must fight out these problems themselves without government interference. Politics he sees as they were during the late nineteenth century. He is a Republican by practice but was not unwilling to go over to Roosevelt for a period and then to change back to the Republicans again. But precisely because of this hostility to the new combination of Fair Deal, New Deal and labor leaders, Lewis and the mine workers represent the real touchstone of the development of the American workers.

During the war with the whole state machine and the general sentiment of the public against him, after a spontaneous walkout of the anthracite miners in the dead of winter, Lewis brought the miners out, sent them back again, brought them out, sent them back again, etc. in a series of audacious challenges to the government in the face of which a man like Roosevelt, commanding a nation at war, was quite powerless. Despite the barrage of propaganda against him, it is equally clear that in 1943 when he was calling these strikes, the large majority of organized labor was sympathetic to him. That is his strength and his significance. Despite his limited political views, the temper of the miners, their defiance of the new combination of labor leaders and government bureaucracy, their readiness to defy public opinion, their instinct for direct action, as when 145,000 miners greeted the Taft–Hartley Act by going spontaneously on strike and saying "Let the Senators dig coal" – all this is a very much more representative sentiment of the temper of the American workers than the constant maneuvers of Philip Murray,

Walter Reuther and the others. That is why Lewis is so cordially hated on all sides. His actions constantly provoke the unstable equilibrium that we have described above into violent oscillations. What he gains for his workers are a constant threat to the need for moderation which besets Murray and the others.

The miners are among the best-paid workers in the United States. And yet at the same time, anyone who has visited the mine area and paid any attention to the actual conditions of labor in the mines knows that in the misery, the poverty, the backwardness of the social conditions in which they live and in the conditions of their life and labor, the great masses of the mine workers are among the most miserable of the industrial workers. So that here with the most successful labor leader of them all, the gains amount to nothing else but a few dollars more. It is obvious that the most militant trade-unionism as such has little to offer in the face of the basic realities of modern conditions of production. Lewis himself and the mine industry and the miners from which he grew, is a very characteristic American. In strength of character, boldness of strategy, tactical skill, he is far and away the most remarkable American of his time. His backward political ideas are bound to be left behind. The iron grip that he holds upon his organization which he runs like a military unit, that too is bound to go. But the spirit, the solidarity and the defiance of society as a whole which characterize both him and his union, that is American to the core. And it is this spirit which exists right through the American working-class movement. Here it will solve the fundamental problems we have posed or the force which will be needed to suppress it will wreck the nation. Such views as these are kept out for the most part of the general political life of the country. People speak of the Depression in terms of markets and higher wages. There is a great deal of talk about government intervention, etc. to save the country from a Depression. But every political figure in the United States, including the late President Roosevelt, on many occasions, has always made it clear that the great masses of the people in the United States would not stand for a repetition of the previous Depression. President Roosevelt and many others seemed to think that the result of an upheaval would be Fascism. Many of them considered that the New Deal was the only possible attempt to hold this off. President Truman has made it perfectly clear that he considers his government is the only safeguard against predatory interests, etc. All these public men speak with a certain amount of caution and phrase what they have to say very carefully. But there is not the slightest shadow of doubt that the great majority of Americans in any positions of responsibility are aware of the strength of the antagonisms which have been described here, and know that upon their resolution rests the future of the nation. Any attempt to present another picture of America to the rest of the world is either hypocricy or a refusal to face reality.

I have concentrated above upon the industrial workers. There are fifteen million of them organized. It should not be forgotten that in some industries where the workers do not work on the assembly line the machine creates conditions sometimes worse than those on the line. Then there are the vast millions of unorganized workers who in one way or another are subjected to the same pressurres. As a matter of fact, the steel workers union has to intervene in some of the smaller industries to modify union conditions so as to allow them to survive. I cannot go here into any details except to say that I have lived in America now for 12 years, have crossed the continent to the coast four times and have lived for periods amounting to months at a time in Los Angeles, San Francisco, Chicago, Washington. I have visited New Orleans and traveled from New Orleans up to Washington. The outstanding feature of my observations has been the pressures on the workers and their violent reaction against these. That will have to wait for more intensive investigation and much of the material on which the above has been based is hidden away in union records, union files, and books by participants in the great struggles of the C.I.O., etc. To complete our rough presentation here only a few more notes are needed.

(1) There are perhaps about 9 million farmers in the United States. One-third of these live under splendid conditions. The remainder are small farmers struggling for an existence. The thing to be noted about them, however, is that they are modern and they know exactly what they want. In the American farmers and the agricultural laborers, there is no hint of that kind of sentimentality and backwardness which one finds, for instance, in a "Bell for Adano" or in Silone's "Fontamara." The American worker wants no bells because they have been in existence in his village for 600 years, nor does he love land for the sake of tradition or for the love of land, which characterizes more backward communities. He wants a good education for his children, a good house to live in, vitamins, a car, television set, and roads not only for his products but so that he can move around freely. He is an industrial worker except for the fact that he works in the country.

(2) The middle classes are to a large extent industrialized and suffer from the same pressures, though very often in different form. As I write, I notice in the morning newspaper that a quarter of a million telephone girls are threatening to strike and the emergence of these middle-class elements with no labor tradition as militant unionists is one of the most remarkable phenomena of the day. They are symptomatic of the millions of department store workers and others who twenty years ago would have considered themselves as completely separate from the labor movement. Still more striking is the following quotation from an article by Dorothy Thompson with which I shall close. The article is headed "Our Fear-Ridden Middle Classes."

Recently, at a party, I ran into an acquaintance I had not seen for several years. I knew him as a graduate of a distinguished university, an editor on a small but established publication, and an occasional writer. I came in; a friend, nodding toward him, said, "Do you know what Jack is doing now? He's just been telling us. He is studying lithography. He's going to be a *printer!*"

Later Jack confirmed this, a bit grimly. "Two times in the last five years I have been kicked out of my job *without any reason being given for it,*" he explained, "and each time it meant several months without a job. In one case two other men were hired to do what I had previously been doing – and since then they have been fired too. As a salaried editor the most I ever earned was a hundred and twenty-five dollars a week, and I regularly took a briefcase of material home to work on nights. I can earn that much, without homework, in the workingman's end of the publication business, and there I can't be kicked out because of a boss's 'change of policy'. I will have more time to write, my family will have more security, and I will have more respect. I am resigning, once and for all, from the most kicked-around class in America – the salaried middle class."

"How does your wife take the news?" I asked.

"My wife is for it. She wants the rent paid, three meals a day for the kids, and thank God, she's not a snob."

To repeat, tiresome as it may be by now, a full and complete study would integrate all this with the proper proportions and balance and such a recognition of the complexities as is possible in an essay of 75,000 words. Enough, however, has been said to show the general tendencies among the workers who, with their wives and children, constitute over two-thirds of the nation. One more chapter remains, and in this I propose to take certain sections of the population, not as industrial units: women, Negroes and intellectuals. This will be sufficient to draw the whole to a conclusion.

7

Negroes, Women and the Intellectuals

We come now to the last chapter of this sketch.

It will have to do two things.

It will have to fill up certain gaps in what after all will be an essay, in which at the best only certain important *aspects* can be treated. At the same time as we are filling up gaps, we have to attempt to make some integration of the whole so that a total impression of society in movement will be left with the reader.

We have so far made clear above all two things. We refuse to treat men as statistics, more wages, more leisure, less unemployment, more goods for consumption, etc. For large numbers of the population these things are still necessary, "a third of the nation," but men have in the past suffered from far greater privations with less sense of frustration, social crisis and doom. It is how they work every day, the material circumstances of their lives, that shape their consciousness; the things by which they live are their sense of perspective, confidence, belief in a social order, its politics, its ethics, etc. We have tried to establish that in principle.

We have tried secondly to show how the general frustrations and bitterness can express themselves where they are least likely to be looked for. If these two points have been made somewhat abstractly, it is because first in an essay, abstraction is imperative, and secondly, the concrete is precisely a finished book and not quotations establishing a general line.

Now, however, we must try to get a little closer to the actual and intimate lives of the population. To do this, we *select* three elements, Negroes, women and intellectuals.

Under the heading of Negroes we deal with what is another major problem in the modern world – the problem of minorities. We shall show why the Negro problem in the United States is the No. 1 minority problem in the whole world.

Under the heading of women we can attempt to see how far the basic conditions we have described affect the most intimate lives of the community, sexual relations, individual personal relations of one human being to another, children, home life, and certain related aspects of social culture. It is a social problem of the first magnitude in every country in the world.

Under the heading of intellectuals we shall deal with the relations of the educated classes to the less educated, the mass, and the relation of the intellectuals to the problems of society as a whole. Between these three we shall within our limits get closer to a more complete presentation of the American civilization.

If previously we dealt with fundamental social relations such as individuality from 1776-1865, and what it is today; with labor relations and the politics that spring from them, we are now dealing with fundamental social *barriers* which are so deeply rooted in civilization so far that to many they seem incurable, the prejudice of the sexes for each other, the inferior situation of women in society; the inferior position of racial minorities, the inferior position of the uneducated. I have not the slightest sympathy and in fact nothing but hostility to all those who preach a doctrine of steady improvement by more education, more democracy (usually by legislation in Congress), higher ideals, etc. This sort of thinking has as much relation to reality as the pre-1914 belief in perpetual progress, increasing rationalism of the human mind, and all that rotten pile of falsehoods which dominated the thinking of Western civilization for over a century and is now in irreparable ruin over half the world and an empty shell in the other half. We have made progress in a certain sense, and the most important aspect is that we have progressed far enough to have to face these questions without illusion, without cant, and in full recognition of the fact that a breaking point in human relations has been reached here as elsewhere. Never before in human history has the antagonism between the sexes; the antagonism between racial minorities and national minorities; antagonism between the "educated" and the "non-educated" been so great as it is today. It is precisely because this is so after a century of "progress" that modern man is so bewildered.

THE NEGROES IN THE UNITED STATES

Through an examination of the Negro question in the United States, we shall accomplish many things. We shall see the relation of racial prejudice to the actual economy of the United States; we shall see it in relation to the political system of the United States, thus giving the economic system more actuality than it has had so far and bringing the political system before us. But to say that the Negro question is an economic or that it is a political problem is at this stage of general political awareness in the United States not to say anything very important and something that may be, in fact often is, very misleading. The Negro question forms a part of that basic social structure and its development which we have analyzed so far. Without some such conception, the Negro question remains a mystery; but at the same time the Negro question will help to make that conception real and alive as few other detached elements or phenomena can do. Thus in addition to its own basic importance, it is important for us who are following this.

The Negro question in the united States is the No. 1 minority problem in the modern world. It is No. 1 because if this cannot be solved, then there is no possibility of the solution of any minority problem anywhere. The fate of six million Jews in Europe, of perhaps twice or three times that number of individuals in the prison-camps of Russia, of Poles enslaved by Germans as a subordinate nation, of millions of Germans and other nationalities uprooted and transported like cattle over wide expanses of territory, the fierce conflict in India, in the United States the uprooting of the Japanese during the war, all this shows that here the world is not moving towards the peaceful enlightened solution of minority or national problems. It is doing the opposite.

The Negro problem becomes therefore a sort of touchstone. America is the wealthiest nation in the world, and stands as the representative banker, armorer and political mentor of one political system in opposition to another which contends with it for world-wide domination. The Negroes are Americans. There never was a minority which was so much flesh of the flesh and blood of the blood of the majority. In language, religion, social culture, education, training, perspectives, the Negroes are Americans and nothing else but Americans. To raise the problem of color alone as a barrier to Americanism is to alienate the greater part of the population of the world, some of whom as in India and China wield important power directly in their own part of the world and not so indirectly in the struggle for world domination. The Negroes do not seek any special privileges, constitution or statehood. All they demand is freedom and equality. The world watches this extraordinary situation. When an American labor publicist visited England some years ago, two questions exceeded all other in the queries made to him, the position of Negroes and John L. Lewis. The American government sent segregated Negroes in the army all over the world, civilized and uncivilized, and thus placed the Negro question squarely before the people of all nations. The whole world and the common people everywhere talk about it, for example, in India it is front-page news.

But it is also a question eating at the heart of the American people, not only at its morale and its confidence, adding to the sense of frustration and impotence. It is one of the crucial pivots of the American political system. Abroad it is a symbol; at home it is not merely a symbol, but a vivid and potent actuality.

Now progress has been made, but as with the women question, it is primarily a progress of realization. Years ago the Negroes had still to struggle to establish themselves as not congenitally inferior to whites. It is instructive to read the old monographs, articles, volumes, disputes on Negro intelligence, tests, the shape of the head, the weight of the brain, etc. Today all that is dead. Those who are intimately acquainted with white Southerners say that even they no longer use the argument of congenital inferiority. The idea that white women in the South are in danger from Negro rapists is also exploded, and it was exploded chiefly by pointing out that of the thousands of recorded lynchings in the South, only 20 per cent of them involved Negroes *accused*, far less convicted, of rape. Negroes have established themselves in all fundamental spheres of American life and won distinction in many. The question now stands naked as one of economic, social, racial domination and now can be seen for what it is, on a par with the labor question and the women question.

Like the workers and the women, the great majority of Negroes are at bottom quite hopeless of seeing within their life-time any equality for Negroes.

First let us face what the Negro question is. It is an economic question; it is a political question; yes, so it is; but it is primarily a question of human relations but not in the common sense of those words. These relations remain a sealed book to the large majority of the nation above the Mason and Dixon line. I know only one book, and that appeared in 1949 and was not widely read, which makes any attempt to express these relations. To put them briefly:

In the greater part of the Southern states where 10 million Negroes live, the vast majority of the Negroes are outside the law. They have no personal rights which a white man must respect. A Negro whatever his status must be prepared to be insulted, beaten up, and if it is found necessary, shot down by white men without possibility of redress by law. A Negro who raises his hand against a white man, whatever the provocation, takes his life in his hands by so doing. The Negroes in the South often refer to the Mason and Dixon line as the Smith and Wesson line. The revolver rules. Regulations about buses, separate accommodations for Negro and whites, etc. are governed in theory by legal procedures. A Negro who breaks them knows that he runs the risk of their being settled on the spot. This is in substantial respects much worse than Fascism, for under Fascism it is the police, the Gestapo, the G.P.U., the state which terrorizes the whole population. In the South it is not the state but the mass of the white population, civilians, any group which knows that it has power of life or death over ten millions of its citizens. The occasional lynching is merely the means by which this power of intimidation is maintained. There is not a normal existence, mere segregation, with an occasional flare-up in a lynching or violence. That is not the South at all. There is at all times, every day, the consciousness in the minds of both white and black, of the fact that a revolver can be brought in to settle *all* disputes. That it is *not* brought in more often is because the Negroes are disciplined to accept, the consequences of non-acceptance are too serious to encourage risks. Many whites also in certain areas strive to prevent the use of power. But it exists, it is the dominant fact in Southern life, and has been for generations. The writer of this as all readers of this outline know, is a Negro, and if it is thought advisable, could give examples of his own direct, personal experiences, extending from New Orleans to Memphis.

To anyone who has grasped this stupendous reality, one of the most astonishing in the history of modern civilized nations, all the agitation and excitement about Civil Rights, a National F.E.P.C. with teeth in it, a Federal anti-lynching bill, abolition of the Poll Tax, etc., all legislation of this kind to be passed in Congress, all this hullabaloo can be seen for what it is, a body of legislation which even if it is all passed, will not alter the fundamental situation. It cannot. The local populations, the local rural administrations, the local municipalities, the local police, the local magistrates, the local state administrations, local juries, will have to be altered and no legislation passed in any Congress will alter these. No Federal administration will hurl itself into a civil war with the states and vast numbers of the population of the South, in a vain and costly attempt to change a situation such as we have described. Let it be said before we go any further that this does not mean that these struggles are vain. Not at all. And the resistance that the South has mobilized against them is clear evidence that something important is involved. The protagonists know that what is really involved is a declaration of position, a statement at least of intention by Congress and the Federal Government. It is an attempt to throw the moral weight of the Congress on the side of the Negroes. It is a lever in the struggle, a very important lever, but it is that and nothing more.

That is where we must begin. There is involved here a revolution in relations comparable only to the revolution which will emancipate labor and the revolution which will emancipate women.

What is it that this system protects? What is it safeguarding? This system protects some of the most precious material interests in the country.

1 The Negro sharecroppers and Negro agricultural laborers are at the mercy of white landlords and merchants, and by this intimidation they not only maintain that domination but extend it over whites as well.

2 Negro labor in industry (and inevitably white labor as well where the two work together) until the spread of unionism was at the mercy of industry.

3 Public funds, mainly, though not exclusively for education, are deflected from Negroes to whites, sometimes in the ratio of 5 to 1.

4 Probably well over a million white-collar and skilled labor jobs which in an equal society would be held by Negroes remain the exclusive preserve of whites.

5 The political oligarchy wield their power in the states and a power infinitely beyond their real social force in Washington and in the nation as a whole through domination over the Negroes and domination over the poorer whites which this Negro domination gives.

6 Banking and investment interests of the North with large investments in the South know that this system protects the status quo and do not wish it destroyed.

7 The political representatives of industrial management in the North are dependent upon the political oligarchy of the South for holding in check and defeating the measures of the welfare state which they consider extreme, such as for example, the repeal of the Taft–Hartley Act.

8 The whole mighty apparatus of government which has now governed the United States for nearly twenty years can be completely upset by the freedom of the popular masses in the South.

Now does anyone believe that so vast and complicated and powerful a system of interrelated interests, safeguarded by the readiness for direct action of millions of whites in the South, protected by their local governments at all levels, does anyone, can anyone in his senses believe that bills passed, in Congress, anti-lynching, Federal F.E.B.C., etc. will change what we have outlined above?

People note the terrific struggles of the Negroes, the manner in which they have forced the issues before the public and forced them into the programs of both parties. They note the mass of information that has been publicized so widely, the wide sympathy that has been aroused, and the fact that the Negro question was a central issue in the 81st Congress, and the struggle over F.E.P.C. dominates this Congress so far. They presume that in time "the Southern bloc" will be defeated and some legislation passed, the whole constituting some sort of progress. Some slight consideration of what has been written above will show the immense illusions contained in the above perspective.

To begin with the present. Why have not the bills been passed despite the clear mandate of the electorate? For the mandate of the electorate is clear. How definitive a change has been reached in the country as a whole was shown nowhere so clearly as by the prompt reaction of the mercurial movie-makers. Sensitive to public opinion they sensed that now they could afford to exploit the Negro question in their own limited fashion for profit and prestige, not only without offending but actually pleasing the public. The only concrete political result so far has been the *strengthening* of the rules by which the Southern Congressmen can filibuster on anti-Jim Crow bills.

Why? It is because the parliamentary process and the political system are absolutely powerless against the system we have described, its ramifications throughout the nation and the gaping holes and cracks it will open in the whole American structure if there were any serious attempt to reverse it. That is why the bills are not passed. It is not a question of "some reactionary Southern Congressmen."

From this we can take the next and far more important step. Even if all the legislation were passed:

(1) It would be passed in such a mangled truncated form and so tied about with legalistic obstacles, so riddled with loop-holes, that it would be useless as a means of changing what it is supposed to change. That a vote of 270 against and 240 for is changed into 270 for and 240 against does not alter the basic relations described above.

(2) And if even, for the sake of discussion, we assume that reasonably sharp legislation is passed, there does not exist in the United States any governmental force to put them into force. What will happen is exactly the opposite of what the light-minded and superficial expect. There will then be created a huge barrier to any serious emancipation. Let us watch this well, for it is a characteristic example of the process by which the modern world is rushing to its doom.

The Federal Government is not an abstraction. It is a huge bureaucratic administration now spending 40 per cent of the national income. In it are represented directly and indirectly vast nationwide interests. These interests have to be maintained in some sort of equilibrium to carry out the main tasks which face it:

1 carry on the "cold war" against Russia and mobilize the nation and Western Europe;
2 struggle to maintain the economy in some sort of equilibrium.

Under these circumstances the Federal Government:

1 organized a military force of 15 millions on Jim Crow lines, bringing Jim Crow forcibly to the attention of the whole nation and the whole world, refuses to make any serious alteration in the status of Negroes in the armed forces and is obviously preparing to organize the nation in a future war upon the same basis;
2 refuses to make any serious alteration in the Jim Crow regulations of the Federal Housing Authority;
3 refuses to take any step to put an end to Jim Crow in Washington;
4 refuses to get into conflict with the state of Tennessee and builds and maintains its atomic project, a project new from the ground up, on strictly Jim Crow lines.

These are the *acts* of the Federal Government and its reasons for them are as clear as daylight. In the present crisis, national and international, it sees not the slightest reason for, and very solid reasons against, undertaking the disruption of the nation which a serious attempt to eliminate Jim Crow from the South will undoubtedly cause. Any legislation that is passed therefore as far as government is concerned, will result in merely adding organizational bureaux, investigators, fact-finders, commissions, etc. (with a liberal sprinkling of Negroes) who become inevitably part of the whole gigantic apparatus of government with all its strains and stresses, its major national and international problems. Its primary function is not to disrupt the economic and social foundations of the country but to perpetuate itself and govern. The good-will or ill-will, the good intentions or bad intentions of the President mean absolutely nothing here. The inevitable result of legislation being handed over to the administration will be that those in charge of it, Negroes or not, with their first loyalty to the adminstration and its primary tasks, will become adjusters, manipulators, fixers, propagandists, educators, but the safest and most dependable preservers and protectors of the essentials of the system.

The process of adjustment is already in progress. The Negro intelligentsia is being combed and groomed to play precisely the role of the labor bureaucracy in its relation to the fundamental problems of the labor process. Not only is this taking place in the government itself. The majority of the very greatest industrial firms in the country, acting through the Urban League, are now carefully selecting a limited number of well-educated Negroes for white-collar posts in industry in the North, where the Negroes as voters have an important political power; and have led the struggles which have brought the Negro question where it is. It would not be too difficult to prove that some of these interests while taking these steps on the one hand, are on the other supporting the maintenance of the status quo in the South. Today Vanderbilts and Rockefellers serve actively on the committees of the Urban League, symptomatic of the changes in popular sentiment over the Negro question. But every accession to the cause of elements of this type means inevitably adjustments at the top and further nails in the coffin of Negro emancipation. For these elements only add weight to the conservative elements in the general propaganda, legislation and bureaucratic conservative adminstration of whatever legislation may ultimately be passed.

Continuing with a rigid selectivity we touch upon certain aspects which illuminate the fundamental relation between this minority question and the basic social structure and development of the nation as a whole. We have sought to emphasize fundamental relations, the great efforts that are made to correct them, and the fact above all which so demoralizes the modern world, that the greater the efforts made, the more terrible are the new forms in which the old social problems reappear. This in fact is the cause of the demoralization and the hopelessness, for if effort produced amelioration and opened out perspectives of hope, there obviously would not be demoralization and certainly not hopelessness.

The Negro question is a very typical example of this. The Negroes struggle against segregation and separation. But every effort that they make results in minor adjustments and greater segregation and separation. This was brought to public notice by Gunnar Myrdal in his *American Dilemma*, the result of a 2.5 million dollar investigation. But Myrdal did not understand it as a fundamental pattern of the modern crisis.

Negroes in the North in particular live in segregated areas, in the great cities, ten, sometimes hundreds of thousands. These communities grow and spread constantly, adding to themselves new territories from which the whites move out. Thus, as Myrdal notes, all-Negro communities who have little to do with whites are on the increase. The government passes legislation prohibiting restrictive covenants for housing. A few wealthy Negroes can thereby move to other neighborhoods. But city municipalities, real estate owners and interests, these are the ones who decide how and where Negroes on the whole should live. They on the one hand and the automatically expanding Negro communities on the other, make nonsense of racial covenants. Negro pressure for living space, for freedom, does not result in their being admitted freely to live where they wish; it results in the pressure being carefully directed towards certain specified areas, "now thrown open to colored," and an increase in segregation. The larger these areas get and the more carefully they are manipulated, the more intense becomes the segregation.

The Negroes and the labor movement and the general liberal forces by pressures and agitation demand equality. Repeatedly as the Negro leaders themselves confess, they are offered increased facilities on a segregated basis and as they confess, they succumb to the temptation. The greater the extent of the segregated areas, the simpler it is to build schools, to open parks, community centers, etc. for the Negroes among the Negroes, staffed to some degree by Negroes.

Thus is created one of the scandalous but inevitable developments in such relations known all over the colored world. There is created a constantly growing vested interest in segregation itself. Negro universities, Negro social workers, Negro institutes, funds for the benefit of Negroes, Negro school systems, Negro representatives in white institutions, Negro representatives on administrative boards and now representative Negroes in white business offices and on technical staffs, Negro war correspondents. We cannot go into details here but the pattern is now well established. And with the growing bureaucratization of all aspects of modern life, the joint pattern of agitation for equality and the resultant increase of facilities by the increase of segregation grows steadily. The analysis of the role the Federal Government will and must play in the administration of anti-Jim Crow legislation is only the fundamental exemplar of what is taking place North and South.

One more question remains and that is to show how deeply embedded in the whole American structure is what on the surface and to foreigners in particular can appear as a racial question to be solved by education, etc. We shall divide this into two parts, the physical facts, so to speak, and secondly the psychological.

(1) The C.I.O. is the most powerful social organization in the nation. Along with the United Mine Workers it can paralyze the economic and political system of the country. All dynamic social progress depends primarily on this. There are over a million Negroes in these two organizations.

(2) There are, as we have said, about 9 million farmers in the United States, of whom about 2–3 million are prosperous, some rich. The vast majority of the others are tenant farmers or small farmers, millions of them being in the most miserable situation. Millions of Negroes in the South are among the most miserable of the farming community.

(3) The urban Negroes, North and South, live for the most part in overcrowded ghettoes, most often in conditions of unbelievable squalor. Here the Negro question is rooted in the all-important housing question.

(4) The most striking phenomenon in American politics is the alliance within the Democratic Party of the C.I.O. and the Southern oligarchy, the two extreme poles of American society. It is certain that this alliance is nearing its end. It is equally certain that the Northern Negroes by their political activity and the political power they wield in many states (where they hold the balance of power) will have contributed as much as, or more than any other single factor in breaking this alliance, one of the strangest in the whole history of politics.[1]

Thus, on all the basic economic and political problems of the day, the Negro, segregated as he is, is an integral part of American life. And it is the contradiction between this fundamental need for complete and total integration demanded by the whole modern development in conflict with the powerful interests which demand and perpetuate segregation that lies the sharpness and the intolerable strains of the whole Negro question.

Finally, to complete the general picture, to make some effort to arrive at some totality, it will be useful to look at certain aspects of the sociology and psychology of the Negroes taken as a whole. They are selected here because they are symptomatic of the nation as a whole.

The Negroes are Americans and in them, in their combined segregation and integration, can be seen indications of the national crisis, strains, capabilities, needs and hopes, as in no other section of the population. It is possible merely to list and not to develop them.

(1) The great unsatisfied desire of the American population is for social organization, free association, for common social ends. It is the only means whereby the powerful and self-destroying individualism can find fulfillment. The Americans are the most highly self-organized people on earth. Every city, every suburb, every hamlet, has organizations of some sort, Elks, Shriners, Rotarians, clubs for everything under the sun. But the Negroes are the most highly organized of Americans. Government statistics show that of some 14 million Negroes in the United States, over 10 million are listed as belonging to some organization. Whatever the variety of these organizations every one has openly or implicitly as part of its program the emancipation of the Negro people. Chief of these is the Negro church. A Negro of oratorical or fluent gifts which, if he were a white man, would give him a good position as a salesman, politician, etc. becomes a preacher. He opens in some small room in a Northern city and gathers a few of the faithful, domestic servants, common laborers, the poorest of the poor, seeking some social organization, some collective life. In fifteen or twenty years, they have built a church, they have property worth $20,000. Choir, Sunday Schools, clubs, classes, excursions, national contacts, local chapters, all are flourishing on a basis of self-government and built on the pennies and dimes of the congregation. Here the Negro is free, free to work out his own purposes and pursuits, free from the unceasing humiliations and domination of the white world. Few aspects of American life are more symbolically significant than this creative social power, excluded from the general world, expressing itself so powerfully within its own narrow environment. It is not religion. It is far more an outlet for the spirit which has made the country and is now frustrated in so many spheres of American life.

(2) The American people as a whole are frustrated in their most essential being and seek release from these frustrations in the ways we have described. No greater torture for an American could be devised than that which the American Negroes suffer, to see others no better than they have elementary rights of which they are deprived. The twisted bitterness of the Negro people is an index of the suppressed angers which permeate the vast majority of the nation. In the passion of the church services and singing of the very poor, in the responses to the great Negro bands in dance-halls and sometimes in theaters in the Negro districts, can be felt a passion, a tremendous elemental social force, which many who note it, like to fancy is primitive, of the jungle. It is nothing of the kind. It is modern Americanism, a profoundly social passion of frustration and violence, characteristic of the nation as a whole as can be seen in the gangster films, radio-dramas and comic strips.

(3) The American people are remarkable for political outbursts such as Jacksonian democracy, the early years of the formation of the Republican

Party, Populism, the I.W.W., outbursts which sought by mass mobilization to rid society of encumbrances at one mighty blow. The Garvey movement despite all its surface extravagances and absurdities was in essence a movement in America, an American movement, with the sweep and the temper and the passion of the American masses when they move.

(4) The American people today and over the past twenty years have been gradually awakened to the necessity of political struggles of a kind they had forgotten. The Negroes are in this foremost. They concentrate on the Negro problem, but individually, in small groups, in organizations, with or without allies, handicapped by the whole actual and traditional barriers against them, they have brought their cause before the nation and the world, won allies and now threaten to give the final blows to the traditional political mechanism by breaking up the Democratic Party.

This is not Negro. It is a symbol of the temper of the American people. The Negroes have their cause simply and clearly posed before them, and the nation, and their segregation forces them and facilitates easier mobilization. But the whole history of America shows that political activity of this kind on their part heralds, is an advance notice of the whole nation in movement.

(5) The American Negroes are today symptomatic of the changed relations in social forces and an index of the basic forces now molding the United States. It was their segregation, their lowly dispersed station that forced them into mining, the steel industry, the automobile industry, cooks and stewards on board ship, etc. Now after thirty years these industries have developed to such a degree that the unions which spring out of them hold in their hands the keys to the American industrial process. The Negroes thus find themselves in the forefront of the social forces contending for mastery in the nation. There are perhaps 100,000 Negro miners in the United Mine Workers. They are unnoticed – the miners move as one.

(6) In more strictly differentiated organizations and in representative individuals the pattern continues. A basic feature of the modern democracy is a grouping like the labor bureaucracy whose function so far in labor relations we have analyzed. The N.A.A.C.P. in Negro relations plays in all essential features within its own environment the same role.

If American intellectuals were attracted into the Communist Party, more Negro intellectuals were drawn to it in proportion. If few have remained, towering among them are Paul Robeson and W. E. B. Dubois. Robeson is in fact on a world scale far and away the most important artist-intellectual associated with the Cominform. But whereas white intellectuals and writers broke away and sought retirement or a refuge with traditional democracy,

Richard Wright and Chester Himes attacked Russian communism and its satellite parties from the left, condemning it not merely for corruption but because it was not revolutionary and betrayed Negro revolutionism – with all their limitations they held up a banner, groping pioneers for a native American radicalism.

Most remarkable of all is the case of Lawrence Dennis. Known for years as the only serious theorist for an American fascism, his career was cut short by the publicity given to the fact that he is a man of Negro ancestry.

The popular writer who in his books has most expressed the modern American feeling for violent, uninhibited direct action and individualistic self-expression is Frank Yerby, a Negro writer.

Richard Wright and Chester Himes first brought to public attention the fact that the Negro in the North suffered not only from physical and legal limitations and humiliations. His intellectual and emotional life were torn and twisted and possessed so that he did not know a moment's peace at any time. Wright and the French existentialists, products of the extreme literary and artistic sophistication, centuries old, of Paris, the artistic center of European civilization, have discovered the closest affinity with each other, and the emotions they describe, despite the fact that Wright's work is exclusively concerned with American Negroes in their own limited environment. The Negro writer represents the extreme peak of *American* revolt against the intolerable psychological burdens placed upon individuals in every part of the modern world.

Such is a brief attempt to present in broad strokes an outline of the concrete totality, economic, political, psychological, and the contradictory antagonistic movement of the relations of one section of the population. Under the heading of minority problems can be seen the intolerable strains and stresses to which the whole nation is subjected.

The next section, on women, cannot attempt to do the same. But it will supplement the foregoing, by trying to represent the manner in which intimate personal relations, beyond the attempts of all legislation and government, are affected and determined by the essential relations which we outlined earlier.

WOMEN

We have to exclude certain substantial elements in the population and choose. We do not propose to take up the women question so far as it relates to the great mass of working women. We shall later make a few observations about them, but that is all. Nor shall we take up those who are wealthy and have domestic servants. We propose to concentrate upon those who are intermediate between these, first, because in two chapters at least, we dealt

212 Negroes, Women and the Intellectuals

with the problems of industrial labor, and we are aiming to embrace as far as possible the great majority of the nation in this study; secondly, because in studying these, we are not so far from the great millions as might appear on the surface. Before 1789 in France, the people who were vocal about equality were *not* the artisans, the merchants, the small urban intelligentsia. They *listened*, or often seemed to be indifferent, while the radical aristocrats and the famous encyclopedists, philosophers, etc., friends of the aristocracy and the aristocratic bourgeoisie attacked what they called the excesses of the monarchical and aristocratic system. In the day of crisis, however, it turned out that the most ardent, the most determined, the most self-sacrificing advocates of equality were precisely those who before 1789 had had very little, practically nothing to say. It is quite certain that the ferment and the ideas about the relations of men and women which were stirring in that section of society I have selected do not represent but are symptomatic of vast stirrings which exist among the tens of millions of the laboring and lower middle-class women.

This section of American women is the envy of its counterparts in all parts of the world who see it glamorized in the movies and in the fashion and women's magazines and novels which between them set the tone in style and manners wherever the English language is read and wherever movies are seen. And the American woman is undoubtedly the freest, the most advanced, with the greatest opportunities for self-development in the world. De Tocqueville and Bryce have drawn attention to the exceptional advantages she has enjoyed throughout the history of the United States. American industry has offered her opportunities, not equal to men's but sufficient to save her from the total economic dependence upon her husband which, in more backward countries, constitutes an intolerable barrier to any pretense of equality. Divorce in many states is easy enough and for the class we are considering a trip to Reno for six weeks, though difficult, is not impossible. They are familiar with men, having had the advantage of co-education on campuses, or if they were not fortunate enough to go to college, have shared in that freedom and easy relationship between the young people of both sexes which is so characteristic of American life. Reasonably good clothes, shoes, cosmetics, the beauty parlor, bathroom, hot water, good medical attention in childhood enable them to make the best of themselves in a way that they can only appreciate if they go abroad and see what their sisters of similar status have to put up with. Vacuum cleaners, frigidaires, the telephone, diaper service, innumerable gadgets and conveniences ease women's traditional burden. Their life is not paradise nor yet the new millenium, but *in comparison with that of women in the past and women in other countries* this stratum is exceptionally well-placed. They are great readers of books and magazines, and as far as the position of women is concerned, their minds are turned forward. And yet these women are the most unhappy, the most torn, the most dissatisfied, the most antagonistic in their relations with men that it is possible to find in history or as far as can be gathered, in other parts of the world.

Equality they have in theory. They can and do embark on careers and win places for themselves in teaching, in the professions, in business. They are severely handicapped by the masculine prejudices, traditions, etc., but they are pushing ahead. If economic crises hit them harder and quicker than they do men, yet crises seem to be in the nature of things. It is not that which disrupts them. The thing that tears them to pieces is that when they examine their equality, they find that it is a spurious thing. This generation more than any other can and does face up to the fact that equal rights with men is not what it appeared to be two generations or even a generation ago.

A baby means in modern civilization three years or more out of a woman's life. If she has money for maids and nurses, she need not go through this period of abstention from her ordinary pursuits. The wife of the ordinary workingman knows from the start that she must accept this. (She is not necessarily reconciled to it, not at all. But so it has been and so it is, so for the time being she accepts it.) But the girl who has gone to college or otherwise had an opportunity to develop her abilities and ambitions is suddenly transformed into a wife, dependent upon her husband, dropping behind in the race, where formerly she had gone side by side with him through high school and college or in the early stages of a business career.

For the woman, for an active woman, is posed the question of the home versus the career, and the career does not necessarily mean a world-shaking one but simply being active in the world, earning some money and not waiting at home as an appendage to a man. No such basic choices ever face an active man. Whether basic biological urges impel women to need babies is excluded here. I cannot go into that. The fact remains that if the couple or the woman or the man, particularly want children, and biological urge or not, that is a natural and normal instinct, equality vanishes.

We are here at the very roots of the modern dilemma. Our parents and still more our grandparents neither expected nor wanted equality. They grew up in a different world. Today, however, equality is not an individual need or the subjective passion of a few intense or rebellions people. *From every point of view it is a social necessity in the modern world.* Industry when, as during the war, it has to make a special effort, calls for labor in general without specification, whatever it can get. Education, primary and secondary, re-duces the distinction between the sexes. Mass political activity, such as it is, embraces the whole population without distinction of sex. The centralization of modern life, industry, communications, press, radio, all drag individuals from a position of social ossification. To accept a priori a subordinate inactive or restricted position in life among our associates – that is today what calls for effort – not vice versa. The husband who goes forth and the little woman at home; the public life and the life of the home, these old distinctions have been shattered among all who have had opportunities, by the blows of modern civilization. The middle-aged women who preoccupy themselves with clubs and lectures, etc. are a pathetic spectacle because fifteen vital years of their lives have gone into bringing up the children. Hence *on the whole* the poor showing of women in politics. Hence the sense of bitterness and the frustration and a feeling of the burdens placed immediately upon women. Many women who are indifferent to "civil rights" burn with rage and impotence at this antagonism between theoretical and practical life which touches them so nearly.

This elementary question of children merely highlights the whole increasing clashing and rasping between the theoretical concept of equality and its actuality. A modern man has grown up in an environment of a man-dominated civilization, education, books, movies, his parents, even the experience of his very early infancy (Margaret Mead has written on this). These have gone to make him what he is. He has as a rule little except the most abstract sense of equality. He and his wife may both work, but almost inevitably the responsibilities of the home fall upon the woman, not only in the material sense of cooking and cleaning but in the sense that except in rare cases, the responsibility for adjustments to differences of personality fall almost automatically upon her. The moment a child comes, or there is any serious disruption of the routine, the steady adaptation of her personality to his can assume a burdensome oppressive and wearing quality which can express itself in forms far removed from the original cause.

Of late years the women in this group have been on the defensive. They are ready to retreat and in fact it appears that they are retreating all along the line. The women's magazines which serve them, such as *Ladies Home Journal, McCalls, Good Housekeeping, Cosmopolitan, Women's Day,* are filled with advice as to "how to hold the man," a proposition the mere statement of which is revealing enough in itself. Still more revealing is the advice given to play up to *him,* listen to *him,* read this or that about *his* work in order to hold *his* interest, when the baby comes be careful to let him see that he is not now a neglected or subordinate factor. Nowhere is converse advice given to the man. These magazines and presumably the women who read them have accepted frankly the fact that man is the dominant sex. But it is impossible for women to grow up in the modern world, be educated in the concepts of liberty and equality, go to modern schools and universitiies, enter into marriage without using the word *obey,* and then find that they have to spend the rest of their lives accommodating their personality to their husband's on grounds that are strictly a priori.

This is the immediate elementary antagonism of the relationship. It is made even worse than it is at first sight because the whole of the past so living in the present, conditions the woman to feeling within her own personality the pressures of submissiveness. This too is in direct opposition to the ideas of freedom and equality for women which she has imbibed from childhood as an individual and from the social environment. The final result is a permanent underlying bitterness and sense of frustration. It is the direct counterpart of the sense of hopelessness and frustration felt by the masses of workers in modern industrial production.

To make the point clear it would be useful to use the method employed earlier and pose *theoretically* in rough and ready fashion the only alternative, a revolution in individual relationships as great as the revolution pointed at in the labor process. Men and women will be equal when from the very start, cooking, washing and other household duties, child care, personal adornment, games, sports, etc. are taught to children by a world which makes no distinction at all between the sexes. The age of chivalry must go and go finally and irrevocably. The world in which a man's brute force was a necessary part of life no longer exists. When a man had to chop wood or be a blacksmith, or saddle a horse, or go hunting for food, women naturally did the cooking, cleaning, embroidering and took over the graces as well as the routine chores of life. It was a division of labor. Today in an advanced civilized household, a woman does the actual heavy work, if any. Only when men by upbringing not so much in words but by social practice can turn their hands to every single social and domestic necessity in the home and not feel it a disruption of their personality pattern to do so, will there be any possibility of equality. Under these circumstances, even a baby in the home does not become automatically the woman's sphere, except for a very few months at least.

Now it is obvious that what is envisioned here is a revolution indeed. And no modern man who observes society at all objectively could deny that on such a basis, if universally admitted and not so much admitted as practiced, man as a social being has everything to gain and nothing at all to lose. The perpetual friction and dissatisfaction are as wearing and deleterious to character development and free and happy association in the man as in the woman. But it is equally obvious that so drastic an overturn in contemporary domestic relations is conditioned upon an equally drastic overturn in economic relations. Man will have to lose his place as the traditional breadwinner. As long as he is this, all talk of equality is a burdensome fiction. And there is no absolute necessity whatever for men to continue as the breadwinner or the provider. At present there are many types of rough work which men do more easily than women (we shall take this up before we are finished) but the ultimate tendency in modern industry is knowledge, skill, mental alertness, flexibility. There are vast branches of modern industry in which women are fully able to take their equal place with men; in the tremendous social test of cities subjected to mass bombing, it is nowhere suggested that women were less able to stand it than men. The revolution in the home rests upon a revolution outside of it. The last war, as great wars always do, shows a clear indication of a future society by the role women played in industry – and willingly. For many millions of women, especially younger women all over the world, work in factories and in farms was an introduction to a new world of freedom, independence and common social experience. In one of the many neglected passages of *Capital* which is so largely concerned with the human relations of industrial man, Karl Marx states that in the factory of the future, men, women *and children* will take part in the work, and thus lay the basis for totally new relations of the family. Modern experiences in the factory show quite clearly that left to themselves a group of workers made allowances for older men, men not physically strong, etc., and it is a very peculiar conception of human nature which does not understand that men, women and children can work together and adjust the work to physical capacities and needs, education and recreation of children, etc. without the slightest difficulty. If this is so for industrial labor, it is obviously much more true of all kinds of labor. Today it is done without strain on many modern farms. But it is obvious that for the personalities of men and women to be altered to permit a genuinely equal relationship requires a total reorganization of *all* kinds of labor relations in the world at large.

Before we go any further it would be useful to establish that many observers have come to the conclusion that some drastic change in society is necessary before the perpetual frustration of modern women (and to a substantial degree of men also) can have any possibility of relief and that energy be turned to more creative purposes, though it is equally true to say that numbers of thinking women look upon the situation as hopeless. As I write, January 30, 1950, I see in the *New York Times Book Review* of January 29 an article by J. Donald Adams which expresses perfectly one of the reasons for the hopelessness which clutches at the vitals of so many millions in the United States. I shall as usual quote extensively from it so that its positive and negative side may illuminate the central point. Adams says of a book by Haniel Long:

Its chief concern, I suppose, is with the maintenance of a free society, and its chief value its emphasis on the fact of individual responsibility. The passage which I quote touches upon a matter no less central to our time than is the survival of freedom. It is one about which far less has been written, about which not nearly enough has been written – the relationship between the sexes in the modern world.

This is absolutely correct. While much has been written, most of it is of the type which deals with more education, restraint, consideration, lengthy and not hasty preliminaries to the sex act, and such like. Adams knows this. He continues:

That may seem like a strange and questionable statement. A great deal has been written on the fringes of this subject, on the obvious results to date of what we refer to as women's emancipation. We have been made more acutely aware, through the drawings of Mr Thurber, and through occasional plays and stories, of the heightened tension in the relationship between men and women, so that we have come to speak of the war between the sexes. But there has been little writing of a creative kind which has really come to grips with the matter of how important this changing relationship is; almost no writing which can be described as constructive.

Perhaps I am blind or unaware, but there seems to me to be little general comprehension among our writers of the fact that women, in their struggle toward readjustment – a struggle which men forced upon them when they brought the industrial age into being – have now arrived at a crucial point, beyond which they cannot go without men's understanding and help. Woman, as Long observes, is being born again, "is delivering herself of herself." And the strain and stress of that experience is, I am sure, the basic reason why women are drinking as much as they are today. It is, too, the explanation of many of the divorces initiated by wives.

Through many centuries it has been difficult for men to see women otherwise than as creatures existing on earth for their comfort, pleasure, and convenience. One evidence of this was pointed out recently by Edith Hamilton in her "Spokesmen of God," when she remarked that "the Bible is the only literature in the world up to our own century which looks at women as human beings, no better and no worse than men. The Old Testament writers considered them just as impartially as they did men, free from prejudice and even from condescension."

The quotation is long but it is so complete and so adequate, it poses the question in terms that have full significance for us who are following this sketch, the individual personality, that it must appear here is someone who grasps the subject. In reality it is typical of modern thinkers of the less superficial kind. He sees the problem but is totally bankrupt in front of it and it is precisely this recognition of vital problems and the utter hopelessness and helplessness in front of them that characterizes our world. The article continues:

The subject upon which Mr Long touches – and I am sorry to present his observations out of their context – must, it seems to me, be one of the great themes which writers will approach during the remainder of this century. It is practically virgin territory; the only creative writing that has been done in it has been of a most superficial kind.

The seeds for such writing were sown nearly fifty years ago by Ranier Maria Rilke in the letters subsequently published as "Letters to a Young Poet." In one of them he remarked that we were only just beginning to look upon the relation of one individual to a second individual without prejudice and realistically . . .

This is fantastic. Adams thinks that creative writers will approach this theme during the next half-century. The fatuity of these thinkers is beyond belief. Joyce, Proust, Lawrence, T. S. Eliot, during the last thirty years approached many other serious problems very creatively. And what is the result? They have increased the sense of demoralization, bankruptcy and hopelessness. What in the name of heaven can creative writers do in the face of what we have been describing? Adams then quotes the letter from Rilke of which we give only one section:

Some day (and of this, particularly in the Northern provinces, reliable signs already speak), some day there will be girls and women whose names will no longer signify merely an opposite of the masculine, but something in itself, something that makes one think, not of any complement and limit, but of life and existence, the female human being.

This advance will (at first much against the will of the men who have been outstripped) change the experiencing of love, which is now full of error, will alter it from the ground up, reshape it into a relation that is meant to be of one human being to another, no longer of man to woman. And this more human love (that will fulfill itself, infinitely considerate and gentle and good and clear in binding and releasing) will resemble that which we are with struggle and endeavor preparing, the love that consists in this, that two solitudes protect and touch and greet each other.

This indeed is the limit of foolishness. Women, it seems, have outstripped men. Love will be more "human" etc., etc. This is mysticism, no less. It is excusable in Rilke, in fact, it is highly creditable to him fifty years ago to have made these observations. To a man who writes about the "cold war" between the sexes and recognizes that today the whole situation is "crucial" to have nothing more to say than this is to confess that for him the situation is insoluble. In the same issue of the *Times* is an advertisement for a new book by Margaret Mead which uses the same phrase "cold war" in referring to the relations between the sexes. I have not read the book but I take a chance and prophesy that it contains admirable and profound analyses by a very able and conscientious mind, but that it will leave the intelligent and experienced reader more hopeless than ever before.

It must be so, because of the simple fact that in all these books the individual is somehow made responsible by his or her own individual efforts to make adjustments to dislocations and antagonisms whose whole roots are in forces totally beyond their individual powers. The changes that are needed are so far-reaching that the writers either dare not or are unable to face them. The changes necessary appear to be, as Elton Mayo said of another sphere, fantastic and utopian. And so they do, undoubtedly, until one looks at what has been happening to the world in the past forty years and realizes that no piddling little reforms and efforts of "creative writers" during the next fifty years can halt the descent and the abyss. And people on the whole know this, they know it very well. It is precisely becuase they no longer believe in any of the little nostrums and medicines that their outlook is so gloomy.

To return to the middle-class women. There is, as we have said, the primary relation in which one personality is compelled day in and day out without let-up to adjust itself to another, to subordinate itself, to accept. And exacerbating this primary antagonism are the physical circumstances of existence.

Americans boast with justice of the high material content of the civilization which can be embodied in the one word plumbing. In reality future generations will and in fact many in this generation recognize already that for modern man the two or three rooms with kitchen and bath, are not a dwelling house at all but a cage.

These interminable blocks of apartments are not related to the needs of the people who live in them. They are related to certain necessities of the economy, first of which is the need to have as many millions of people packed together as closely as possible to get them to work in the huge industrial concentrations as quickly as possible. This is the first and fundamental motivation in modern building, and there is no escape from it because under the present circumstances those who would protest loudest at any change would be the people who suffer most from it. Secondly, there is the question of squeezing the utmost value out of every square inch of land which follows from the first necessity. Thirdly, there is the question of transportation bound up with the first two. Just as today governments deal with food more and more in terms of vitamins and calories necessary for life, i.e., to be able to work, so for generations regulations deal with how many windows, distances between houses, etc. The result is that the modern individual (or the modern couple) of moderate means faces the physical conditions of existence worked out to a degree which gives no faculty of self-determination or choice whatever. The circumstances of work, of transport, of home and life, are determined. The individual must fit into them. To recall de Tocqueville, this modern individual's grandfather or great grandfather did not live this way. Life was a heroic adventure for anyone who wanted to act. For the modern individual it is a deadly routine. And for the woman whether she stays at home or goes to work, the personal frustration and anxiety never ceases. *For the responsibility of making something tolerable and interesting out of this formidable apparatus of mechanized routinized living devolves by social tradition and practice upon her.* Society constructs a huge apparatus whose determinant force is getting masses of people to work and back with the utmost convenience and despatch, for the sake of industry. Into this structure, with every square inch mapped, the woman is thrown with a man and given the impossible task of overcoming the handicaps inherent in the whole structure.

Both herself and her husband are people sensitized by modern civilization to social and psychological needs far beyond men and women of previous generations. Yet they are subjected to the remorseless discipline of the society. The personalities, stimulated and at the same time cheated, can only express themselves in violent clashes or suppressions within the two rooms, kitchen and bath. Hitler who understood much of the frustrations of modern life did not like to see modern apartments built because as he said, they bred communists. So that the modern middle class woman with all the needs of free self-expression which her upbringing and social education have fostered, finds the whole burden of modern civilization brought to bear within the narrowly limited confines of two rooms, kitchen and bath, expressed in her handicapped relation with a man who bears in every atom of his physical and emotional life the stamp of the antagonism, contradictions and anachronisms of the society around him. Children which are often conceived in order to help cement the marriage can be a source of added anxiety and conflict. With all the advantages of modern science in childbirth, prevention of diseases, etc., there is the fact that within the modern home in the modern world, the demands of rearing one child unfit the mother for doing much else. The bringing up of children in a modern city means that merely for the child to get fresh air demands what amounts to a daily expedition; the child of a few years must play on the pavement. Privacy for the individual in the home, almost impossible before, now becomes quite impossible. For the woman in particular, self-development comes to a halt. You do not need statistics for this. Simply sitting in the park and watching the harried faces and manners of young married women is enough. Thousands upon thousands refuse to have children altogether, which does not in the least mean that they have solved any fundamental problem, for the wife or the husband frequently want children. Many women fight a constant, never for a moment forgotten battle against their husbands (and themselves also) on this question of children. In the middle of the nineteenth century only exceptionally gifted, bold, adventurous women had these problems. Women married and settled down to bear children and be complementary (and complimentary) to their husbands. Today that is over. Modern society has created modern woman, and now a stage has been reached where a reckoning is being made. It must have come as a shock to many to read Mrs Roosevelt's autobiography and realize that fortunately placed as she was and successful a woman as she appears to have been she too felt and resented the pressures outlined above. Of the great millions of working women whom I have omitted from this analysis, it is sufficient to say this: there is nothing of the highly publicized conflicts and difficulties of middle-class women, and the basic problems described here which do not apply with tenfold force to the vast majority of the working women or wives of working men in the United States. From the stimulations of the modern world they are not excluded nor for that matter are farmers in remote areas. The film, the daily paper, the radio, the Diesel engine subjects them to the same pressures as their college-educated sisters. They are less vocal, protest less. History has repeatedly shown that this is not because they feel less but because they see no way out.

It is impossible here to treat the question of sexual relations. Yet to write of a civilization and avoid it is impossible. What I propose to do is to take up certain related aspects which together will convey a total impression. I take it for granted that in the modern world the only possible solution of the basic relation between the sexes is that women must become human beings first and women afterwards. The whole of modern civilization is driving towards this, the modern woman feels it at every stage.

Greece of the great age, it may be noted, did not give full equality to women, but the highly cultivated Greeks of that age sought adequate companionship in two ways, homosexuality and a peculiar group of women, the most famous of whom was Aspasia, the friend of Pericles. These women broke openly with the restrictions upon their sex and gave up all advantages of a protected domesticity. They studied philosophy and politics and educated themselves like men and became the companions of the distinguished Greek citizens. Aspasia in particular was famous for her political skill. Pericles worshipped her, Socrates visited her. Some Greek citizens even brought their wives to her salon, and yet at the same time her house was a center for young women who followed her profession. We shall take up the question of homosexuality later, for it is a critical question in American sexual relations. For the time being, and here it is sufficient to reassert that modern society has now reached a stage where it must either turn backwards or women must become free independent human beings, in every way, and the whole sexual relation recreated upon this basis. But nowhere in the world is there so powerful a subjective onslaught upon this conception as in the United States, the country where women have reached so far in the pursuit of equality.

There is a cult of women as women in the United States which must be stated before any attempt can be made to draw any conclusions, however tentative. Its most obvious manifestation is in the field of advertisement and public relations. Women, their legs and their breasts, are called into service to sell everything from insecticides to aeroplanes. No political meeting, convention or public meeting or display is complete without stars, starlets, models; no magazine can do without its cheese-cake. In all the really popular novels, and in many of the best of the crime stories, a man sees a woman once, and her "shape" at one glance is sufficient to send him on a career of crime or its analogue. It is the correct thing, the expected thing, to whistle or otherwise express open admiration at the "shape." Love, but love in the form of the "shape," and the sweater rules all. Saint-Exupéry has noted that on the radio in the United States 75% of the songs are about love, while in France he claims 75% of the songs are about politics. This extraordinary glorification of the "shape," the sweater, and "romance" is completely removed from the preoccupation with women which distinguishes or up to recently distinguished the Latin countries. There women as such were discussed frequently by men in terms of the elemental function, but by men who did not believe for one second in any theory of equality either abstract or concrete, and by women who did not believe it either. This cult of women as women in the United States is of another order. Its origin I may discuss later, but its consequence to progressively minded women of the middle class in particular, with whom we have been concerned, is ruinous. The very thing that they want, to establish themselves as individual human beings with rights to independence and self-development as human personalities, and upon that basis to build an intimate relationship in which their total personalities as women are no more or less special than the total personality of the man, that is being assaulted day in and day out, every hour of the day, by all the mechanical means of communication at the disposal of a powerful industrial civilization. As usual, with any powerful social manifestation, even those who see it for what it is, are affected by it within themselves. It is one of the most powerful barriers to any attempt to build a genuinely human relation.

What is its origin, whence it draws its strength, it is impossible to discuss adequately here and now. But it is so all-pervading that it would be a mistake to presume that it is due "purely" to advertisers, etc. As we said earlier, there is a great deal of Whitman in this, and Whitman cannot ever be ignored in any consideration of the modern American people. It can also be approached from the angle that it is a violent reaction against the absurdities and exaggerations of nineteenth-century Romanticism which produced some rare specimens in the United States. It is a reaction, in all probability, also against puritanism. But this writer, with all due caution, leans strongly to the belief that it is of the same type as the welfare state; Voice of America paeans to democracy, labor bureaucracy, gangster films, film stars, etc. All these, varied as they are, are very real but synthetic constructions, projections from a harsh reality and an attempt to overcome that reality without touching fundamental relations. it is a substitute but a substitute that does not fall from the sky but springs organically from below, from the reality itself. It finally ends in becoming an iron barrier to the very needs it sought to satisfy, if even partially. This specious adoration of romance in the shape of sweaters and legs seems to evidence a recognition by the people of America of the role of sexual relations in life, a consciousness of great need, and at the same time a consciousness of a complete inability to satisfy that need. Not only the heavy drinking of women but divorce statistics, the marriages that are holding together because of the children or because another marriage will probably only be the same, "men are like that," and the cult of psychoanalysis, all these are some of the considerations within which the statistics of Kinsey must be examined.

Finally there is the question of homosexuality, and it is brought in here for convenience as much as for the fact that it occupies a special place in the intimate relations of American life. Gorer in his book on the American character has some interesting pages on this as an American phenomenon. It is not that more Americans are homosexual than people of other nations. It is, as he reports, that Americans have a unique attitude to it. They hate it, they denounce it, they are on guard against it. The American Army, he states, excluded avowed homosexuals and he claims this was the only army to do so. Private conversations and inquiries have also yielded the information that men are beaten, pushed away, exposed on charges of homosexuality among Americans, where the average European would express his distaste by shrugging his shoulders and turning aside.

There are other considerations. Melville relates a homosexual episode at the beginning of *Moby Dick* with an ease and lack of self-consciousness which is amazing in a writer of that period writing for his public. But even more strange is the case of Whitman. Whitman's poems at first glance seem to be full of a defiant homosexuality and he has been widely accused of this. Yet there is another view. John Adington Symonds, a homosexual himself, wrote to Whitman as one friend to another. Whitman, an old man then, wrote back in horrified terms, denying any imputation of sexual irregularity of that kind. It is not at all to be excluded that Whitman had a conception of intimate relationships between men, which he might have considered extravagant or adventurous or revolutionary or an integral part of a fully developed human being, but which he did not consider to be sexual irregularity. This kind of friendship, appearing in these two writers, and the peculiar attitude of American officialdom and the American people as a whole to homosexuality, seems to indicate some unusual attitude characteristic and a specific product of the United States.

I have been careful to write *around* the sexual relation, for I am aware of the difficulties involved. The difficulties in regard to homosexuality are even greater. By the time this sketch is developed into a finished book, I shall be more in a position to decide what to write, how far to go, and whether to write on it at all. But so far at least, I have a line of investigation consonant with the whole method of which this book will be an expression. It is this. Women have always had a special place in the United States, respected as women have been in no other modern country. But the American male has had a passion for human relationships, social and personal, general and intimate, and it is this which above all constitutes the high civilization of the United States. He has not been able to create or establish this relationship with women. Whitman, Melville, Poe in their writings present a picture of relationships with women which is worth a chapter in itself. Poe in particular, in story after story, killing them and then bringing them back to life again.

Under these developing social circumstances there has been a powerful impulse to intimate friendships with men but hedged around by a safeguard of stern prohibition against this intimacy becoming perversion.

There should be considered in this connection one of the outstanding features of World War I and World War II, the development of what has been called "comradeship" among the men. Also at times in reading or listening to the few who will talk about it, it appears that all the squalor, the blood, the inhumanity, were recompensed by the consciousness of the relation, unknown it seems among modern men in times of peace. Also to be taken into consideration is the Greek attitude toward friendship between men – a Greek did not think it possible between a man and a woman, except a woman who had broken with all respectable ties.

This is sufficient for the time being. The writer believes that hidden here are avenues of investigation to new relationships among men and new relationships between men and women, both sexual and otherwise. And here for the time being, the matter will have to stay.

This has been a difficult section. More than ever here it has been a question of indicating ideas. Some may, in fact, will be developed farther; others excluded, new ones embodied. But certain fundamentals remain. First, there is no question of the organic connection between what has been discussed in previous chapters and the most intimate private lives and personal relations of the American people. There can be no separation of them. The life of modern man has been split into separate fragments and his whole life and personality need to be integrated. Secondly, there is nothing specifically American about this. All that is American about it is that in the United States these world-wide tendencies and developments have reached their sharpest expression. Finally, though there is no special need to develop this point, the reader will go badly astray if he does not bear it in mind. We have treated this question as a question of the home. We have emphasized its roots in the whole social environment, but it is not only rooted there. From the home it returns to the economy. Hitler and the modern totalitarians in general seek to solve the frustrations by boldly denying equality. "It is the business of women to bear children and serve as recreation for the tired warrior." That is the first stage. The totalitarian propaganda machine gets to work to drive this into the minds of men and women alike. But it does not stop there. War and production for war is the main motive force of world economy as a whole. The women are driven to produce children. And more children. But as the war becomes urgent, they are once more dragged out of their homes and shoved into industry wherever they are needed. In unemployment crises they can be sent home again to lessen the unemployment figures. Thus in Russia we have the combination of women in industry and the most reactionary laws in relation to divorce, abortion, etc. Thus the totalitarian solution is a double exploitation of women, far surpassing the exploitation of previous civilizations. Here as elsewhere the cruelty of modern civilization for objective reasons surpasses all others. Nor does this apply only to working women. Quite the contrary. There is evidence to show that at critical periods both Russia and Germany lined up the women of the middle class and drove them into industry wherever the war machine needed them. Britain, it must be repeated, has the laws on the statute books, but while all the experts say that the economy can never be planned without their enforcement, the Labour Government in time of peace has not dared to enforce them.

THE AMERICAN INTELLECTUALS

This section of this final chapter is the section before the last pages of this sketch. Those last pages will be entitled: *The American People and the Next Stage*, for I do not by any means intend to shirk some tentative prognosis of the next stage of development. This section on the intellectuals belongs to the first two, because there can be no real picture of the American civilization without some picture of the more or less purely intellectual processes at work and the alignments, actual and developing, among these.

At the same time this section forms a natural bridge to the last one – the American people and the next stage. Because I propose to draw to a very sharp contrast one of the decisive contrasts of the ideas presented here. In fact, this is the most important from a theoretical point of view. It is this: the American intellectuals have nothing to say that is new. They will make no special contribution to the future of American society, they formulate no new doctrine, reactionary, progressive or otherwise. So far as they are matters of intellectual organization and theoretical expression, the basic doctrines of today are already formulated in Europe, the Communism of Marx and Engels, Fascism, Catholic Humanism, the Socialism of the British Labour Party, the doctrines that come from the Moscow regime and its satellite parties all over the world, and recently Existentialism. The American intellectuals *follow*. Since Woodrow Wilson enunciated the doctrines of intellectual cooperation, America neither among its ruling classes nor its intellectuals has had anything to say. At this very moment, despite the enormous power of the American government, its spokesmen, the man on whom it depends and has depended for years to give some dignity and color to its international politics is an Englishman, Winston Churchill.

On the other hand, in the section on film, popular music, etc. we showed the creative power inherent in the masses of the American people (which does not exclude at all the fact that gifted individuals have to produce individual works); from the war there came two works of really nationwide significance, the drawings of Mauldin and the journalism of Fyle. Somewhere within their commonplace exterior, these two caught some of the war, as it was to the ordinary soldier and as the ordinary civilian wanted to know about it. Yet both these men are in style and content absolutely of the people. By intellectuals I do not mean them. Jean-Paul Sartre, Lewis Mumford, Walter Lippman, H. G. Wells, Hemingway, Norman Mailer, Senator Douglas of Illinois, Hutchins of Chicago, John Dewey, Beatrice and Sidney Webb, Einstein, Picasso, Ramsey Macdonald, all these are intellectuals. But Ernie Fyle and the Mauldin who drew the war cartoons were not. They were men of the people, doing a job, an ordinary everyday job which the people wanted done. I have to make this distinction clear because it is the whole thesis of this book that the intellectuals as such, as they have expressed themselves in Europe, and as every sign shows they will express themselves in America, have and will have nothing to say to stop the pattern I have described here, the crises, mass upheavals and struggles, and then the erection of huge bureaucratic concentrations which bring an intensification of the evils which they sought to correct. Not only are they powerless before the process. The intellectuals contribute to it, and then either drown themselves and their doubts and hesitations in it or desperately seek a retreat in their own individual psyches, Existentialists in France or psychoanalysis in the United States.

Opposite to this I shall pose as an elemental sociological force the instinctive rebelliousness and creative force of the modern masses. We have seen its forerunners in the United States in the middle of the nineteenth century, slave revolts, underground railroad, Abolitionist movement, Harper's Ferry, rescues of slaves and of escaped slaves, reforms of every kind, Bloody Kansas, the formation of the Republican Party and the first national mobilization for the Civil War. By 1862 as an *organized* mass movement it was practically over. In 1858 the force of this movement dragged Lincoln into it and made him a national hero. Wendell Phillips once said that every single argument used by the parliamentary and respectable official opponents of slavery had been worked out originally by the band of outcast Abolitionists. The intellectuals had a role to play as I have tried to show in Chapter 2.

The question, the vital question, is whether some such movement today (and the modern masses have an inherent power infinitely greater than those who worked between 1830 and 1860) whether this movement is bound to end in the vast oppressive bureaucratic militarist structures which mean without a doubt the end of civilization.

So that I pose the two: the intellectuals, the men who are the guardians of the traditional ideas and develop new ones; who do not necessarily wield power but who express in scientific, artistic and political form the ideas which spring from new economic and social developments. And on the other hand, instinctive mass movements such as Jacksonian democracy, 1830–62, the C.I.O., movements which have leaders and sometimes distinguished intellectuals, but which are best exemplified by the formation (to be seen within the period) of the Republican Party which was an example of free association if ever there was one, born exactly no one knows where, springing up out of the ground with not one single national politician or leader of any status having anything to do with it, until *after* it was formed and people saw its power. Finally this must sink in. Up to say 1852, only 9 years before the final crisis, no one of any political stature knew that a new party was on the order of the day, that the Civil War would be the greatest war the modern world had yet seen, and that at the end of the war a new America would have been born.

The premises and logical consequences of this view I shall develop later. It is enough that I state it, so that here and for these purposes we know where we are going. And here an interjection: if some who are reading this Ms. are startled at this, I would like to remind them

(1) that I am not asking them to join anything or do anything;

(2) there must be at least some alternative ways of thinking to (a) the type of ideas which build the New Deal, the Square Deal, the Fair Deal, the United Nations, atom bombs, hydrogen bombs, all of which solve nothing, or the opposition of the Republican Party which is torn by whether to oppose the Truman policies or to say that it can carry them out better, in other words no real opposition except in the struggle for place and power; (b) joining up with the Stalinists as so many tens of thousands of intellectuals in Europe and all over the world have done; (c) turning the back on both and seeking to find some way out in Catholicism or probing one's own private unconscious.

But although this Ms. may merely chart ideas, life itself is somewhat more demanding. Most of the readers of this Ms. (which is not at all intended for any publication whatever) are members, more or less, of the intellectual classification. The alternative courses of action, and choices portrayed here will inevitably be their own, as intellectuals in Russia, Eastern Europe, Germany, Spain, Portugal, China, Indo-China, Indonesia, have had to choose, and in France and Italy have either chosen or are trying to decide.

The intellectuals today from one point of view have not been so important in the world for 500 years certainly, and perhaps never in the world before. The reason lies in the structure of society. The tremendous mechanization and socialization of production, distribution, and all aspects of consumption, the reduction of the mass to an immense accumulation of units, concentrates at one end of society knowledge, organization, power to organize and control the immense mechanism. The less the intelligence, initiative, knowledge required from the mass, the greater the concentration of scientific knowledge required from those who guide, control, organize. The division between manual mechanistic labor and scientific intellectual labor was never so great as now. But if the mass is deprived, not only in industry but in politics, of any initiative, its need for intellectual guidance, education, knowledge, etc. is not lessened. We have dealt with that earlier. In addition to the actual organization of socio-economic processes, there has arisen the necessity for a gigantic organization, the production and dissemination of ideas. The immense mechanization and socialization of *things* has lifted *ideas* to a new importance. The war of propaganda is the contemporary barbarism which corrupts and destroys and poisons what in reality is a very high stage in the development of man. The function of supplying this becomes the function of intellectuals.

Thus the development of society itself has created a situation where on the one hand is the increasingly undifferentiated mass, and on the other, the organization of science, technology, social, political and administrative management which becomes the preserve of the intellectual worker. Free enterprise, socialism, Stalinist communism, this is the social reality today. In the nineteenth century it was not so.

To repeat what I said earlier. Although this section is headed American intellectuals, for the most part it will have to trace European conditions and movements, for there, as is characteristic of Europe, the tendencies have reached full maturity. The best way (here) is to treat fully the European developments and then show their American counterparts which are at present embryonic and clear enough, but not fully enough developed to be easily analyzed in themselves. In fact, except in the light of European developments, they make little sense.

Now if we for the moment use the empirical method and look at the world around us, cautiously, and as far as that is possible, without preconceived ideas, we shall see that in Russia, the constitution defines the population, workers, peasants, intelligentsia; but in Britain where there is private property and capitalists, the organizers are the immense body of labor leaders and intelligentsia who form the Labour Party and the administration. In all the satellite states of Europe an immense bureaucracy of intellectuals under the guidance of the party rules. The same is rapidly developing in China. It is one of the two most striking features of America since 1932 – the gigantically developing bureaucratic organization of government which now spends about 40 per cent of the national income. The second is of course the labor movement, *and the two are inescapably tied together.*

The ruling bureaucratic organizations can be divided roughly according to function: politics and government; industrial administration; propaganda and information, "entertainment;" and the labor bureaucracy. Every year sees them automatically growing larger and extending their functions. They compete within themselves as the newspaper chain competes against another; they compete with one another, as for example, in the United States, the organization of the press as a whole competes with, opposes the bureaucratic organization of the Truman administration, but it is to be noted that the Republican Party proposes only that instead of spending 40 per cent of the national income, a Republican government would spend only 39 per cent. This from the bitter opponents of "statism." When the Republicans are asked: what will you change, they have no answer. You have complicated relations such as the relation between the labor bureaucracy carrying out the function of disciplining the workers for industry, while representing the workers in their conflicts with the industrial administration; the same labor bureaucracy united with the political administration, etc. But the whole modern tendency is towards integration; and under pressure of civil war, inside the country or international war, the tendency toward integration is accelerated. Its ultimate point is where the government bureaucracy, the administration of industry, the organization of ideas; propaganda and entertainment, and the labor bureaucracy are fused and disciplined under one central leadership. That is the totalitarian state. Its distinguishing political feature is the totalitarian party and the totalitarian party is in essence the state of the various bureaucracies coalesced into a forced unity. The world is a very complex place, and ideas, least of all ideas stated here with so much concentration, cannot encompass reality. But without general ideas everything is chaos, and the above is the modern development. It can take place as it did in Germany by completely reactionary elements destroying the traditional labor movement, but immediately restoring a labor bureaucracy of its own. It can be the result as in Russia of a genuinely proletarian communist revolution in the original sense of those words. This revolution accomplished tasks which needed to be accomplished in feudal Russia for centuries, but was crushed by the growth of the bureaucratic tendencies. In Britain we have the labor bureaucracy taking over the government and a fusion between the labor and administrative bureaucracies which then proceeded to nationalize certain industries which includes substitution of the labor and government administrative bureaucracy for the traditional industrial bureaucracy. This is done under the impetus of the mass labor movement. In France today we have two basic types facing each other and paralyzing the state, on the one hand, the De Gaullists, on the other, the Stalinists. The Gaullists in power will defend in words traditional capitalism, private property, etc. The Stalinists in power will undoubtedly destroy private property. There are immense differences between them, but this much unites them – their distinguishing ultimate destiny and very conscious aim is the completely bureaucratized militarized totalitarian state and the population enslaved. Undoubtedly the old individualistic capitalists retained some of their power in Germany; they have none in Yugoslavia, Poland or Czechoslovakia. But to call these men as they were in Germany examples of free enterprise is not very intelligent. The outstanding change in the social structure is the centralization, the bureaucratization, the incorporation of the great mass of *intelligentsia* into the unit which governs, manages, instructs, organizes the great undifferentiated mass. As we have seen it, the power of this governing body can be taken over from the old industrial class, the landowners, the military without destroying these; it can come from the labor leaders who have the power over the mass. The new governing force is in itself powerless but with the help of one or the other of these fundamental forces, it can gain power and embody in itself the directive forces in the state. This group is of course a body of conflicting forces, sometimes it is divided into two, each half following one of the two camps of the United States or Russia. It can purge itself of its outstanding enemies with extreme violence. But in its essence as a social composite, by the time it reaches any maturity, it represents a fairly well-defined section of the nation. In Czechoslovakia, once it was clear that the Communists were in power to stay, hundreds of thousands, in all nearly two millions joined the Communist Party. A Social-Democrat like Nenzi in Italy, where at one time it looked as if the Communist Party would win, led a huge mass party into an alliance with them; at the height of the Communist Power in France, the old Social-Democratic leadership like Jouhaux went along with them. Communist decline and the Marshall Plan funds have detached them for a while but with a swing in the pendulum, they will go back again. And in fact the whole ECA program and the program for the armament of Western Europe is based upon this simple reality; the intellectuals, the political leaders and educated opinion in Western Europe have made it quite clear that if in a coming war they are to be overrun and then liberated *afterwards*, the people or enough of them will prefer to go with Stalin. Given arms, etc. they may fight to preserve themselves but democracy as they have known it for thirty years does not mean that much to them. The only ones the United States can really depend upon to fight on its side are the real militarists and Fascists who see red at Russia because they seek to destroy the working class movement at home.

Very little publicized is the letter Churchill wrote to Roosevelt *after* he had sworn that we would die on the beaches, in the streets and in the hills. There he told him clearly that Britain had to be defended, because if it was defeated, those who would form a government would have to give Hitler the fleet, etc. That the admitted leaders of the old regime, some tens of thousands or even more, would be liquidated; that the leaders of the war effort in Britain expected and, there is no need to doubt, many were ready to face it. But a nation consists of 40 million people and it would have had to accommodate itself to a Hitlerism dominant in Western Europe. It will accommodate itself to Stalinism similarly placed. And the great mass of intellectuals *go with the power*. When every allowance is made for the immense different origins of Hitlerism and Stalinism, in fact the more these different origins are emphasized, the more remarkable becomes the astonishing similarity of the matured state form, the bureaucratic centralization, the totalitarian regime, the power of the secret police, the attempted dehumanization of the mass of the people.

This is a brief, rough, brutal (but for our purposes entirely adequate) outline of the movement and direction of the world in which we live. (And it is this that creates the hopelessness, for the great majority of the people do not want that world, and we can agree in advance that most of the intellectuals do not want it either.)

Now to look at America. The basic social forces outlined above are here. We have on the one hand, the tremendous industrial and financial concentration, the great farmers and plantation owners, etc. But although they own and draw profits, their industries, etc. are run by vast social concentrations of managers, scientists, technologists, administrators, etc. Thirty years ago if Henry Ford had disappeared, his business might have disappeared with him. Today Henry Ford II could be expropriated and it would make no difference to the actual running of the plant. No one knows this better than the industrialists themselves. Hence their frantic appeals to the public against socialism, communism, regimentation, etc. Max Lerner, in a quotation we gave in the Introductory chapter, talks about the "paranoid sense the conservatives have of living surrounded by dangers." The conservatives are infinitely more intelligent than he. This Ms. has been written in vain if it is not clear that they with their daily experiences, the relationship with workers and labor leaders, know that they are in danger, that an economic or war crisis can unloose a flood which will end in their elimination. They know the workers. Lerner does not. Turn again and read the debates between Reuther and X in Chapter 6, and also Chapter 4. The slave-owners were for thirty years filled with reassurances from their Northern commercial friends and governmental colleagues from the President down, that their slave property was safe. They saw that it was not and they were right. To the great industrialists it seems that they may go and the huge bureaucratic organizations which remain and must remain will have new masters, and this they see as the beginning of a terrible tyranny. Equally present is the already huge and growing governmental bureaucracy with its enormous power. Government is not a few hundred men in Congress. Ambitious intellectuals, scientists, technicians, organizers, administrators of all kinds swarm in the government. They rule and are driven by an irresistible momentum, more power is impelled in their hands every day.

More significant than all of these is the growing power of the labor leaders. If a critical situation were to force the unity of the C.I.O. and A.F. of L. and create the united labor movement as it is known in Europe and elsewhere, American society will feel an impact such as it has never known before. These labor leaders are now active in politics and Roosevelt's "Clear it with Sidney" is evidence of the power they held as far back as 1944. There are still some old hands like Lewis and Hutcheson who are Republicans. The new type is a political type of whom Reuther is the pre-eminent representative,[2] and *Life* did not err when in reporting his victory at a U.A.W. convention, it said that he and his friends had other victories in prospect at a convention of the Democratic Party or of their own Labor Party.

This is gospel truth. The A.F. of L. has recently undergone a political transformation. Its leaders are not only in national politics. They, along with men from the C.I.O., are the last active enemies of the Communist Party *in Europe* where their agents work tirelessly. They now dominate an international trade union movement comprising millions. They hold the whip-hand in the Democratic Party. A split in the Democratic Party would not only throw the Southerners out. It would do far more. *It would release the Southern masses for the first time to have politics of their own*, and this politics would undoubtedly be the politics of the labor movement. The next logical step is political power and the fusion of the labor bureaucracy with the government bureaucracy. It would throw America into mortal crisis.

The American intellectuals are caught within these inexorable forces. Numbers of them are already within the bureaucracies, some of the new labor leaders are indistinguishable from the intellectuals, and this tendency will grow. At present the intellectuals or political types like Justice Douglas, Senator Humphrey, Senator Douglass, young Roosevelt of New York, the younger economists, professors, writers, historians (David Lilienthal, Stuart Chase, Harry Hansen, Arthur Schlesinger Jr.) journals like the *New Republic* and the *Nation*, gravitate between the labor leadership and the administration. The great press, Luce publications, etc. are politically outdistanced, the combination, not fusion as yet, of labor leadership and the administration has them beaten. These conservatives are all united with their labor enemies for the "cold war" but they have nothing to say of any importance on fundamental issues except "Voice of America" and Vote Republican. Whereas in Europe, the issues are clear, clear to the extent that great political organizations with doctrines offer some road, in America everything is in chaos except: Get out the vote; prepare to win the war (though we doubt if we shall survive it and we doubt that the war even if won will get us anything, though perhaps it is better to win than to lose). The confusion, the strictly intellectual confusion, is immense. Important public figures, not philosophers but active public men whose words carry weight constantly strike great blows at the shreds of internal peace and confidence that remains. I shall give only two examples. One is by General Eisenhower who, speaking with his immense authority on war, informs the public that to defeat Russia would be one thing and asks: Where are we to get thirty million men to hold the country down afterwards? At the same time a man almost equally authoritative in his own sphere, Bernard Baruch in an article published in the millions in the *Saturday Evening Post*, declared flatly that there is no longer any clear border between peace and war and America must make up its mind to lose its liberties and be regimented in peace so as to be ready for war. At the same time, not a soul knows if within a year a tremendous depression will not fall upon the country.

To plan or not to plan, to acquiesce in the militarization of the state and the tremendous growth in the power of the F.B.I. or not? Is all the steady encroachment upon civil liberties necessary for protection against a few thousand Communists? This new power of government, dominating all spheres, the ceaseless conflicts between capital and labor, the inadequacy of Congress to handle a simple obvious necessity like Civil Rights for Negroes, the great victory of Communism in China: Is the world going Communist? Is American money sufficient to counteract what Communism has to offer? What is our democracy that we can offer it? To plan or not to plan? Without plan are we headed for a mighty depression? And isn't it clear that planning means the final blow to all concepts of liberty and individualism as we have known it?

This is what faces American intellectuals, the more liberal-minded ones, and the great mass of the American people are in general of what may loosely be called a genuinely liberal turn of mind. The American intellectuals do not know, they do not even know what they want, and they are drifting. But they are drifting in a pattern. Europe during the last thirty years faced the same crisis, and to see the American patterns that are emerging we shall have to examine rather closely the European patterns as they have developed. They are of the very structure of the mind of the modern intellectual, they exist in the United States as in Europe and the period ahead of us will see their growing maturity.

The European intellectuals developed out of the crisis in roughly three directions. We shall take them one by one with the American counterpart of each. We shall then sum them up as a whole.

The first which has developed very powerfully in France, that great center of *literary* movements, is Existentialism. Existentialism is not in essence a literary movement. It is the expression of the complete impossibility of the intellectual being able to associate himself fully with any social or political grouping in society. He turns in upon himself, what *he* does, the state of his own soul, the morality of his own actions, *his* suffering, *his* pain, *his* nausea, *his* grief, *his* indecision, these are the fundamental reality of life. He will know ultimately what his life has been at his death. Meanwhile what matters is the decision that he takes at every stage.

This has been growing for years in Europe among the intellectuals. In so brief and concise a summary as this, we select one statement by Sartre as most characteristic: "We were never so happy as under German occupation." Here is the whole concentrated. *Then, most intellectuals knew what to do*, join the Resistance, and so they did, and coming out of the libraries and cafés, performed heroically. *They knew what to do.* But facing DeGaulle and the Communists, American domination or Russian, the old suicidal doubts, the incapacity to decide has overwhelmed them again.

And in America? America is a country whose chief expression of itself is active, purposeful intervention, for the purpose of accomplishing. Hence the refuge of modern American intellectuals is psychoanalysis and the examination of themselves as individuals, their internal conflicts, the unplumbed depths of their consciousness where they hope to find "Peace of Mind." Unlike the French they propose to "cure" themselves, but the sickness is the same, a sickness in face of society. Psychoanalysis is one of the great scientific discoveries in the twentieth century and an integral part of modern man. It is a preliminary to the integration of the human personality (without which modern man's society will go from catastrophe to catastrophe). It is part of that process of mastery of the mind which is one of the signs that man has reached the stage where he *must* live a truly human existence. But it is impossible to believe, and the writer has nowhere seen any hint that Freud and the men who made this science, believed it to be the refuge from social ills and the football that American intellectuals have made of it. The will, the intelligence, the faculty of decision, endurance, fortitude, these are repeatedly abstracted from the personality *in its social environment* and placed at the door of the psychoanalyst. To which must be added the following: that judging from conversations and popular articles the drastic conceptions of (for example) Freud as he repeated them in the last book he wrote, these are not taken seriously by those who live in an atmosphere composed of their neuroses and the neuroses of their friends. It is an emasculated body of ideas within which they live. It is not a scientific consideration at all. It is essentially a social counterpart of what in France has taken the form of Existentialism.

It is for this reason that the work of Wright in particular, and to a lesser degree, *Lonely Crusade* of Himes is so important. Wright claims that he had been thinking and feeling like the Existentialists long before their work appeared. *Lonely Crusade*, a portrait of a militant Negro labor organizer, is completely Existentialist in sentiment. Neither Wright nor Himes are Existentialists. The motive force of their work is the social emancipation of the Negro people. But they show that within Negroes, and not merely intellectuals, the apparent hopelessness of their situation engenders sentiments akin to those the Existentialists make their main concern. This has far-reaching implications for modern society as a whole and American society in particular, but I cannot go into that here.

The second European tendency, ignored at first, but now after the war, seen to be of extreme importance, is Catholic Humanism. This must be observed carefully, for what it signifies goes far beyond the more blatantly reactionary aspects of the Catholic Church. Rauschning, the German who joined Nazism and left it, has told us his own development in the early days of Nazism with the utmost candor and insight. It is particularly valuable because he describes the process when the German intellectual was at much the same stage that the American intellectual is today. The people whom he represented had up to the time of the great crisis not participated in public life.

The great crises brought into the political arena elements that had shown no inclination until then of playing any active part in political life. Just as the masses of the lower middle class suddenly became interested in politics and crowded into Nazism, so sections of the educated classes felt compelled to play their part in public life. It was not Nazism but necessity that made these classes politically-minded and brought them into action – the necessity born of the inadequacy of the political leaders and the failure of essential problems to find a solution.

The ideas of these men, and the undeniable energy and vitality and devotion of some of them, carried away not a few of those who had their doubts of the movement. One had the feeling that may perhaps be described as revolutionary par excellence – the feeling that the opportunity had come for creative work to which it was worth while to devote one's whole life and strength.

There was a sudden awareness that they lived in a period when leadership was needed. Now note what tore them from their intellectual pursuits. See how it corresponds to the situation we have been following:

There were the disturbing signs of a new time – the masses, the growing collectivism, the growing primitiveness, the decline in spiritual standards, the sequelae of the more and more radical technical revolution, the change in men, the mechanization of life, the growth of gigantic industrial organizations. There were also the material changes, the efficacy of the new instruments of power, the senselessness of small territorial systems, the dwindling of space and time. There were the new means of amusement and edification, permitting an undreamed-of influencing of the subconscious mind of the masses. These means of amusement – wireless, cinema, sport and so on – turned into means of domination for those who could manipulate them.

All fixed standards had disappeared. It was particularly visible for them in the youth. Now note here the rejection of the old individuality, the rejection of the old social and ethical standards and the need for new ones.

These young people are no longer content with the relativity of all standards. They no longer feel it to be an enrichment of their lives to have access even to the remotest stimuli and truths. They demand fixed standards, unambiguous judgments. They demand a faith. They are different, too, in another critical point from us old people, for whom the individual personality was the central element in the passage through life. Compared with our sophistication, these young people are primitive. On the other hand, they are more definite and more active. We have had in Germany for a long time a sort of striving after "superpersonal realities." The "individualist age" is a despised one. These young people live, in a growing and growingly extreme measure, in reaction against intellectualism and sophistication. At first the movement was romantically pantheist. Then it went over to ideas of a new "organic" or rational association with the superpersonal realities of state, society, people, stock, race or class. Today all these ideological crutches are thrown aside, and the individual acknowledges the duty of absorption into the existing superpersonal reality of the new community of party, collectivity, state.

The intellectuals had discovered that the rationalism of the nineteenth century by which America lives today: science, industrial progress, individuality, opportunity, democracy, everything constantly getting better and better, they had discovered that this was finished. There was the need for a Christian basis instead of the enlightenment of rationalism. A "new political and intellectual elite," a "body of leaders who would throw down the frontier posts of the past party formations," this was needed. Thereby there would be restored the idea of human imperfection to replace the idea of human perfectibility which is the real utopianism. Place and status, accepted loyalties, established standards would be restored. Equilibrium and measure, the judge rather than the legislator would be the ruler.

The movement towards totalitarianism "either in the form of the state of social services and totalitarian democracy with an integral social and economic planning, or in that of the state of total mobilization with an unlimited imperialism" – this movement would be supplanted by "independent sectional spheres with the functions of order." This would mean the legitimizing, as it were, of the "indirect powers" that are burdensome to the state and lead it astray; in other words, making them joint holders of sovereignty. This might lead to a new equilibrium. It would be a "pluralist" community, decentralized corporations of "mutual help and self-administration."

All that stood in the way of this ideal was the masses. The masses refused to be led by these educated people.

We were simply forced by an elemental natural compulsion, to look about for a mass basis. . . .

They found it in the Nazi party. As Rauschning tells us, they reached the point of judging virtue by necessity. He asks:

Can you place yourself in that situation? What would have been your feelings, in such circumstances, in regard to the Nazi movement? You have certainly heard all sorts of objectionable things about it. You let them pass; you say to yourself: "They are young men; we will teach them. Not everything is as hot in the eating as in the cooking. Young birds of this sort learn to moult – to turn over a new leaf." You will add: "A very unsavory set of leaders, rowdies en masse among the old party comrades, and then that appalling program with its stupid paragraphs. But there is energy at the back of it, rhythm and new life. There are hundreds of thousands full of good will, of passionate devotion. That is political capital: it must not be squandered, it must be got into the right hands."

They felt that they had to "unite with a revolutionary element in order to attain the opposite of a revolution." They were determined to "get through this period of revolutionary Nazism as quickly as possible." "Many things could be achieved through the party's strong disciplining which without it might have ended disastrously." Again he gives us the key:

There was also the phenomenon of the masses. How was it to be got rid of as a political force and a menace to any political order? We hoped for help from Nazism in this. We proceded from the reflection that the masses can only be overcome through themselves. They must be made non-political by a mass movement, and then set limits to themselves, or, rather, give themselves a new form, in which they are no longer masses, but an articulated, ordered community, with a public function, though a restricted one.

I cannot stay to emphasize the points. But it is clear that the general picture he paints, the new social developments, are as like Modern America as it could be.

A Catholic Humanist tendency is one of the most active intellectual currents in the United States today. It centers around Robert Hutchins at Chicago University. It is not their neo-Thomism that is important, though no doubt it nourishes them. Hutchins and Adler are Americans. They have organized a militant humanism and they have taken it to the public in activities symbolized by their "hundred best books." They have had an immense influence on university education and they have fought the liberal rationalism of Dewey wherever they have met it. Hutchins proposes to "restore human dignity to the person." The latest step of the Chicago University Press is a series of publications, reissues of Kant, Early Theological Writings of Hegel, Cicero *(On Duty)*, etc., Leibnitz (it is to be noted that Kant was no Catholic). From neo-Thomism, through Cicero and Kant to their courses on "the hundred best books," the intellectual attack is comprehensive and vigorous and goes far beyond the bounds of a narrow doctrinal Catholicism.

Hutchins has recently issued the first number of a quarterly journal called *Measure*, whose essence may be summed up in the comment of one of the contributors, John U. Nef, a professor of Economic History and Chairman of the Committee on Social Thought at the University of Chicago:

It is the task of intellectual leadership to impress on the peoples of the earth a sense of their common humanity. By their nature, scientific inquiry, engineering and surgery are inadequate means to such an end. Intellectual leadership is a function of the thinker, the artist and the man of letters. Authority cannot perform this function; it can only suppress it.

We are not gods but men. Let us conform to our measure. Only by recognizing that human experience is by nature tragic, can we hope to make the overwhelmingly powerful engines science has given us instruments fit for human use.

Measure is published in cooperation with the Henry Regnery Publishing Co. and Regnery himself is a member of its Board of Editors. Since 1945 this publishing house has issued monthly pamphlets (the series was initiated by a pamphlet of Hutchins') and is also the sponsor of the Humanist Library which includes studies of Ortega y Gasset, best known for his work *The Revolt of the Masses*, and T. S. Eliot, best known of the lost generation intellectuals who found their way to the Catholic Church. They have international ties. Raymond Aron, who represents this tendency in France, has written a pamphlet for them. Many of the "educated class" which emigrated from Germany write for them. While most of the works noted above are written for the intellectual aristocracy, the same ideas are published in popular form through the Signet and Mentor pocket books. Among these are Whitehead's[3] *The Aims of Education*, J. W. N. Sullivan *The Limitations of Science*, two symposia on "The Christian Interpretation of World Problems," edited by William Scarlett, Bishop of Missouri (Protestant Episcopal Church), contributors to which include, among others, Victor Reuther, Sumner Welles, Anna Eleanor Roosevelt and Paul Hoffman. The best seller among the non-fiction titles[4] of this press appears to be *Human Destiny* by the biophysicist, Lecomte du Noüy. Du Noüy continues the tradition of the famous scientists, Eddington and Jeans, in using the limitations of science to prove religion. But whereas the work of the latter was mainly cosmological or limited to a metaphysical interpretation of the natural world, Du Noüy has extended this to a popular propaganda for the Christian solution to social problems. Moreover, he has pursued the Christian Humanist conception of moral education to the political conclusion of the need for leaders. He writes:

The task of correcting the deformations he has observed and of seeking the way to avoid them in the future devolves on the educated, moral and evolving man, *no matter what his profession.*

. . . we are obliged to fashion leaders, and, as intellectual qualities are not distributed equally, we must prepare two different methods for gaining access to consciences. The first must rest on the most plausible interpretation of scientific facts and on a precise knowledge of the goal to be attained. The second, on the knowledge of human psychology and on the preponderance of sentimental ideas. The first must be employed to prepare the teachers who will be responsible for the orientation of the coming generations. The second less intellectual and more emotional, will enable the leaders to reach the very heart of the masses.

It must be noted that this book, after its first publication by Longman's Green in 1947, was on the nation's best-seller lists for 18 months. It was enthusiastically reviewed by the religious and secular press, by philosophers, scientists and educators. Since its appearance in pocket book form, it has been sold in hundreds of thousands, perhaps millions of copies.

But the most significant member of this school for us is no less a person than Peter Drucker. Yes, Peter Drucker. As indictment it is difficult to exceed his detailed and comprehensive indictment of capitalist *production*. The propagandist strength of this current is that modern rationalism cannot stand up against it al all. As Rauschning said, looking at the rough, brutal Nazi youth:

Are they not, then, nearer, even in their error, to the real truth of a superpersonal order in human life, than we old and hard-boiled individualists and liberalists with all our lives centered in democratic freedom and in the arrogant assumption that we alone can represent democracy.

Now I have not the slightest intention of imputing a neo-Fascism or future Fascism to Hutchins, Drucker and the others I have mentioned. In fact I propose to impute to them, as far as I impute, the opposite, a great belief in democracy. The proposals of Drucker, in fact, in his book of 1943, were for decentralization and self-government, etc. What is important is that their German counterparts joined the Nazi movement because *they were looking for a mass basis to carry out their ideas which were absolutely useless otherwise.*

The masses, and above all, the workers, wanted a superpersonal ideology. The Catholic Humanists would give it to them but from above by means of the Nazi party. Who wishes to assert the sincerity of these Catholic and humanistic intellectuals can have it. What we should look at is the poverty, the miserable poverty of this humanistic conception which did not turn in immediate revolt from the barbarous inhuman evil that Nazism showed from its beginning. No, this doctrine offers nothing.

The current in America is, however, worth watching. America is not Germany nor France nor Italy. The appeal here will be not only to Catholic intellectuals but to many intellectuals, Protestant or atheistic, seeking some doctrine by which to shake themselves from the bankrupt nineteenth-century rationalism. In Europe where some parties that base themselves on some such doctrine have appeared and even won power as in Italy, they do nothing. They turn out to be just another of the old makeshift democratic parties that brought Europe to ruin. They live positively by American aid and negatively by anti-Communism. Neither of these can be looked upon as permanent commodities.

In America this intellectual current is flourishing and vigorous which means it feels some nourishment in the social subsoils. In a period of rapid social and political realignments it could be the rallying point of sizable political groupings. But it means nothing, is getting nowhere. It has to *join* something. And in his article in *Collier's* Drucker made it clear where his fine theories end: in the camp of the labor bureaucracy – and the labor bureaucracy because it is the only force in America so far which commands a social movement that does more than voting.

But that is not the only road for Catholic Humanism. In 1948 there was published by this very Chicago Press a book called *Ideas Have Consequences*, written by Richard Weaver who teaches in the college of the University. The jacket of the book, unlike the usual dignified blue and gray which distinguish the publications of this press, was a garish montage of such newspaper headlines as "Leap Kills Steel Scion," "Riot torn India free today," "Guns Roar in Palestine," "Jail 1000 Strikers," "Holy War Cry Grows," "100,000 Idle as Strikes Sweep U.S.," "Peace Jams Divorce Courts as War Marriages Explode." The jacket of the book also carries favorable comments by such intellectuals as Reinhold Niebuhr, John Crowe Ransom, Paul Tillich, Cleanth Brooks, Norman Forester. The latter's comment is particularly striking:

For thoughtful persons who do not know what to think – for those who are lost and are aware that they are lost – this is a book that will suggest some new anchorages.

The book itself is as serious a counter-revolutionary manifesto as I have seen in the United States. Its counter-revolutionary philosophy is exceedingly profound and consistent in its attack on nominalism (the philosophic basis of nineteenth-century rationalism), empiricism and materialism. It embodies a method of thought with deep historical roots in the most reactionary aspects of all the idealist philosophers and is as penetrating a summation of the conclusions of idealism as I have seen in the modern world. The author knows his subject and writes with a counter-revolutionary drive which draws all those who hate the masses together into a theoretical center. All that we have deduced from analyzing the logical course of Mayo, Hutchins, Drucker, Mumford, and the others, is here made explicit and removed from the realm of speculation.

Weaver begins with the modern world:

First, one must take into account the deep psychic anxiety, the extraordinary prevalence of neurosis, which makes our age unique. The typical modern has a look of the hunted. He senses that we have lost our grip upon reality. This, in turn, produces disintegration, and disintegration leaves impossible that kind of reasonable prediction by which men, in eras of sanity, are able to order their lives. And the fear accompanying it unlooses the great disorganizing force of hatred, so that states are threatened and wars ensue. Few men today feel certain that war will not wipe out their children's inheritance; and even if this evil is held in abeyance, the individual does not rest easy, for he knows that the Juggernaut technology may twist or destroy the pattern of life he has made for himself. . . .

Added to this is another deprivation. Man is constantly being assured today that he has more power than ever before in history, but his daily experience is one of powerlessness. Look at him today somewhere in the warren of a great city. If he is with a business organization, the odds are great that he has sacrificed every other kind of independence in return for that dubious one known as financial. Modern social and corporate organization makes independence an expensive thing; in fact, it may make common integrity a prohibitive luxury for the ordinary man, as Stuart Chase has shown. Not only is this man likely to be a slave at his place of daily toil, but he is cribbed, cabined and confined in countless ways, many of which are merely devices to made possible physically the living together of the masses. Because these are deprivations of what is rightful, the end is frustration, and hence the look upon the faces of those whose souls have not already become miniscule, of hunger and unhappiness.

The quotation, again, is long but it is necessary to realize how passionately Weaver views the actuality, in order to appreciate how all-embracing are his conclusions. Starting from this actuality, Weaver has made an analysis of its philosophical roots in nominalism (William of Occam) and the rejection of the Platonic conception of the reality of ideas. He repudiates even Aristotle's conceptualism which attributes reality to both matter and form. He calls for a return to the One from the Many – the totalitarian doctrine of the German philosopher, Schelling. He seeks to restore dualism or a wedge between the material and the transcendental, with the latter dominant. Upon these methodological conceptions, he bases his more popular philosophy of a need to return to a confession of guilt, a recognition of obscenity, a restoration of piety.

His hostility to the workers as seeking to emerge from their difficulties is absolute, although framed in the ideology of hostility to their fragmentation in modern industry. Labor, he says, is a prayer, it is therapeutic. The trouble with the modern world is that it bases itself on the idea that the world owes the worker a living, it worships comfort, it promises security, it does not enforce discipline. We have to return to the idea that strikes are "conspiracies."

Demagogic leaders have told the common man that he is entitled to much more than he is getting; they have not told him the less pleasant truth that, unless there is expropriation – which in any case is only a temporary resource – the increase must come out of greater productivity. Now all productivity requires discipline and subordination; the simple endurance of toil requires control of passing desire.

He hates the middle classes and makes them responsible for the materialism and utilitarianism which dominate modern life. With this is coupled an attack on finance capital, liberalism, civil liberties, the modern press, radio and movies.

He shows every sign of hostility to Negroes. Throughout his book, as he propagandizes for a return to hierarchy, he employs the words "discrimination" and "measure," not specifically against the Negroes but as a means of enforcing superiority rather than equality. He attacks jazz, linking it with the Negroes' "spontaneity," with "formally repudiating restraint by intellect and by expressing contempt and hostility towards our traditional society. . . Jazz sounds often as if in a rage to divest itself of anything that suggests structure or confinement." His hostility to jazz extends even to Beethoven because of the latter's sympathy for the French Revolution and because of his "introduction of dynamism and strains of individualism" into music.

Weaver is against an equalitarianism in society as a whole or betwen the sexes. He is opposed to democracy and calls for an aristocracy, of the hero, of the soldier and the priest, and of a caste like the old Southern aristocracy. He calls for woman's return to the home and family while praising her "superior closeness to nature, her intuitive realism, her unfailing ablity to detect the sophistry in mere intellectuality." His dislike for democracy extends to the American frontiersmen because they threw off restraints. He attacks Mark Twain for his anti-conventionalism and admires the Founding Fathers insofar as they resisted too great democratization. His heroes are Nietzsche, Kierkegaard, Peguy, Spengler, Rauschning, Ortega y Gasset, Milton (insofar as the latter was for an elite) and Cromwell, for the same reason.

Fraternity, according to Weaver, must supplant equality.

The ancient feeling of brotherhood carries obligations of which equality knows nothing. It calls for respect and protection, for brotherhood is status in family, and family is by nature hierarchical. The essence of cooperation is *congeniality*, the feeling of having been "born together."

Weaver is not writing for the sake of analysis only. He says:

Because we are now committed to a program which has practical applications, we must look for some rallying-point about which to organize. We face the fact that our side has been in retreat for four hundred years without, however, having been entirely driven from the field.

The central slogan of this program?

One corner is yet left. When we survey the scene to find something which the rancorous leveling wind of utilitarianism has not brought down, we discover one institution, shaken somewhat but still strong and perfectly clear in its implication. This is the right of private property, which is, in fact, the last metaphysical right remaining to us. The ordinances of religion, the prerogatives of sex and of vocation, all have been swept away by materialism, but the relationship of a man to his own has until the present largely escaped attack.

How fleeting would be such a program for the restoration of private property we have seen under Hitler. The conception, closely linked to regionalism and decentralization, is also aimed at inspiring the agricultural middle classes. What stands out in Weaver's book is rather his appeal for "some passionate reaction," the deadly seriousness of his statement:

We have to inform the multitude that restoration comes at a price.

The aim of this restoration is discipline and hierarchy, "political authority regularly into the hands of the wise," "some source of authority," "some center," "the virtue of subordinating self to communal enterprise." Weaver's hostility to Russia is based, not upon its totalitarianism, its discipline and its elite (which he praises) but his conviction that it too caters to the principles of comfort and freedom from want, whereas for Weaver "freedom from want and fear would reduce man to an invertebrate."

I have gone into Weaver's book in such detail because (1) he begins where every serious thinker must begin today, with the alienation in society; (2) takes a consistent philosophical position and calls for a "passionate reaction" based upon this position; (3) is evidently a rallying-point for such intellectuals as Niebuhr, Ransom and Brooks who have given favorable notice to his book; and finally (4) because he is clearly an American Rauschning who would have no hesitation in linking himself up with any mass movement which promises to discipline the masses whom he hates so violently. It is absolute blindness not to see that with America as it is, as we have described it, any serious dislocation of the unstable existing system would result in the unleashing here of the passions of which this book is a philosophical presentation.

The third intellectual current in Europe is the most important of the three. It is the movement which we know today as the Cominform. It is the most important not only for Europe and the rest of the world, but for the United States. But here we must be careful. The United States at present and in the foreseeable future is not in any danger from the Cominform or its American representatives. It is not only that the F.B.I. and the labor bureaucracy have purged them from the labor movement and instituted a reign of terror over them. In unions like the U.A.W. and the N.M.U. the workers saw them go gladly, being sick of their gangsterism, their manipulation of the union for their own purposes, their duplicity, their shamelessness. Stalinism in the shape of a party of the Cominform is no serious contender for power in the United States. But what Stalinism represents in the world is not dead in the United States and only the analysis of Stalinism in Europe will help us.

What is this monstrous apparition now ruling or controlling some 800 million people, and so powerful in key countries like Italy and France? The answers do not come pat.

The Russian Revolution and the parties of the Communist International in the early days were a great revolutionary upheaval and social manifestation that sought to reorganize the world along the lines, economic and social-humanistic, of traditional Communism. By 1929 the Russian Revolution had been radically transformed, and capitalism from 1924–9 seemed to have embarked upon a new prosperity. But the crisis of 1929 coming after the war and the revolutions of 1917–23 hit the world like a thunderbolt. The perspective of a satisfactory system under capitalism collapsed in Europe and today is kept alive only because of American injections. But the failures in 1917–21, the transformation of the Russian Revolution, the brutal nature of the dictatorship, posed the social question in a new form. What exactly was the future of Europe? What did the proletariat have to offer in *economic* development? The first Russian five-year plan awakened enormous interest and side by side with the collapse of Europe, the well-propagandized successes of the plan turned the minds of masses and intellectuals alike towards Russia. The dictatorship was excused on account of the economic successes. The *political* issue for Europe hung on Germany, where the Communist Party with at one time nearly 450,000 members seemed on the verge of seizing power and opening the victory of Communism on a continental scale. Vast millions in Europe on the whole, workers and intellectuals alike, were ready to follow a victory in Germany. Then came the catastrophe, collapse before Hitler, the rise and spread of Fascism and the threat of war.

Few writers on Europe have grasped what then took place in Europe, the climax of the terrible experiences of the twenty years from 1914 to 1933. The conception of proletarian dictatorship as an uprising of the masses, workers councils, societs, socialism as a form of democracy deeper and more extensive than capitalism, this began to disappear from the minds of writers and theorists everywhere except for small political minorities. Planned economy became the synonym for socialism, and the struggle between Russia and Germany became the symbol of the political struggle for Europe. *Soviet Communism* by Sidney and Beatrice Webb, 1934, symbolized the new stage, both in its conception and its reception. The plan was the thing. Freedom would come after.

From that time through all the twists and turns of policy, Popular Front, Stalin–Hitler Pact, it became more and more clear that there were new social types emerging in Europe and the world. The most characteristic was the Stalinist Party-man, functionary or labor leader. It is perfectly obvious today that he was no repetition of the old Social-Democracy. He was and is the mortal enemy of private capitalism and the outstanding representatives of the old bourgeois class. He sought above all to influence the workers and he spent his life among them – he knew where the sources of his power lay. He was ready to nationalize the capitalist property when he could do so safely.

But he was no revolutionary of the school of Marx and Lenin and Trotsky. He did not believe in the mass uprising, in socialism or communism as an expression of the release of vast creative social energies in the great mass of the population. For him the masses were rank and file soldiers, workers to be led and disciplined and planned. He did not depend upon them to seize power, not in Europe. His source of real power was the Stalinist regime and the Red Army. He depended upon them for victory. (Not even in America do the Communists believe in any uprising by the American workers. They depend solely on the idea of defeat of America by the Red Army, and then aided by the Red Army, the tremendous prestige of Communism victorious over the world, to seek communist allies and impose their domination on the American people.)

This European Communist joined with the bourgeoisie or opposed the bourgeoisie as was convenient and necessary for Russia, for without Russia he conceived himself as lost. He was not and is not a venal person. He is a man animated by a doctrine, the abolition of private property, the creation of a world state, beginning with Europe, planning the economy, disciplining the workers, totalitarian. That is his summation of the experiences of 30 years. He lives for this and dies for it. There is no duplicity, cruelty, assassination of character or person, betrayal of a nation (looking forward to winning it back after) which he will not commit. That is precisely what happened in Spain. The great masses of the workers and peasants in Spain in 1936 revolted with the most violent social upheaval the world has yet seen. Workers, peasants and many middle-class elements simply took over every-thing in at least two-thirds of Spain. But the Communists invaded Spain in force, and in accordance with their larger plan of supporting the democratic countries, i.e. whoever would ally with Russia, against Fascism, at that time Germany, Italy and Japan, they devoted their main efforts to the destruction of the Spanish Revolution.

This is the type of labor leader and party functionary or party man who was destined to become the new leadership of the decisive elements among the workers. We did not know then, but we have no excuse for not knowing now that great numbers of labor leaders, technicians, administrative types and intellectuals who seemed devoted to democracy, faced with a serious crisis, would go with them, accepting their monstrous doctrine as the next stage of human society.

The analysis we have made in early chapters of the crisis in American society applies (with all the necessary historical complexity) to Europe with added problems of long historical origin. Europe has been crying for years for organization, nationally and internationally. A society creates, i.e. by the very fact of its existence, shapes certain types of personalities to its needs. The technicians, sick at the chaos in industry, the administrative supervising types, all those who could see that capitalism in Europe had nothing more to offer, knew the corruption and bankruptcy of the old ruling classes, and feared or hated or despised Fascism, looked upon the Stalinists sympathetically and in the crisis of 1944 rushed to join them in France and Italy, and it must be insisted upon, the Social-Democracy and the vast majority of the union leaders were prepared to go along.

The European intellectuals in France and Italy poured into and around the Stalinist Party. Americans who have any illusions about this should cease shouting at Stalinism as if it were some loathsome disease that educated people caught by accident. The intellectuals, for whom Existentialism and Catholic Humanism are the only alternatives to Gaullism, *accept* Stalinism and Stalinism in power will win over, intimidate and bludgeon the majority into acceptance.

From their base in the working class (we shall take this up in a moment), these men of plan and totalitarian power offer the intellectuals today posts in their vast party and union apparatus; tomorrow they promise places in the bureaucracy and power. They know the Existentialist tendency and the helplessness of these intellectuals well. They know that they are caught between the bureaucratic organizations which run society and the bureaucratically dominated workers' organizations below. They know their feeling of impotence, their need to *do* something, to make contact with some reality that is *effective*.

The Stalinists tell them: either link your fate to the working class and *especially to its vanguard*, or face personal disintegration. Roger Garaudy, member of the French National Assembly and Stalinist leader, has written a pamphlet *Literature of the Graveyard* with this as its main thesis. He tells the intellectuals: You need a faith; we give you one in the common man. You feel the need for creative construction? We give you Stalinist Russia where everybody is engaged in developing the productive forces. You need a chain into which your personal action can fit? We give you the party. You need to get out of your study. Our program is activism for all the progressive forces. Break with us and there is nowhere you can go – except to the Existentialists, confessing that your personality has disintegrated – or to another movement like the Gaullists.

They do not hide their totalitarian aims and methods at all. In France in

1948 there was an open discussion about the freedom of discussion which the intellectuals can enjoy in the party. Casanova, a French Stalinist, writing about the responsibilities of the Communist intellectuals, says:[5]

To remain modest before the party, that is not to debase yourself. Personal recognition of the party for all that it gives and makes of each one – this very simple sentiment cultivated by the thousands of militants – can be avowed *shamelessly* before the others. Self-respect is naturally contained therein.

He concludes:

Rally around all the ideological and political positions of the working class, defend under all circumstances and with the utmost resolution *all the positions of the party,* safeguard our sense of sufficiency, cultivate in ourselves *the love of the party* in its most conscious form, *the spirit of the party,* and give to the proletariat the *supplementary reasons and the new justifications* which you can lend it by your more probing work. Then "an immense field of free initiative and of free creation will open before all those who can master these prerequisites to all science, all art, in this stage of social development."

This is the doctrine plain and straight. Look again at the words emphasized. They mean, shut up, do not question, accept the Moscow line, use your knowledge to go and find "supplementary" reasons and "new" justifications why what we tell you is correct, go and look in art, literature, history, science, for proof that we are right, the *we* being the party men. And this they say before they have the power. The French intellectuals know what they are in for and take it.

This brazen but absolutely confident doctrine answers very powerful needs in these intellectuals, needs which the party expresses and consciously cultivates. The intellectuals feel accumulated in themselves tremendous knowledge, science, technique, means. They have to fasten on to certain social purposes and ends. The rationalistic premises of their scientific method make them hostile to the Catholic Humanists. And in the party they find all the vulgar materialist ends of power over nature, social relations and a science of man.

Burgum (author, *The Novel and the World's Dilemma*), *an American intellectual who helps edit Science and Society,* expresses it very simply. There are pessimist writers like Hemingway, Joyce, Kafka; and then there are optimists like Whitman. What must distinguish modern optimism, however, is the stress on the need to achieve democracy, not by easy and assured triumph but by a struggle between liberalism and reaction, between the majority and the minority. Isolation and the quest for quixotic perfection must be supplanted by "warm contact" and "immediate activity."

The Stalinists offer these intellectuals "energy, violence and a humanitarian conviction," "the complete sense of security of the man who has made a decisive acquisition, the validity of which is guaranteed each day in practice" (Garaudy). The alternative, they never fail to point out, is the "unhappy and dual conscience of a Radek or a Bukharin." "If my joining the Communist Party is the beginning of my freedom, my betrayal would be the beginning of my agony." Through "adherence and creation," through positivism as contrasted with scepticism, by joining with the martyrs who die for a cause, by link to a collective workshop, by losing yourself in social enthusiasm, you will find yourself.

The terrible thing about this doctrine is that, philosophically, there is not the slightest thing that is *new* about it. It is the old rationalism with which Descartes ushered in the age of individualism, control by man over nature, inevitable progress, etc., though in his day and for centuries, especially against feudal and aristocratic obscurantism, it played a great role. But it placed body and mind in separate compartments, i.e. the mass of ordinary men on one side and intellect, knowledge, science, method, on the other. It heralded the division of the human personality by the industrial processes of capitalism which has now reached the extraordinary stage that it has all over the world. The Stalinists have not the slightest use for totally integrated social man as the unit, economic and political, of a completely new reorganization of society. They, without pretence, seek to join the intellectual as intellectual to the worker as worker. They consciously set out to build a party and a mighty bureaucratic structure in which intellectuals and intelligentsia and leaders of labor and official propagandists will use science, knowledge, etc. to plan. This huge structure will rest upon the backs of the workers who will be moved here, there or wherever necessary "according to plan." They do not pretend that there will be anything democratic about this regime. They know that it will be held together by iron bands, the bands of the army and the secret police. In country after country, when they have entered, it has been noticed that they find some of their best cadres among the Fascists, Iron Guardists, police and army of authoritarian or fascist regimes. These regimes will collapse ultimately. They solve neither economic, social nor psychological problems. They integrate the personality by destroying it altogether. They destroy the very basis of progress in the productivity of labor; the police state is an economic burden and a psychological cancer. But before they are destroyed, they will cost humanity much, for they are not accidents; they are the desperate attempt to resolve antagonisms which have matured and for generations now are tearing at each other in every sphere of society.

To understand the Stalinists as a social manifestation, we must exclude the idea that they are leaders of the proletarian masses in revolution. They will fight civil war in China, in Indo-China, in the Malay States, i.e. after a great war in peasant countries, when they are certain that there is no possibility of intervention by any great power such as America. But in 1923 they refused to lead the German workers; they had nothing to do with the general strikes in England where they had little power; in 1933 they collapsed before Hitler, and in Germany they had mighty forces. They played no part in the initial uprising in Spain which took place against their wishes and they joined it only to suppress it. They played no part in the fighting of February 17, 1934, when Paris was saved from the Fascists by workers in the streets; they were taken by surprise in the sit-down strikes in France in 1936 and were active in bringing it to an end; despite the great forces at their command in 1927 they capitluated to Chiang Kai-shek. Revolution as Cromwell, the French revolutionaries of 1789, Marx, Lenin, etc. understood it, that is entirely foreign to them. They are men of a *resistance* movement in war, but they and the Red Army massacred the Warsaw Resistance Movement in 1944 because Polish workers and peasants had made it entirely clear that they aimed at a socialist Poland, independent of Anglo-American influence and of Russia. They seized power in Eastern Europe under the protection of the Red Army. Elsewhere as in Italy and France, they have lost influence because workers are sick and tired of their perpetual chatter about revolution when they obviously don't mean it. Their "peace policy" is in reality a war policy, a preparation for a war they believe inevitable. They will seize Paris and Rome but the Red Army must be there. In Czechoslovakia, when they did move into action, they carefully hand-picked action committees, sent them out on tasks, and when they came back, dismissed them.

The great masses they led in Italy and France in the immense parties and in the unions find in them an obstacle and a source of tremendous confusion. For a vast revolutionary concentration like 2.5 millions of people in Italy are a natural outcome of modern society and the collapse of Fascism. If there had not been a single Communist in Italy, it would have taken place just the same, in the same way as it took place in Spain in 1936. The Communists are on the alert to place themselves always at the head of these tremendous social upheavals. But their long record shows exactly what they represent, men who have been educated and trained in a collapsing capitalist world and have broken with it, but, after the experience of 1914–34, no longer believe in mass uprisings, workers rule, etc., which they consider Utopian. They are prepared to create order out of chaos, plan economy, rule and discipline workers, and for *this* they understand that they need Russia and the Red Army. Hence their blind obedience to the Kremlin. They are the fully conscious men of the centralized bureaucratized totalitarian solution to the fundamental problems of the day.

The above is a rough analysis based upon many years of observation of Stalinists of various types in different parts of the world and a reasonably close study of their writings. I wish to repeat here that we are dealing with intellectual currents and we are seeking intellectual currents in Europe to understand intellectual currents in the United States and also the social forces they represent, although these intellectual currents have not fully appeared as yet in the United States. The reader must bear in mind what we have written about the Catholic Humanists, how vigorous they are in the United States and *what they did in Europe*. Here there has very recently been published a book by A. Rossi, *A Communist Party in Action*. This book has been written by an ex-Stalinist in France who has observed them very closely both from the inside and from the outside. Now as you read, note whom the Communist Party appeals to and why.

Rossi makes it clear that the working class does not form the nucleus of the Communist Party in France. The party agitates the workers:

It *does* midwife . . . working class demands. It *does* in backing up those demands vigorously play the championship role that the other parties . . . fail to claim for themselves. . . . It *does* in this way maintain close contact with the workers. But this is not the aspect of the party's strategy that wins it the hard core of militants who are notoriously drawn from elements . . . who do not need to have their interests defended in the manner which is described.

The men whom the Stalinists attract are:

. . . men who in large part because of the relatively high standard of living they enjoy have developed a high degree of awareness vis-à-vis the social and economic situation in which they are caught up. They are men who have come to realize the alienation of the working class from French society, i.e. the fact that the workers under the French capitalist system are treated as a commodity. They are men who have gained insight into the necessity of escaping from the position of inferiority that alienation implies, have sensed the central importance of the question of property and the question of power, and have caught a glimpse of the values that may one day restore men to a French life. . . . The party . . . knows how to play upon the hopes and anticipations concerning the future dignity of men and while it puts these anticipations to work for ends that are not really theirs, it keeps them convinced that their fidelity to it is their fidelity to what is best in themselves.

Rossi has observed closely the dilemma of the French intellectuals:

The French intellectual of our time is, for one thing, weary of not being able to take sides on the big problems of modern society. He is for another thing eager to shake off his feelings of inferiority in the presence of the men of action. The role he has been trained to play is that of doubt, that of constant readiness to reopen any question, that of never permitting oneself any but the most tentative conclusions. . . . Taking orders from the party leaders, knuckling under to party discipline gives him a

welcome sense of certainty.
What apparently strikes his fancy in Marxism is its emphasis upon offering simple explanations for everything.

The predilections of the intellectual is for "general ideas" and he has a "fondness for schematization" which he finds in the Stalinist doctrines. The intellectual feels isolated. The party caters to its members' "primitive or if you like, basic need to belong." Hence the party tends to thrive in societies whose members are no longer held together by the bonds of "moral principle and purpose."

Where unity can be had on no other terms men finally seek it in some political movement that is able and willing to impose it.

The party does not ask the intellectuals, as party men to give up their professions. In fact, they are encouraged to retain academic positions which lend prestige to the party. But it gives these intellectuals a feeling of contact with the mass.

As a party dignitary he discovers in himself an orator capable of evoking wild applause at great party meetings.

Rossi goes into detail about the organization of the party nuclei to go to the masses and "become the mouthpiece of the popular dissatisfaction, the tribunes of the people." Using these militants as a core, it seeks to mobilize the masses into committees in all quarters and in every sphere. It makes inseparable French politics and Soviet politics, uses the Red Army and the Soviet Union as a vital center, combines immediate agitation against profiteers and capitalists, emphasizing the betrayal of France by these elements, together with promises of a march to world revolution by the Soviet Union and the Red Army. It has taken over the French tradition of Descartes, and appeals to the intellectuals to play the same role for France today as the intellectuals of the Enlightenment did for the French Revolution. Rossi describes how the French Communist Party, scorned by the Comintern before 1930, became a mass force after the Depression hit France about 1930 and with its Popular Front policy in 1935 acquired a base in the petty-bourgeoisie.
Rossi has observed the French Stalinist intellectuals well but his conclusion reveals that the French intellectual who repudiates Stalinism is in imminent danger of falling into the camp of DeGaullism. He calls upon the workers to "put less emphasis on the class struggle, emphasize the community interest," and "adapt this general interest as their program and accept the building of the community as a responsibility that they share with all

their fellow-men." His final words:

This means first of all attacking that sickness in the minds and hearts of its sons who must relearn the human values that are France's most precious possession – and the gauge of its greatness.

The translation of Rossi's book into English was made by a former functionary of the American State Department, Wilmore Kendall, who also writes an introduction to the text. Kendall praises Rossi for his insights into the compulsions which push the French intellectuals towards the Stalinists:

Above all, his point is never how wicked they are, how inconsistent, how shamelessly they are willing to follow the latest shifts in party line.

From his study of Rossi he advises the Americans:

We are very wide of the mark indeed when in planning the means for combatting the growth of the Communist movement, we fix attention more than incidentally upon the data of the economists, the size of the national income, the distribution of that income, the ownership of property, or rely more than incidentally upon the skills of the economist.

What alternatives does he offer? He refers to Weaver, whom we have quoted so extensively above, because the latter has recognized the need for a moral purpose in society.

The character of the existing political communities that renders necessary their transformation (because it creates the strategic opportunities that the communists exploit) is their purposelessness, their failure to make demands upon their members, i.e. their inability to infuse meaning into their members' lives.

And finally, he comes to the same conclusion in politics that Mayo came to in industry:

The skills we need in the struggle against the Communist movement are clearly those of which Plato and Rousseau called the Legislator, i.e. those of the political theorists whose business we should define with them of building the political community whose members willingly accept a single belief-system.

Here is an American intellectual who has observed Stalinism in Europe, studied it, is not unaware of its barbarities and its corruption, and to combat it, he proposes precisely that conception of an intellectual elite which the Stalinists have cultivated and express, and "a single belief-system" administered by that elite. This member of the American administrative hierarchy, repudiating the concept of economic man, is immediately tempted by its complementary opposite, the totalitarianism of modern idealism.

The American intellectual does not today face the temptations of Stalinism in its outer form, in the historical dress it has so far assumed. And the reason is not far to seek. The decisive cadres of Stalinism have appeared in Western Europe in countries which, in the Stalinist view, are unable to stand by themselves. They guide all their politics by the needs of Russia, the power strong enough to dominate Europe, suppress the masses and fight off a rival imperialism. In the colonial countries of the Far East, similarly, Stalinism is powerful for the same reason – the leaders of native revolutions fear isolation. But now that there are no longer many illusions about Russia and the arena is being cleared for the world struggle between Russia and America, labor leaders and intellectuals in America, above all places, have no need for the Cominform *for they have no need for the protection or assistance of Russia*. They live in a country fully able to take care of itself and initiate world policy, not submit to it. There was a time when some were attracted to Stalinism because they saw it as a revolutionary force in Europe and the enemy of Hitlerism. That is not so any longer.

But, it is necessary to repeat, these intellectuals face the same basic social problems, and if the Existentialists and the Catholic Humanists are in the United States, the Stalinist type labor leader and intellectual is here also.

Begin with today. As labor leaders, Murray and Lewis are at opposite poles. John L. Lewis rules his union and his immediate subordinates with an iron hand. But it is not generally known that Murray has the same authoritarian grip upon his own union. He addresses his wage-committee of hundreds of men like a little fuehrer. N.M.U. rank and filers fought a desperate battle to defeat the Stalinists, but on installing Curran as leader, he immediately turned around and aided by police and goon squads made a shambles of his opponents high and low, in a way the Stalinists had never dared to do. Dave Beck, a labor czar on the West Coast and second to Tobin in the teamsters' union, has no truck with democracy at all, but is liked by many industrialists for the iron discipline he maintains over the workers. Reuther spares no pains and ceaselessly cuts away at the splendid democratic traditions of the U.A.W. In the C.I.O as a whole, we repeat, the brutality and the ruthlessness of the purge of the Stalinists is unprecedented, absolutely unprecedented, in the history of labor except in Stalinist countries.

These American labor leaders, as far as the workers are concerned, *today already* show every sign that, given the necessary circumstances, they will control the workers with as iron a discipline as the Stalinists. In fact, as far as discipline and authoritarian control are concerned, this writer would like to know exactly what are the differences between Curran, Dave Beck, on the one hand, and the Stalinists on the other.

254 Negroes, Women and the Intellectuals

But the American labor leaders are now only at the beginning of their career. At present, Reuther, for example, is always bowing and scraping before Justice Douglas, young Roosevelt, and others like these who come down and address the union on ceremonial occasions, gaining political prestige for themselves and helping Reuther to keep the restless workers quiet in the Democratic Party. We repeat: nobody today wants to rock the boat for no one knows what lies around the bend. But Reuther, for example, is no Samuel Gompers, nor is he any Sidney Hillman. If, as is likely, he succeeds Murray as President of the C.I.O., his career will only then be really beginning. Given economic crisis, or an intense social dislocation, the stratum that Reuther represents will not perpetually hand around cap in hand to liberal politicians who are today dependent upon labor. The next stage is political power.

There is no need for any great argument here. The simple way to approach it is negatively. Who believes that the present political alignments will continue indefinitely? No one. For if people believed that, there would be no crisis or sense of crisis. America is now vulnerable from economic crisis, the conflict between capital and labor, and the whole quivering world situation. Labor has emerged in every part of the world as a *political* force. It is not possible to believe that the most powerful labor force in the world, surrounded to the eyes by crises of all types and entangled in politics, national and international, will not *have* to act. Unlike *Life* in its analysis of Reuther, I am not speaking of his *personal* plans, though he and numerous others, labor leaders and liberals, have repeatedly declared that they favor a labor party – when the time is ripe. The basis of my conclusions is the objective situation. They will act only when impelled, but act they will or forfeit their leadership of the workers and that they will not do. But the more they are projected into political action, the more necessary it is, it will be, for them to discipline the workers in industry, to purge the unions of opponents like X, to control the right to strike, to build the bureaucratic machine and to rule. In Britain a workers movement long disciplined by unions and a political party, has been handled with extreme skill and yet, without American aid, Britain today would be in chaos. But the basic tensions in American life, the temper, the passions, the violence, have never been disciplined at all. The C.I.O. was formed to give the workers mastery in the shops. As we saw, the strikes are chiefly periodical explosions of intolerable rage and anger. The labor leadership has no alternative but on the one hand, to lead labor and the Negroes, small farmers, youth, old people and the middle class who will go with it, and at the same time, in the face of a total social crisis and international disorder, *discipline* the turbulent force in its rear. *That discipline* is the condition of any success it can have with the rest of the population.

What of the intellectuals? *They have to go alone.* They have no analysis, no perspective. They fastened on to Roosevelt, they believed that here

America would perhaps show a way to the rest of the world. They know better now. But the terror they are in was shown by the crisis which broke out among them before the 1948 elections, not only when reading but believing the big press (which it was clear the masses of the people did *not* do). They screamed for General Eisenhower, not party men like Jimmy Roosevelt who think in terms of power, but liberal intellectuals, economists, publicists, thinkers; these men did not know the General's politics nor his ideas on anything. The General said nothing and there was no need for him to say anything because he said he was not a candidate; as far as I can remember his only statement on public issues was made in his capacity as a soldier that he was opposed to equality in the army for Negroes. But the liberal intellectuals chased after him until he brushed them and all other importunities aside. Today the man they were hoping would save them from the Republican Party is the most effective proponent of Republican politics. Contrast this with the manner in which the great mass of the population, battered by press, radio and pollsters, kept its mouth shut, went its way and gave a victory to the party which in its eyes represented "the people."

Nothing new, no new doctrine is coming from these intellectuals. They are destined for a parallel fate to that of the intellectuals, organizers and administrative elements in Europe in relation to the Communist Party. They will attach themselves to the labor bureaucracy and bring all their science, knowledge, etc. to assist the labor leadership in building a mighty bureaucratic centralized apparatus, to resist extreme reactionaries and die-hards, on the one hand, and above all, on behalf of the interests of labor, to discipline labor, so as to organize and to plan. This is not a concrete prophecy. But it is a line of direction. By the complicated ways history works, with all the unpredictable complexity of actual events, with all the differences between the traditions of Stalinism and the United States, with the great conflicts which would retard the movement here, only to project it violently forward there, and vice versa, despite all this, the inevitable direction of society as it is, is towards the vast centralized bureaucratic state in which labor leaders and intellectuals of all types will form a solid governmental mass, controlling labor in the factories, administering the state, with vast resources and power to influence press and radio, controlling the armed forces and the F.B.I. The reader who doubts this should spend a few minutes comparing the Federal Government in 1932 with what it is today.

There is of course another alternative. Republicans and the great industrialists may attempt to impose themselves and their conceptions upon the government and the people, either by electoral means or by force. Electorally they seem unlikely to succeed. If they attempt it by force, it means civil war. But whatever the outcome, the end will be a massive centralized bureaucratic state directing the national life. Many liberal intellectuals will make their peace with and join such a state of the most authoritarian type. James

Burnham, a former active Trotskyite, now preaches a doctrine of suppressing Russian Communism and its satellites by force and imposing the American way on the world. Their ideas are not important. But Burnham visited Malraux, DeGaulle's right-hand man, had conversations with him, in which Burnham found a surprising lot to agree with; which is particularly strange, for few people in France know what are DeGaulle's policies except that this Fascist aims at power and disciplining the French people. But Burnham published these conversations in the *Partisan Review*, a magazine of the literary left, was mildly rebuked by one of the editors, and continues to write in the review and be one of its editorial directors.

So the majority of the intellectuals drift along, knocking from pillar to post and finding themselves in the strangest places. They can tell no one anything, for they have no coherent ideas on anything. Let us conclude with a glimpse at one of the best of them. He is Robert Lynd, a deservedly world-famous *sociologist* (note this), obviously very able, passionate, sincere and courageous. He attended an education conference of the U.A.W. and made an address which has attracted attention. Here are some extracts to give some idea of its tone and content. Note the prefatory remarks by Victor Reuther:

It has stimulated discussion throughout the union and has given an increasing number of wage earners in the shops where our union is organized an insight into the workings of government and economics that has enabled them to make connections and to acquire understandings of events which they believe to be fruitful.

Lynd begins:

What all of us who are interested in labor are after is to make our economy deliver all of those goods and social securities that a twentieth-century economy can deliver; and that a democratic nation's economy must deliver if the nation is to pretend to call itself a democracy. The difference between a generation ago and now is that today we *know* that national planning will work; that it can give us high-level full employment year after year in peacetime, and social security for all our people at all of the exposed points in life; and that we can plan democratically. The United States can do these things now provided it is willing to do what it takes to plan democratically. The question we all face is: Will it do what it takes?

Now note where he sees the main danger:

In respect of the handling of both organized labor and government, it is highly probable that American business leaders learned directly from what they saw their German opposite numbers do. Big industry in Germany brought Hitler and his Nazis in power in order to break the power of German labor and to free German industry from the rising burdens of regulation by a democratic government and of taxation for social legislation. German capitalism in trouble was showing the way which capitalism, in trouble all over the world, was to take. This involved the recognition that, in the tightening pressures of the twentieth century – between nations internationally, and internally within each nation between industry and labor – the economic and political systems of a nation have got to work together. National states cannot afford anything less than maximum efficiency in their economic affairs, while national economies require strong and continuous backing from the state apparatus. For the economic and political systems to try to coerce, and thus frustrate each other step by step, has become too inefficient, unreliable and nationally dangerous. And, once a big advanced industrial nation like Germany had shown the way to ease its pressures by linking up industry and government, the business leaders in other nations began to follow.

Either democracy will move in on our private economy, socialize it and run it for the purposes of democracy, or big business will move in on the democratic state, take it over, and run the whole works for the profit of big business.

What has organized labor got to put up against this? Mark you, these men who are doing this thing are not fascists – yet. They're patriotic Americans, and the Nazis and the big German manufacturers were patriotic Germans. William Allen White, the well-known Kansas editor who died five or six years ago, said of these same men as he watched them clawing and jockeying for war contracts in Washington in 1943: "For the most part, these managerial magnates are decent, patriotic Americans. . . . If you touch them in nine relations of life out of ten, they are kindly, courteous, Christian gentlemen. But in the tenth relation, where it touches their own organization, they are stark mad, ruthless, unchecked by God or man; paranoics, in fact, as evil in their design as Hitler."

What does Lynd propose?

If labor is to seize the intiative, I am convinced that it has got to go political. And I don't mean reward your friends and punish your enemies. I mean go political all out and through and through. I mean a labor party.

National planning is a powerful democratic weapon lying open to your hands. Business won't touch democratic planning, for that is the thing it is fighting and the last thing it wants.

And he concludes:

I believe liberal democracy, the nineteenth-century straddle between political democracy and capitalism, is finished, and that from here on we are either going to have a lot more democracy, or a good deal less. And labor looks to me like the only force in contemporary society big enough and strong enough to save democracy for us Americans.

Lynd is a nineteenth-century rationalist still. He, a sociologist, does not hint at, nowhere shows any sign of the world-wide conflict *between the workers and the bureaucratic-administrative-supervising castes*. He shows no sign of understanding that the elementary problem of modern life is to unite once more in the human being labor and intelligence, knowledge, science, etc. instead of continuing to separate them into the undifferentiated mass, on the one hand, and the concentration of all intellectual, scientific and organizing power on the other. He was applauded, but if he had spoken of what was nearest to the men, from their point of view, the roof would have come down, his name would have spread from one end of the country to the other, in the shops he would have earned the permanent hatred of the bureaucracy.

Lynd is no Stalinist, but his speech could have been written by one. If the whole speech is read, it can be seen that here is an intellectual conscious of his isolation and burning to make contact with some social force, the labor movement. But he conceives the whole process *philosophically*, exactly like the Stalinists. Here is the typical intellectual *joining the workers*. He will place all he has at the disposal of the workers, i.e. of the labor bureaucracy and thereby he reinforces the very barriers which keep the workers down.

It is necessary to point out that Lynd has made a great step forward. He has posed the question in terms of socialism. He has warned against Fascism, and it is obvious that he is ready to go to the end as he sees it. But it is equally obvious that he does not pose the real crisis. He does not see it. It is noticeable, I repeat, that a Stalinist could say precisely what Lynd is saying, and at the same time be preparing to clamp the iron vise upon the workers. It should also be noted that one of Lynd's colleagues, F. O. A. Matthieson, an author of a very fine and liberal-minded study of American literature of the nineteenth century, has stated in print that if he were in France, he would join the French Communist Party. Caught in the rationalist past of America and unable to break through to the fundamental relations of production and all that is involved therein, the whole philosophical ideology underlying an intellectual so ready to work with labor as Lynd leads him straight to the type of social change which is represented by the Stalinists in Europe, and which is inherent in the whole situation of the labor leadership in the United States.

The sense of hopelessness among the intellectuals exists because they are hopeless. At the beginning of this section I made it clear that nothing was coming from them and nothing can. And the American intellectual is worse off than all the others. The absence of a mass political labor party which all modern developed countries have had for two or very often three generations – this America has not got. In France the non-Fascist intellectuals can revolve around the Communists or go back (for the time being) to the Third Force; in Britain they circulate in and around the Labour Party. In America there is nothing. They are lost absolutely.

As I write these pages, I read in today's (February 6, 1950) *New York Herald Tribune* Walter Lippman's column commenting on the universal fear and despair that the atom bomb and America's plan for the hydrogen bomb is generating all over the world. He writes:

It is not too much to say that the reason why so little has been published abroad about this strategical revolution is that the people who understand it have been stunned by it. Again and again I was told when I asked about it in Britain, in France and in Germany, that they did not dare to think out loud about a problem which was at once so terrifying and so insoluble.

And then he says:

But that paralysis will surely pass. The human instinct to survive will impel men to think their way out of this predicament.

In the same issue of the paper is printed the Republican platform for 1950. The Republicans base their appeal to the American people on the issue of human liberty and dignity of the individual as follows:

We shall not passively defend the principles stated here, but shall fight for them with all the vigor with which our forefathers fought to establish what we now seek to advance and perpetuate – human liberty and individual dignity.

We pledge that in all we will advocate and in all that we will perform the first test shall be: does this conduct enlarge and strengthen or does it undermine and lessen human liberty and individual dignity.

The American intellectuals can make neither head nor tail of this. The very same issue of the paper is filled with defiance of Truman and the Taft–Hartley Act by the miners. The American liberal intellectuals are pledged to the repeal of this act but yet are absolutely bankrupt before the determination of half a million miners not to be coerced by an act which the country voted to repeal in the last elections. After 15 years of John L. Lewis and the miners, the American intellectuals do not know what to think or say.

And finally, so far as Europe is concerned, the *Daily News* columnist John O'Donnell, in the most widely read paper in the United States, taunts the American intellectuals with the following quotation from the *New Statesman and Nation*, telling them that this is the way "the leftist intellectuals in the present Labour Government are thinking:"

So far as we know there is no feverish demand in this country for bigger or better bombs. The British people know perfectly well that, even if America and Russia might survive an atomic war, Britain and Western Europe would not. Morality and self-interest alike should compel us to mediate in this fatalist rearmament race.

So that these intellectuals face the fact, as we have pointed out in this sketch, that their solitary allies, the intellectuals of Western Europe, have no such fundamental belief in democracy as these Americans would like to believe, to strengthen their own doubts. The *New Statesman* statement is only another indication of the fact that the Western European intellectuals are prepared to let American democracy and Stalinist totalitarianism fight it out and join up with whatever side is victorious. These are the ones who are supposed to give leadership to the masses.

8

The Transition

Transition, because as soon as we explore what is meant by the complete bankruptcy of the intellectuals, in the very course of exploring it, we shall arrive at final conclusions. The total failure, inadequacy, gloom, despair, subservience of the intellectuals, is the philosophical and social complement to the total rejection, by the workers and the mass, of being merely automata, mechanized units. Society in the shape of labor, production (in its comprehensive sense) on the one hand, and science, organization, art, intellect, on the other, has broken down in both halves. The duality of modern rationalism which Descartes began is no longer viable in any sphere. That formidable "we," "the party," which Casanova told the French intellectuals to obey, *that* rules, and it rules because either as Fascism of Stalinism (I repeat, the differences between them are great and have immense political consequences), the "we" who rule are the men who control and discipline the great working mass of the population. The intellectuals as such can join these, work for them, do the work they want done, but freedom, free speculation, the primary condition of intellectual work, that they have no longer. In America, free America, the pronouncements which matter are by the President, the Atomic Energy Commission, Philip Murray, John L. Lewis. The intellectuals have plenty to say, but chiefly, as we have shown, of how hopeless the whole situation is. To do anything, they must *join* something and *serve it*. And this something is a mighty centralized bureaucratic organization which from its internal structure and the similar organizations at home and abroad with which it is in conflict, pursues an almost impersonal policy. The pitiable plight we have analyzed in the last section is not accidental or due to deficiency of intellect or character. It is the plight of a social grouping *for which the world no longer has any use.*

It was one of the finest products of the age of rationalism. In the Middle Ages the intellectuals served an organization, the Church. But the rise of capitalism and with it bourgeois rationalism gave them their ideological freedom, printing gave them a mass audience. The first was Dante and then century after century, there followed a magnificent roll-call: Petrarch, Erasmus, Calvin, Rabelais, Montaigne, Shakespeare, Hobbes, Bacon, Descartes, Molière, Leibnitz, Rousseau, Jefferson, Montesquieu, Kant, Hegel, Marx and Engels, Adam Smith, Ricardo, Comte, Shelley and Beethoven, Goethe, Whitman and Melville, Garrison and Phillips, Victor Hugo, Darwin, Dostoyevsky, Freud – the list chosen at random merely indicates the role played by intellectuals. They came from all classes, they functioned in all spheres, they went sometimes into politics, some like Marx and Engels created new philosophical systems and acted on them. It is absolutely false to consider the intellectuals merely as great individual men. They were all, each and every one, the product of a great intellectual ferment, of social conditions, the high peak of thousands of lesser men and connected by a thousand threads with the active life of their time. Even the superb Pascal, priest and religious maniac as he was, took religious controversy from the cloisters of the church and carried it to the people. They explained society to itself, were its conscience, the organizers of its ideas, they charted the new discoveries, they resisted and endured, were heroic or subservient, but they filled a role, and an independent role within the social limitations of their particular time. Today? They are as we have described them. The most miserable of all are the scientists. They are slaves if ever there were any, mutinous and rebellious sometimes in words, but slaves. They make atomic discoveries and bombs and then go home and cry. When Germany was defeated, the contending powers each captured where he could, some of the most highly developed and trained scientists, the most highly developed and trained minds the world has ever known, and put them to work in Moscow or Washington. They work, do as they are told, find what they are told to find, like any laborer at a dollar an hour. And in free America, if anyone of them dared to defy the authorities and declare he would have nothing to do with a bomb which would kill a quarter of a million people, the whole machinery of politics and propaganda would set to roll and leave him utterly crushed. He would probably find it impossible to continue scientific work at all. And yet, the real dilemma is in his own mind, he does not know whether he ought to or not. The *Journal of the Atomic Scientists* is one of the most pathetic publications in the world.

The intellectuals (as a group, of course; many individuals can see) do not know what has happened to them. If they did, they would not be as they are. *What is to take their place?* They cannot conceive of a world in which they, as intellectuals, do not play an intellectual role, so powerful are the social practices and established patterns of over five centuries of European civilization. But such a bankruptcy cuts them off from seeing the changes that are taking, that have already taken place. The world as they know it has changed, but they are blind to it. In the Introductory chapter I quoted a review by Max Lerner of Brogan's book on America. The blindness of the old and the emergence of the new (unknown to the writer, Lerner), are there.

Lerner says that the serious writer on America will have to answer why "we" Americans who have built up such mighty power structures fear power. There speaks a typical American intellectual. Who is this "we" who fear power? The great industrialists, the men of finance, etc.? Lerner believes that they as Americans fear power, today, 1950. Was there ever such a gross illusion? It is possible to say that up to the late nineteenth century, American individualistic capitalism, with its vast opportunities, did fear power which would hamper it; it made use of the traditions of 1776–1865. But today big industrialists know the need for power, their own power, political power. They are trying for it at home and abroad.

But bad as that is, it is the lesser half. The great masses of the American people no longer fear power. *They are ready to allocate today power to anyone who seems ready to do their bidding.* They defied all the barrage of propaganda about statism and regimentation and collectivism and voted for the government in 1948. They want Truman to have not less but *more* power, so long as they think he will use it to do what they want. The old America is gone at both ends of society, but Lerner still lives in it.

Again he says that "we Americans" have a way with machines, but flee from the psychic realities. Again, utterly untrue. In the violent development of industrial, mechanical and technical skill, under the banner of democracy, Americans had neither time nor energy to investigate psychic realities. The constant fluidity of classes, the splendid physical achievements, prevented the crystallizations and needs of Europe which faced the writers with the task of probing deeply; some few individuals, baffled by the whole business did "tragic and interior" writing but could not relate this to the society and therefore as we said earlier, the writing itself suffered. But today? Running away from psychic realities? No intellectuals in the world run so much after the psychic realities of their own souls as Americans. The concern of the great mass with what their *work* does to them as *human beings* – that is the greatest psychic reality of all. The total bankruptcy of the dominant rationalist mode of thought is here seen in all its purity. Lerner believes that the miners have continually challenged official society in war and peace for 50 cents a day more. He is wrong. The great mass of the people are preoccupied with psychic realities but in the closest relation to social realities, and the Republican Party with its flamboyant pledge to judge everything by human liberty and the dignity of the individual understands that much.

He says again that "we" are at once "idealistic and tough," "moralists and pragmatists." This phrasing shows that he is referring to that duality which has been so often noted in American life, the grand phrasing, the idealistic aims, and the rapid disregard of these when faced with a concrete opportunity, there were so many. It was a very real characteristic of America and many have commented on it, very often with amusement and cynicism. That duality, however, is on its way out among the large masses of the American people. Tough and pragmatist they still are in that they wish to *accomplish and* brush aside or resolutely tackle obstacles. But the vast majority of them take social idealism and social morale seriously. They believe in social equality, in economic justice, in a genuine freedom, in governments doing what they promise, in assistance for the poor and underprivileged. And they believe in action for these things. That was the secret of the hold Franklin Roosevelt had in the minds of the masses of the American people, they believed in his idealism and that he had a moral approach to society while at the same time he was a good politician and tough. All the power of the press could not break the Roosevelt hold. In the minds of the American people that old duality is over.

Lerner asks why with "our" genius for organization we have such a contempt for intellect. How blind can a man be? The American masses, it is true, have the national genius for organization. It is part of the historical development of the nation and they cannot lose it. But contempt for intellect? Today the millions in America have a passionate desire for knowledge, for historical knowledge, for library knowledge, for political knowledge, for everything which will help them to *understand*. Where does Lerner live? The great barons of the nineteenth century up to Henry Ford, with the vast physical opportunities before them set the tone and the millions who lived so tumultously, both found empiricism enough. But that is over. The America of today, the workers, the farmers, the middle classes, the men who were in the army, have no contempt at all for intellect. For personal culture in the European sense, yes, but for intellect? No.

Finally, Lerner asks: What inner strength is there in Americans and their culture which will prevent them from completing the trajectory of Rome and its collapse? See the Philistinism, not of Lerner as an individual, but of the whole worn-out, useless group of intellectuals to whom he belongs. To compare the American people to Romans. The great mass of the Romans were in the days of the decline slaves, backward agriculturists, or a city mob. The splendid peasants and artisans of the early city-state were gone. Now look at the people in America today who work. Forget for a moment the rulers, the owners, the enormously wealthy, and the great body who are always attached to these. Take the industrial workers, the unorganized workers, the farmers, the clerical assistants, the small functionaries, the vast majority of the nation which has nothing but lives from day to day. When or where was there ever such a powerful body of men and women, when and where was there such "inner strength" in a nation? It is not their weakness that is ruining civilization. It is *conflict* that is ruining us. It is the consciousness of strength in the mass and the need for full self-expression that in seeking to burst the traditional limits of society can bring society to ruin. Lerner, a characteristic representative of the American liberalistic rationalist tradition, is totally blind to all this. He writes books like *It Is Later than You Think*, he is aggressively liberal, progressive, etc. But in this brief analysis of what he thinks of his own country, we can see why the intellectuals are as they are. For men who are so lost to contemporary society, what is there to do but to run to Existentialism or bow their heads to "authority" and place their talents at its disposal. Lerner lives in a kind of hothouse of his own. But even when the intellectuals see what is happening they are more baffled than ever. Their solution: more welfare, higher social security, two weeks free vacation instead of one, and so on.

We have to make it clear that their intelligence as such is not in question. Nothing could be more ruinous than to believe that they are not intelligent enough to see; or as Julien Benda wrote twenty years ago, that the intellectuals have committed "treason." Nothing is wrong with their "intelligence." What is wrong with them can be stated thus. They are unable to conceive of the workers as anything else but workers and therefore are unable to conceive of themselves as anything else but intellectuals. No intelligence in the world can enable a social grouping to think of itself as something which must be abolished. In fact, up to a point, the more intelligent they are, the worse for them. When an intellectual seriously envisages modern production, what it takes in science and organization to produce atomic energy, it seems to him that you can promise workers and fight for full employment and better education (and sometimes after the crisis) more leisure and preserve his voting rights and everything under the sun, except – the one thing the worker wants – not to have vast changes in the productive system every single one of which reduces him more and more to a mechanism. But alas! The more you try to satisfy him outside production, the less amenable he is to what takes place inside production. And worse still, it is becoming clear that not only the daily struggles but the very size and weight of the mighty productive machine, and all the complications it brings with it, impose intolerable burdens upon the economy itself as an economy, and education and housing have to be stinted.

We now have to show, difficult as that is, how these very conditions (1) limit not the intelligence but the creative imagination and artistic powers of the modern intellectual; and (2) how those who manage, however partially, to break through them, find their powers extended beyond all the possibilities that can be conceived by the rationalistic method. This is extremely difficult to do, but at this stage, we have a certain background and by sticking rigidly to the concrete, the actual, we shall be able to enter upon the conclusion in a few pages. Now for the artistic imagination (and I leave aside the undoubted relation between this and intelligence).

During the last thirty years, literature all over the world is dead. Joyce,

Proust, Lawrence, T. S. Eliot, all were mature before 1914. Some believe that there have been such periods in the past and this desolate gap will be filled some time. That is as true as the idea that there will be "real peace" sometime.

The great writers I have mentioned all describe *decadence*. They point to the decline of a civilization. But unlike Dante, Balzac, Shakespeare, they have no glimpse of what is new; they see nothing *emerging* except further decay and disorder. I am speaking here not of Eliot's Catholicism, monarchy, etc. I am speaking of his *writing*, as Shakespeare saw the new individualist man of bourgeois society, however much he dressed him up in feudal trappings. Now some writers did have a tremendous *sympathy* for the mass; and out of it came some remarkable books, e.g. Silone's *Fontamara* and *Men From Nowhere* by Malaquais. Some other intellectuals like Malraux and Koestler wrote books that apparently dealt with revolutionary ideas and social movements. But a careful reading of *Man's Fate* shows that Malroux is primarily concerned with his own soul; and brilliant a book as *Darkness At Noon* is, it is perfectly clear that for the writer, the masses are not seen very differently from the way the Stalinist bureaucrats he describes see them. Malraux and Koestler are organically individualistic, and from their failure as intellectual *types* to find the solution of their problems, by turning to the mass movement, there is an easy transition to *authoritarianism*. Let us merely note here that in the breast of *every* modern intellectual exist powerful tendencies to Existentialist emotions and ideas. But equally present are the authoritarian complement. Both are inherent in the history of modern production and the rationalism which has sprung from it, particularly since Rousseau. And they will swing between these forces, often combining both, until they have mastered an integrated humanism in which man as producer becomes the center of human theory and practice.

The Audens, the Spencers, all turn to the mass movement but without any integrated philosophy, they turn away. As writers, as creative artists, all of these find themselves limited, baffled, they do not develop, they shrivel. And, as usual, the most fruitful example to take is one of the best of them, a man already referred to, Norman Mailer.

Here is a young man, 25 years of age when he wrote his book, who has enormous gifts and the very best characteristics of the American writer. He sees the limitations of parliamentary democracy, he strives to see each individual life as a life. He describes in the best tradition of Melville the daily ordinary activities of men in their different social spheres, before they joined the army and in the army; nothing is finer than his description of how the men have to march and pull and labor and get tired and have to go on and on – it is the military parallel to the labor in the factory. *In his writing*, it is clear that Japanese are ordinary men like the Americans. His description of them expresses a genuine internationalism. He sees modern war for what it is. He is realistic but he has vision and imagination – the whole conception and execution of the attempt to climb the mountain shows an unusual artistic instinct. All this in a young man of twenty-five.

Why then does the book not sweep the reader away and open a new vision for its reader, excite trained and sensitive critics with the feeling that a new artistic personality has arrived, as Chopin's music did, or Montaigne's essays, or Balzac after the early apprenticeship, or even the early Kipling or Joyce's *A Portrait of the Artist as a Young Man?* With every reservation, due to a very difficult subject, I submit the following: This gifted writer works within the intellectual limitations of his time. The spaces and urges which give dynamism to an artistic consciousness are lacking. The opposition that he sees to democratic decline and democratic decay are the fascistic Croft and the artistic force with which he describes him, shows that this evil man has fascinated the imagination of the writer. Croft he *knows* will not open any new perspectives for mankind. But Croft he sees as the new power. And it is for this reason that he pours such bitter scorn on the uncertain liberal-Marxist intellectual, and for this reason that he is quite blind to the supreme fact: that the utter negativity of the lives of the masses he describes, the ultimate character of the negativity, must *of necessity* contain in itself a force to correct that negativity. For if they, as he sees them, modern men in a modern world (not ancient slaves) do not contain in themselves somewhere an overpowering desire to live differently, to change, to be fully human, then civilization is lost indeed, and, which is what concerns us here, Mailer's gifts are enclosed in a wall of unbreakable steel. He can only turn back upon himself. If the people can do nothing and merely accept, then he as a writer is lost. He cannot *grow*.

We can see this quite clearly in Melville. In 1850 Melville, in seeing Ahab in the America of that time, saw dynamically. His book represents the world as it was and the world as it was going to be. It had a tremendous *movement*. Melville did *not* leave the reader uncertain. He carried everything to its conclusion and made it clear that Ahab would ruin civilization. Now today, 100 years later, young Mailer can only *repeat* Ahab in Croft. He dare not say as Melville said, that Croft (and his economic, financial and military counterparts – they are in the book too) will ruin civilization. He cannot say that today it would be a capitulation to existing forces, to a living threat. Emotionally (and as a political person) Mailer is opposed to this evil. The forces which Melville could not see because they did not exist, exist for Mailer today, but only as external forces, the labor movement, politics, Marxism. He does not see them dynamically as Melville saw Ahab in embryo and let his imagination go to make him a symbolical character. In their artistic consciousness, wherever it is that creation takes place, Mailer is still where Melville was, although he may join a revolutionary political movement and die on the barricades. Here we have a perfect example of the needs, aims, desires, confusions, limitations of the modern intellectual and the American intellectual in particular. Mailer is young, he is entirely of the new generation; he appears to have escaped Stalinism and faced the world without blight. Not a line written here implies that by reading the correct books or studying economics or following a "correct" political policy, he will "understand" and "write better." God forbid that anyone should read such nonsense in what I am saying. Artistic processes live and develop in far deeper layers of consciousness than that. Racine, after a lifetime of writing psychological drama for the court, and a period of retirement, was asked to write plays for a girls' school to perform and wrote *Athalie*, perhaps the greatest play in French literature and one of the great revolutionary dramas of the world.

I have to add here that I am very much aware of the inherent difficulty and complexity of any such analysis as this. Great dramatic literature, not only as drama, but with dramatic qualities, demands among other conditions a society where people act independently, freely; they do not so act today; but Mailer *did* find someone: Croft.

Furthermore a new society will fuse the individual and the collective – we have lost the models and the feeling for that type of work after 500 years of individualism. There are other considerations I cannot touch on here. Yet I think it is still true to say: (after making all allowances) (1) Melville, after *Moby Dick*, declined, wrote little and concerned himself with incest and salvation of the individual by the search for personal morality, etc., all the things we are familiar with today; and (2) the modern writers all go the same way. The walls that surround them have to be broken and they as a group cannot break them, though a single individual can do anything. Mailer's future career will be one of the most revealing indications of the modern development, whether he will be contained or will break through. But that concerns his fate as an individual writer. The intellectuals as a group cannot break through. It will take more than intelligence to break down walls which are very high and very strong.

To see now the reverse, imperfect, limited, shot through with contradictions but yet clear, let us ask ourselves a question about America. Who is the man who in the new epoch which began in 1929 has most stamped his consciousness upon the nation and the world as representative of the nation, who in his personality and actions expressed, symbolized such powerful sections of the social movement that his actions have affected the material lives, ideas and consciousness of the people more than any other man of his time? The answer comes easily – Roosevelt. And what does Roosevelt signify in the United States? The welfare state with all that it aims to do and all that it cannot do – we need not go into that again.

And then who is next on the list? Which American citizen has had the most powerful impact materially and otherwise upon his fellow-Americans?

There may have to be some searching but the ultimate answer is inevitable – it is John L. Lewis. I do not see how anyone else can be substituted for him.

Now Lewis's immense limitations have been referred to, and a complete study would have to probe into him more deeply than has been done here. What we have to see here is only one thing: what is the secret of the enormous power he wields, which has made him able to challenge the full force of the government and official opinion in peace and in war, and repeatedly keeps the whole nation waiting anxiously as to what decision he will make in the perpetual conflicts between him and the government. The American intellectuals who study Kafka and Dostoyevsky, and read and write books about Lenin and Stalin with such eagerness, have never even taken the trouble to try to understand Lewis.

The source of Lewis's power is very simple. *He follows the miners and the miners alone.* Follows them? Yes, *follows them.* There is not the slightest trace of paradox here. In 1949 Alinsky published a biography of this extraordinary man, and he shows how in 1935 Lewis was little different from Green and the other leaders of the A.F. of L. in his attitudes to government sponsorship of collective bargaining. But when the tumultous spontaneous actions of the workers began, Lewis *followed.* He declared for the C.I.O. and this great social movement was launched. When the war began (and in the period before), Lewis was a member, though a recalcitrant one, of Roosevelt's labor-management committee. Then in 1943 came a spontaneous strike of Pennsylvania miners. Lewis changed his attitude and defied the government in a series of strikes in the midst of the war. All the labor leaders have solemnly declared their opposition to Taft–Hartley and hire lawyers and ask the workers to put their faith in the Democratic Party. When the bill was passed, nearly 150,000 miners went on a spontaneous strike. Lewis has declared open war on Taft–Hartley and had the words "able and willing" inserted in the contract, taking the position that no government law or legislators could force men to work if they do not want to. The whole bibliography shows that this labor leader, blind as he is to so much, has learned one thing, to look carefully and listen to what his men want; and then, *on the basis of that,* to challenge whatever stands in the way. The result is a power and a field for the exercise of strategy, boldness and courage, an inner fortitude which is unshaken by the abuse and vilification of practically the whole press and his labor colleagues; he has evoked a fanatical loyalty among his men on union affairs and leads half a million men against overwhelming odds in an unending series of titanic battles which dwarf everything that is taking place in America today.

For Lewis is posing the question: will the workers retain the right to decide how and when they shall work, or is the government to do it? And all know that the vast millions of workers, organized and unorganized, are heart and soul in sympathy with Lewis, and that only the iron grip of the labor leaders holds them in check.

Furthermore Lewis has repeatedly tried to *unite* the labor movement. But he wants it done on his terms, and these terms are: for the whole movement, readiness to challenge the government and the employers as his mining union challenges them.

This is the spectre in American society. That the labor movement should find itself uniting under a leadership which, like John L. Lewis, bases itself upon the instinctively expressed desires of the mass and then acts in accordance. Against Lewis is ranged every social force in the country. As we have shown, the labor leadership is headed for governmental power and symbolical of this welfare-state bureaucratized concept is Reuther. Lewis by his *political* confusion and meanderings unnecessarily complicates his almost intolerably difficult position. But he has held it now for nearly fifteen years, and he has held it for the reasons we have described.

And the intellectuals? You can see what they do *not* stand for by their attitude to Lewis. They analyze Kafka and Lenin, they form committees for miserable sharecroppers, for intellectuals starving in Europe, they form little "ginger" organizations like Americans for Democratic Action, they expand sympathy for revolutionary struggles everywhere, they meditate deeply upon Jefferson democracy. But this, under their eyes, they turn away from. They do not grapple with what Lewis represents, they do not try to explain him to themselves, far less try to analyze the premises and conclusions of his acts and illuminate these for him. They allow him to be vilified in the press as "Shakespearean ham" without coming to his defense. They form no committee to defend the miners. They try to distinguish between Lewis and the miners. They are against Taft–Hartley, but they prefer to win at the election and then lose in Congress rather than see the full implications of Lewis's "able and willing." All in all, his actions irritate them; they wish him out of the way. And the basic reason is simple. Lewis, *for the reasons we have given, is the exact* antithesis of the modern intellectual.

But that is not all there is to Lewis's struggles. Not only are *the organized workers for him*. In the South his name is a legend among all the Negroes and millions of poor whites. And the middle classes look on fascinated. At the height of one of Lewis's great struggles and just after the mine disaster at Centralia, even women's magazines carried long articles full of real sympathy for the miners. Their general tenor was that people, Americans, should *not* live like that. And by implication they understood Lewis. Finally, that admirable journalist, Dorothy Thompson, whose political ideas make no coherent sense whatever, but who at her best is a very faithful reflector of the fears and hopes and instability of the petty-bourgeois, she, in the course of one of the perpetual crises, wrote a brilliant article analyzing Lewis and the miners. She saw him not as a ham or arrogant labor czar, but a man who even in his language was moved by an Old Testament sense of intolerable wrong, and a stern implacable demand for justice. And in her naivete, she posed the question: What do the miners want? Let us know and let us see if we can fix it, and put an end to these continual explosions that threaten the whole nation. She grasped at any rate that it was not 40 cents more per day that would settle this unsmiling insoluble conflict.

What do the miners want? It is an admirable question. Lewis does not know – he could not answer that question. His enormous strength comes from the fact that he understands at least what the miners do *not* want, any kind of capitulation to employers or government. This separates him from all his contemporaries and lifts him so that he towers above them all. This places us very near to, in fact, on the threshold of conclusions.

Conclusions

Conclusions, because to a work of this kind, there can be no single conclusion, no recipe for salvation. What do the miners want? What do the people want? Let us look at one of them, as he sits in the evening listening to his radio. He is a unique product. The radio is characteristic of him. He can by a switch, listen not only to gangster stories but can hear international statesmen and distinguished publicists telling him that the whole edifice of modern civilization and government exists for him and is dependent upon his will, his needs and his decision. This is a very remarkable thing. More remarkable is the fact that this man who listens, does not consider it strange that he should be considered as the arbiter. He has received a good education, not only in books but in the life, the highly organized life around him. He has information. Such a mass of periodicals, newspapers and cheap books are now at his disposal as to give him the opportunity of learning as much as he has energy for. Hundreds of millions of cheap books are now sold, and hundreds of thousands are reading Flaubert, Dostoyevsky and Dreiser, taking them to the factory in the paper-backed editions.

He is quite accustomed to the idea of revolution and like the American citizen a hundred years ago, he has had to be familiar with conceptions of underground, mass revolt against authority, distinctions between the mass of the people and the government. They are not only in every newspaper, on every radio, but his own government constantly indulges in analyses of this kind. He is filled with a deep cynicism about the ability or the intentions of leaders to do anything for him. It is noted by those familiar with the union movement that the really unskilled production worker does not attend union meetings. He will rally to the defense of the union if it is attacked. And he will come out on strikes. But the regular business of the union, he pays no attention to and that is not because he, as so many Philistines think, is stupid or apathetic, but because he knows that that organization will do nothing for the things that affect him most vitally.

As a private individual he is very confident of himself in relation to other individuals. In my own sphere I know a man who brings laundry to the house every week, a butcher in a small way, two men who run a small grocer's store, an architect and many workers. *You cannot tell the difference between them.* The architect is interchangeable with the man who brings the laundry. The younger men who have been in the army seem to have been cut from one mold. The civilization is a dollar civilization. Good. *He* has money, that's all, there is no other difference between him and me. The women have to use cheaper materials but between them and the very rich there is no wide gap in the general style of the clothes they wear. It was not so thirty years ago.

These are among the more fortunately placed of the workers and the lower middle class. Below them are many millions who live in poverty and want, sometimes in horrible poverty, but, astonishing thing, in America their ideas are absolutely those of the people just above them in station. Sharecroppers who live in hovels, on getting some money continue to live in the hovel but buy an automobile. Characteristic is the tale of the young couple just married who are so poor that they have nothing but a television set. Speak to the poorest mother in the park, or to a sharecropper's wife in the depths of the South. More often than not, through the radio and the newspaper, they are acquainted with the latest theories on vitamins, child-care, etc. Man and woman have a passion to master technical things, to know about them, to do, to tackle a concrete difficulty and solve it.

(There will be space in a finished book for signs of the unmistakable revolt against the prevailing conditions of American life in the most intimate personal things: architecture – the revolt against the two rooms and a half – the apparently simple but profoundly revolutionary demand for the whole house or apartment to be built around the kitchen; the already established practice of cooking food at home, as can be seen in every newspaper – the revolt against packaged food and mechanized eating.)

Cultured they are not, in the old European sense, and that is one of their chief virtues. The American bourgeoisie created nothing in that sphere and thus the masses today are not in any way dominated by a sense of inferiority. Furthermore European bourgeois culture, so remarkable in its day, is today an incubus, a weight, an obstacle. The American people, the great body of them, are ignorant of many things their European brothers know. But in *social* culture, technical knowledge, sense of equality, the instinct for social cooperation and collective life, the need to live a full life in every sphere and a revulsion to submission, to accepting a social situation as insoluble, they are the most highly civilized people on the face of the globe. They combine an excessive individualism, a sense of the primary value of their own individual personality, with an equally remarkable need, desire and capacity for social cooperative action. And when you consider the immense millions of them, they constitute a social force such as the world has never seen before. Their power has been seen only in snatches so far. About 1935, the C.I.O. took up the question of discrimination against Negroes, because it was impeding union organization. In fifteen years more has been done to alter the status of Negroes than in the previous century. While their leaders hesitated, the white workers went to the Negroes' houses and neighborhoods and won them over.

And these people are convinced that something is "wrong." I use the phrase in quotes because two or three years ago the reporters of *Time* made a survey of the state of the nation. There was full employment, everything was normal, but the consensus of opinion was that something was "wrong." What? The average man did not know, but something was "wrong." We have explained sufficiently what we think is "wrong." We have avoided discussion of the more personal characteristics of the American people. We have preferred those aspects which belong to world tendencies. But within the last dozen years, the always volatile, restless, aggressive American individual, has now reached a pitch of exasperation, suppressed aggressiveness, anger and fear which irresistibly explode in private life but represent a profoundly social situation. The signs of an accumulating social explosion are everywhere.

We shall now do three things and quite briefly: (1) indicate what we think will happen *next*; (2) indicate what the general aims of the masses will be; (3) indicate if and how they will ever be achieved at all.

(1) The most important of these is what is likely to happen next, by which I mean, what definitive stage in the development is now due to appear. It seems to me that just as the Republican Party arose from underfoot to push aside the old parties that between them had led the country into the crisis, so the next stage, in two years or five, in ten, that does not matter, is a new political party. But this will be a party such has never been seen in the United States before. If I judge the American scene and the American temper correctly, it will comprise many millions of members; it will be such a mass mobilization as that which the Stalinists captured in Italy and France, but with a special violence peculiar to the civilization we have described. But though it will take a part in parliamentary politics, its inherent aim will be to break the practice of confining politics to merely voting for legislators. Too much in life and death is at stake, is going on, and the people excluded – that is eating at the heart of the American people. *They* want to know, to decide, to act. They will certainly want to begin in industry, for it is organized labor that will form the core of this party. Americans will rush to join something at last, something where they can express their national genius for organization, their terrible need for collective action, their national characteristic to roll up the sleeves and get to work to fix things that are wrong.

One more prediction can be made. When this movement comes, it is the labor leadership and the intellectuals rallying to them who will strive with might and main to reduce it to a tame purely political party, to vote, go home and leave it to the leaders to build the most powerful welfaring of welfare states. A new stage will have been reached.

Beyond that it is stupid to predict. There may be counter-mobilizations to crush this attempt of the people themselves to become the state. This party may be provoked by a fascist mobilization. The party may come during or after a war, it is not impossible that it may come before. But the sign that the permanent crisis is at last up for resolution will be the appearance of this new mass political organization which will seek to make politics an expression of universal man and a totally integrated human existence.

(2) Those who succeed in leading it will do so because they will have learnt to formulate the needs of the people and to be foremost in the struggle for them. But the whole impetus will come from the mass, its concrete actions, its attempt to break the bonds and traditions of centuries.

What are these needs? Once the spell of routine is broken, they will appear with extreme rapidity and develop with even more startling speed. It must be remembered that no one, not a single soul, guessed what the French masses, so passive in 1789, would demand in 1792. The thing was beyond human imagination. The same in Britain in 1645. But we can learn from history.

The demands will not be too far from what I barely outline here. They may go beyond them: (a) complete control and management of industry by workers. There is no need to elaborate this; (b) complete technical education for all men and women so as to abolish the distinction between management, supervision, office workers and mechanized workers. Americans know that if the government could train and educate 15 million people during the war in two or three years, in a dozen years they could strike such a blow at inequality that it could never recover again. Every worker would be a highly skilled engineer with scientific training. This is just below the surface in the United States.

True there is dirty and heavy work. Research is needed for cancer, but miners, for example, know that a billion dollars per year given over to technical and engineering research by highly trained scientists who are miners could totally alter the conditions of mining. Furthermore, with their instinct for equality and practical gifts, it will not take them long to discover that certain types of hard work are for younger men, who can take their turn; they learnt the complicated business of war in two years; with basic scientific training they could master any process.

Migrant labor for agriculture is today a curse. Millions of young people from the towns could go to it, every summer, and in the very center of the agricultural areas can be built the great universities with regular classes. Nothing prevents it. It is perfectly possible to begin all this tomorrow.

The vast majority of Americans would embark on it as on a great adventure, building and rebuilding and reorganizing the whole social structure. But they will have to do it themselves, a democracy of equals, with relations of a subtlety and intimacy that we know nothing about. They will create a new society, new, and the chief thing new about it will be that thought and action will be united – the worker as such and the thinker as such will disappear.

Intellectuals can join this and many will though many will fight it. They can serve *this* movement. But the primary creative force will be the collective actions of the mass seeking to solve the great social problems which face them in their daily lives. Intellect will play a high role, higher than ever, but it will be the intellectual activities of millions of men, dealing with realities. Intellectuals will be of use to the extent that they recognize the new forces but as a class they will recognize it only when they see and feel the new force. The role that they played between 1200 and today will be over, because the condition of that role, the passive subordinate mass, will be undergoing liquidation in the very action of the mass which will be creating a totally new society, an active integrated humanism. The ideas demanded and the will to achieve them unfold one from the other, and with the consciousness of power, ideas, hopes, wishes, long-suppressed, because thought unattainable, but now come out into the open – that is the process. We devoted considerable space to the Abolitionists in the middle of the nineteenth century. But the great masses become abolitionist now; themselves to wipe away the conditions of their own slavery. These cannot be abolished by anybody else.

Utopia? It is possible that it is. But to those who think so, I recommend a reading of Weaver's book and particularly the names of the people who have praised it on the jacket. See the kind of Utopia they are thinking about, and then remember that over vast areas of the world, that and similar tyrannies have had or are having their day. Hitler in particular thought that what I outline is Utopia and believed that was the source of all the evil in the world, and his main purpose was to substitute something else for it.

(3) And what are its chances? I believe in the instinct of humanity to survive and that this is the only way it can survive. The modern world is organizing itself scientifically at such a speed that either it must be ruled in totalitarian fashion or by a new conception of democracy beyond anything we have known. Lenin, whose writings on the experiences in Russia constitute an example of objectivity, profundity, realism, combined with a wide vision that makes them unique, said in 1918:

We can fight bureaucracy to the bitter end, to a complete victory only when the whole population participates in the work of government.

That is it. *The whole population* or totalitarian bureaucracy. What he went on to say is illuminating:

In the bourgeois republics not only was this impossible, but *the very law prevented it*. The best of the bourgeois republics, no matter how democratic they may be, have thousands of legislative hindrances which prevent the toilers from participating in the work of government. We have removed the hindrances, but so far we have not managed to get the toiling masses to participate in the work of government. Apart from the law, there is still the level of culture which you cannot subject to any law. The result of this low cultural level is that the Soviets, which by virtue of their programme, are organs of government *by the toilers* are in fact organs of government *for the toilers*, by means of the advanced stratum of the proletariat and not by means of the toiling masses.

Here we are confronted by a problem which cannot be solved except by prolonged education. At present this task is an inordinately difficult one for us, because, as I have frequent occasion to say, this stratum of workers who are governing is an inordinately, incredibly *thin* one.

No such backwardness exists in America. If the masses cannot govern, then nobody ever can.

The present writer *advocates* nothing. This is an objective analysis. But this much can be said. There will be no peace, no cessation of crisis, there is no haven ahead. *It will be many, many years before the whole world is reorganized*, and whoever believes or claims to believe that there is some possibility of emerging from the crisis on a world scale without blood, suffering, wearisome struggles, on a national and international scale, whoever says this is a charlatan or a fool, most probably the former.

Two men who made a life-study of revolution have said words on this which ought to be remembered. In 1881 Karl Marx wrote very harshly against those who wanted to predict the future of socialist revolutions. He said:

Scientific insight into the inevitable disintegration of the dominant order of society continually proceding before our eyes, and the ever-growing passion into which the masses are scourged by the old ghosts of government – which at the same time the positive development of the means of production advance with gigantic strides – all this is a sufficient guarantee that with the moment the outbreak of a real proletarian revolution, there will also be given the conditions (though these are certain not to be idyllic) of its next immediate *modus operandi* (form of action).

And Lenin in 1918 said of the coming of socialism:

It must never be forgotten that violence will be an inevitable accompaniment of the collapse of capitalism on its full scale and of the birth of a socialist society. And this violence will cover a historical period, a whole era of years of the most varied kinds – imperialist wars, civil wars, within the country, the interweaving of the former with the latter, national wars, the emancipation of the nationalities crushed by the imperialists and by various combinations of imperialist powers which will inevitably form various alliances with each other in the era of vast state-capitalist and military trusts and syndicates. This is an era of tremendous collapses, of wholesale military decisions of a violent nature, of crises. It has already begun – we see it clearly – it is only the beginning.

This too was in 1918. We have had 32 years of it. That is the world as I see it today and tomorrow. I shall do no more predicting than that, it is totally unnecessary here. If I have not used the terms socialism or communism, it is because what I write about is so different from Attlee's Britain and the monstrous barbarism that Stalinism controls or prepares for, that I preferred to deal with the thing itself.

So these are the rough ideas. The whole is to be ruthlessly cut, quotations yanked out, written for the average person, in 75,000 words or less.

References

Alinsky, Saul 1949: *John L. Lewis: an Authorized Biography*. New York: Putnam.
Auden, W. H. 1948: *The Portable Greek Reader*. New York: Viking Press.
Barclay, Florence Louisa 1910: *The Rosary*. New York: Putnam and Sons.
Beard, Charles 1913: *An Economic Interpretation of the Constitution*. New York: Macmillan.
Beard, Charles and Mary 1937: *The Rise of American Civilization* (2 vols.). New York: Macmillan.
Benda, Julien 1928: *The Treason of the Intellectuals*. Trans. Richard Aldington. New York: William Morrow.
Braun, Kurt 1947: *Union Management Co-operation: Experience in the Clothing Industry*. Washington DC: Brookings Institution.
Brogan, Dennis 1944: *The American Character*. New York: Alfred A. Knopf.
Browne, Sir Thomas 1906: *Religio Medici and Urn Burial*. London: Methuen.
Bryce, James 1920 (1894): *The American Commonwealth* (2 vols.). New York: Macmillan.
Burgum, Edwin 1947: *The Novel and the World's Dilemma*. New York: Oxford University Press.
Burke, Edmund 1981: *The Writings and Speeches of Edmund Burke: Volume 2 Party, Parliament and the American Crisis 1766–74*. Oxford: Clarendon Press.
Burnett, William Riley 1929: *Little Caesar*. New York: The Dial Press.
Bush, Vannevar 1949: *Modern Arms and Free Men: a Discussion of the Role of Science in Preserving Democracy*. New York: Simon and Schuster.
Caldwell, Erskine 1940: *Tobacco Road*. New York: Signet.
—— 1934: *God's Little Acre*. New York: Signet.
California Personnel Management Association 1948: *New Problems and Rising Costs in Management Relations: a Report of Significant Addresses at the 18th Pacific Coast Management Conference*. San Francisco.

Cantor, Nathaniel 1945: *Employee Counseling: a New Viewpoint in Industrial Psychology.* New York: McGraw-Hill.

Casanova, Laurent 1949: "Responsabilites de l'Intellectuel Communiste", *La Pensee* (Jan.–Feb.): 120–2.

Chapman, John Jay 1921: *William Lloyd Garrison.* Boston: Atlantic Monthly Press.

Drucker, Peter 1942: *The Future of Industrial Man: A Conservative Approach.* New York: John Day.

Fitzpatrick, Bernard 1945: *Understanding Labor.* New York: McGraw-Hill.

Frazier, E. Franklin 1949: *The Negro in the United States.* New York: Macmillan.

Fryer, Lee 1947: *The American Farmer: His Problems and His Prospects.* New York: Harper.

Garaudy, Roger 1948: *Literature of the Graveyard: Jean-Paul Sartre, François Mauriac, André Malraux, Arthur Koestler.* Trans. Joseph Bernstein. New York: International Publishers.

Gardner, Burleigh 1945: *Human Relations in Industry.* Chicago: R. D. Irwin.

Gibbon, Edward 1783: *The History of the Decline and Fall of the Roman Empire.* London: Folio Society.

Gorer, Geoffrey 1948: *The American People: a Study in National Character.* New York: W. W. Norton.

Hammett, Dashiell 1934: *The Maltese Falcon.* New York: The Modern Library.

Heron, Alexander 1948: *Beyond Collective Bargaining.* Stanford: Stanford University Press.

Hersey, John 1944: *A Bell for Adano.* New York: Alfred A. Knopf.

Himes, Chester 1947: *Lonely Crusade.* New York: Alfred A. Knopf.

Jaeger, Werner 1948: *The Theology of the Early Greek Philosophers.* Oxford: Clarendon Press.

Johnson, Robert Wood 1947: *People Must Live and Work Together or Forfeit Freedom.* Garden City, NJ: Doubleday.

Joyce, James 1926: *The Dubliners.* New York: The Modern Library.

—— 1942: *Portrait of the Artist as a Young Man.* London: Cape.

—— 1946: *Ulysses.* New York: Random House.

Kinsey, Albert et al. 1948: *Sexual Behavior in the Human Male.* Philadelphia: W. B. Saunders.

Koestler, Arthur 1940: *Darkness At Noon.* London: Cape.

Laski, Harold 1948: *The American Democracy: A Commentary and an Interpretation.* New York: Viking Press.

Lecomte du Noüy, Pierre 1947: *Human Destiny.* New York: Longmans, Green.

Lenin, V. I. 1943: *Selected Works, Volume 11.* Ed. J. Fineberg. New York: International Publishers.

Lerner, Max 1938: *It Is Later Than You Think: the Need for a Militant Democracy.* New York: Viking Press.

Lewis, Wyndham 1948: *America and Cosmic Man.* London: Nicholson and Watson.

Lewisohn, Sam 1945: *Human Leadership in Industry: the Challenge of Tomorrow.* New York: Harper.

Long, Haniel 1950: *A Letter to St. Augustine: After Re-reading His Confessions.* New York: Duell, Sloan and Pearce.

Lynd, Robert 1949: "Class Stratification, monopoly and propaganda myths", *UAW CIO Ammunition* vol. 7, no. 2 (Feb.), 42–4.

Maier, Norman R. F. 1946: *Psychology in Industry: a Psychological Approach to Industrial Problems.* Boston: Houghton Mifflin.

Mailer, Norman 1948: *The Naked and the Dead.* New York: Rinehart.

Malaquais, Jean 1943: *Men From Nowhere.* New York: L. B. Fisher.

Malraux, Andre 1934: *Man's Fate.* (Translation of *La Condition Humaine*). New York: The Modern Library.

Marx, Karl 1929: *Capital: a Critique of Political Economy.* (Translation of the 4th German ed). New York: International Publishers.

—— 1936: *The Poverty of Philosophy.* New York: International Publishers.

Matthiessen, Francis Otto 1941: *American Renaissance: Art and Expression in the Age of Emerson and Whitman.* London and New York: Oxford University Press.

Mayo, Elton 1933: *The Human Problems of an Industrial Civilization.* New York: Macmillan.

Mead, Margaret 1928: *Coming of Age in Samoa: a Psychological Study of Primitive Youth for Western Civilization.* New York: William Morrow.

—— 1949: *Male and Female: a Study of the Sexes in a Changing Society.* New York: William Morrow.

Melville, Herman 1851: *Moby-Dick: or the White Whale.* New York: Harper.

Miller, John 1945: *Origins of the American Revolution.* London: Faber and Faber.

Mitchell, Margaret 1936: *Gone with the Wind.* New York: Macmillan.

Myrdal, Gunnar 1944: *American Dilemma.* New York: Harper Brothers.

Nyman, Richard Carter 1949: *Foundations for Constructive Industrial Relations.* New York: Funk and Wagnalls.

Ortega y Gasset, José 1932: *The Revolt of the Masses.* New York: Norton.

Parrington, Vernon 1927-30: *Main Currents in American Thought: an Interpretation of American Literature from the Beginnings to 1920* (3 vols.). New York: Harcourt Brace.

Phillips, Wendell 1863: *Speeches, Lectures and Letters.* Boston: J. Redpath.

Porter, Gene Stratton 1909: *A Girl of the Limberlost.* New York: Grosset and Dunlap.

Rauschning, Hermann 1940: *The Voice of Destruction.* New York: Putnam.

—— 1942: *Men of Chaos.* New York: Putnam.

Roethlisberger, Fritz and William Dickson with Harold Wright 1939: *Management and the Worker: an Account of the Research Program Conducted by the Western Electric Company, Hawthorne Works, Chicago.* Cambridge, Mass.: Harvard University Press.

Roosevelt, Eleanor 1949: *This I Remember.* New York: Harper.

Rossi, Augustin (Tosca, Angelo) 1949: *A Communist Party in Action: an Account of the Organization and Operations in France*. Trans. Willmoore Kendall. New Haven: Yale University Press.

Scarlett, William (ed.) 1946: *Christianity Takes a Stand: an Approach to the Issues of Today; a Symposium*. New York: Penguin Books.

Siegfried, André 1927: *America Comes of Age: a French Analysis*. Trans. H. and D. Hemming. New York: Harcourt Brace.

Silone, Ignazio 1948: *Fontamara*. Trans. G. David and E. Mosbacher. London: Cape.

Stowers, Harvey 1946: *Management Can Be Human*. New York: McGraw-Hill.

Sullivan, J. W. N. 1949: *The Limitations of Science*. New York: New American Library.

Sward, Keith 1948: *The Legend of Henry Ford*. New York: Rinehart.

Tocqueville, Alexis de 1945 (1835–40): *Democracy in America*. (2 vols.) Trans. Henry Reeve, revi. by Francis Bowen, ed. Phillips Bradley. New York: Alfred A. Knopf.

Tolstoy, Leo 1898: *What is Art?* Philadelphia: H. Altemus.

Turner, Frederick Jackson 1947: *The Frontier in American History*. New York: Holt.

Walker, David 1829: *David Walker's Appeal, in Four Articles Together with a Preamble, to the Coloured Citizens of the World, but in Particular and very Expressly to Those of the United States of America*. Boston: Published by David Walker.

Warner, W. Lloyd 1947: *The Social System of the Modern Factory: The Strike, a Social Analysis*. New Haven: Yale University Press.

Weaver, Richard 1948: *Ideas Have Consequences*. Chicago: University of Chicago Press.

Webb, Sidney and Beatrice 1936: *Soviet Communism: a New Civilization?* New York: C. Scribner's Sons.

Webster, Daniel 1853: *The Great Orations and Senatorial Speeches of Daniel Webster*. Rochester: W. M. Hayward.

Weschler, James 1944: *Labor Baron: a Portrait of John L. Lewis*. New York: William Morrow.

Whitehead, Alfred 1929: *The Aims of Education and Other Essays*. New York: Macmillan.

Whitman, Walt 1928: *The Eighteenth Presidency: Voice of Walt Whitman to Each Young Man in the Nation, North, South, East and West*. Montpellier: Causse, Graille and Castelnau.

—— 1948: *The Complete Poetry and Prose of Walt Whitman*. New York: Pellegrini and Cudahy.

Wilkie, Wendell 1943: *One World*. New York: Simon and Schuster.

Wilson, Augusta Evans 1859: *Beulah*. New York: Derby and Jackson.

Winsor, Kathleen 1944: *Forever Amber*. New York: Macmillan.

Yerby, Frank 1949: *Pride's Castle*. New York: Dial Press.

Appendix

The Americanization of Bolshevism (1944)

To Bolshevize America it is necessary to Americanize Bolshevism. It is time to begin. But we do not begin by writing some articles in *L[abor] A[ction]* about the Bolshevik and Menshevik struggle in 1903, trying to make the readers "party-minded" by describing what our five comrades in X did or the seven in Y nearly did. No. We begin by getting a theoretical orientation and basis. Nothing can be more misleading than the idea that Americanization means seeking historical examples of revolutionary American parties and American heroes of labor with which to "inspire" the American workers and season our journalists.

Every great revolution is a truly national revolution, in that it represents not only the historic but the immediate interests of the nation and is recognized as such. But every party which leads such a revolution is also a national party rooted in the economic and social life, history and tradition of the nation. Its own class ideology is cast in the national mold and is an integral part of the national social structure. In my article on Sidney Hook (signed AAB, July, October 1943, *N[ew] I[nternational]*), I tried to show how truly Russian and national was Lenin, the greatest internationalist of the age. The Bolshevik Party was the same. And we shall see, it was so from the its very beginning. The W[orkers] P[arty] is not that. It is a long, long way from that. It has got to turn its head in that direction. A huge task if ever there was one, calling for the theoretical and practical energy of a high order.

As usual, our only model is Lenin, the leader of the only effective Bolshevik Party which history has known, and like the one we aim at, built from the ground up.

Lenin spent six years in preparation for his task, mastering the volumes of *Capital* that had appeared, *Anti-Duhring*, etc. He arrived in Petersburg in

1894 and from that time to 1914 his life's work was to translate Marxism into Russian terms for the Russian people. The Russian revolutionary movement has a long tradition behind it, Herzen, Belinsky, Chernyshevsky, men famous in the revolutionary movement and in Russian literature as a whole. Lenin took care to build on that tradition. His method of doing so was to do for his generation what they did for theirs, teaching Marxism to the Social-Democratic Party and the Russian people in spacious terms. Here is a rough summary of his work.

1 The most thorough exposition of [the theory of] Historical Materialism that exists in his long reply to Narodnik falsification of Marxist theory. In vol. 11 of his *Selected Works*, extracts from his study fill nearly 200 pages. It is dated 1894, is probably his first major work, is couched in Russian terms and is unsurpassed to this day.

2 His controversy with the Narodniki on the future development of Russian capitalism fills volumes. In the course of it, he made contributions to the analysis of *Capital* which remain for the most part unknown and far less understood in Western Europe and America. Yet it was Marxism applied strictly to the Russian economy.

3 He wrote *The Development of Capitalism in Russia*, a book of many hundreds of pages. It was a direct application of the most abstract Marxian economic theory to Russia.

4 His work on party building, *What Is To Be Done?* is Russian in conception and execution, Marxist classic though it is.

5 His special work on the Agrarian Question in Russia stands alone. It is a masterpiece of Marxism, but on Russia.

6 His study of American agriculture, made in 1913, is a unique masterpiece. He did it specially to illustrate certain aspects of the problem of Russian agriculture.

It is on this that the Russian Social-Democratic movement lived. These were the theoretical and propagandist foundations of the party. This was the work which guided the agitational press of Bolshevism. The Bolshevik Party was rooted in the day-to-day work, in industrial and mass struggles[,] to a degree compared to which our modest efforts can claim comparison only in good intentions. Only an armor-plated ignorance could think of the Bolshevik leader as anything else but an advocate of mass activity. But as a leader he considered it his special task to provide those thousands of party leaders, propagandists and agitators with material and method by which they could educate themselves and others. In this way, as Trotsky says, he also educated himself.

This was no work of an exile. It began from the day he came to St. Petersburg, writing leaflets about conditions in a factory, reading *Capital* to small circles of Russian workmen. In his propagandist work he was nakedly, unashamedly, and belligerently theoretical. In his study of the development of capital in Russia, he prefixed an essay on Marx's economic theory so as not to have to refer to the theory too often in the text, which nevertheless is packed with quotations from *Capital.* This was the Leninist method. It is the only method for building a Bolshevik Party. It is the only way to combat bourgeois ideology. It was necessary in Russia fifty years ago, where large sections of the population were permeated by hostility to Tsarism and the existing regime and where a long line of great writers had influenced and developed the revolutionary tradition. Furthermore, in the 'nineties Marxism swept Russia. Marxist books were bestsellers.

Compare the modern United States, the most bourgeois country in the world where the workers are permeated with bourgeois ideology. Isn't it clear that we today need to begin this work? Isn't it clear that without it the party cannot even begin to become a mass American party? How ridiculous it would have been if Lenin had been told that the articles about unions in the *ISKRA* were teaching the Russian workers Marxism.

And we?

Let the reader now look at the list of pamphlets, brochures, etc. published by the Pioneer Publishers in the old days, from the "Draft Program of the Comintern," "Germany What Next," "The Chinese Revolution," "The Spanish Revolution in Danger," "Whither France," etc., etc. and the corresponding articles in *The New International.* That was one period, one party, aiming at one group of workers and contacts. We have made a big turn to the masses. But in our theoretical conceptions and our practice, how vast is the difference! The great danger is that we shall just say "Well, let X write a pamphlet, or Y write two. Then when we get some more forces we shall write some more." That approach is false to the core, empirical, superficial and a positive obstacle in the progress and development of the party. We shall not get very far that way.

AMERICAN OR NOTHING

The more we consider this question the more we can see the special character of the problem with which we are faced in the United States.

The classics of Marxism are European in origin and content. They require more than an ordinary knowledge of European history and particularly by an American worker. In the 1928–38 days it did not matter much where we began with the Communist Party members and the radicals. Today when we have to give a class or a piece of literature to a contact, we begin perhaps with *The Communist Manifesto.* For us who aim at becoming a mass party this in five cases out of six is anomalous and will increasingly become so. Every European worker of today who reads *The Communist Manifesto* with his European experiences, his school studies and the daily life around him, social, political, literary and artistic, at once experiences a tremendous illumination that has solid concrete associations. A French worker who reads *Class Struggles in France, The Eighteenth Brumaire* or *The Civil War in France;* a German worker who reads *Revolution and Counter-Revolution*, or *The Peasant War in Germany*, finds the history of his own country made significant for him as never before.

Capital is not only a study of abstract capitalism. It is the history of English capitalist development and there is no finer introduction to the history of Great Britain. The last section on Primitive Accumulation is the historical garment of the logical capitalist development of Western Europe. For the average American worker these books as a beginning are alien. Doubtless if he reads one he is impressed with its power and brilliance and learns something. But what they cannot give to him in sufficient measure is that sense of reality of the development of his own country, that feeling that in addition to the daily class struggle, he is part of something beyond himself that is the beginning of theoretical Bolshevism and the rejection of bourgeois ideology.

Such historical data, knowledge, general reading, social experiences as he has, the structure in which his theoretical experiences must grow, are American. We have to begin now, not to write a few pamphlets but to build up the American counterparts of *The Communist Manifesto, The Eighteenth Brumaire*, and perhaps even more important, the American counterpart of *What Is To Be Done?* We do not wait until we become a large party to do these things. This is the way to prepare ourselves and all our supporters for the gaining of forces and the building of the revolutionary party. If in time among our efforts, we can manage at last to get one such solid pamphlet that does for United States history or the development of the labor movement or any such topic what these pamphlets do for Europe, and catch some of their spirit, we have the possibility, not only of immediate response but, in time, of reaching an ever-widening circle of concrete rewards.

This is precisely what Lenin set out to do with a grandeur, breadth and vision that are astonishing even after years of familiarity. In every field he posed proletarian ideology against bourgeois ideology. It is impossible to build an American mass party with our propaganda consisting of Marx on France and Germany, Lenin on Russia and Trotsky on Stalinism and Spain; supplemented by the present *Labor Action*. It is impossible for a number of average workers to become Bolsheviks unless on the basis of some systematic penetration into American development. Good Stalinists, yes. Good Trotskyites in the old days – the very old days? Perhaps not today, for what we are doing, NO.

That is the first point. The second is less easy to grasp but more important in the long run. For the implications of this orientation go much, much deeper. Not only do raw workers need this Americanization. *The party members from the highest to the lowest need it also.* No one has any serious grasp of Marxism, can handle the doctrine or teach it unless he is, *in accordance with his capabilities and opportunities,* an exponent of it in relation to the social life and development around him. The dialectical progression, the various stages of development, the relation between the economic basis and the superstructure, history, economics and philosophy, all the principles and doctrines of Marxism were evolved from a profound and gigantic study by its founders of European history, of European politics, of European literature, of European philosophy. The principles have universal application. But to the extent that the conditions from which they were drawn are not familiar to the Marxists, they remain to a greater or less degree abstract, with infinite potentialities for confusion and mischief.

Either the would-be Marxist must have some serious knowledge of European history in its broadest sense, constantly renewed, amplified and developed, or the principles of the doctrine must have been incorporated, worked over, and made to live again in a study of the economic structure, social development, history, literature and life of he country with which he has been many years familiar. Only then is he on the road to becoming a serious exponent and contributor to the doctrine. In fact and in truth [it is] only until one had dug the principles of Marxism for himself out of his own familiar surroundings and their historical past that the Marxism of Marx and Engels, Lenin or Trotsky and the famous European Marxists truly stand out in their universal application. Not only is this so. It would be a miracle if it were not so. Not only is it so for analysis, for propaganda or for agitation. It is, abstracted from the question of personality, the basis of Socialist confidence and Bolshevik morale. The Bolshevik solidity which must be the core of those who may come to us, the capacity to stand all pressures, must be rooted in a deep, rich, wide concept of American development. The masses may not need it. But for the party cadres of this period it is imperative.

To the degree that we teach this to masses, we develop and reinforce the hostility to American bourgeois society which is the objective result of capitalism in this stage of its development. Proletarian ideology is not merely a matter of theoretical analysis. It is the weapon and armory with which we must arm and surround the American working class and particularly those who face the enormous tasks confronting us in the present period. Unless it is rooted in the American environment and in such terms as the American worker can grasp, we cannot lift them above the instinctive class struggle, sharp as that will inevitably become. Isn't this what Lenin meant by the socialist consciousness which the party carries to the working class?

Every principle and practice of Bolshevism [needs] to be translated into American terms. Historical materialism, the Marxian economic analysis, the role of the party, the relation between democracy and socialism, the relation between the trade union and the party, reformists and revolution, the role of Social-Democracy, the theory of the state, the inevitability of socialism, every single one of these can be taught, developed, demonstrated from the American economic, social and political development. The American Revolution, the Civil War, the Knights of Labor, the Populist Movement, the Southern economy, the tremendous history of the C.I.O.; the development of the two major parties, the political and social contributions of Paine, Jefferson, the Wilson Administration, the New Deal, the NRA, the American dollar civilization, the rise and decline of the American Socialist Party, Eugene Debs, John L. Lewis, the Marxist analysis of all this is the material of our education, of our propaganda, of the creation of a Bolshevism which will break a path for us to the American masses. The ideas and principles of Marxism must be boldly and uncompromisingly presented to the American workers. The great European classics must be used, not only for their own sake, but as a means of explaining the American development.

With such a party, we shall not be able to educate our members and give to those with whom we come in contact what they will increasingly be looking for. On the basis of our mass work, when they come to us, they will be able to feel that they belong to us. This is not only a necessary and imperative supplement to our work, it is our special contribution to the American labor movement. The two complement each other and complete what is known as scientific socialism. If one aspect is ignored, neglected or superficially dealt with, then the other assumes an unchecked momentum of its own and does not even bring the rewards which the efforts lead us to expect. . . .

CONCLUSION

At the meeting on the American question which preceded the 1944 convention, I listed three propagandist points as ones on which we should center our attention.

1   The Americanization of Bolshevism
2   The Stratification of Production
3   Internationalism

Points No. 2 and 3 will have to wait. I have tried here to abstract propaganda and agitation and education from work among the masses. But such an abstraction has all the one-sidedness of an abstraction. In actual life the mass work will guide and shape the theoretical approach at every stage. Contact with the proletariat usually results in that. But the theoretical work will guide the mass work also. . . .

Let me here conclude with the question, propaganda, agitation in its relation to the fundamental question of the building of the party.

The American mass party will not be built by us or by the Cannonites.

Groups of Virginia miners, West Coast sailors, Southern sharecroppers, Pittsburgh steel workers, all sorts of "left" formations will coalesce in time and hammer out a unified organization. They will bring their qualities. Our task is to form such a strong nucleus that the coalescence will take place around us, or even if that does not take place, our special contribution will be Marxism and the theory and practice of Bolshevism. But to do this we have to gather a nucleus of a few thousands, of whom 75% will be American workers, men and women, instinctively hostile to bourgeois society, who are workers, have been workers and who have no other prospect in life except to be workers. They and only they can build a mass party. They are the only real mass propagandists and agitators, day after day. They exist in tens of thousands already and capitalism will create more and more thousands for us. But they need to be given, not prospects of a happy life and higher wages, but a method of thought and a conception of social development that makes their own lives and efforts intelligible to them in national and international terms. They need to know that in Marxism and the revolutionary party they have something which, even if far from being completely understood, yet is theirs. Proletarian thought, proletarian method must [be] for them a challenge to the bourgeoisie at all points, defeating it in theory as the workers will one day defeat it in practice. For them it must be a theory which marks off those who adhere to it from all others giving them pride and confidence and the consciousness of a great superiority to all however influential or famous who do not accept Marxism. That is Bolshevism. That is what Lenin in his day and with his problems from the start strove to create.

It is with such people that we can in time grow rapidly. From now and henceforth there will be increasingly rapid breaks in the national consciousness and in the social development of the working class. This class will increasingly throw off substantial numbers of workers breaking with the traditional and petty-bourgeois ideologies. If within their own environment and of their proletarian origin, there are trained and conscious Marxists, each of these can form at critical stages the rallying center of dozens and perhaps scores of adherents. The workers in the US have no allegiance to any traditional workers parties as have the workers of Europe. Broadly speaking, the whole field is open, and by laying the necessary foundation with thoroughness and confidence we can legitimately expect the American workers as they respond to declining capitalism will find it impossible to pass us by.

CONCRETE PROPOSALS

Obviously from the whole argument above, *this will be no list of articles or proposals for columns which solve the difficulties of the party.* I therefore merely indicate the following as immediate concrete steps for the next period in the direction outlined. Here I must revert to what is proper logical order[:]

THE NEW INTERNATIONAL

A. Through straight articles or book reviews, we need a preparation for indispensable pamphlets:

1. A series of studies of the American Labor Movement. AF of L and IWW and then AF of L and CIO.

2. The Civil War as the American bourgeois revolution. (Trotsky wanted to write a History of the Civil War.) This is the theoretical basis for the coming social revolution.

3. The American Revolution of 1776. From here flow all the ideology and current social thought of the country: Constitution, Bill of Rights, Founding Fathers. We have to start breaking that up, as Marxists.

From this should come in time two full length pamphlets:

1. "The Communist Manifesto" of America, an analysis of America['s] development from 1776 to today.

2. An analysis of the labor movement and its role in American history with special emphasis on the AF of L and the CIO.

These should be our permanent standby. They should last forever – or at least until socialism, and all our classes should begin with them and *immediately after, side by side, The Communist Manifesto, etc.* They must bear our stamp, our label.

B. *The whole theoretical discussion of accumulation, with a practical application to the economics of the government spending, must begin. If we do two or three articles in a year, we have done well. But we must begin.*

C. The Socialist Party, the beginning of the CP in this country, the Third Party; studies of these, not academic but in the Leninist manner, for our own education and the education of the workers, must begin to appear in the journal. With articles on Bolshevism and its beginnings, as a historical standard of comparison, we shall begin to create theoretical premises for an American Bolshevism and in time do our own "What is to be Done?"

D. The writings of Marx, Engels, Plekhanov and the other classics on Dialectical Materialism must find a place in the paper. Not every month or every three months but steadily, so that we consciously begin to illuminate our own work with the Marxist scientific method.

We, being what we are, the above divisions are in descending order of importance. American development comes first in time and energy and space. But we have to work systematically at the other, too.

ARCHIVES

Here are two things we have to do:

A. The writings, letters, etc., of Marx, Engels, Lenin, Serge, Trotsky, on America have a value far beyond their scattered character. They must be collected, annotated and published. "Lenin on Britain" is a famous and very precious volume in Britain. Lenin's two letters to the American workers, for example, should be at once reprinted in the paper.

B. We have to start reprinting and annotating some carefully chosen classics of American revolutionaries. For example, David Walker's *Appeal*, Speeches of Wendell *Phillips*, etc.

THE NEGRO QUESTION

Here, as Marxist interpreters, the field is ours – Negroes and populism, Booker T. Washington, Frederick Douglas, the Garvey movement, whatever serious work we do here will not only educate ourselves but will be gobbled up by the Negro people, masses and intellectuals alike, and progressive white workers.

PARTY PAMPHLETS

We need two at once:
1. What is the Workers Party?
2. The Labor Party

They should be serious pamphlets both cast in a *historical* mold. Both pamphlets should be carefully coordinated, so that the reader who reads them both should have a clear but briefly stated idea of the development of the labor movement and of the function of the two parties. Closely linked with this must be the publication of a formal Declaration of Principles and general program. This is a crying necessity.

LABOR ACTION AND THE PAMPHLETS

A substantial section of the paper must reflect in popular form the work done on this propagandist effort. Some of the pamphlets or extracts from them must *actually appear week after week in the paper. Articles in the* NI *can be summarized with suitable extracts.* The party program and explanatory articles must constantly appear in the paper. There must be a constant tie-up, literary, political and promotional between the *NI, the solid propagandist pamphlets and the paper.*

Reviews of books should play an important part in the paper. They must not be watered down. Two reviews which have appeared or will appear in the *NI* have every place in the paper, one by Shachtman on Wilkie's *One World* and another on Wechsler's study of John L. Lewis. *Life, Time, The Saturday Evening Post, Collier, Look,* constantly have articles of the most serious type by highly qualified writers who do not write down. These are read by millions. A recent article in *Life* on "Capitalism and the Free Market" is a case in point. These and not articles in the *New York Times* should be the target of systematic, comprehensive and fully Marxist replies by *L[abor] A[ction]. Life* writes on the free market? Good. We write the Marxist view of the free market. The *Saturday Evening Post* writes about cartels and monopolies? Next week we write one or two articles on monopolies and cartels exposing their superficiality and preaching our own view. We say that the classic work on monopolies is Lenin's *Imperialism.* We refer to our book service. We refer to a current article in the *NI.* We denounce cartels, *but* we teach, we explain, we deliberately lift the worker above his daily struggles.

EDUCATION

The above document is not a a programmatic document. Once the theoretical necessity is grasped, then the organizational arrangements, the courses of study, etc., are, to start with, a matter of collaborative effort. This, however, must be said. This document repudiates entirely that conception of education which sends out documents about the speeches of Roosevelt and lists of war profits and war scandals.

From: J. R. Johnson [C. L. R. James], "Education, Propaganda, Agitation: Post-War America and Bolshevism" (October 1944), Pts. II and IV.

Literary Executor's Afterword

It seems to me the idea of our civilization, underlying all American life, is, that men do not need any guardian. We need no safeguard. Not only the inevitable, but the best power this side of the ocean, is the unfettered average common sense of the masses. Institutions, as we are accustomed to call them, are but pasteboard, and intended to be, against the thought of the street.

Wendell Phillips, 1859

It was the American civilization that had begun to spread itself thick and pile itself high, in short, in proportion as the other, the foreign exhibition had taken to writing itself plain . . .

Henry James, *The American Scene*, 1907

If in addition to his grand physique, his skilful work, and his noble character, he were a civilized human being, then there would be some hope for the world which Melville sends to its doom. But splendid as he is, the primitive Queequeg cannot save society.

C.L.R. James, 1950

PREFACE

America bears a heavy responsibility for C.L.R. James. It was in America that he found the bonds of personal and political association that allowed him to overcome his dread of isolation. Culturally, America provided him with the freedom and opportunity to demonstrate his mastery of the discourse of modern civilization, as he had earlier mastered the principles of English literature and English cricket in the West Indies. America also presented James with his greatest political and intellectual challenge. Confronted with the Stalinist degeneration of official Marxism and the stagnation of official Trotskyism, James set himself the task of rethinking the fundamentals of Marxist theory. The resultant achievement would bear the strong imprint of American society. With the publication of the present work, it is now possible to appreciate how distinctively American as well as universal in scope was the body of Marxist ideas that C.L.R. James helped to create in the United States.

The various aspects of James's strategic relationship with America and the contours of his thought are plainly visible throughout the present prospectus. It is for this reason that its text is so valuable and helps so greatly in clarifying not only his ideas and their sources, but also the connection between his developing thought and American society. In addition, the present work serves as an important reminder of a bygone time when serious political thought was conceived and carried out with a public audience in mind. Although it was not written for publication, *American Civilization* marks a significant stage in the fruition of James's theoretical efforts, beginning in 1941 and continuing throughout the forties and fifties, toward clarifying the relevance of Marxism to America at mid-century.

Since a large and crucial part of what made his ideas so original rested upon what he discovered in America, the present work now fills a critical void. It was in America that James ultimately came to appreciate and experience most forcefully the phenomenon of popular autonomy. "The American people," James declares, while "ignorant of many things their European brothers know," are

in *social* culture, technical knowledge, sense of equality, the instinct for social cooperation and collective life . . . the most highly civilized people on the face of the globe. They combine a sense of the primary value of their own individual personality, with an equally remarkable need, desire and capacity for social cooperative action. And when you consider the immense millions of them, they constitute a social force such as the world has never seen before.

I

In the late summer of 1982, I was beginning to examine the state of various collections of James's papers. On a visit with a former associate of James, Nettie Kravitz, in Detroit, Michigan, I happened upon a box that contained an old onion-skin copy of the present prospectus. It took only a short time, after an initial inspection, to recognize that the massive transcript of 327 pages had been written by James. Ms. Kravitz, whom I had been interviewing, was among "the limited circle" of friends to whom James entrusted numbered copies of the text for their comments.

In 1983 I wrote recommending its publication to Margaret Busby, co-founder and then editorial director of Allison & Busby, which had just reissued James's *Notes on Dialectics* the year before. As the individual responsible for initiating publication of the series of Selected Writings of C.L.R. James, Margaret became James's publisher of choice in his final years. (Until then, the individual responsible for keeping in print most of the key documents of James's political tendency in the United States was Martin Glaberman, who published them under the imprint of Bewick Editions.)

Quite apart from the intrinsic merit of the prospectus, I sensed that there was some sort of relationship connecting *Notes on Dialectics* with the newly discovered work. From references in the text, it appeared to have been composed *circa* 1949, i.e., the year after *Notes on Dialectics* was written. If for no other reason, the sheer consanguinity of the two documents as well as their being formally titled "Notes" seemed to make them almost parallel texts. It was for this reason that I recommended to Margaret Busby *seriatim* publication.

Nothing came of my proposal in 1982, though the existence of the prospectus was noted in the bibliography that accompanied *At the Rendez-vous of Victory*,[1] the third in the series of James's *Selected Writings*. Then, five years later, in 1987, the idea was revived by the present editors, Anna Grimshaw and Keith Hart, who, with James's approval and support, collaborated in preparing the text for publication. The prospectus is now published here very much as it was written by James forty-three years ago. Only minor editorial interventions have been made in the text, for example, supplying chapter titles missing in the original and correcting spelling and punctuation. An appendix containing an excerpt from James's October 1944 manifesto, *Education, Propaganda, Agitation: Post-War America and Bolshevism*, has been added for the light that it sheds on the origins of James's concerted effort to deal with Marxism in the context of American society and American history.

II

By birth Trinidadian, a colonial by upbringing, and by education an intellectual trained in the tradition of English liberal humanitarianism, C.L.R. James came of age, intellectually and politically, in an era that was to witness the destruction of some of the most cherished beliefs of European civilization, especially the civilizing ideal of liberal education and the inevitability of progress. James summed it up as "the Gospel according to St. Matthew, Matthew being the son of Thomas, otherwise called Arnold of Rugby."[2] At this stage and for a long time, the United States was no more than a distant nation and a symbol of various virtues and vices: "Matthew Arnold still had possession."[3] Twenty years later all this would change. It was America that really changed James.

By the time that he finished school in Trinidad at Queen's Royal College in 1918, James entered a world torn by crisis, roiling from the moral collapse caused by the unprecedented slaughter of the First World War. The victorious Russian Revolution also threw bourgeois Europe into a profound state of doubt. Over the next two decades, the Western world was dominated by the specter of socialist revolution and fascist counter-revolution.

James took his stand as this epic struggle was approaching its apogee. For a man of Renaissance-style intellectual background and interests, James was already an anomaly in an age that confined intellectuals to ever more specialized branches of knowledge. An autodidact pursuing "the best that Western Europe and America had produced in literature and politics," James after 1929 followed the path of social revolution. Amidst the social misery inflicted by the Depression, James linked himself to the cause of the world proletariat and to the coming struggle for colonial independence. It was a commitment from which he did not retreat; and he never submitted to the world as it was organized.

In what would turn out to be our last conversation via telephone between Los Angeles and London, James talked about how he would like to be remembered. "Just say I was a West Indian who did his part," he remarked. He died a year later, on May 31, 1989, at the age of 88, in Brixton, South London, where the last nine years of his roving life as a revolutionary were spent in the embrace of the black British community. He was honored with an impressive national funeral in Trinidad, organized by the Oilfields Workers' Trade Union, and attended by several thousand people.

Following the memorial in the packed auditorium of the OWTU headquarters in San Fernando, at which James's fellow West Indian writer and friend, George Lamming, delivered the eulogy, James's catalfaque was driven in procession across the island to his hometown of Tunapuna, where he was buried. Other memorials for James were also held in various Caribbean territories and in cities across North America and in Great Britain.

In the obituary published in *The Times*,[3] James was described as "an author and political activist who became something of a legend in his native Trinidad and throughout the Caribbean." Indications point today, however, to the fact that there is a growing interest in James that reaches well beyond the West Indies. The life and thought of this remarkable West Indian has now become the subject of scrutiny on the part of a growing body of students, particularly in the fields of cultural studies and studies of post-colonial literature.

To appreciate James's revolutionary thought, however, it is necessary to understand the man in his totality. From the beginning, his thought ranged widely across diverse areas of intellectual, cultural, and political engagement – education, sports, fiction, social and literary criticism, politics, journalism. These various facets of James's early life constitute, singly and collectively, a complex of ideas and experiences, all of them expressed with a rare versatility of prose style, that would prepare him for his later career in the revolutionary Marxist movement.

Before arriving in America, he had already intellectually established himself in Britain, within five years of leaving Trinidad, as a novelist, journalist, historian, anti-colonial activist, and Trotskyist militant. James's original conversion to Marxism had occurred in England in 1934, about one year after he had commenced his reading of Trotsky's *History of the Russian Revolution*,[4] a single-volume abridgement of which was published in England by Victor Gollancz in 1934. In an unpublished autobiographical reminiscence, James describes what most impressed him about this work:

> Trotsky in *The History of the Russian Revolution* was not only giving details of the revolution itself, but he was expounding the Marxist theory of historical materialism. He referred to the Greeks and the Romans, to the Reformation, the Renaissance and the French Revolution – he made Marxism and the Communist Party the climax of many centuries of historical development. Trotsky referred not only to historical events and personalities, but he made references to literature as expressing social reality and social change. *The History of the Russian Revolution* gave me a sense of historical movement: the relation of historical periods to one another.

At the same time that he was immersing himself in Trotsky's immense *History of the Russian Revolution,* James was also reading, *in tandem* it would appear, another major historical classic. This was the highly controversial *The Decline of the West*[5] by the nationalist German philosopher, Oswald Spengler (1880–1936). A one-volume English edition was also published by Oxford University Press in 1932, the same year that James arrived from Trinidad as an aspiring writer. James was fascinated by Spengler's philosophy of history, which closely mirrored, it must be noted, the depressed mood of the bourgeoisie in the crisis that engulfed it following the First World War.

"I did not accept the decline that Spengler preached," James recalls, "but I did absorb from him, too, the strong sense of historical movement, the relation between different historical periods and different classes." Spengler's thesis that capitalism breeds imperialism, which in turn breeds war, would certainly have been of special interest to James. Far from being unique, Spengler's influence, it should be noted, was profound among the educating reading public throughout Latin America, where *The Decline of the West* proved to be one of the most important intellectual experiences during the thirties and forties.

What James did was pull Spengler's ideas out of their pessimistic German context and modernize them by relating the thesis of the decline of the West and its civilization to the vindication of contemporary political, economic, and social movements. This background forms the context for the appearance of Spengler's name in the list of European philosophers who are described by James in the introduction as "Europeans of a concrete environment, and yet were recognized as signposts in the advance and retreats of the human race."

In order to understand the appeal that Spengler exerted, it is necessary to point out that James had very recently joined in the discourse of civilization which is the theme of *The Decline of the West*. James's intervention took the form of a radical critique of British colonial rule in the West Indies. Published as *The Life of Captain Cipriani: An Account of British Government in the West Indies*,[6] it represented the clearest statement up to that point of the West Indian claim to independence, and today serves to remind us how James's thinking was, from the beginning, influenced by his experience of colonialism.

"What the stranger unacquainted with these islands must get very firmly into his head," James writes, "is that these people are not savages, they speak no other language except English, they have no other religion except Christianity, in fact, their whole outlook is that of Western civilization modified and adapted to their particular circumstances."[7] Membership in Western civilization was what, in James's view, endowed West Indians with the capacity to govern themselves.

The experience was not all positive, however. "This lack of tradition, this absence of background, is in one sense a serious drawback. It robs the West Indian of that national feeling which gives so much strength to democratic movements in other countries." Obviously, there was more to the question than merely belonging to Western civilization. "The question must be squarely faced," James declared. "What sort of people are these who live in the West Indies and claim their place as citizens and not as subjects of the British Empire?"

III

James landed in the United States from England in October 1938. Initially, he had proposed to spend only a few months lecturing in the US at the invitation of the leader of the recently organized Socialist Workers Party (SWP), James Cannon. Instead of a short stay, however, he quickly became a leading figure in the American Trotskyist movement and remained in the US for fifteen years.

As American historian Henry Steele Commager illustrated a short time prior in his overview, *America in Perspective: The United States through Foreign Eyes*,[8] America has long animated a strong interest in visitors. The number of foreign visitors who have written books is quite staggering, running literally into the thousands. Included in this number are works by such notable English travelers to America as Mrs. Frances Trollope, Charles

Dickens, Harriet Martineau, Leslie Stephen, Anthony Trollope, William Cobbett, Goldwin Smith, Matthew Arnold, James Bryce, and H. G. Wells, among others.

To the best of our knowledge, however, there does not exist another work of comparable scope produced by a black visitor to the United States. The closest example in this regard would be James's West Indian compatriot, Edward Wilmot Blyden (1832–1912). Blyden's arrival in the United States, in 1850, from St Thomas in the Danish West Indies (later Virgin Islands) marked the beginning of an illustrious career in the service of the African American community in the United States as well as in the service of Africa.

Disenchanted after being rejected for admission to Rutgers' theological college, Blyden sailed for Liberia, in 1853, with the assistance of the American Colonization Society. He did not return for another decade to America, but during that time Blyden published a powerful anti-slavery pamphlet addressed to America in *A Voice from Bleeding Africa*.[9] Blyden would eventually rise to great height as the African nationalist *non pareil* in the latter part of the nineteenth century. During an extremely active career as writer, statesman, politician, ambassador, Pan-African diplomat, professor, and university administrator, he returned a total of seven times on various missions to the United States.[10]

Blyden's involvement in the political debates within the African American community and his views concerning the return of Africa's exiles are contained in *Christianity, Islam, and the Negro Race*.[11] James was heir to the tradition of African vindicationism adumbrated by Blyden in the nineteenth-century, shaped to a significant degree by the racism that was endemic to American society. Blyden's thought would provide the springboard for succeeding generations of West Indian activists and thinkers, including a distinguished retinue of Pan-African activists such as Henry Sylvester Williams, J. Robert Love, W. A. Domingo, Marcus Garvey, Richard B. Moore, and George Padmore.

The interest in America which animated most European writers was the question of America's future. Where previous authors, beginning with Crèvecoeur's "What is an American?" in *Letter from an American Farmer* (1782), approached their subject from the perspective of American character and national characteristics, James looks at America as a society that is caught in a profound crisis. James dates the beginning of the crisis to the stock-market crash of 1929: "The blight (and the turn to murder and violence) which has descended upon the American people since 1929 expresses the fact that the bottom has fallen out of the civilization; men have no confidence in it any longer, and are brought sharply up against the contradiction between the theories, principles, ideas, etc."

James sees raging within the American character a deep fissure, which produces a widening conflict manifesting itself daily in the struggle "of the mass exposing its rage, anger and hostility, its desire to smash the impasse in which it finds itself, and [which makes] this the outstanding new characteristic" of American society. James finds this conflict portrayed all through popular culture which represents "modern Americanism, a profoundly social passion of frustration and violence, characteristic of the nation as a whole as can be seen in the gangster films, radio dramas and comic strips." It is this view of America in social crisis that, ultimately, distinguishes James from authors of the naive cult of America as well as the detractors, who have been legion. Indeed, James's text has as much in common with Thomas Paine's *Common Sense* (1776), which mobilized the American people for revolution, as it does with the literary fare of foreign visitors to the United States.

James's presence in America also closely parallels the influx during the thirties and forties of leading European cultural and intellectual figures, mainly Jewish exiles from Germany and Central Europe, whose influence helped to reshape the artistic and cultural landscape of America. The fact remains, however, that James's prospectus is unique in the literature of what Max Lerner refers to as "the Idea of American Civilization."[12]

It was highly improbable that the present text, forged as it was in the stultifying atmosphere of the Cold War, could have been published at the time it was written. Written by a black foreigner and independent Marxist, who claimed the intellectual right to interpret the complexity of American civilization, it represented in every respect a fundamental challenge to the zealously guarded interests of the American status quo. Written before the emergence of the modern civil rights movement that would transform American political consciousness, before the rise of the New Left, at a time also when the notion of an independent, critical Marxism had been all but submerged by the clamor of super-power rivalry for world mastery, the prospectus of the contemplated work, in a practical sense, had nothing going for it except its ideas.

Today, ironically, James's legacy faces a different problem, which stems from the tendency to move away from the interpretation of James as a revolutionary Marxist. The effect is, ultimately, to make of James a safe and respectable academic, whereas, in fact, he was to the end an unrepentant revolutionary, who achieved his latter-day reputation without ever earning any formal academic degree. The contemporary down-playing of James's Marxism is reminiscent of the process that caused Lenin in 1917 to observe caustically: "What is now happening to Marx's doctrine has, in the course of history, often happened to the doctrines of other revolutionary thinkers and leaders of oppressed classes struggling for emancipation. . . . After their death, attempts are made to turn them into harmless icons, canonize them, and surround their *names* with a certain halo for the 'consolation' of the oppressed classes . . . while at the same time emasculating and vulgarizing the *real essence* of their revolutionary theories and blunting their revolutionary edge."[13]

In December 1947 a warrant for James's arrest was issued in Los Angeles, California, by US immigration authorities seeking his deportation. James voluntarily surrendered himself and was released under bond. Finally, on July 3, 1953, at the height of the McCarthyite witch-hunt, James was forced to leave the United States, after a protracted and lengthy series of immigration examinations, trials, and unsuccessful appeals, making all attempts to fight his deportation futile. Two years before his departure, however, as if anticipating the prospect of his imminent expulsion, James penned the present prospectus. It was – to borrow a phrase from *Mariners, Renegades and Castaways* – a "natural but necessary conclusion" to his American sojourn.

One measure of the importance that James attached to his continued connection with America can be gleaned from the comment that the publication of his book on Melville occasioned. Writing to Howard P. Vincent, one of America's leading Melville scholars at the time, most notably the author of *The Trying-Out of Moby-Dick*,[14] James spoke wistfully of being overtaken by events. "I had looked forward to my book appearing in the normal manner and discussion developing normally, reviews in the press, articles in literary magazines, etc. . . . I now find myself in the unfortunate position when I may be forced to leave the United States in a few weeks without having had a discussion or real interchange of ideas in any shape or form about Melville with American Melville scholars."[15] Ten years later, upon his re-reading the book, Vincent would describe *Mariners, Renegades and Castaways* as "a highly charged work, full of a wonderful appreciation of Melville's genius, of *Moby-Dick*, but even more important (but because connected with them) is the affirmation of life as expressed by Melville in the appreciation of whales and crews."[16]

IV

Originally entitled "Notes on American Civilization," the prospectus appears to have been written over a single stretch of approximately 6–8 weeks during the winter of 1949–50. James explicitly informed a small circle of acquaintances to whom he passed copies that it consisted of a set of notes that represent "a preliminary view of an essay that I propose to write for the general public." He emphasizes that the work was not intended as "a full and complete study," but simply as "the best way to convey certain ideas." It would be "one closely interconnected logical and historical exposition . . . for the average reader, in 75,000 words . . . and written so that it can be read on a Sunday or on two evenings."

While a bit longer than James's original intention, the work nonetheless reflects his belief that a revolutionary Marxist point of view should be presented free of jargon, in a form that the general reading public could read, understand, and even accept. It attests to that "organic relation between the creative imagination of an artist, the receptivity of a public and the connection between them" which he finds exemplified in American popular culture. The introduction affirms, as a basic theoretical premise, the necessity for the artist to meet the consciousness of the audience with a consciousness of the artist's own: "When modern popular art is free, free in the consciousness of the artist that a vast public is ready to assemble together to listen to him, a whole new phase of art will begin."

In the course of its unfolding, the early self-imposed limitations of the prospectus gave way before a momentum that transformed it into a full-fledged political and cultural manifesto. What starts out as an exploration of American civilization changes almost imperceptibly, in the fifth chapter, into something overtly revolutionary, which has as its goal the mobilization of a mass political movement. It takes place, significantly, in the chapter that describes the struggle for mastery of production, in which James declares that "the industrial workers and their future are the basis of the whole edifice." In structural terms, we really have the result of *two* processes conjoined through the sheer sweep of James's prose and novel insights to appear like a seamless whole.

The expansion of the prospectus beyond the original aim was congruent with the basic theoretical orientation and purpose of the author. "I have long believed," he writes, "that a very great revolutionary is a great artist, and that he develops ideas, programmes, etc., as Beethoven develops a movement."[17] It would be more accurate, perhaps, to compare *American Civilization* to a series of preludes and fugues, successively stating several related yet contrapuntal themes, which gradually build up into a complex whole, with distinct divisions and stages of argumentation, but dominated at its core by a single major theme.

The unifying subject of *American Civilization* is the relationship between Marxism and American intellectual life at mid-century. In the United States, the Trotskyist milieu was then notable largely because it gave special encouragement to discussion of the American question in radical circles. This was especially the case with the group of intellectuals involved in the early years of American Trotskyism, principally James Burnham and Dwight Macdonald. It was an intellectual and political project that was almost unique in American radicalism, and one in which Trotsky himself also played an important role.

"From 1929 to his death," James commented in 1947, "Trotsky fought for a comprehensive theoretical presentation of the perspectives and tasks of the American revolution." James pointed out that "the letters, memoranda, conversations, etc., of Trotsky" were, in his opinion, "the most precious arsenal of analysis of the United States ever made, [and] must form the basis for a revolutionary attack upon every phase of American bourgeois production, social life, and thought." (James's use of Trotsky, it is necessary to point out, should be understood as primarily polemical, directed as it was *against* the policies pursued by the American Trotskyist movement; as James himself notes, in *Notes on Dialectics*, "Much of our past quoting of Trotsky is for tactical purposes."[18]) Nonetheless, Trotsky's support of the general idea of translating Marxism into American terms was clearly seen by James as a vindication. Trotsky, in responding, albeit critically, to radical journalist V. F. Calverton's pamphlet *For Revolution*, had declared: "To Americanize Marxism signifies to root it in American soil, to verify it against the events of American history, to explore by its methods the problems of American economy and politics, to assimilate the world revolutionary experience under the viewpoint of the tasks of the American revolution. A great Work! It is time to approach it with the shirtsleeves rolled up."[19]

Within months of his arrival in America, in February 1939, James informed Trotsky that he was thinking of writing a book "addressed chiefly to the American Negro" that was to be written from the perspective of "the [American] Negro and the present world crisis." It was serialized as *Why Negroes Should Oppose the War!* in the *Socialist Appeal* (official newspaper of the SWP), in ten installments between September 6 and October 3, 1939, and published immediately afterward in pamphlet form by Pioneer Publishers.

A perusal of the outline that James presented Trotsky in 1939 reveals that James's preoccupation with "the American question" had its origins in Trotskyist inner-party debate. During the years that followed, James made it central to every theoretical discussion. It is also significant that James's analysis of America should have begun with the relationship of African Americans to America. James's understanding of America was, in fact, rooted in an appreciation of African Americans, whom he saw not only as an integral part of the development of the United States, but also as a potential agent in the process of transformation.

The fifteen years that James spent in America were the years most critical for his development as an original Marxist theorist. "In 1940 came a crisis in my political life," he recounts. "I rejected the Trotskyist version of Marxism and set about to re-examine and reorganize my view of the world, which was (and remains) essentially a political one." In the factional struggle that reached its climax within the SWP convention in April 1940, over the disputed question of support for Russia, James voted with the minority of the SWP that split with Trotsky and the national committee over the latter's defense of the Soviet Union as a workers' state in spite of its alliance with Nazi Germany. Along with the minority, James split from the SWP after the convention in May 1940. The minority proceeded to set up its own separate organization, known as the Workers Party (WP), carrying with it the former theoretical organ of the SWP, the *New International*, as well as launching its own newspaper, *Labor Action*.

Despite his political differences with Trotsky in 1940, however, James would remain deeply involved in the Trotskyist movement in the US over the next decade, defining and refining his distinctive theoretical stance and the mode of literary and political praxis that it engendered. He first staked out his political ground in a resolution on the Russian Question presented to the first WP national convention, in September 1941. In the resolution, James called for a fundamental re-evaluation of the theoretical tenets of Trotskyism. Arguing that, in the absence of proletarian revolution on a world-scale, there had occurred the restoration of capitalism in Russia, James rejected the characterization of Russia as a bureaucratic collectivist order, which was the view of the WP majority. Instead, he put forward the revolutionary position that Russia was, in fact, a state-capitalist society, one in which the bureaucracy had become the new masters of state-run production, providing it with the basis of its political power. At the end of the convention, James and other like-minded persons came together and established their own political tendency. Referred to as "Johnsonites," deriving from James's party alias, "J. R. Johnson," the group formally became known as the "Johnson–Forest Tendency" in 1945.

V

The connection of James's Marxism to an exploration of American society was first clearly illustrated in the essay which he penned in response to Wendell Willkie's *One World*,[20] written, with the support of President Roosevelt, to convince Americans of the need to abandon their old isolationist attitudes. James's critique, "The American People in 'One World:' An Essay in Dialectical Materialism," which appeared in the July 1944 issue of the *New International* (the theoretical journal of the Workers Party), was a first attempt to show how the principles of dialectical materialism might be applied to the "transformational change" that James anticipated would follow the end of the Second World War in the US. "The essence underlying each social order is exactly the opposite of its appearance on the surface," he argued. The appearance disguised what was a developing contradiction. "The power of Washington as capital of the world rests on no sound foundation," he declared, adding that "the imperialist American grandeur is the mark of imperialist American doom."

Although the essay was linked ostensibly to the publication of Willkie's *One World*, James was also using the occasion to respond to Charles A. Beard and Mary R. Beard's *The American Spirit: A Study of the Idea of Civilization in the United States*,[21] in which the authors decried "the denationalizing, universalizing process which blends the various peoples of the earth into the unbroken unity of internationalism."[22] James's attention, however, would have been particularly caught by the Beards' attempt to show the incompatibility of Marxism with civilization: "By its very origin and nature as an interpretation of history, the Marxian invention called dialectical materialism clashed with the idea of civilization, as Prussianism clashed with the French Revolution and afterward with the conquering Napoleon."

James would also have been particularly sensitive to the Beards' charges of intellectual failure. "The repudiation of American civilization was direct and explicit in the creed of Marxian communism as developed in the United States," the authors declared. "A large proportion of the propagandists who advocated it on this continent were themselves of foreign origins, immediate or recent – men and women reared in the civilizations of Europe from the Channel to the Siberian steppes." The Beards' then finished up their indictment by pouring scorn on the feeble attempts of Marxists to assimilate the American experience:

The utterly alien nature of Marxism was illustrated by the fact that neither foreign born nor native Marxists produced any significant contributions to thought in relation to American history or economy. Attempts of communists to rewrite American history and to make "good comrades" out of Jefferson and Lincoln, besides betraying an unfamiliarity with relevant facts in the case, usually fell into the category of elementary declamations. . . . With sheer force substituted for the process of enlightenment, moreover, the reconciliation of Marxism with the idea of civilization in the United States was practically impossible.[23]

It was precisely to effect just such a reconciliation that James set out in 1944 to write *Education, Propaganda, Agitation: Post-War America and Bolshevism*,[24] a work which provided not only the basic statement of James's minority tendency within the WP on matters of political organization, but also the first explicit statement by James that his goal was to achieve "the Americanization of Bolshevism." James had obviously taken to heart the shortcoming identified by the Beards; the long journey that would eventually lead to his composition of *American Civilization* had begun.

VI

The idea of Americanizing Marxism had been around since the thirties, however. It was a particular goal of V. F. Calverton and other contemporary literary radicals, such as John Dos Passos, Edmund Wilson, Kenneth Burke, Max Eastman, and Sydney Hook.[25] John Dos Passos, in Calverton's *Modern Quarterly*, wrote in 1932, "Somebody's got to have the size to Marxianize the American tradition or else Americanize Marx."

Calverton's ambitious *The Liberation of American Literature*,[26] and *For Revolution*[27] were both steps in this direction. His most concerted attempt, however, was his *The Awakening of America*,[28] described by the author as "the first extended Marxian history of America." The first and only volume to be published of what was projected to be a three-volume work, it focused self-consciously on "those incipient class struggles that embodied the early outcroppings of the rebellious spirit and prepared the way for the Revolutionary War and the establishment of what today is known as the democratic tradition." This search for a usable past was the cornerstone of thirties' attempts to Americanize Marxism.

On November 6, 1944, the *New Republic* published a review of D. W. Brogan's *The American Character* by Max Lerner. Providing an incisive commentary that went well beyond the limited scope of the book, the review noted that "*the* American problem . . . still needs someone to define it," and added pointedly, "Whoever . . . will write an important book on America today . . . will have to face much tougher questions of economics and social theory, of national psychology, of politics and metaphysics, than Mr. Brogan has set for himself." Lerner finished with the pithy comment that "the problem of America is the key problem in the modern destiny."

A measure of the importance of Lerner's review can be judged from the fact that James would introduce *American Civilization* with an explicit reference to it. Responding to his own question, "What exactly do I propose to do that is new?", James quotes approvingly from Lerner's review and goes on to conclude – "Some basic approach of this kind I have had in mind from the beginning and Lerner is correct in saying that no such book has been written about modern America."

Following the end of the Second World War, James would continue to clarify his ideas with such articles as "The Tasks of Building the American Bolshevik Party,"[29] to which the young Irving Howe, at the time a member of the WP's youth wing, wrote a spirited rejoinder. In July 1947 James identified as a basic problem of American radicalism the "inability to assimilate the principles of Bolshevism owing to the absence of any conscious revolutionary perspective in the United States." "This deficiency," he declared, "is rooted in the whole history of the country."

Writing in 1947, James argued that Marxists needed "to find a basis in American society to concretise and develop the political and organizational principles of Bolshevism," if they were to be able to transcend the "moods and tendencies of American petty-bourgeois radicalism." The attempt to ground Bolshevism in the American revolutionary sub-soil was reflected in James's 1948 draft resolution on the Negro question presented to the thirteenth convention of the SWP. The text of the resolution has attained historic status as a watershed document in the development of Marxist thought in America.

James's entire analysis rested on the independent nature of the black struggle in America. "The Negro people, we say, on the basis of their own experiences, approach the conclusions of Marxism." The instinctual movement of blacks in their struggle for freedom was made synonymous with the tradition of Bolshevism. But there was more to the question than this. "It is not only Marxist ideas; it is not only a question of Bolshevik-Marxist analysis. It is not only a question of the history of Negroes in the US" In social terms, what James attempted to demonstrate was that the black movement had a dual character: the independent black movement had "a vitality and validity of its own," but it also had the potential to "intervene with terrific force upon the general social and political life of the nation," which made it "an aspect of the struggle between the bourgeoisie and the proletarian movement." This latter was the most important of James's points. According to the report, the independent black movement had "a great contribution to make to the development of the proletariat in the United States, and that it is in itself a constituent part of the struggle for socialism." Declared James, "the policies of genuine Bolshevism are now ready to compete fully armed in the tremendous battle that is raging over the Negro question in the United States."

James's report represents one of the most original applications of Marxism to American conditions ever made. It also sharply distinguishes his contribution from the static views of the traditional white left as well the liberal intelligentsia with its melting-pot theory of American race relations. James clearly apprehended the black problem as a touchstone of the larger American society: "It is a symbol of the temper of the American people. The Negroes have their cause simply and clearly posed before them, and the nation, and their segregation forces them and facilitates easier mobilization. But the whole history of America shows that political activity of this kind on their part heralds, is an advance notice of the whole nation in movement."

VII

After the SWP's July 1948 convention, James left New York and headed for Nevada, where he would spend the next several months. He used the time not only to secure a divorce, but also to undertake a basic reappraisal of the combination of theory and organization that was Bolshevism. The results of this undertaking are recorded in *Notes on Dialectics*.

The change that issued from James's theoretical effort was profound. "The whole propaganda and agitation must revolve around the destruction of the bureaucracy," he decided. "By this means every serious problem of those which are wearing down the revolutionary movement can be placed on a new basis."[30] The destruction of the labor bureaucracies thus became the top theoretical and organizational priority. It gave in consequence an entirely new meaning to the concept of Bolshevism. "The proletariat cannot adapt these bureaucracies to its use," James was adamant. "The main task, in fact the only task of the proletariat, is itself to eliminate them."[31] Socialism was thus no longer defined, politically, in vanguard party terms; instead, it was reconceptualized on the basis of drawing "an unbridgeable gulf between the great masses of the proletariat and the bureaucracies everywhere."[32] This was not a retreat from the struggle against capital, however, but a new imperative in consequence of the transformation of the proletariat in the era of state capitalism.

On the basis of this analysis, James concluded that the goal of socialism would now have to change. It was the concrete experience of the American proletariat that would provide the basis for the break with the arrested state of socialist political discourse. "It is an unsettling sight," James acknowledged. "But our stomachs must be strong. At least we have learnt this much. Lenin wrote *State and Revolution* and never stepped down an inch from it. But that was thirty years ago. We have our *State and Revolution* to *write – our* Notion."[33]

Ultimately, in my view, it was with *American Civilization* that James set himself the goal of writing an American counterpart of *State and Revolution*. "Lenin wrote his little book. And from that moment, that moment and no other, *not before*, his programme, his concrete work, in Russia, was devoted to the elucidation of *State and Revolution* in Russian conditions."[34]

Lenin's "little book," written in hiding in Finland in August and September 1917, was not published until 1918. Its seventh and final chapter, which was to be devoted to the analysis of the revolutionary events in Russia in 1917, was never completed; only the first two sentences of it were ever written. Like Lenin, who wrote *State and Revolution* as a challenge to the Marxist movement, including his own party, James found himself isolated on the American Left as he set about to modernize Lenin's concept of a workers' state, as well as simultaneously hounded by US immigration authorities with an order of deportation. And like Lenin, James looked to the social movement which he believed was imminent to demonstrate the validity of his analysis. James's prospectus represents, as was the case with Lenin's collection and explication of the texts of Marx and Engels on the state, the theoretical working out of a definite set of ideas on the mass mobilization of workers and the arming of the anticipated revolutionary forces with these ideas. "Lenin did not wait for all the workers to form soviets before writing *State and Revolution*," James notes.[35]

Why did James feel so strongly that it was necessary to update Lenin? The answer was given in *Notes on Dialectics* in 1948. "Johnsonism is a quarter of a century older than *State and Revolution*. We are not there any more." He goes on to say: "We are beyond *State and Revolution*. I can summarize where we are in the phrase: *The Party and Revolution*. That is our leap. That is our new Universal – the abolition of the distinction between party and mass. In the advanced countries we are not far from it in actuality. . . ."[36] The same warning regarding the pitfall of theoretical redundancy was repeated in August 1950, when James in *State Capitalism and World Revolution* recommends that "we have to draw a new universal, more concrete and embracing more creative freedom of the masses than even *State and Revolution*."[37]

It cannot be emphasized too strongly that the 1950 prospectus while it is addressed to the topic of American civilization, had as its principal theoretical objective the need to clarify, under post-Second World War conditions, in James's words, "the theory of the state and the relation of the workers to the state – the idea of the workers' state."[38] This was the essential question that Lenin's 1917 *State and Revolution* was concerned with and it was what James's essay on America was the preparation for.

American Civilization, then, represents a specific, concrete application of the new notion of socialism developed earlier by James in *Notes on Dialectics*. "The same transference from Russia that Lenin made for the world in 1917," James declared in 1948, "that same transference we have to make from Russia of 1917-23 to the world of 1948."[39] The American prospectus of 1950 embodies the results of the theoretical transference that James had made to Lenin's thought two years earlier. He was confident that it could be understood by the general public because it represented the popular experience. "In the U.S.A. the proletariat is ready for this," James argued. "In its great masses it hates the bureaucracy with an abiding hatred."[40] The battle for socialism would be waged against the bureaucracy in production. Significantly, the 1950 text concludes with James discussing Lenin and the problem of bureaucracy as the basic impediment to the achievement of socialism: "Lenin, whose writings on the experiences in Russia constitute an example of objectivity, profundity, realism, combined with a wide vision that makes them unique, said in 1918: 'We can fight bureaucracy to the bitter end, to a complete victory only when the whole population participates in the work of government.'" James exclaims at this point: "That is it. *The whole population* or totalitarian bureaucracy."

Lenin's explanation of the cultural roots of the political difficulty faced by the nascent Russian workers' state allowed James the opportunity to compare it with the level of culture in the United States. "No such backwardness exists in America," James insists. Like de Tocqueville's volumes that were written "to teach democracy [in Europe] to know itself, and thereby to direct itself and contain itself,"[41] the goal of James's study of American society was informed by a similar political objective. Motivated by the quest to understand the reasons for the failure of socialism in Russia as the basis for assessing the feasibility of its consummation in America,

James resorts to an explanation based on the premise of convergence. Any assumption of American distinctiveness was jettisoned in this reasoning.

The same principle shows up in the appraisal of American Abolitionism as "perhaps the highest peak reached by the United States intellectuals in the foreshadowing of the future of the world of today and in indicating how deeply all great world currents are integral to the United States as a nation." It is also contained in the description of what James viewed as emergent totalitarian tendencies within the United States, which convinced him that "the close study of the United States will explain most easily to the people of Western Europe why totalitarianism arises, the horrible degradation it represents, its terrible cost to society, the certainty of its overthrow." Finally, the principle of convergence is applied to the examination of European intellectual currents "to understand intellectual currents in the United States and also the social forces they represent, although these intellectual currents have not fully appeared as yet in the United States."

VIII

Between November 1945 and March 1946, a series of large-scale strikes erupted in several major industries leading to a curtailing of production and a first round of wage increases. A total of 4.5 million workers struck this year, crippling the coal, auto, electric and steel industries and interrupting rail and maritime transport. Then, in April–May 1946, a second major wave of strikes hit the coal mines and the railroads; before they could be settled, the government was forced to seize control of the railroads (May 17) and the coal mines (May 20), the latter after employers rejected a government-negotiated contract.

This was followed in June 1947 by passage of the draconian Labor Management Relations Act (Taft–Hartley Act), passed by the US Congress over President Truman's veto. It limited the power of labor unions by placing severe restrictions on the use of the strike, the closed shop rule, and political activities of labor; it was intended, in short, to roll back most of the gains made by workers under the Roosevelt New Deal. A third wave of postwar labor unrest occurred in April–July 1948 in the coal, railway, and steel industries; strikes were only stopped through government action and a third round of sizeable wage increases.

In October 1949 500,000 steel workers struck; the workers agreed to return to work only after the steel firms agreed to provide fully funded pensions. "The union leaders now use the militant mobilization for the pension demands," James comments, "but the men were not militantly for pensions except as these became a symbol of the permanent struggle as to who will rule production."

The strikes transformed James's entire political outlook. James responded to the first and second waves of postwar strikes with an essay on "The Social Crisis in the US and the General Strike" published in May 1946. A year later he writes: "On the American scene the proletariat during the past two years by its actions has given ample warning to the revolutionary movement that it has entered upon 'the years of decision.'"

The post-war strikes actually had their origin in the wildcat strikes against the no-strike pledge in the auto industry and mining during the Second World War, the story of which is set out in Martin Glaberman's *Wartime Strikes*.[42] In *Notes on Dialectics*, James refers to "the miners in 1943 [speaking] by their actions for the *whole* proletariat,"[43] referring to the May 1943 strike of 500,000 miners to protest the government's wage freeze, a stoppage that was only called off after Roosevelt placed the soft-coal mines under federal control. Moreover, the concluding proposal that James makes for establishment of committees of miners rested on "the miners' actions of 1943" as emblematic of the national unity of the American proletariat.

The prototype for James of the mass mobilization of American workers, however, was embodied in the sit-in strikes and the militant CIO movement of 1935-37. "The CIO was formed to give the workers mastery in the shops," James declares. One measure of the importance of the sit-in strikes and the CIO for James can be found in the frequency of references to them that abound in *Notes on Dialectics*. Here James describes the CIO as "far more party than union" and expresses his "expectation that in the United States the party [of labor] will be the CIO politically transformed," going so far as to see it "in relation to a revolutionary international."[44]

The whole phenomenon of the CIO was not only inextricably linked in James's mind with the concept of America; it was also the basis of the bold political projection enunciated at the conclusion of the prospectus. "All dynamic social progress depends primarily on this," he argues. In this context, one of the major achievements of the *American Civilization* prospectus is its retrieval of the origins of the CIO from obscurity, which it restores to its place of historical importance. "When the tumultuous spontaneous actions of the workers began," James emphasizes, referring to the sit-in strikes and the response of the mineworkers union, "[John L.] Lewis *followed*." In fact, James's prospectus is a challenge to labor and social history, with its affirmation that the original idea of the CIO "will have to wait for more intensive investigation," while calling attention to the fact that the material for this undertaking will be found "hidden away in union records, union files, and books by participants in the great struggles of the CIO, etc."

In the text James connects the CIO directly with "the great strikes" of the post-Second World War era. From this tremendous wave of strikes James's analysis of the working-class movement in America leapt boldly forward. "The CIO won acceptance. But it solved nothing fundamental. The great strikes of 1946 showed that." The heart of James's analysis of American civilization is based fundamentally on his attempt to clarify what was involved as far as the creative achievement of this new stage of worker mobilization was concerned. "There is obviously gathering among the workers a tornado of anger and determination to bend production to their will which will put the formation of the CIO to shame," James declares.

The necessity to clarify his political perspective on this postwar crisis was the thing that pushed James to extend his theoretical work, of which *American Civilization* is one expression. He lays particular emphasis in the text on the strikes, which he deems to be "explosions of intolerable rage and anger" on the part of workers. The cornerstone of James's analysis of America was lodged in the struggle of the American worker. "What is most striking is the unanimity of all industrialists, journalists, professional investigators, university professors, on the simple fact that the workers, not merely in coal-mines but throughout industry, have reached a definitive stage in relation to industry," he declares in the chapter dealing with the experience of the industrial worker. It was a new understanding brought home by what James describes as "the great strikes of 1946" which made clearer what was involved. "There is obviously gathering among the workers," James postulated, based on the unprecedented wave of the post-war strike movement, "a tornado of anger and determination to bend production to their will which will put the formation of the C.I.O. to shame." In July 1947 James wrote that "American capitalism and the American proletariat are each the most powerful representative of the international class struggle which will result either in the common ruin of the contending classes or the socialist reorganization of society."

IX

It should also be noted that several of the key ideas of James's prospectus were already contained in *The American Worker*,[45] comprising the experience of a production worker in the factory that was accompanied with a philosophical analysis by Ria Stone (Grace Lee Boggs), the whole introduced with a preface written by a Detroit union-committeeman, Johnny Zupan. *The American Worker* was only one of several important publications that the Johnson–Forest Tendency issued during the three-month interim period in the summer of 1947, between the time it resigned from the WP and it was formally readmitted into the SWP.

This brief interim period was a fecund time for Johnson–Forest. The group was now free of political constraints for the first time. It used the opening created by the transition from the WP to the SWP to publish an extraordinary array of materials which the group had been steadily working on for some time. Among the publications that it issued were *The Balance Sheet: Trotskyism in the United States 1940–47* (August 1947); "Dialectical Materialism and the Fate of Humanity," James's introduction to the collection *World Revolutionary Perspectives and the Russian Question* (September 1947); and *The Invading Socialist Society* (September, 1947). Twelve separate issues of the *Bulletin of the Johnson Forest Tendency* were also published.

The foundation of much of *American Civilization* can be found in the pages of *The American Worker*, particularly in the latter's sensitive analysis, within the section "The Reconstruction of Society," of the ideas contained in Elton Mayo's *The Human Problems of an Industrial Civilization.*[46] It presages the attention that James was to give to Mayo's work in the diagnosis of production relations and the thought of American industrialists that he presents in the present prospectus.

Most importantly, there appears in *The American Worker* an exposition and application of the concept of "alienated labor" derived from Marx's *Economic-Philosophical Manuscripts* of 1844. These early essays, written in Paris, represent the first version of his theoretical system, which he called the "critique of political economy." Crammed with original insights, they contain the initial working out of Marx's key idea of the self-creation of humanity through material labor and its consequences. It is what provides the theoretical framework of *The American Worker*. Unlike other later commentators (Althusser, for example) who tried to make an antagonistic separation of the early and late Marx, James would use the 1844 manuscripts in order to illuminate Marx's *Capital*. In fact, Johnson–Forest became notorious in the WP as the group that was always holding classes in *Capital*.

A short time prior to publication of *The American Worker*, the Johnson–Forest group published during the so-called interim period the first English translation of the three most important of Marx's early essays – "Alienated Labor," "Private Property and Communism," and "Critique of the Hegelian Dialectic" – in mimeographed form under the title *Essays by Karl Marx Selected from the Economic-Philosophical Manuscripts.*[47] This Johnson–Forest translation, partial though it was, preceded by many years the appearance in 1964 of Martin Milligan's full English translation of these critical texts.[48] It has been said that "no intellectual event since his death altered the reception of Marx so much as the publication of these manuscripts."[49]

The first draft of the Johnson–Forest translation of the *Economic and Philosophic Manuscripts of 1944* was actually prepared as early as May 1943. It was carried out by Raya Dunayevskaya who was first made aware of their existence through reading Herbert Marcuse's *Reason and Revolution: Hegel and the Rise of Social Theory.*[50] A fresh translation was undertaken by Grace Lee Boggs, this time using the authoritative German edition in *Karl Marx–Friedrich Engels: Historisch-Kritische Gesamtausgabe.*[51] The Johnson–Forest group ultimately published this latter translation in the summer of 1947, after trying in vain "to awaken particular interests" in the possibility of their publication. In addition to Marx's 1844 essays, Grace Lee Boggs also translated portions of Marx's formerly unpublished manuscripts of 1857–58 known as the *Grundrisse*. The Johnson–Forest group also began to receive translations of sections from an American living in Germany named Evrard. This was almost thirty years before there was any public awareness of its existence and the first English translation appeared.[52]

"We hope, we are confident," James writes in his preface, "that somewhere there is a response waiting for us." "Every political line that we have written has been fertilized by the concepts contained in these translations and the others we are unable to reprint," he reveals. Writing in 1962, James would underscore yet again the strategic importance that Marx's concept of alienation occupies. "We have here to go back," he writes in the section of *Marxism and the Intellectuals* dealing with the American working class and the subject of the reorganization of work, "to what socialism is and what it is not. When Marx was laying the foundations of his theory over a hundred years ago, he and Engels did a profound analysis of work. His analysis has never been approached, far less surpassed or even developed. We know part of it popularly as the alienation of labor."[53] The first explicit reference to them by James to appear in print came in his 1946 essay "After Ten Years: On Trotsky's *The Revolution Betrayed*."[54]

James concluded his preface to the essays by emphasizing the link between their theoretical content and the corroborative experience of American factory workers: "We have been stimulated to find that those of our colleagues who work in factories and who share our ideas," he remarks, "have found that the great masses of the American workers feel and think in a way that invest these century-old essays with a meaning and significance that they could never have had, however assiduously they were merely read and merely studied. . . . If these essays have helped us to understand Marxism and them, they too have helped us to understand these essays and Marxism."

X

In my view, any accurate understanding of what James is actually doing and saying in *American Civilization* is contingent upon recognizing the central role played in its formulation by Marx's twin concepts of alienation and self-activity of "*socialized man*, the *associated producers*," first articulated by Marx in 1844 and the premise upon which he would erect the entire structure of his analysis of capitalist production later found in *Capital*. James makes an allusion that confirms this interpretation, when he refers in the prospectus to Marx's *Capital* as being "so largely concerned with the human relations of industrial man," illustrated in this instance by what Marx had to say about "the factory of the future, [where] men, women *and children* will take part in the work, and thus lay the basis for totally new relations of the family."

According to Marx, alienation is produced by "the act of estranging practical human activity, labor," under a variety of circumstances. These circumstances occur in (1) "The relation of the worker to the *product of labor* as an alien object exercising power over him;" and (2) "The relation of labor to the *act of production* within the labor process."[55] These first two are fundamental, and from them follow two other aspects of alienation, namely, (3) estrangement "from man his own body, as well as external nature and his spiritual aspect, his *human* aspect;" and (4) as "an immediate consequence of the fact that man is estranged from the product of his labor, from his life activity, from his species-being is the *estrangement of man* from *man.*"[56]

It is instructive to note how closely James follows this definition of multiple estrangement in interpreting the artistic achievement of Herman Melville, who James finds "worked out an entirely new conception of society, not dealing with profits and the rights of private property (Ahab was utterly contemptuous of both), but with new conceptions of the relations *between* man and man, between man and his technology and between man and Nature."[57]

Employment of Marx's concept of alienation is what, fundamentally, distinguishes James and the Johnson–Forest group from other Marxists on the American Left during the forties. John Patrick Diggins indirectly confirms this disjunction when he notes, in *The Rise and Fall of the American Left*: "What was curious about the discussion of Marxism in the late thirties and early forties was the absence of any mention of 'alienation'. The Old Left was not aware of the younger Marx of the 'Economic and Philosophic Manuscripts' (1844), where one finds the first conceptualization of alienation rooted in the monotony of industrial work."[58]

James *was* very much aware of the 1844 essays of the young Marx. In *Notes on Dialectics*, he emphasizes just how fundamental these essays were to his thinking: "Note how the things we emphasize, alienation, creativity, etc., are looked upon by other people not as the basis but as mere features, particulars."[59] In *American Civilization* James applies the concept of alienation specifically, using it to examine the labor process, the role of intellectuals, and the struggle by blacks and women for human relationships in society. "Today we are once more at an age when universality is on the order of the day," James declares. "But today universality *begins* with man in the labor process." His emphasis upon the role of intellectuals as agents in the disciplining of workers makes them part of "the labor bureaucracy in its relation to the fundamental problems of the labor process."

The prospectus tries to understand also the basis of the "profound alienation from society" of contemporary American literature with "its inability to satisfy either itself or the national need." By basing his analysis fundamentally upon the phenomenon of estrangement, James's work is able to achieve psychological truth and sociological depth:

> Upon a people bursting with energy, untroubled by feudal remains or a feudal past, soaked to the marrow in a tradition of individual freedom, individual security, free association, a tradition which is constantly held before them as the basis of their civilization, upon this people more than all others has been imposed a mechanized way of life at work, mechanized forms of living, a mechanized totality which from morning till night, week after week, day after day, crushes the very individuality which tradition nourishes and the abundance of mass-produced goods encourages.

At the same time, by basing his philosophical outlook on Marx's *Economic-Philosophic Manuscripts*, James is able to postulate an alternative to "alienation in society" by utilizing and applying the concept of human emancipation found in Marx's 1844 essays. When James refers in the text, for example, to "the creation of man as an integral human being, a full and complete individuality with the circumstances and conditions of that fully integrated individuality," he is using the concepts and language spoken by Marx in the Paris manuscripts.

This is also true for the concept of integrated humanism that features so prominently in *American Civilization*. "The role that they [intellectuals] played between 1200 and today will be over," James asserts, "because the condition of that role, the passive subordinate mass, will be undergoing liquidation in the very action of the mass which will be creating a totally new society, an active integrated humanism." The concept of integrated humanism represents a theoretical condensation of Marx's concept of "reintegration or return of man to himself, the transcendence of human self-estrangement" and the account of communist society given by Marx in the essay "Private Property and Communism," in the *Economic-Philosophic Manuscripts*, in which Marx describes "*Communism* as the *positive* transcendence of *private property*, *as human self-estrangement*, and therefore as the real *appropriation of* the *human* essence by and for man; communism therefore as the complete return of man to himself as a *social* (i.e., human) being – a return accomplished consciously and embracing the entire wealth of previous development." Marx continues: "This communism, as fully developed naturalism, equals humanism, and as fully developed humanism equals naturalism; it is the *genuine* resolution of the conflict between man and nature and between man and man – the true resolution of the strife between existence and essence, between objectification and self-confirmation, between freedom and necessity, between the individual and the species."[60]

XI

Extremely significant for the theoretical perspective that James presents in the prospectus is the fusion that he effects in assimilating Marx's concept of association, described by Marx in the essay "Private Property and Communism," to the phenomenon that de Tocqueville ferreted out in America: "Americans of all ages, all conditions, and all dispositions, constantly form associations . . . religious, moral, serious, futile, general or restricted, enormous or diminutive . . . to give entertainments, to found seminaries, to build inns, to construct churches, to diffuse books, to send missionaries to the antipodes. . . ."[61] In a reflection of this synthesis, James states in a footnote that appears in *Beyond a Boundary* that Marx and Tocqueville are "two of the acutest minds of the time."[62]

"De Tocqueville's interesting appreciation of this American phenomenon," according to Frederick Jackson Turner, of extra-legal, voluntary association was also "one of the things that impressed all early travellers in the United States."[63] Turner describes some of the social forms that association among the early pioneers took:

The log rolling, the house-raising, the husking bee, the apple paring, and the squatters' associations whereby they protected themselves against the speculators in securing title to their clearings on the public domain, the camp meeting, the mining camp, the vigilantes, the cattle-raisers' associations, the "gentlemen's agreements," are a few of the indications of this attitude. It is well to emphasize this American trait, because in a modified way it has come to be one of the most characteristic and important features of the United States of to-day. . . . These associations were in America not due to immemorial custom of tribe or village community. They were extemporized by voluntary action."[64]

Turner calls these associations "aspects of early backwoods democracy" which arose from "the power of spontaneous association" on the American frontier. Here in these associations was the historical basis that provided the conceptual springboard for launching James's theoretical synthesis of Marx's concept of "direct association" with the American tradition. He does this without making explicit in the text that this is the historical and theoretical bases of the "free association" that he expounds in the text.

Marx's account of the phenomenon of "direct association," which appears in the 1844 manuscripts, is the philosophical justification for the concept of "free association" that James applies in *American Civilization*. It is easy to see how James made the theoretical leap once it is situated in the context of Marx's exposition. Marx states: "Social activity and social enjoyment exist by no means *only* in the form of some *directly* communal activity and directly *communal* enjoyment, although *communal* activity and *communal* enjoyment

– i.e., activity and enjoyment which are manifested and affirmed in *actual* direct association with other men – will occur wherever such a *direct* expression of sociability stems from the true character of the activity's content and is appropriate to the nature of the enjoyment." To this he appends the added caution:

> Above all we must avoid postulating "society" again as an abstraction *vis-à-vis* the individual. The individual is *the social being*. His manifestations of life – even if they may not appear in the direct form of *communal* manifestations of life carried out in association with others – are therefore an expression and confirmation of *social life*. Man's individual and species-life are not *different*, however much – and this is inevitable – the mode of existence of the individual is a more *particular* or more *general* mode of the life of the species, or the life of the species is a more *particular* or more *general* individual life.[65]

Marx's explication of the concept of association is taken up and applied by James, when he asserts, for example, that in America the individual "showed an altogether exceptional capacity for free association, in industry, in politics and for any other purpose. Individuality and universality achieve a fusion unknown elsewhere." "The great unsatisfied desire of the American population," James argues, "is for social organization, free association, for common social ends." He gives as a concrete manifestation of this social urge the Negro church situated "in some small room in a Northern city" where can be found gathered together "the faithful, domestic servants, common laborers, the poorest of the poor, seeking some social organization, some collective life." Marx develops and applies the concept of association when he writes about changing "from top to bottom the conditions of industrial and political existence, and consequently the whole manner of being of the associated producers."[66] James simply expands this notion by making the "associated producers" synonymous with the totality of the popular classes.

James's application of the concept of association would later prove central to his interpretation of Melville's *Moby Dick*. In writing of what might otherwise appear from the outside as the motley crew of the *Pequod*, James tells what happens when you part the veil: "They are meanest mariners, castaways and renegades. But that is not their fault. They began that way. Their heroism consists in their everyday doing of their work. The only tragic graces with which Melville endows them are the graces of men associated for common labor."[67]

The concept of free association as the cultural and moral ethos of workers precedes by at least a decade E. P. Thompson's investigation of the analogous phenomenon prefigured in the "moral economy" of eighteenth-century rioters and protesters. According to Thompson, the food rioters' of the eighteenth century acted from implicit moral judgments about economic relationships founded in their minds upon some traditional notion of rights and obligations that were violated by capitalist market practices.[68]

In James's analysis there is one important difference, however. The violation of the moral consensus is not wrought by impersonal market forces; instead, it is instituted from within the sphere of work and it is maintained by the power of the bureaucracy that uses it to discipline workers and control production. Production relations and not market relations are the key for James.

XII

The Johnson–Forest minority resigned from the WP in 1947 in order to rejoin the SWP. James's group had for some time been strongly in favor of reunification between the two wings of the movement. It was a conviction that was greatly strengthened when the SWP promulgated its "Theses on the American Revolution," adopted at the SWP's convention in late 1946. As the basic postwar document of the SWP, the political statement strongly resonated with James's views on the postwar crisis of America. At the July 1947 conference of the Johnson–Forest group, held on the eve of rejoining the SWP, the American theses of the SWP were explicitly acknowledged. "The SWP at its last [1946] convention has brought forward," the conference resolution declared, "as a new stage of development for the American movement, programmatic perspectives for the revolution in the United States; what has been missing since 1940 can therefore now be made clear: theoretical unity or difference around the strategic orientation of the American party in its struggle for the American revolution."

What the SWP in 1946 was embarking upon was the difficult task of attempting to transform itself from a propaganda organization into a mass political party. James supported this objective. However, he was also convinced that a fundamental requirement for building such a party in the United States was the development of a body of Marxist ideas on American society. The basic condition of such an undertaking was intimate acquaintance with the activity of the American working-class. James's organization was his anchor and the vehicle that provided both the connection with the American working-class and the community of ideas upon which he and his colleagues drew in developing their distinctive body of Marxist ideas in the forties. It is extremely important to emphasize this point, since it is so easy for intellectuals today to overlook it.

At the time that he wrote *American Civilization*, then, James felt that he wished to go directly to the public with his views. He had enough of the sectarian existence that was his lot as a minority functioning within the two branches of the tiny Trotskyist movement in the United States. As a minority in the WP and then the SWP, James's group could not strike out on its own in public, even while it sought to demonstrate what adoption of such a stance would mean in the form of articles published in the theoretical organs of the *New International* and the *Fourth International.*

In 1950, therefore, James set himself the aim of breaking through the intellectual confinement that enmeshed the entire sectarian Left in America. It was a bold and empowering vision, which required James to transform his political group from a theoretical tendency into a propaganda circle openly propagating its theory of the self-activity of the working class.

The posture of James and his associates up until the time that he wrote the present prospectus was politically sectarian, operating within the confines of a political sect away from the mainstream. In view of this ideological restriction, the idea of going to a bourgeois publisher with a proposal or a manuscript would have been utterly unthinkable. This attitude changed in 1949, however, as James felt the enthusiastic audience response during his nationwide lecture tour of that year. The present prospectus bears all the signs of a work intended for a popular audience. It represents the first substantive attempt to reverse the sectarian stance of Johnson–Forest. From operating essentially underground while he awaited the outcome of his deportation case, James was now looking to take his ideas before the wider American public.

American Civilization thus marks the turning-point of James's political activity in the United States, the culmination of a protracted process of theoretical exploration and growth. The premise of the Leninist vanguard party was now rejected. "All this setting up of little splinters as parties for workers to join, which will little by little grow, that is the quintessence of stupidity," James declared. "We have no such illusions any more, thank God."

The present prospectus constitutes an important preparatory step in James's ultimate break with official Trotskyism in the United States. In 1948 James had experienced a slight foretaste of the freedom to "write and develop ideas as Marx and Lenin used to write and develop ideas," as he relates in what would eventually become *Notes on Dialectics.*[69] When the break with the SWP was finally made official, in July–August 1951, it was eighteen months after James completed the text of his prospectus.

After formally resigning from the SWP, Johnson–Forest reorganized itself as the *Correspondence* editorial committees. *American Civilization* was instrumental in laying the groundwork for this new, independent phase of political activity. James was even at this point preparing to go public. As he elsewhere noted in connection with Lenin's writing of *State and Revolution*, "Lenin did not keep his theory in his book or in his head. *He went to the masses with it.*"[70]

Like everything else that he wrote in the United States, James's ideas were developed out of contact with American workers. The goal was to create a Marxism that would be relevant for the present. The work of transforming these ideas into written form was a process conducted in association with political colleagues. "As is customary in the Marxist movement," James would attest in recalling the writing of *Facing Reality*, "the ideas contained in the book and the book itself were planned and written in close collaboration with all who were members or close associates of our movement."

What James has to say about American civilization is not simply a cultural critique nor a personal document: it represents his view that world capitalism had entered a new stage, namely, state capitalism, which posed the social question in terms of the struggle for control over the labor process. Without understanding the primacy that he attaches to the industrial workers, it is impossible to arrive at an accurate assessment of the significance of the present work. It is the feature that makes James unique among the great Marxists of the twentieth century, who, with the exception of Lenin, have very little of significance to say about the industrial working-class of America. Unfortunately, as James acknowledges, the record of intellectuals, particularly American intellectuals, in "recognizing the power of the working class is very bad."[71]

James later acknowledged that "It took more than ten years, but by 1952 I once more felt my feet on solid ground, and in consequence I planned a series of books. The first was published in 1953, a critical study of Herman Melville as a mirror of our age, and the second is this book on cricket."[72] If James's book on Melville announced his intellectual independence, his prospectus with its lengthy section on Melville, represents its foreshadowing. More importantly, if we accept the dichotomy that James asserts, then the present text sits astride both halves of his political career. It is the literary marker demarcating, on one side, the prior period of allegiance to the Trotskyist movement, and, on the other, the achievement of political independence that was soon to follow composition of the prospectus in 1951. It forms a significant part of that "solid ground" to which James refers.

At the beginning of Chapter 7 of *American Civilization*, James pauses to inform the reader: "We come now to the last chapter of this sketch." When he refers again, later in the same chapter, to the expectation that a quotation would have "full significance for us who are following this sketch," it confirms his fundamental practice of circulating everything to members of his political organization to elicit their discussion and modification, even those things that would be published eventually under his own name. To the extent that the prospectus lays out the literary path along which James was to move in the fifties, the prospectus of *American Civilization* served as both a sounding-board and a sketchbook for the works that were to follow. Although executed in an extremely short time-span, its significance was long-term, containing the basic intellectual agenda that James was to continue to amplify throughout the crucial decade of the fifties that in reality forms the apogee of his career.

XIII

James's fifteen-year sojourn in the United States allowed him to acquire a familiarity with American past and present American culture, sufficient for him to ground his application of Bolshevism to America in an American usable past. James identifies a group of representative 19th-century intellectuals – Whitman, Melville, and the Abolitionist crusader Wendell Phillips – whose relationships with American society he compares with the position of contemporary intellectuals in the United States:

(1) Whitman: a singer of loneliness and Democracy with a capital D.
(2) Melville: prophet of destruction.
(3) Abolitionism: advocates of mass revolution.

James is concerned in the prospectus with demonstrating the superior value of the latter two tendencies. *American Civilization* attempts to demonstrate how their roles in twentieth-century American culture and society have been inherited and are reproduced by the modern popular arts and the insurgent movements of the American working class.

The book constitutes James's appeal directed at American intellectuals, whom he hoped to influence as he was preparing his break with official Trotskyism. "Most of the readers of this Ms.," he carefully notes, "are members, more or less, of the intellectual classification." It explains the attention that the prospectus lavishes upon the young Norman Mailer, whose critique of 20th-century America's bureaucratic totalitarianism, in *The Naked and the Dead*, strongly appealed to James. The remarks on Mailer are in the nature of an intellectual rescue mission.

At a time when James was looking to leave behind his sectarian existence and reach out to a wider audience, *American Civilization* might have served as a beacon to guide a new post-war generation of intellectuals. As it happened, however, James would have to wait for almost another two decades, before members of the rising radical wing of the black freedom movement and the New Left in the US were to rediscover his particular brand of revolutionary Marxism. They embodied the sort of intellectual engagement that James was already in 1950 forecasting as a component of the struggle for popular emancipation.

In the introduction discussing the significance of Herman Melville and Walt Whitman, he remarks: "In any estimate of contemporary culture, studies of the past or speculations into the future, their work is indispensable." The shift in perspective from past toward "speculations into the future" is further hinted at when, in the second chapter of the prospectus James comes to discuss the movement of American Abolition and concludes that "it is perhaps the highest peak reached by the United States intellectuals in the foreshadowing of the future of the world of today and in indicating how deeply all great world currents are integral to the United States as a nation."

For James, then, the source of "the evolution of American Bolshevism" was to be the American Abolitionist movement. "Out of America, with no assistance from any alien tradition but from the very genius of the country," he declares, "emerged this clearly recognizable replica of the early Christians, the Puritans, and later the early Bolsheviks, types which have appeared only when fundamental changes are shaking a society to its depths." The abolitionist Wendell Phillips, James went on, "in his context and in his political programs showed the same breadth of view, the revolutionary conception of democracy, and political ruthlessness which are associated with what is loosely called Bolshevism." Speaking in the immediate aftermath of John Brown's raid at Harper's Ferry, Wendell Phillips also recognized that there was an intimate connection between American civilization and the struggle for emancipation. "For the last twenty years," he declared, in Brooklyn, New York, in November 1859, "there has been going on, more or less heeded and understood, in different States, an insurrection of ideas against this limited, cribbed, cabined, isolated American civilization, an insurrection to restore absolute right [of justice]."[73]

XIV

At the outset of the prospectus James's focus is upon the threat of totalitarianism. He informs the reader in his introduction that "I find the American pattern to be the dominant social pattern of our time and in this conviction I give a fairly detailed treatment of totalitarianism in the world at large and totalitarian tendencies in the United States." At the conclusion of the text, however, the reader is informed that "the sign that the permanent crisis is at last up for resolution will be the appearance of this new mass political organization which will seek to make politics an expression of universal man and a totally integrated personality."

A parallel trajectory can be traced along the path that starts with James asking early in the introduction of the prospectus: "What exactly do I propose to do that is new?" From this initial question, James proceeds to ask – "Why has the United States failed to produce men who planted flags in unexplored territory?" For the answer to these questions, James turns to an analysis that attributes the cause of the failure to the dismal failing of

American intellectuals. But this comes at the beginning. The focus later shifts, again in the pivotal sixth chapter, as James asks – "What is it that the people want?" The same question is recapitulated in the conclusion of the text. "What do the miners want? What do the people want?" asks James.

This same shifting movement appears in James's discussion of the Abolitionist movement – "the first great independent expression of the American genius." When James reaches the conclusion, he picks up the theme of Abolitionism, but it is greatly expanded. From a discrete phenomenon, characterizing a distinctive stage of American history, Abolitionism is transformed at the conclusion of the text into a political metaphor for a process of liberation universal in scope. "We devoted considerable space to the Abolitionists in the middle of the nineteenth century," James recalls for the reader. "But the great masses become abolitionist now; themselves to wipe away the conditions of their own slavery. These cannot be abolished by anybody else." Unless this continuing movement and development within the text of *American Civilization* is appreciated, it is difficult to understand the connection bridging James's dissection of the past with his bold projections into the future. It is this connection that unifies the present statement as a singular piece of political analysis.

In 1952, James announced, in his study of Herman Melville, *Mariners, Renegades and Castaways*, that "my ultimate aim, and my book on Melville is merely a preparation for it, is to write a study of American civilization." Spurred on by celebration in 1951 of the centennial of the publication of *Moby Dick*, James interprets Melville's literary classic of the monomaniacal pursuit of the great white whale as the prophetic allegory of American civilization, forecasting the totalitarian threat to the human personality and the viability of American civilization in its struggle with the specter of totalitarian domination coming not from Russia but from within American society.

"The house in which Ahab had lived, and this house was American civilization of the nineteenth century," James decides, "this house had fallen into ruins about him."[74] In keeping with the apocalyptic vision of the book, James interprets Fedallah's prophecy that "the wood of Ahab's hearse can only be American" to mean that "Ahab will bury himself in the wreck of American industrial civilization, symbolized by the line and the whaling vessel."[75]

Three years before writing this, in 1949, James began a series of public lectures on such topics as *Herman Melville and American Culture, Walt Whitman and American Culture, New Currents in Historical Thinking and Research,* and *The American Negro: Touchstone of American Civilization.* He lectured "to all types of audiences, workers, intellectuals, church members, whites and Negroes, students, hundreds at a time," in such cities as New York, Detroit, Pittsburgh, Philadelphia, San Francisco, and Los Angeles.

Culminating in April 1953, James capped his public speaking career in the United States with a series of three remarkable lectures at Columbia University entitled *The American Vision*, in which he spoke about Walt Whitman, Herman Melville, and the group of contemporary authors – Richard Wright, Norman Mailer, James Jones, and Ralph Ellison.

The prospectus forms an important accompaniment to the lecture tours that James undertook in the United States from 1949 until 1953. With the birth of a son in April 1949, James was also trying to generate additional income for the upkeep of his family (he married Constance Webb in 1948). If his public lectures caused his writing pace to slow down, however, it also greatly stimulated his creative energies. This was especially the case with his public lectures on Herman Melville. "What stood out was the readiness of every type of audience to discuss him, and sometimes very heatedly, as if he were a contemporary writer."[76] The public response to his lectures made James aware of a certain irony: "Foreigner as I am, it was from me that many of them gained their first enthusiasm and interest in Melville."

After he returned to England, in 1953, James prepared and circulated a lengthy prospectus for a series of lectures which he again proposed to give on "The American Civilization." He followed up this statement with a detailed eleven–page outline for a book that he hoped to write for the European public, to be entitled "The American Civilization: Its Place in History."

In 1956 he completed a second investigation of "American Civilization," written in collaboration with members of his American organization. With the outbreak of the Hungarian Revolution, in October 1956, this work was put aside in favor of an account of the Hungarian workers' councils that was published eventually as *Facing Reality*.[77] During this same period James also embarked on the writing of *Beyond a Boundary*, which, following his five-year involvement in West Indian politics, was published to great critical acclaim in 1963. This latter work descends from the same intellectual lineage to which the present prospectus belongs.

XV

In the present text, James cites numerous topics that he proposed to take up and amplify in the finished work. These include (1) "the Populist outburst at the end of the [nineteenth] century;" (2) the relationship of "Emerson, Thoreau and the Transcendentalists to Whitman, Melville and the Abolitionists;" (3) "the great popular tunes, the famous blues;"(4) "the sexual relation" and "the question of homosexuality [as] a critical question in American sexual relations;" (5) "architecture – the revolt against the two rooms and a half;" and, finally, (6) "inflation, bad housing, seasonal unemployment (as opposed to the Depression which undermined confidence in the whole economy), racial prejudice, the dislocations of war, the struggles in the factories, struggle over civil liberties, etc."

The one topic that is noticeable by its absence from this list is sport, even though there are fleeting references to it, for example, in the suggestive remark that "the [totalitarian] state integrates every aspect of life, production, politics, entertainment, aesthetics, sport into a single whole and imposes these with the utmost ruthlessness upon the mass of the nation." The absence of any explicit discussion of American sport may simply have reflected James's lack of direct experience; without such experience, he would never be able to participate fully in the popular passion that they aroused in the way that he could in regard to the game of cricket. The same principle holds true for these other sports that he enunciated in relation to cricket: "The aesthetics of cricket," he observed, "demand first that you master the game, and preferably, have played it, if not well, at least in good company."[78]

It is in the present prospectus, specifically in the section on Ancient Greece, that James would draw the connection between popular culture and cricket. It was suggested by W. H. Auden who, in his *Portable Greek Reader*,[79] likened classical Athenian drama to modern popular entertainment. "The nearest modern equivalent," Auden pointed out, "is not any work of the theater, but a ball game or a bull-fight." James picks up the idea and runs with it: "The idea that he [Auden] is trying to convey is correct," he affirms, "the Greek masses went to the theater as if they were going to the World Series, Independence Day and a film festival all combined." Participation was the key and "to get the idea of participation," James states, "we must go back to Auden's image of the ball-game but even that is not enough. Perhaps a mass-revival meeting of Negroes just relieved from slavery would give another avenue of understanding." James would later apply this idea with very pleasing results in *Beyond a Boundary* (1963), in which the same Audenesque insight is utilized to buttress the analogy of cricket spectators with the popular audience in Greek drama. "W. H. Auden compares the Greek crowd to a Spanish crowd at a bullfight,"[80] James repeats there exactly what he stated earlier in *American Civilization*.

The continuity of this aesthetic judgment with *Beyond a Boundary* is made explicit in the dedication of the latter work to Learie Constantine and W. G. Grace, where James states that "this book hopes to right grave wrongs, and, in so doing, extend our too limited conceptions of history and of the fine arts." Again in the chapter celebrating the latter's accomplishments, James recognizes as the measure of Grace's true greatness not simply the fact that Grace "had enriched the depleted lives of two generations and millions yet to be born," though that was certainly important, but that Grace "had extended our conception of human capacity and in doing all this he had done no harm to anyone."[81]

XVI

American Civilization forms the bridge between the theoretical work that Johnson–Forest carried out during the forties and the statement that represents its theoretical culmination, *State Capitalism and World Revolution*, which appeared during the summer of 1950, as *Discussion Bulletin* No. 4 of the SWP, not more than six months after James had finished composing his prospectus. Originally prepared for a conference of the Fourth International in Europe, *State Capitalism and World Revolution* was, in James's words, "not a political resolution of the traditional type, but a long overdue restatement of Marxism for our day."

In analyzing the nature of contemporary industrial societies, and emphasizing the revolutionary potential of the working class, *State Capitalism and World Revolution* draws extensively upon the two chapters of his American prospectus that are the axis on which the edifice turns and that describe the struggle of workers to control production. "The Mode of Labor in the United States," the title of chapter 5 of the resolution, summarizes the data presented in *American Civilization*.

The American prospectus of 1950 also became the source for *Mariners, Renegades and Castaways: The Story of Herman Melville and the World We Live In*, the writing of which James actually completed in November 1952. The present text, particularly the section on popular culture and Greek civilization, also supplied the theoretical underpinning for *Beyond a Boundary*, which was substantially completed by 1957 but not published until 1963. Finally, the ideas presented in the 1950 prospectus are reflected in the joint statement published in 1958, in the aftermath of the Hungarian Revolution, entitled *Facing Reality*, in the sections dealing with the United States and the struggles of American workers, African Americans, and women.

XVII

While the bulk of the prospectus was probably produced during the first couple of months of 1950, in terms of political inspiration and theoretical conception it was a work that reflected the experience of forties' America. One giveaway, for example, is the fact that television is hardly mentioned. Although the first television sets became available to American consumers in 1946, the language of television was still being invented in the late forties and early fifties. In point of fact, James makes mention of the story of the popular radio personality Mary McBride who "took one look at herself on television and fled from it." According to James's explanation, it was because "One glimpse of her might destroy her hold over the millions who listen." The present text mirrors this pre-television era of American culture.

The prospectus also accurately reflects the forties' defiant sentiment, a mood that one historian of the period interprets as "an unmistakable sense of displacement, a feverish running away, a bitterness that reveled in the harsh, the mocking, the blatant."[82] "The American intellectuals can make neither head nor tail of this," James argues, applauding "the defiance of society," which, in the case of the coal miners and their leader John L. Lewis, is described as being "American to the core." This popular attitude of resistance so characteristic of the forties was perhaps best expressed in the dissonant musical phenomenon of be-bop – "the intense, high-speed revolution that has become jazz's most enduring style."[83] By separating the revolution in popular music symbolized by be-bop, it has become all too easy to identify the forties with the buoyant melodies of Rodgers and Hammerstein musicals, forgetting that the forties were a socially turbulent as well as stylistically innovative time for American society mirrored in the impact of jazz on popular attitudes and tastes. The zoot-suit phenomenon, which became the dress of choice of African American and Hispanic hipsters in the forties, was emblematic of the new defiant mood. It was a profoundly anti-elitist attitude. James vividly captures the ethos of this era when he states: "This much is certain, the America I have seen and studied in a dozen years will never accept an elite. If by any chance an elite should establish itself after what will be one of the bloodiest civil wars in history, the human, social and economic forces it will need to maintain itself will assuredly result in the collapse of civilization."

Popular élan, supple and intricate relations within the plant, and solidarity between plant and community – these traits are what provided the impetus behind the great sense of autonomy and inner freedom that most Americans experienced during this period, which they exhibited in displays of fearlessness as well as genuine curiosity about world-embracing ideas. "The America of today, the workers, the farmers, the middle-classes, the men who were in the army, have no contempt at all for intellect," James remarks. "For personal culture in the European sense, yes, but for intellect? No."

Most commentators do not look upon the forties in this manner, although this was very much the way that James and the members of his organization experienced the era. Members working in the plants supplied an important stimulus in development and refinement of the group's ideas. The impact of this shared experience and insight upon James's *American Civilization* was profound. There are several allusions made to this exchange of information and perspective that resonate in the prospectus. It can be heard in the description of a typical miner's attitude toward participation in the union: "It is noted by those familiar with the union movement that the really unskilled production worker does not attend union meetings. He will rally to the defense of the union if it is attacked. And he will come out on strikes. But the regular business of the union, he pays no attention to and that is not because he, as so many Philistines think, is stupid or apathetic, but because he knows that organization will do nothing for the things that affect him most vitally."

It would not be exaggerating to say that for James the forties was a kind of redemptive experience. He derived tremendous satisfaction and sense of vindication from the social movement that he felt himself keenly a part of. The depth and quality of worker networks forged within the plants of the forties among individuals coming from extremely diverse social backgrounds meant that the labor bureaucracy was met with strong shop-floor resistance. Students, women, blacks, Chicanos, hillbillies, intellectuals, artists – it seemed that almost everyone had some kind of contact with the plant in the forties. The plant thus was a practical, day-to-day experience, not an intellectual or abstract question. The same was true for vets in the army, but it was life in the plant that really held the key to the culture of forties' America.

If the first half of the decade of the forties represented a hopeful hour for popular initiative and autonomy, the postwar half reflected a mood of national anxiety. Suddenly, the feeling of hope and confidence gave way to a sense of self-doubt and fiendish reality. It is a transformation that is still difficult from this distance to appreciate. James's text records both these outlooks, the buoyant optimism immediately following the defeat of Nazism and the eroding sense of gloom. "When or where was there ever such a powerful body of men and women, when and where was there such 'inner strength' in a nation?" James asks. And he replies: "It is not their weakness that is ruining civilization. It is *conflict* that is ruining us. It is the consciousness of strength in the mass and the need for full self-expression that in seeking to burst the traditional limits of society can bring society to ruin."

XVIII

A problematic aspect of the prospectus is the support which it appears to give to the view of America as somehow the special creation of American males. "Women have always had a special place in the United States, respected as women have been in no other modern country," James acknowledges, then goes on: "But the American male has had a passion for human relationships, social and personal, general and intimate, and it is this which above all constitutes the high civilization of the United States. He has not been able to create or establish this relationship with women."

Depending on how one reads this statement, it could be interpreted as either a critique of otherness or as a limitation of James's analysis. If it is the latter, such a view privileges the male subset as the driving force of the entire American population, a view which has the effect of diminishing America's stark social divisions, inequalities, and conflicts when men are seen as the virtual representatives of the culture as a whole.

James's omission of women from the intellectuals and authors discussed in the text also raises the important issue of canon. Because the figures that he presents are nearly all male, the result is that the voice of women is absent from the text. Although James devotes a significant section of the prospectus to an analysis of the struggle of American women for equality, there are no voices of women. By including William Lloyd Garrison, Wendell Phillips, and Frederick Douglass, it is true, James's canon represents an important expansion over what existed at the time, but its overwhelmingly male focus still represents a major limitation.

James's unbounded enthusiasm for the subsequent literary achievements of African American female writers in the seventies, moreover, makes the absence of any real female voice in the prospectus all the more surprising. There are only two exceptions to the absent voice of women, found in references *en passant* to the autobiography of Eleanor Roosevelt, *This I Remember*,[84] and Margaret Mead's *Male and Female: A Study of the Sexes in a Changing Society*.[85]

The absence seems all the more contradictory in view of the fact that it was James who insisted to his political organization that *Correspondence* devote a section in the newspaper to women. He insisted also that it should be edited by women, a responsibility which was given to the Los Angeles branch of the group. In fact, it could be argued that the woman's section of *Correspondence* during the fifties was theoretically way in advance of the women's movement and the New Left of the sixties. It departed sharply from the old socialist slogan of equal pay for equal work and dealt with issues of the family, relations between husbands and wives, child-rearing, etc. One of the most popular articles that would ever appear in *Correspondence* was something called – "I prefer a man who is backward," which rejected the idea of the superiority of the middle-class male in relation to women.

The treatment of the "women question" in *Correspondence* is reflected not only in the preparation of the section, but also in the role that it played in the writing of *A Woman's Place*. Co-written by Selma Weinstein (later James) and Filomena Maria Daddario, with assistance from Vivian Hall, *A Woman's Place* was published in February 1953 in Los Angeles. It was among the early voices that would help to pave the way for the new women's literature to emerge in the sixties and seventies. A profound yet simple statement of the problems and oppressive conditions faced by American women, it was James who insisted that the authors should be left alone by the rest of the organization in order that they might feel free to write what they wanted to.

If James's prospectus reveals a point of view that was quite rare on the American Left at the time, it also drew upon de Tocqueville's *Democracy in America*, with its considerable attention devoted to women in American society – "mistresses of their own action" is how de Tocqueville refers to them – which provided James with the conceptual building-block upon which he elevates his views of American women. More importantly, however, the prospectus reflects the salient role of women in Johnson–Forest, notably Raya Dunayevskaya, Grace Lee, Freddy Paine, Constance Webb, and, at a later date, James. The participation of women in Johnson–Forest was the real source of the sense of immediacy that can be felt in James's treatment of the subject in the text. When James observes that "De Tocqueville and Bryce have drawn attention to the exceptional advantages she has enjoyed throughout the history of the United States," his statement was a mirror of the reality of the Johnson–Forest organization, which enjoyed, as a result of the participation of the women in leadership, definite advantages in the quality of its life as a political group, not the least of which was the discussion of women that went on within it.

Despite his modernity and his support for the claims of women to equality, however, James was not a feminist. The problem of canon is best exemplified in the context of James's response to the suggestion made by the reviewer in the *New York Times Book Review* of January 29, 1950, J. Donald Adams, who observed that there was a subject "about which not nearly enough has been written – the relationship between the sexes in the modern world." James welcomed Adams's observation as being "absolutely correct," but he was frankly skeptical about the reviewer's prediction that the subject of women would become "one of the great themes which writers will approach during the remainder of this century." "It is practically virgin territory," Adams declared. James responded: "Adams thinks that creative writers will approach this theme during the next half-century. The fatuity of these thinkers is beyond belief. Joyce, Proust, Lawrence, T. S. Eliot, during the last thirty years approached many other serious problems very creatively. And what is the result? They have increased the sense of demoralization, bankruptcy and hopelessness. What in the name of heaven can creative writers do in the face of what we have been describing?"

What this reveals is the unconscious assumption, common to both James and Adams, that creative writers somehow meant male writers. Within a very few years of this exchange, a new generation of creative women writers as well as the developing feminist movement would challenge this situation of literary hegemony, ultimately exploding the assumptions of male discourse and laying the basis for an assault upon the canon as a bastion of male privilege. The publication in English, in 1953, of Simone de Beauvoir's landmark work, *The Second Sex*, signalled the start of the movement that paved the way for the international groundswell of feminist writers, activists, and scholars whose voice would transform the discourse of men and women in the latter half of the twentieth-century.

The tremendous storm of controversy generated by publication of de

Beauvoir's *Le Deuxieme Sexe* in 1949 would have reinforced the significance of these earlier views. Like de Beauvoir, James integrates the struggle of women as part of the class struggle, at the same time that it is linked, as in de Beauvoir's analysis, to the struggle waged by blacks for equality. "There is involved here a revolution in relations comparable only to the revolution which will emancipate labor and the revolution which will emancipate women," James states, in describing the importance of the black struggle; it exists "on a par with the labor question and the women question." Women's experience in the process of production resulting from war-time labor shortages was an emancipating experience, transforming their potential as a revolutionary social force in their own right. "For many millions of women, especially younger women all over the world, work in factories and in farms was an introduction to a new world of freedom, independence and common social experience." And speaking of the sense of frustration that women feel, James explains that the struggle of women is "the direct counterpart of the sense of hopelessness and frustration felt by the masses of workers in modern industrial production." "To make the point clear," James asserts that the resolution of the struggle of women will only be found in "a revolution in individual relationships as great as the revolution pointed at in the labor process."

XIX

In spite of the insight that the prospectus reveals into the nature of production relations, James's predictions concerning the political futures of key labor leaders would eventually fall wide of the mark. In the case of Walter Reuther, who later became head of the CIO but ended up being politically eclipsed by George Meany, James's prediction proved wrong. James contends in the prospectus that "the labor leadership is headed for governmental power" and that the labor leader most symbolic of "this welfare-state bureaucratized concept" was Reuther. Likewise, James saw John L. Lewis as wielding "enormous power which has made him able to challenge the full force of the government and official opinion in peace and in war." Lewis for his part simply faded away after the war.

In actuality, James's prediction of the increasingly powerful role of the labor movement in American politics – "the next logical step is political power and the fusion of the labor bureaucracy with the government bureaucracy" – failed to come about. Since the 1980s, the American labor leadership and union movement as a whole have floundered in disarray and have suffered steady decline.

The same paradoxical combination of short-term anticipation and long-term analysis is reflected in James's penetrating analysis of American intellectuals. It is also sociologically very suggestive: "The outstanding change in the social structure is the centralization, the bureaucratization, the incorporation of the great mass of *intelligentsia* into the unit which governs, manages, instructs, organizes the great undifferentiated mass." Likewise, his comments about the integration of intellectuals as part of the labor bureaucracy, "to assist the labor leadership in building a mighty bureaucratic centralized apparatus, to resist extreme reactionaries and die-hards, on the one hand, and above all, on behalf of the interests of labor, to discipline labor, so as to organize and to plan," is highly suggestive, even if it might need to be amended and updated.

James's designation of intellectuals into three groups, composed of Catholic Humanists, Existentialists, and adherents of the Cominform, also dates what is otherwise a still very relevant discussion of the role played by modern intellectuals in overall social planning and production. (The Communist Information Bureau or *Cominform* was established in September 1947 by the Communist Parties of the Soviet Union, Yugoslavia, Bulgaria, Rumania, Hungary, Poland, France, Italy, and Czechoslovakia to co-ordinate the activities of European Communist parties; it was originally headquartered in Belgrade, with Marshal Tito as its *de facto* leader.)[86] Intellectuals identified with these three groupings have long since ceased to carry any political or ideological weight. James was of the view, however, that they would continue to exert a dominant influence.

Written before the start of the modern civil rights movement, which was signaled in December 1955 with the Montgomery bus-boycott, the event that catapulted Martin Luther King, Jr., to national prominence, James's text antedates one of the most historic turning points in modern American politics. Because of its proximity and partly due to James's keen sensitivity to the mood of the African American community, the prospectus resonates with the sound of the struggle that would shortly arise and transform America.

James adopts a skeptical view of the previous civil rights strategy based on federal enactments to succeed in outlawing the legalized system of white supremacy in the South. "Let us face what the Negro question is," James writes. "It is an economic question; it is a political question; yes, so it is; but it is primarily a question of human relations but not in the common sense of those words. These relations remain a sealed book to the large majority of the nation above the Mason and Dixon line." Basing his critique on the analysis of racism presented in E. Franklin Frazier's recently published *The Negro in the United States*,[87] James implies that only a fundamental social movement has the capacity to transform the South. "That is where we must begin. There is involved here a revolution in relations comparable only to the revolution which will emancipate labor and the revolution which will emancipate women." In this sense, James was clearly prophetic in his estimate of what the struggle for black freedom would require if it was to challenge the entire system of racial oppression in America.

Where James's view fell short, however, was in his underestimation of the range and power of the actual movement that he predicted. In its mobilization of the entire country, particularly in its ability to enlist the authority of the federal executive, the civil rights movement went well beyond what anyone in 1950 thought was feasible in overturning the system of segregation. As James viewed it, however, the federal government would not enter the struggle on behalf of the struggle to overthrow segregation. The limitation of this political forecast, existing side by side with his otherwise accurate assessment of the imminence of the movement, is especially ironic.

"To anyone who has grasped this stupendous reality, one of the most astonishing in the history of modern civilized nations, all the agitation and excitement about Civil Rights, a National F.E.P.C. with teeth in it, a Federal anti-lynching bill, abolition of the Poll Tax, etc., all legislation of this kind to be passed in Congress, all this hullabaloo can be seen for what it is, a body of legislation which even if it is all passed, will not alter the fundamental situation," James argued. From this assessment, he extrapolated a political scenario that was categorical in its denial: "No Federal administration," he asserted, "will hurl itself into a civil war with the states and vast numbers of the population of the South, in a vain and costly attempt to change a situation such as we have described." Yet this was the underlying political strategy of the whole civil rights movement in the South.

The success of the civil rights movement in changing the nature of politics in the South and in America as a nation, however, should not obscure the fact that the problem today is that, as James said in 1950, "a body of legislation, which even if it is all passed, will not alter the fundamental situation." It is not that nothing has changed or that the changes that have occurred have not been valuable. It is that nothing *fundamental* has changed.

XX

A similar test of the accuracy of James's forecasting ability was presented by the events of the Cold War which form the political backdrop of the text. James comes close to subscribing to the Cold War mystique of Americanism, particularly when he argues for the credulity of "the official opinions of a very substantial organized body in the United States [which] revolve around the thesis of the freedom of the individual, in business enterprises but elsewhere also, and free association." He sternly warns: "To sneer at this means to misunderstand the past of the United States and the tremendous power of this idea which is and will always remain a part of the national tradition."

At first glance, James seems to be supporting the Cold War version of the myth of American exceptionalism, but it is clear from the text that he understood the ideological agenda behind its manipulation by "those who rule, guide and instruct the United States and the people of the world about the United States." He certainly was not taken in by the oft-repeated slogans of "free individuals, free enterprise, science, industry, Democracy – that is[,] the Voice of America and this at a time when every thinking mind in America is pondering over the outcome of precisely what these terms signify for American and human civilization."

Perhaps the affirmative tone of his statements was designed to render his underlying critique more palatable to a popular audience at a time when the prevailing anti-communist hysteria throughout the United States condemned such views as heresy. As James was to explain a couple years later in the conclusion of *Mariners, Renegades and Castaways*, his prospectus was "also a claim before the American people, the best claim I can put forward, that my desire to be a citizen is not a selfish nor a frivolous one."[88]

The Stalinist totalitarian order that James inveighs so mightily against, however, no longer corresponds to the contemporary world of Eastern Europe and the former Soviet Union. James spent many years observing "Stalinists of various types in different parts of the world" and making "a reasonably close study of their writings," which was put most notably to advantage in his *World Revolution 1917-1936: The Rise and Fall of the Communist International.*[89] Stalinist parties had scored impressive gains in Western Europe and in Asia at the time that James was writing – the victory of the Chinese Communists had just occurred a few months earlier in 1949.

James's analysis of Stalinist totalitarianism follows David Rousset's *L'univers concentrationnaire,*[90] the first book to make the crucial identification between Nazism and Stalinist totalitarianism, a question that James struggles to clarify in the note that comes at the end of his introduction. "In this volume there is made an identification of the regimes of Hitlerism and Stalinism under the common name *totalitarian,*" he asserts, but then follows the warning:

It must be understood that this implies no identity of the regimes. The characterization has been made merely to emphasize the ultimate social consequences of any kind of regime which does not develop along co-operative creative lines, developing the creative spirit of the mass. Politically speaking the differences between Stalinism and Fascism, particularly on a world scale, are of immense, in fact of decisive importance.

James's account falls midway, chronologically, between, on one side, George Orwell's *Nineteen Eighty-four, a Novel,*[91] and, on the other, Hannah Arendt's *The Origins of Totalitarianism,*[92] and Theodor Adorno *et al.*, *The Authoritarian Personality.*[93] James's involvement in the analysis of totalitarianism forms part of this wider post-war intellectual project. It has been overlooked because it remained unpublished. Now that it is available, it can be evaluated as a missing piece of this rich mosaic of post-war theory.

The death of Orwell, on January 21, 1950, occurred while James was in the middle of composing his prospectus. James had known Orwell during the thirties in England. Both men shared the same publisher, Secker and Warburg, and were together on the same political side of the barricade during the Spanish Civil War tragedy. Orwell's own valiant struggle against Stalinism in Spain, forcing him ultimately to flee that country in fear of his life, was vividly recounted in *Homage to Catalonia*.[94] Many critics consider this to be one of Orwell's best books.

If, as V. S. Pritchett believed, Orwell's *Nineteen Eighty-Four* marked the end of the literary movement of the thirties, perhaps James's analysis of totalitarianism also marks a sort of political and intellectual homage to Orwell from America. James's statement that "the close study of the United States will explain most easily to the people of Western Europe why totalitarianism arises, the horrible degradation it represents, its terrible cost to society, the certainty of its overthrow" shows an awareness on the part of James of the potential of a European audience for his work. It would thus complement the discussion of totalitarianism that Orwell's work had already done much to help understand. James was attempting to advance the analysis still further: "I aim at showing," he informs the reader in the introduction, "that the apparently irrational and stupefying behavior of people in totalitarian states is a product of modern civilization, not merely in terms of the preservation of property and privilege but as the result of deep social and psychological needs of man in modern life."

What is novel for this time is James's insight into the disintegrative character of totalitarianism, in the form of the Stalinist system, a prophetic view of its demise that counterbalances the assessment of its seemingly absolute character. This was quite rare among political commentators of the forties and fifties on the Left. The prescient quality of James's analysis, now borne out by events in Eastern Europe and the former Soviet Union, is perhaps best summed up in his statement: "These regimes will collapse ultimately. They solve neither economic, social nor psychological problems. They integrate the personality by destroying it altogether. They destroy the very basis of progress in the productivity of labor; the police state is an economic burden and a psychological cancer."

XXI

In my view, the most significant limitation of the prospectus stems from the absence of any discussion regarding automation and its impact upon workers. James did not foresee the enormous dislocation that was to result from the massive introduction of the new technology of automation, which began in earnest in the early fifties. This does not mean, however, that he would have been surprised by its consequences, even if it is missing from the prospectus. Marx's comment in the *Communist Manifesto*, and later repeated in *Capital*, to the effect that capitalism is revolutionary because it is constantly revolutionizing the means of production, and with them all the social relations associated with them, was fundamental to his thinking. Technological change has always resulted in setbacks for the working class, but James would not have doubted for a moment that the class had the capacity to recover and create new forms of organization to deal with the changed situation.

The term "automation" was coined around 1946 by the automobile industry to describe the introduction of automatic devices and controls to mechanize production lines. But it was the development of the electronic digital computer UNIVAC I (Universal Automatic Computer) in 1951 that ushered in the new technological era. The consequence for American workers would be enormous.

The analysis in *American Civilization* rests on a perspective of the industrial working class as stable and solidified in heavy industry. In reality, the American working class was about to begin to undergo a period of extremely rapid transformation. Automation went beyond anything that James anticipated; on the contrary, he was of the view that the strength of American labor unions in such heavy industries as mining, steel, and automobile, had developed to the point where they "hold in their hands the keys to the American industrial process." James was aware that something was stirring, however, for the alternative that he presents in the prospectus is both stark and implies rapidly advancing technology. "The modern world is organizing itself scientifically at such a speed," he asserts, "that either it must be ruled in totalitarian fashion or by a new conception of democracy beyond anything we have known."

What the introduction of automation technology in machining, chemical processing, metallurgy, assembly, and electronics manufacturing was to effect was a major reorganization of industrial work, while at the same time replacing mainly semi-skilled and militant workers (machine operators, assemblers, etc.) with machines. Whereas unionization of heavy industry inaugurated a brief era during the late thirties and forties during which workers held much of the power to determine the pace and staffing of production, supported by a shop-floor system of power and authority in the form of stewards and committeemen, from the late forties and early fifties management employed automation to recapture much of its authority. What is important to stress is that this effort by management aimed at regaining control of the shop-floor was indirectly facilitated by the leadership of American unions. With its focus on wage and fringe benefit issues such as pensions, the union leadership abandoned any pretense at participating in the setting of production decisions.

The result was a rapid restructuring of production that destroyed the traditional worker networks that had provided for a considerable amount of autonomy in the production process during the forties. In addition to displacing large numbers of skilled workers, automation simultaneously laid the basis for creation of a permanent underclass in America made up primarily of blacks and members of other minority groups. The massive automation that took place in the auto industry in the fifties disguised this trend due to the changed racial composition of the auto workers in the Detroit metropolitan area which now became, in the majority, black. The theoretical void that exists for the most part within the Left today in regard to automation and the development of the even more advanced technology of robotics and the impact of both on the restructuring of the labor process is not accidental. The intellectual collapse of the Left is nowhere more apparent than in this failure. In any attempt to overcome it, however, James's theoretical legacy, with its concentration on creative forms of association within the labor process, and the self-activity and autonomy of persons in confronting social relations, becomes indispensable.

XXII

Two schools of historical practice, both of them in the Marxist tradition, proved important to James in the conceptualization and writing of *American Civilization*. Numerous allusions to their influence are to be found scattered throughout the text. The first was the historiography of the English Civil War of the 1640s, specifically the historiography of the radical egalitarian sects of the era such as the Levellers and Diggers. The second was the school of historiography associated with the study of popular movements in the French Revolution.

The combined influence of both schools is reflected throughout the prospectus but nowhere more forcefully than in James's statement at the conclusion of his discussion of the American Abolitionist movement. In emphasizing the radicalism of Wendell Phillips' leadership, James points out how "the policy of seizure of the land by the Negroes was known in the South among the Negroes as a Wendell Phillips," and is reminded, furthermore, of Phillips' idea of organizing a party to challenge Lincoln's government. "By degrees the power of the North asserted itself, and for the same reasons that the Republican party superseded the Abolitionists, Lincoln's government was never challenged from the Left." Then comes the clarifying statement which shows the clear influence of both the English Revolution and the French Revolution. "The great national crises in social upheavals are caused by challenges to revolutionary governments, not to established ones. It was the challenge of Lilburne and the Levellers to Cromwell; of the Paris Commune to the Committee of Public Safety and Robespierre which marked the most desperate crises of the revolutionary regime. It never came to this in the [American] Civil War. But the Abolitionists and Phillips in particular show that in the United States, such an embryo, such an anticipation of extreme revolutionism had developed."

A year or two later, the same fusion of historical perspective would be expressed. In the prospectus announcing his final American lecture tour, the list of possible topics all deal with American subjects with the exception of one lecture, entitled *New Currents in Historical Thinking and Research*. The main focus of the lecture is the English and French revolutions, and to these James adds the subject of the American Civil War, a topic which, coincidentally, the present text does not treat in any depth, a surprise considering James's view that "whatever is socially significant in literature and the arts [of America] takes its roots from the United States which came to an end in the Civil War." It is possible that James was equating the Civil War with the Abolitionist movement which he discusses at some length in the prospectus.

Two years before, James sought to identify the origins leading to the contemporary ascendancy of the petit-bourgeoisie as a class grouping. In *Notes on Dialectics* he claimed to have found its origins in the English Revolution of 1640-49. At the conclusion of a lengthy analysis, he advances the view that democracy was "*not* the creation of the French revolution, but of the British petty bourgeoisie, the petty bourgeoisie of radical small farmers and artisans."[95] The following year marked the celebration of tercentenary of the English Revolution (1649–1949), and James produced a lengthy two-part essay on the role of the Levellers in the English Civil War. Writing under the pseudonym of G. F. Eckstein, the first part, entitled "Cromwell and the Levellers," appeared in May 1949 in the *Fourth International*.[96] The second part, "Ancestors of the Proletariat," was published in the September 1949 issue.[97]

Besides demonstrating a novel integration of the popular literature of the Levellers with an analysis of their revolutionary politics, the first instalment indicates the important connection which the analysis of seventeenth-century English events had for James's subsequent discourse on contemporary America. The point could not have been made more explicit. "The same process can be observed in the French Revolution," he writes, "and the most striking historical example of it is the long-drawn out battle in the United States today over the interpretation of democracy. At the first serious clash it will be discovered that the battle over bourgeois parliamentary democracy covers social conceptions and aspirations to which this type of democracy is entirely subordinate, and nowhere will this be more marked than among the great masses of people."

For his essay, James draws upon and positively acknowledges the recent research of such outstanding scholars as A.P.S. Woodhouse, A. D. Lindsay, Don Marion Wolfe, William Haller, and Godfrey Davies. He also notes, but takes strong issue with, the analysis of British Communist historians published in the special April 1949 tercentenary issue of *Modern Quarterly* devoted exclusively to the so-called Puritan Revolution. In this same context, James refers also to the British *Communist Review* issue of March 1949 focussing on "the Great English Revolution" as well as the 1948 issue of the American *Science and Society* which published the British Marxist historian Christopher Hill's essay, "The English Civil War Interpreted by Marx and Engels." Also contained in the same issue of *Science and Society* was a lengthy article by Herbert M. Morais on "Marx and Engels on America," which James would not only have seen, but might also have acted as a stimulus to his own thinking.

Finally, at the conclusion of the overall essay, James closes with a celebratory statement that positively links the historiography of the English Civil War with the second of the two historical schools that we have referred to. Referring to the Levellers as "these bold revolutionaries," James also designates them "the brothers of the *sans-culottes* and the *enrages* of the French Revolution and the Russian Bolshevik workers of 1917," the Parisian social and political revolutionaries.

XXIII

As with the revolutionary movement in the case of the English Civil War, a significant feature of *Notes on Dialectics* is the examination by James of "the French Revolution in Historical Logic."[98] Central to the whole discussion was an analysis of the complex and unstable relationship, before it finally disintegrated, of the popular movement with the revolutionary dictatorship under the leadership of Robespierre and Saint-Just, to whom there is a poignant reference made in the present text. After recalling the impact of Saint-Just's famous utterance at the height of the French Revolution that "happiness is a new idea in Europe," James adds the statement that "America had already shown the idea to the world – in America."

It is significant that James uses the French Revolution to explain what could be expected in America: "No one in the world dreamt that underneath the France of 1789 had developed the passion for equality which was to burst forth in the French Revolution (to take one example) and help tear down the age-old structure of monarchy, aristocracy and clergy," James assures the reader. He goes on: "Yet historians after the event could go back and trace the stages by which this growing passion was developed, established itself below and in the interactions of the old regime, its advances and retreats, the disguises it assumed, and how and why it became so much a constituent part of the nation that finally it burst forth as it did."

This appears in Chapter 6, the second of the two chapters devoted in the prospectus to dealing with industrial workers and their struggle for control of production. Then, in his summing up near the end of the chapter, James again draws the parallel with the popular movement of the French Revolution. "This that we have put here so roughly, so unambiguously, is not everything but everything springs from there," he observes, while noting that "it took 100 years before French historians recognized plainly that the French Revolution was a social revolution springing from depths that affected the ultimate social lives of the great majority of the population."

Finally, at the end of the prospectus James again compares the coming American struggle with the historical examples of the English Civil War and the French Revolution. Referring to the social needs underlying the mass mobilization that he forecasts taking place in America, James writes: "Once the spell of routine is broken, they will appear with extreme rapidity and develop with even more startling speed. It must be remembered that no one, not a single soul, guessed what the French masses, so passive in 1789, would demand in 1792. The thing was beyond human imagination. The same in Britain in 1645. But we can learn from history."

These repeated statements found in his 1950 prospectus strongly indicate the presence of definite historical models in the social analysis that underlies James's vision of America. If anything, the importance that James attached to the French Revolution grew with the passage of time. "After fifty years," he writes in 1989, "the French Revolution means more to me than it did at the beginning of my serious studies." In *American Civilization* James makes explicit reference to the two giants of French revolutionary historiography – Jules Michelet (1789–1876) and the French socialist Jean Juarès (1859–1914). The reference foreshadows the appraisal that he would make in the expanded bibliography accompanying the second edition of *The Black Jacobins: Toussaint L'Ouverture and the San Domingo Revolution*. James writes there that "many pages in Michelet are the best preparation for understanding what actually happened in San Domingo."[99] Michelet's monumental *Histoire de France* (1833–67), with its lyrical Jacobin, almost messianic, ethos, and the author's heroic effort at rescuing from obscurity ordinary lives, made him, in James's sight, "the greatest historian of them all" among the great historical school of the French Revolution.

Michelet was a constant inspiration to James's own historical imagination, with its radical, Jacobin tone stamped upon all that he wrote. He was also, along with Marx, the chief inspiration for Jean Juarès, whose multi-volume *Histoire socialiste de la Révolution française* (1901–04) provides the impetus behind all modern studies of the French Revolution. Juarès, in addition to establishing "once and for all the economic basis of the revolution," exhibited "a sympathetic understanding of the great mass movements."

The zenith of French revolutionary historiography was reached with the great Georges Lefebvre (1874–1959), whose studies represent, according to James, "the crown of this work of over a century."[100] James singles out for special mention Lefebvre's mimeographed lectures to students at the Sorbonne. These are the same lectures that Richard Cobb argues "are, in my opinion, far the best introduction to the general history of the [French] Revolution."[101] Lefebvre's career of scholarship, James concludes, "would be difficult to parallel."[102]

XXIV

James's interest in the historiography of the French Revolution became more than a theoretical interest in 1948, when he was asked by Daniel Guérin to translate the latter's recently published *La Lutte de classes, sous la première république, bourgeois et "bras nus" (1793–1797)*.[103] The US immigration commissioner who wrote the first rejection of James's appeal against deportation was to include in his statement of rejection a reference to the fact that James "was now engaged in translating from the French a history of the French Revolution."[104]

A political study of the revolutionary *sans-culottes*, Guérin's book gave fresh theoretical impetus to James's preoccupation with the creative role of popular movements in the history of revolution. It forms the backdrop to the recurring transference that James makes from 1948 onward to the French Revolution and the parallelism that he draws to the role of the popular classes in the United States. In the bibliography to the 1963 edition of *The Black Jacobins*, James gives high praise to Guérin and his work which he describes as "a brilliant, original and well-documented iconoclastic study, which centres around the conflict between Robespierre and the various mass movements."[105]

In the late forties, James formed a close relationship with Daniel Guérin who spent two years (1947–49) visiting the US on a fellowship from the French government. Guérin and James met on several occasions in New York during this period. An anecdote recalled by Guérin of one of their meetings provides a social context for what must have been a mutually stimulating and intellectually rewarding relationship for the two men:

There was a small French restaurant in New York called the Paris-Brest, a very charming popular-type restaurant with typical checked table cloths. It was owned by a couple from Brittany. French sailors from the warships used to frequent the place, but not to eat a meal since they could not have afforded it; the patronne used to offer them free liver *pâté* sandwiches. I invited James to this restaurant. He was a bit apprehensive about a cold reception but was amazed by the warm welcome he received, the first time from a white restaurant. There was still much racial prejudice, even in New York, in those days.[106]

Up to the time of his visit to the US, Guérin was best known for his analysis revealing the class and economic determinants in fascism's march to power in Italy and Germany. Published in French in 1936 as *Fascisme et grand capital*,[107] the book quickly established itself as a classic in the Marxist canon on fascism. It was translated into English and published in America under the title *Fascism and Big Business*.[108] Dwight Macdonald wrote the introduction. As an admirer of James's *Black Jacobins*, Guérin helped to arrange for its translation into French by Pierre Naville. Published in 1949 by Gallimard as *Les Jacobins noirs*, it was reviewed by Louis Ménard in the February 1950 issue of *Les Temps Modernes*.[109]

"James was interested in my evolution," explains Guérin, "because of the spontaneous and anarchistic tendencies in my principal work *Lutte de classes, sous la première République*," which Guérin commissioned James to translate. Unfortunately, after completing only three chapters, James was forced to discontinue the work.[110] A copy of the original transcript of James's partial English translation of Guérin's book was found in the same place and at the same time as the copy of the transcript of the 1950 American prospectus was discovered. Extensive sections of the translation were duplicated and circulated within James's group for discussion and political education.

Guérin spent his two years (1947–9) in the US conducting research for the study of America that he was to publish upon his return to France. *Où va le peuple Américain? [Whither the American People?]*[111] would cost Guérin his visa to the US, thus preventing his return to America and the completion of the work by hampering the writing of the third volume. Three excerpts from the work in progress were published in Jean-Paul Sartre's *Les Temps Modernes*.[112] Prior to that, in August–September 1946, it had published an impressive double-issue devoted exclusively to the subject of "USA."

It seems probable that Guérin would have shared with James his ideas of *Où va le peuple Américain?* in the hope of eliciting his comments prior to publication. Whether or not James was shown the manuscript of Guérin's book, Guérin does refer in his first volume[113] to James's *Trotskyism in the United States, 1940-47: The Balance Sheet*. In the second volume, however, Guérin makes frequent and repeated references to essays by James and his colleagues, notably Freddie Forest (Raya Dunayevskaya) and William Gorman, dealing with the struggle of African Americans. All of these essays were published in the *Fourth International* (theoretical organ of the SWP) over the two year period 1948–50.

Despite the use made by Guérin of the writings of James and his colleagues, however, it appears from the context that James was critical of the second volume of *Où va le peuple Américain?*, in particular the section treating

"La Révolte nègre," which was shortly afterward excerpted, translated into English, and published separately in the US, under the title *Negroes on the March: A Frenchman's Report on the American Negro Struggle.*[114]

Guérin mentions in the text of the English edition of the excerpted work that he received a letter from a "correspondent" in the US disagreeing with the views expressed concerning the alleged African background of American blacks' ethnic and cultural features. Guérin upheld the view advanced by Melville J. Herskovits in his landmark *The Myth of the Negro*,[115] which boldly argued for recognition of the African origins of African American culture. In the American publication of *Negroes on the March*, Guérin attaches a special appendix, entitled "Has the American Negro an African Background?", in which he responds to the criticism. Guérin's "correspondent" had argued that "The Negro is a constituent part of American society. He has no culture but Anglo-Saxon culture. There are no ethnic barriers standing in his way."[116]

From the content of the views expressed as well as their literary style, it is plain that James was the "correspondent." Throughout all of his writings and speeches, James took the position, as was stated in the 1952 descriptive overview of his popular lecture, *The American Negro: Touchstone of American Civilization*, that "the social characteristics of the American Negro are, above all, American. The very segregation of the Negroes intensifies these characteristics and makes the American Negro a touchstone to the development of the American people." The fact that Guérin refrains from naming James as the author of the letter was purely precautionary, in order to guard against its possible use in the deportation proceedings that were then underway in America against James.

The basis of intellectual reciprocity between James and Guérin, even in the presence of such disagreement, was still considerable. In fact, James sets out the plan of his American prospectus and the hopes that he entertained for publication of the eventual manuscript in a letter that he wrote to Guérin dated January 17, 1950. It is a unique source for reconstructing the development of the present text. At the same time, on account of the abundance of relevant data marshalled by the author, Guérin's *Où va le peuple Américain?* provides the essential empirical backdrop to many of the key political issues discussed in James's prospectus, particularly as they concern the position of the labor bureaucracy.

In the preface to his first volume, Guérin also asserts a point of view that is very similar to that of James: "America, thanks to mass production and the high level of its technology is in the act of creating the material basis for a kind of civilization such as has not yet existed on the planet: a *mass civilization [civilisation de masses]*, a civilization for everyone and not, as in old Europe, for the privileged few."[117] (*"Civilisation de classe ou civilisation de masse"* was also the title of an article by Guérin, published in France, in

1930, in *Révolution Prolétarienne.*)[118] Guérin ends the preface of his 1950 work with a promise that the conclusion of his study will analyze more fully "the *mass civilization* with which America today brings hope to the world." The original concept was borrowed by Guérin from Lucien Romier, whose formulation of the "Phenomena of Mass Civilization" was constructed on the basis of his analysis of American civilization to be found in *Qui sera Maître, Europe ou Amérique?*, a book that was a model of narrative brevity, theoretical clarity, and incisive originality.

A similar awareness of the transforming power of mass production had been enunciated by yet another French observer, André Siegfried – "a very intelligent European," according to James – whose *America Comes Of Age* (1927) ends with a remarkable statement on the incompatibility of individual freedom with mass production. "It is a remarkable passage, written in 1927," James observes in the prospectus, but one that was limited by the fact that the author failed to comprehend that "this was not a matter of art and self-expression but a question of the essential day-to-day lives of civilized men, wearing them down and against which they are revolting."

Guérin's presence in America might well have served as an additional intellectual catalyst for James in the late forties. Their relationship supplied him with valuable contact with French intellectual currents, affording him particular insight, as James reveals in the text of the prospectus, into the movement of French existentialism as well as making clear to him the dominant position among left-wing intellectuals of the French Communist Party. Moreover, James's analysis of American society draws heavily upon the example of revolutionary movements in the French Revolution embodied in the phenomena of the *sans-culottes*, *enragés*, and *sociétés populaires*. These were the substance of Guérin's *La Lutte de classes sous la première République, bourgeois et "bras nus" (1793–1797)* which Guérin asked James to translate. In 1958 James would cite Guérin's book as "the finest study of the activities of the working class during the French Revolution."[119]

James's *American Civilization* prospectus represents, from this broader perspective, a novel extension of French revolutionary historiography into American history. The objective, it must be emphasized, was never for some purely intellectual exercise. It was guided by the attempt to comprehend the struggle of American workers for mastery of production in light of the modern obstacles that confronted them. "The question, the vital question," James decided, "is whether some such movement (and the modern masses have an inherent power infinitely greater than those who worked between 1830 and 1860)-[,] whether this movement is bound to end in the vast oppressive bureaucratic militarist structures which mean without a doubt the end of civilization."

XXV

At the most general conceptual level, the idea of American Civilization is one that today is hardly ever used, a decline in usage that has been especially marked since the American Bicentennial was celebrated in 1976. To the extent that it continues to have intellectual currency, the concept appears mainly as a refraction of the image of the United States in the discourse of foreign commentators, viz., K. Ohashi *et al.*, *Amerika no bunka [American Civilization]*,[120] Andre Kaspi *et al.*, *La civilisation américaine.*[121] Foreign consumption of the idea was inevitable in light of the very significant role that immigrants played in the development of the United States. Many influential authors such as Oscar Handlin, Charles and Mary Beard, Edward Sapir, and Franz Boas, writing on cultural anthropology have also stressed the immense role of European immigration in the development of humanistic studies, mass culture, and mass society in America. Conversely, these authors also dispute the myth of Anglo-Saxon culture in the formation of American culture.

It is the placing of the needs of common humanity at the center of social concern that ultimately redeems the concept of American civilization and transforms it from the discourse of Americanism into criticism of American society. By the late forties, this change was already apparent in Harold Laski's *The American Democracy*,[122] the final chapter of which was entitled "Americanism as a Principle of Civilization" (chapter 14). In clarifying "the complex relationship between the European tradition and Americanism,"[123] Laski helps us to understand how the concept of American civilization was generated out of the process of cultural negotiation between American identity and the dominant idea of European cultural provenance. With the end of the Second World War, however, this trans–Atlantic transaction was finally settled – in America's favor: "What is at least certain is that Americanism will never again be an outer province, as it were, of the European idea."[124] "The conclusion to which this leads is, in its essence, simple," he declares. "It is that the peculiar complex of qualities we call Americanism is now subject to much the same forces as the peculiar complex we call Europeanism."[125] The "forces" that Laski had in mind were fundamentally social: "Americanism must come to mean the same thing for the sharecropper of Arkansas as for the stockbroker on Park Avenue in New York City, for the steel worker in Pittsburgh as for the corporation lawyer in Wall Street, for the senator from a Southern state like Alabama as for a senator from a Northern state like Vermont, if, indeed, the house is to stand."[126]

The corollary of this new definition of Americanism put forth by Laski was political – "free change, where there is a majority will for free change, as the technique by which the content of Americanism is defined." The allusion to Americanism by James in the text – "To raise the problem of color alone as a barrier to Americanism is to alienate the greater part of the population of the world" – closely parallels Laski's social definition of the concept. James certainly was familiar with Laski's book, which he describes in the introduction as issuing from "a renewed attempt by foreign commentators to grasp the essence of the American civilization." Included in the list are Dennis W. Brogan,[127] Geoffrey Gorer,[128] Wyndham Lewis,[129] and "a full study by Harold Laski."

James expands the concept of American Civilization as social critique which he premises upon the struggle of ordinary people for association and self-representation. He is careful to distinguish clearly his own views on American society from what he considers to be "the inadequacies of the liberal sociology of Dewey, Beard and Parrington." "That is why I devote," he explains in another place in the text, "substantial space to the lives of the great masses of the people in factories, offices, and department stores, their home lives, and seek a co-relation in this with what is so lightly called the 'entertainment industry,' but what is in reality one of the most powerful social and psychological manifestations of the American life and character." It also supplies the key to the value that James places on Melville who, in his view, "described common men as they have been described in no modern literature." To cite another example, James was of the view that the films made during the Second World War were important because of "the attention given to the actual life of the common man."

From this perspective, James's *American Civilization* represents not only a notable attempt to extend cultural and social analysis to hitherto much neglected material. Embracing a whole range of cultural phenomena that had been dismissed up until then by American Marxists as being either too trivial or misguided, James demonstrates how this evidence of popular culture could be studied and the criteria whereby the new material could be interpreted in politically meaningful terms.

XXVI

By the end of the Second World War and with the immense cultural changes that followed in its wake, a countervailing tendency began to unfold making the myth of American exceptionalism less and less tenable, however. America's ascension to the role of champion of the West struggling against Soviet communism, while it reinforced the sense of national mission, made the notion of America as a special case in international politics unfashionable.

Paradoxically, the place where the idea of American exceptionalism continued to have considerable intellectual appeal was within post-war American historiography. This was especially true of the "myth-and-symbol" scholars and historians whose work came to fruition and flourished throughout the fifties and finally tapered off in the sixties.[130] The intellectual mission of this generation of American scholars was to a significant degree nurtured and shaped by influences of pre-war literary movements that laid the intellectual foundations for American cultural criticism.

The paradigm of the "myth-and-symbol" school was based on the notion that all interpretations of American culture must focus on what is uniquely and distinctively American. From the galaxy of scholars who rose to prominence after the Second World War, scholars such as Perry Miller, Henry Nash Smith, David Potter, R.W.B. Lewis, Marvin Meyers, Roy Harvey Pearce, Charles Sanford, Leo Marx, and Alan Trachtenberg, would come a flood of important books that very rapidly and firmly established the "myth-and-symbol" genre of American scholarship. In this context, James's *Beyond a Boundary*, with its metaphor of the game of cricket, represents, figuratively speaking, the counterpart of the American "myth-and-symbol" school of American historical consciousness.

XXVII

James's prospectus serves as literary and historical evidence of the legitimacy that the concept of American civilization had acquired from the thirties and up through the forties. Such intellectual legitimacy as the movement attained by 1950, however, still had to contend with the "unmistakable disdain of American society" that James detected not only within intellectual circles in Europe but also in America. "Until the latest phase of American economic and political power forced unwilling and self-interested recognition upon them," James notes, with the Marshall Plan and NATO obviously fresh in his mind, "the universities, intellectuals and organized culture of Europe paid no organized attention to American literature, art, history or civilization." But if this was the case with the intellectual elite in Europe, the situation was hardly better in the United States. "The serious students of philosophy, literature and culture today in America are far more familiar with and interested in Dostoyevsky and Kafka, Picasso and Matisse, Kierkegaard, Heidegger, Marx and Freud, the philosophy of Existentialism than they are in the literature, art and philosophy of the United States."

James's objective in the text was not simply to deplore but to try to overcome the theoretical inadequacy of previous attempts to address this critical situation. He believed that what he had to say was new. It is this quality of theoretical intervention that explains the manifesto-like quality of the prospectus. It is now possible to see how James's ideas about American society belong to that same cluster of insights which the American scholar George Lipsitz recently lamented as constituting "a lost opportunity for scholarship and criticism" in the evolution of American Studies.[131] The trio of figures whom Lipsitz had in mind were Ralph Ellison, Chester Himes, and Charlie Parker, but James fits readily into the same category of missed opportunities. Indeed, James's comment concerning the significance of Chester Himes and Richard Wright as individuals holding up a banner of "betrayed Negro revolutionism,-" making them "groping pioneers for a native American radicalism," provides additional weight to what Lipsitz decries as "one of those many 'turning points' in history that failed to turn."[132]

James's acquaintance with Wright also provided him with a powerful intellectual stimulus. James was so excited by the discussion that evolved in the course of their first meeting in 1945 that he was afterward moved to write: "I have been wavering about writing a book. But I shall hesitate no longer. By the time they have recovered from his autobiographical novel (*Black Boy*), I shall hit them across the eyes with a historical study."[133] Once again, as was true in 1939, the African American question, which, according to James, "neither white America *nor black America* has faced . . . for the deep fundamental thing that it is in the life of the *nation* as a whole,"[134] gave renewed impetus to his long-contemplated intervention. In a very real political sense, *American Civilization* was ultimately the product of James's long-standing preoccupation with the significance of African Americans as a key critical for explaining the dynamics of American society.

Most importantly, James's manuscript crosses the cultural and political divide in American Studies. James crosses it most forcefully in his critique of the Philistinism of the intellectuals for thinking that workers are "stupid or apathetic." It is reflected in his comment on the failure of American film to address major social issues of the day and in his confidence on the readiness of popular audiences to see such issues dramatically portrayed. "Imagine now the Philistinism which would profess to believe that the American masses could not understand it inasmuch as they were not 'educated' enough as yet. They would understand it only too well."

James also crosses the divide in cultural criticism and cultural discourse in the nature of his appreciation of the significance of Herman Melville. At the time of his writing the post-Second World War Melville revival was in full-swing. "He is being recognized at last," James comments, but goes on to say that "nowhere have I seen anything like justice done to him as an interpreter of the United States and a guide to contemporary society and contemporary art as a whole."

Another area where the divide is crossed is James's novel attempt at integration of the literature of the middle of the nineteenth-century with the popular arts of the twentieth-century: "I propose to show that here is not mere shoddiness, vulgarity, entertainment. On the contrary. Here, after the writers of the middle of the nineteenth century, are the first genuine contributions of the United States to the art of the future and an international art of the modern world."

The emphasis placed by James upon the writers of the middle of the nineteenth century (Poe, Melville, Hawthorne, Whitman, and Emerson) strongly points to the influence of Harvard scholar F. O. Matthiessen (1902–50) whose monumental study *American Renaissance: Art and Expression in the Age of Emerson and Whitman*[135] revolutionized the whole study of American literature and "did more than any other book to set the American canon as it would be taught in American universities after World War II."[136] James acknowledges the value of Matthiessen in the prospectus, describing him as "an author of a very fine and liberal-minded study of American literature of the nineteenth century," who, he is obliged to note, "has stated in print that if he were in France, he would join the French Communist Party." Matthiessen committed suicide in 1950.

Matthiessen's work marked the culmination of a critical revolution in the study of American literature that had begun building after World War I. Its chief goal was the creation of a national literary identity for America through the rewriting of American literary history from the point of view of the tradition of democratic thought rather than from the previous perspective of regional and political divisions. Largely responsible for the definition and development of the critical study of American literature in the thirties and forties, Matthiessen propounded a radical theory of literary interpretation that was directly linked to the search for a usable past.

Although at this stage it is only a hypothesis, it seems possible that James's 1944 stated goal of achieving the "Americanization of Bolshevism" could have been informed or reinforced by Matthiessen's *American Renaissance* with its challenge to repossess a "literature for our democracy."[137] Matthiessen would have been especially important to James for the reason that it was Matthiessen's book that effectively launched the Melville revival in the United States (by far the largest section of *American Renaissance* is taken up with the discussion of Melville.[138] Matthiessen also laid the foundation for the modern critical interpretation that James would adapt and expand. In *American Renaissance* the political symbolism of Melville's *Moby Dick* is already present. "Responsive to the shaping forces of his age as only men of passionate imagination are, even Melville can hardly have been fully aware of how symbolical an American hero he had fashioned in Ahab," Matthiessen decides, adding: "He is the embodiment of his author's most profound response to the problem of the free individual will *in extremis*."[139]

This is James's thesis in a nutshell, as can be seen in the statement made in *Mariners, Renegades and Castaways* that Ahab "has been trained in the school of individualism and an individualist he remains to the end."[140] It was the adaptation and expansion of Matthiessen's paradigm into the present that James would make his most notable contribution, based on his bold interpretation of Ahab as symbolical of the modern trend toward destructiveness, on the one hand, and, on the other, the crew of the *Pequod* as embodying the power of social regeneration. Referring to the scene when Ishmael the narrator is at the helm of the *Pequod* at night and he is reflecting upon the ship's crew working below, James declares:

That at first sight is the modern world – the world we live in, the world of the Ruhr, of Pittsburgh, of the Black Country in England. In its symbolism of men turned into devils, of an industrial civilization on fire and plunging blindly into darkness, it is the world of massed bombers, of cities in flames, of Hiroshima and Nagasaki, the world in which we live, the world of Ahab, which he hates and which he will organize or destroy.[141]

In the absence of Matthiessen's *American Renaissance*, James's lethal reading of Ahab and redemptive vision of the crew in Melville's *Moby Dick* may never have succeeded in the interpretive range which it attained. Andrew Delbanco, introducing the new definitive text of *Moby Dick*,[142] affirms the continuing significance of James's interpretation: "As the Trinidadian writer C.L.R. James suggested long ago," he writes, "Melville's political vision of the mirrored fanaticism of ruler and ruled was to be most fully realized in Europe and only fitfully approached in the United States."[143]

Matthiessen's *American Renaissance* illustrates the significance of the study of American literature for the evolution of James's ideas concerning not just Melville, but, more generally, the "Americanization of Bolshevism." James's prospectus is built upon just such an extrapolation from literature to politics and back again. In his discussion of the literary expression of the nineteenth-century in relation to the cultural expression of the popular classes, James asserts that "it is in the study of these and the outbursts of American social and political action in the same period that there can be seen the beginnings of tendencies which have now reappeared with tremendous concrete force both among intellectuals and in the artistic fare of the masses."

A similar transference occurred in the case of James's reading of Melville scholar Henry A. Murray's landmark edition of *Pierre or, The Ambiguities.*[144] In a letter dated March 7, 1953, that was addressed to another Melville scholar, Jay Leyda, James attributes great value to Murray's work: "In his introduction to *Pierre*, he [Murray] says specifically[,] '*Moby Dick*, for instance, was the super[]best prophecy of the essence of Fascism that any literature produced.' To me, *that* is what matters, in *1953*." Murray's essay represented a major turning-point in the shaping of James's perspective regarding the political symbolism of Ahab. For James, the great fictional characters of literature such as Melville's Ahab were "characteristic social types" who were also indicative of "the age which was to follow." It is precisely the symbolic factor that James finds to be missing in the character of Croft in Norman Mailer's *The Naked and the Dead*.[145] "The forces which

Melville could not see because they did not exist," James recognizes, "exist for Mailer today, but only as external forces, the labor movement, politics, Marxism. He does not see them dynamically as Melville saw Ahab in embryo and let his imagination go to make him a symbolical character."

The greatest expression of James's synthesis of the literary tradition with political analysis came, in fact, in his bold intervention into the field of Melville scholarship with his *Mariners, Renegades and Castaways*, written in 1952. James declares his political perspective on Melville without any apology. "What the writing of this book has taught the writer," he declares, "is the inseparability of great literature and of social life. I read Melville during the great historical events of the last seven years, and without them I would never have been able to show, as I believe I have done, that his work is alive today as never before since it was written."[146]

James reveals another important influence in shaping his interpretation of Melville in the valuation he gives of D. H. Lawrence's *Studies in Classic American Literature*.[147] In his 1952–53 lecture prospectus, James remarks: "Melville and the other great American writers of his period give to Western Civilization of the last quarter of a century *a view of itself* as exists nowhere else in such concentrated compass. D. H. Lawrence first saw this, and despite his quirks and obsessions, his book on American literature though published over thirty years ago, is still the only book which recognizes what American literature of 1840–1860 signifies for contemporary Europe."

Yet another important allusion in the text which reveals how James gleaned ideas from American literature to buttress his political outlook on American society was the reference to Vernon H. Parrington, dubbed by one recent scholar as the "Intellectual Founder of American Studies."[148] James uses Parrington to emphasize the creative quality of the American Abolitionist movement. "A finished book will have to relate Emerson, Thoreau and the Transcendentalists to Whitman, Melville and the Abolitionists," he cautions, but then adds: "Sufficient to say that even Parrington says that the soil which produced Emerson also produced Garrison – they were complementary parts of the same movement." It was Ralph Waldo Emerson, the great spokesman of the Transcendentalists, who, speaking just after the outbreak of the Civil War, gave voice to the urgent need of the hour. "The evil you contend with has taken alarming proportions, and you still content yourself with parrying the blows it aims, but, as if enchanted, abstain from striking at the cause," Emerson admonished his audience gathered at the Smithsonian Institution in Washington, D.C., in January 1862. Foreshadowing the policy that Lincoln would eventually adopt some six to eight months later, Emerson declared: "Emancipation is the demand of civilization. That is a principle; everything else is an intrigue."[149]

If Matthiessen's *American Renaissance* finally established the legitimacy of American literature, Parrington's *magnum opus, Main Currents in American*

Thought: An Interpretation of American Literature from the Beginnings to 1920,[150] established the legitimacy of studying American thought. "With that act," comments Gene Wise, "the integrating study of American culture was to enter a new era." James's integrating vision of American culture and politics was also no different; it exemplifies, in my opinion, "how an integrating 'American Studies' might be done."

XXVIII

James's vision of American civilization was in a significant way predicated upon an analogy with his own West Indian colonial experience. This cultural identification is echoed in the chapter on the popular arts, when, for example, James makes the observation that "the great masses of Americans are backward in 'culture' in the European sense; but in the essential needs of modern civilized man as we have described him, they are the most advanced people upon the face of the globe."

What we have in this statement, in my opinion, is the revolutionary Marxist speaking in the voice of the colonial vindicationist. In the course of *Notes on Dialectics*, the two facets of James's politics are united around the vindication of Lenin, when James asserts that "It will be many years before justice is done to this amazing, this incredible man. He took the *Russian* soviets and created a new Universal, for the *world.*"[151] The challenge of cultural vindication was always of paramount importance for James in his capacity as a colonial. It was what inspired the struggle in the thirties that James conducted for West Indian self-government. In the concrete circumstances of the United States, James would discover a depth and breadth of cultural mastery that took vindication to new heights. The criterion of mastery is employed throughout to vindicate American civilization. "The crisis of Ahab," he states near the beginning of *Mariners, Renegades and Castaways*, "is that of a civilization which has recognized that it is on the way to complete mastery of the arts and sciences of civilization."[152] Its possession is also what assured him that Americans were capable of achieving a major new advance toward a higher stage of social existence as "part of that process of mastery of the mind which is one of the signs that man has reached the stage where he *must* live a truly human existence."

James locates the symbol of mastery, ironically, among what Melville terms "this my savage crew" aboard the *Pequod.* James sets out to vindicate the primitive savages that form part of the crew – Queequeg, Tashtego, and Doggo: "They are the representatives of the three continents where primitive men were still found. The men are masters of their craft, brave and skillful as virtuosos. But over and over again they perform the bravest acts, far beyond the line of duty. Whenever anything remarkable is done, one of them does it." Such a conception went beyond strictly aesthetic ideas. It rested upon a critical understanding of the strategic position occupied by certain individuals standing outside the mainstream of civilization. Illustrating the point concretely, by reference to the characters and plot of Prometheus, Lear, and Ahab, James wrote to the Melville scholar Howard P. Vincent:

I am convinced that it is not at all accidental that all three are men of a certain maturity, that they are engaged in mortal conflict with forces symbolical of an outwork society, that the scene of the conflict is set in remote places outside the boundaries of civilization, and that at the critical moment each is surrounded by followers who are themselves outside the pale of civilization – disinherited men or women. Mankind is once more "unaccommodated man."

Here can be seen one of the earliest instances of the enunciation by James of the twin concepts of cultural boundary and mastery from the colonial perspective, to which he was to give full literary expression in *Beyond a Boundary* ten years later. The same concept was also embodied in James's discussion of Melville's concept of nature. James believed that Melville had gone beyond seeing nature as simply symbolizing the goal of the struggle for mastery, to encompassing the idea of society divided "into two spheres, the stable society of the land; and the society of the sea," which together represented "the shifting boundaries of man's need to go further and ever further."

The problem that *American Civilization* seeks to explain is the crisis that resulted from the loss of that sense of mastery that Americans underwent with the advent of large-scale capitalist industry following the Civil War. It is a crisis that James is able to articulate and empathize with very completely for being himself an "unaccommodated man" from the colonial realm.

> Thou art the thing itself:
> unaccommodated man is no more but such
> a poor, bare, forked animal as thou art.[153]

Once again, the crew of the *Pequod* serves for James to symbolize this earlier phase: "They do their work splendidly, the ship is kept in fine shape, the whole crew does its daily work heroically, to recall de Tocqueville's phrase." Symbolizing the transition from this early achievement also were America's two greatest artists of the nineteenth century – Walt Whitman and Herman Melville. In the case of the former, "The old heroic individualist *activity* was going and Whitman, the intellectual, passionately wanted to be one with his fellow-men." In the case of the latter:

The old heroic individualist America he knew; but he could see as artists see that the old individualism was breeding a new individualism, an individualism which would destroy society. . . . Melville saw, and indeed on the basis of his experiences, could see no solution whatever, but it is noticeable that this American, this product of the heroic individualism of 1776 to 1850 had no sympathy whatever with intellectualism or escapism of any kind.

With the end of the American Civil War, "the freedom, the energy, the heroic quality of the individual pursuing his daily vocation" was lost. It was forfeited on the floors of America's factories in the period of rapid industrialization. Renewal could come about, according to James, only through its extension into the realm of work, but "caught in this contradiction and under the pressure of the labor organizations, the state actually proposes now no longer freedom but security; security for children; against sickness; better housing; for the rural areas technical education and fixed prices; for full employment; for vacations and pensions for the infirm and aged. There can be no more striking contrast to the heroic frontiersman, trader, sailor and artisan striving to be a capitalist, of the early days."

An example of renewal for James was achieved by the CIO, the aim of which was "to give the workers mastery in the shops." At stake was the future of American civilization: "We face a problem that goes to the very roots of our civilization, of the intimate and at the same time social lives of the great majority of the population." James goes on:

This is the fundamental conflict. There is on the one hand the need, the desire, created in him by the whole mighty mechanism of American industry, to work, to learn, to master the machine, to cooperate with others, in building glittering miracles that would achieve wonders, to work out ways and means to do in two hours what ordinarily takes four, to organize the plant as only workers know how. And on the other hand, the endless frustration of being merely a cog in a great machine, a piece of production as is a bolt of steel, a pot of paint or a mule which drags a load of corn.

XXIX

The two strands of James's analysis in terms of association and culture are joined at the point where his exploration of the antagonisms of American society connect cultural experience with the creativity of American social movements. This perspective stands in sharp contrast with the conclusions voiced by the generation of post-Second World War American social critics such as David Riesman, C. Wright Mills, William H. Whyte, Daniel Bell, Christopher Lasch, and Richard Sennett.

Although these critics recognized the spreading domination of the economy and society by large-scale bureaucracies, they nonetheless mourned the loss of the older entrepreneurial spirit of American individualism. "However their analyses differed in detail," Elizabeth Long has pointed out, "all of these critics agreed that the transformation of a relatively decentralized economy into a centralized and interdependent set of interlocking bureaucratic hierarchies had left little room for the entrepreneurial endeavor, style, or character."[154] Fearful of the ever increasing social conformity bred by mass society – "the men in the gray flannel suits, the country-club Christians, the organization men, the frightened herd that composed the lonely crowd"[155] – the social critics of the fifties would try in vain to discover some vision of moral transcendence that could salvage the values of traditional individualism and revive older forms and values of community.

By contrast, James saw a quite different social reality, something that eluded their sophisticated instruments of opinion measurement and sociological profiles. Instead of passivity and sterile conformity, James recognized signs of tremendous creativity embedded within popular culture, reflecting the striving for autonomy and free association that he posited as occurring within the sphere of production relations.

It is important to point out that James was able to theorize the dynamics of popular culture in the way that he did because he starts out his analysis not upon the premise of individualism but upon the craving for free association that he identifies as the principal American character trait. James takes the view that this was de Tocqueville's most important insight into the working of American society. De Tocqueville, says James, "the most remarkable social analyst, native or foreign, to examine personally the United States in the first century of its existence," saw that the American individual "showed an altogether exceptional capacity for free association, in industry, in politics and for any other purpose." The result was that "individuality and universality achieve a fusion [in America] unknown elsewhere."

By adopting as his starting-point the norm of association as opposed to the norm of individualism, James is able to invoke the imperative of community that the other critics tend to dismiss. "It is the only means whereby the powerful and self-destroying individualism can find fulfillment." A new society was required to re-unite the individual and the community, since, "we have lost the models and the feeling for that type of work after 500 years of individualism."

James looked upon modern individualism as the antithesis of true individuality, which he credits as the real achievement of the earlier America. Basing himself upon Frederick Jackson Turner, "the most popular writer of the advancing industrial age," James argues that by the turn of the century the rupture with the American past of "heroic individualism" was complete. "[Turner] saw the actuality and the future in a manner impossible to the limited vision of Bryce." The influence upon James of Frederick Jackson

Turner's book on the significance of the frontier in American history and the specific character of American civilization was great, indeed. Turner's frontier thesis dominated historical thinking in the United States until Charles and Mary Beard's *The Rise of American Civilization* broke its monopoly in 1927.

Although Turner's ideas have subsequently undergone a good deal of criticism, with Marxists in particular stressing the role of ideological class conflicts, his theory of the importance of regions was reflected in the emphasis that James places on regional divisions and consciousness, which he describes in the first chapter of his prospectus as the basic impediments to American national consciousness, which, James argues, was the necessary condition for a strong national culture. James likewise wholeheartedly embraces Turner's discussion of the democratic nature of the country, particularly the prominent role that Turner assigned to the contribution of popular associations of the western states. The crisis of American civilization, as James saw it, was fundamentally a crisis resulting from the struggle to overcome the impediments erected against free association within the relations of capitalist production.

XXX

Denied in the realm where it most mattered, i.e., in the process of work, the struggle to achieve autonomy was transferred to the realm of representation, energizing popular culture. Spontaneously and without any political organization, popular culture became "a world movement towards the creation of man as an integral human being, a full and complete individuality with the circumstances and conditions of that fully integrated individuality."

The sphere of popular culture now became a terrain of contestation. "The film, comic-strip, radio-drama are a form of art which must satisfy the mass, the individual seeking individuality in a mechanized, socialized society," writes James, "where his life is ordered and restricted at every turn, where there is no certainty of employment, far less of being able to rise by energy and ability or going West as in the old days."

Conversely, the actuality of popular culture offered a model of integration by demonstrating a parallel fusion – "an immense social and artistic movement which points a broad arrow to the future and the integration of the social and aesthetic aspects of life." "It is the writer's belief," James goes on to declare, "that in modern popular art, film, radio, television, comic strip, we are headed for some such artistic comprehensive integration of modern life, that the spiritual, intellectual, ideological life of modern peoples will express itself in the closest and most rapid, most complex, absolutely free relation to the actual life of the citizens tomorrow."

While this may have sounded utopian in 1950, it has long since become an everyday reality, so that it is routinely taken for granted today. James was among the first cultural theorists to delineate the dual process of contestation and quest for integration within the domain of popular culture. "In observing the content and form of the popular arts in America today, with their international success," he asserts, "it is possible to deduce the social and political needs, sufferings, aspirations and rejections of modern civilization to an astonishing degree."

His analysis closely resembles the argument put forward by Walter Benjamin in his pathbreaking 1936 essay, "The Work of Art in the Age of Mechanical Reproduction."[156] There is no evidence to suggest that James actually knew of its existence at the time that he was writing, and yet his analysis arrives at the essential conclusion of Benjamin regarding the communicative meaning of modern expressive art. "The popular film, the radio, the gramophone, the comic strip, the popular daily paper and far more the popular periodical constitute a form of art and media of social communication which through mass production and the type of audience produced in the United States constitute a departure in the twentieth century as new in civilization as the art of printing in the fifteenth," James recognizes. "It has transformed the production of art."

But while James's discussion strengthens Benjamin's basic thesis of the contemporary "de-aestheticization" of art, he was sensitive to the surrender of the critical function in the new, mechanically reproduced popular arts, particularly as it was reflected in the "violence, brutality, sadism" that engulfed popular entertainment after 1929. "In such a society," James declares, "the individual demands an aesthetic compensation in the contemplation of free individuals who go out into the world and settle their problems by free activity and individualistic methods." He goes on: "Impotent rage, anger and frustration which can find expression only in a popular art of blood, destruction, torture, sadism[,] and an outlet for cheated, defrauded personality in vicarious living through a few striking personalities, these are the basic results in the only field where the masses are not free but at least have some choice in deciding."

From the perspective of cultural theory, such statements replicate, ironically, the criticism levelled against Benjamin's position by Theodor W. Adorno (1903–1969) in the latter's own landmark 1938 essay, "On the Fetish Character of Music and the Regression in Listening."[157] It is worth noting that James's criticism of what he takes to be the failure of the modern popular art is illuminated by an evaluation comparing the artistic achievement of Greek drama with that of "the modern American film" as a guide to "the future of modern art and society" and their capacity to achieve social and aesthetic integration.

A classic today of the sociology of art, Adorno's essay is a polemic directed explicitly against Benjamin's position. It applies the Marxist theory of reification to enunciate the negative, regressive aspect of mass culture. James, for his part, tempers his enthusiastic embrace of the ideological values purveyed in the popular arts. He recognizes the negativity of the mass culture industry: "No," he declares, "we have to examine more closely the conditions in which these new arts, the film, and with it the comic strip, the radio and jazz have arisen, in order to see exactly why they become an expression of mass response to societal crises, and *the nature and limitation of that response.*" In criticizing what he took to be "the failure of popular art today," James attempts the difficult task of differentiating and maintaining the dialectical unity of success and failure:

It would seem that deprived of any serious treatment of the problems which overwhelm since 1929 the modern masses have reacted in two main ways. They have fostered on the one hand an individualistic response to violence, murder, atrocities, crime, sadism; and on the other they have pertinaciously fostered and encouraged by their money and interest this creation of synthetic characters. Through them they live vicariously, see in them examples of that free individuality which is the dominant need of the vast mass today. Not only in their artistic but in their public lives these stars are the real aristocracy of the country and they perform one essential function of any genuine aristocracy. They fill a psychological need of the vast masses of people who live limited lives.

James affirms his essential optimism, however, regarding the continuing validity of the aesthetic function of art. It is this conviction that enables him "to imagine a social situation in which by means of fine artists and gifted performers, there will be an almost day-to-day correspondence between the ordinary experiences of many millions of human beings and their transmutation into aesthetic form." This would inaugurate a new stage in the development of modern popular art, but one that is conditional upon "the consciousness of the artist that a vast public is ready to assemble together to listen to him."

James connects the political urge concealed in the trend toward aggression in popular art with the violent frustration originating inside the labor process. "Far deeper social forces are coming into action," James observes in this connection. James also traces to the contradiction of labor the collapse of Greek drama because of the latter's failure to deal with it: "The Greeks of the fifth century aimed at universality. They accomplished the miracles that they did but they failed because they did not, they could not, take into account one particular aspect of universality – how a man labored."

Theoretically, what James was attempting to explain was the role of popular response in the process of cultural production. He seems to be arguing that this response was a reflection of the struggle for association and autonomy within the sphere of everyday labor. The outcome of this productivist theory of aesthetics becomes a dual theory of cultural autonomy, providing a synthesis of the polar positions advanced by both Benjamin and Adorno. It constitutes, in my opinion, a significant theoretical advance.

XXXI

Recognizing that any real freedom of the individual, as understood by Americans before the Civil War, had ceased to exist "except in the most abstract terms," James sought to comprehend the social antagonisms that he perceived were building up beneath the surface calm amid the unprecedented materialism of the post-war era. Approaching American society from the perspectives of daily life and work, and unfettered by the ideological blinders of either the entrepreneurial model of American individualism or the bureaucratic model of socialism, James perceived the making of an immense social crisis.

"Within the last dozen years," he declares, "the always volatile, restless, aggressive American individual, has now reached a pitch of exasperation, suppressed aggressiveness, anger and fear which irresistibly explode in private life but represent a profoundly social situation. The signs of an accumulating social explosion are everywhere."

Instead of a sterile, conformist, and blandly materialistic American culture, James found in the vibrancy of the "popular arts" – films, comic strips, soap operas, detective novels, jazz music, blues – the achievement of an unsurpassed autonomy in the realm of cultural production that succeeded in winning popular allegiance because it mirrored for the vast majority of the population the goal that it was daily struggling for, namely, free association in order to control the work process within American factories and offices and fields.

James was aware of the novelty that his analysis presented. He acknowledged the difficulty, particularly at this stage of its presentation and in its present form, that readers of the prospectus would be faced with: "The whole concept is of unusual (though not insuperable) difficulty, especially as this is the first tentative statement. There will be some overlapping and repetition. It cannot be as easy to grasp as [it would be] after it has been re-written half-a-dozen times and thoroughly discussed."

James's viewpoint on the radical impulse underlying American popular culture stands in such marked contrast to the cultural conservatism of the social critiques of mass culture emanating from the post-Second World War generation of social critics as well as assorted "New York intellectuals" – Sidney Hook, Dwight MacDonald, Mary McCarthy, Richard Hofstadter, Irving Howe, Alfred Kazin, Daniel Bell, Lionel Trilling and Diana Trilling, and others – that it is almost unique. It is precisely what also enhances its value and relevance to the current reappraisal of American Studies as an intellectual project.

XXXII

James crosses the cultural and political divide in American Studies by virtue also of the integration that he achieves in his analysis of the variables of class, race, and gender. Beyond this act of theoretical integration, he demonstrates their linkage with popular culture. In this respect, James's *American Civilization* stands as a watershed document in the transition away from the prevailing "myth-and-symbol" school, which was to a great extent responsible for establishing the legitimacy of American studies as a discipline, and points toward its displacement by contemporary theory in the new post-modern era, broadly-speaking, of American Studies.

The problem of representation and knowledge grounded in ordinary life, the moral economy of work, the mundane practices of everyday life in conflict with bureaucratic social institutions – these are the concerns that a couple of decades later have come to distinguish the practice of the new generation of American studies scholars from those of the "myth–and–symbol" school that preceded them in the forties and fifties. In this sense James anticipates these later developments already in 1950.

James's prospectus was also innovative in the use that it makes of the Marxist concept of alienation to analyze the social antagonisms of American society. It is the organizing, core concept that holds the various parts of the prospectus together and allows it to navigate back and forth between class and ideology, race and bureaucracy, gender and the production relations, popular culture and mechanization. It is also the reason that the pages of *American Civilization* remain so alive. As the social question has come to be defined increasingly by the regimentation governing all spheres of social life, the relevance of James's use of alienation as the central organizing concept for studying the problems of American society becomes apparent.

XXXIII

The lasting value of James's *American Civilization*, however, is what it reveals about James and the world in which his mind and spirit moved. Its basic message was not different from the author's own need which was to overcome isolation. (The Latin root of "isolation," it should be noted, is *insula* or island.) Through his writing and ideas, James was always seeking to overcome the isolation that he warns of throughout the text as the affliction characteristic of intellectuals. "Many European intellectuals write for common men, organize for them, and will readily die for them, do everything for them in fact except meet them as men," James reflects.

The prospectus delineates "the new isolation *of the intellectual,*" which James sees best exemplified in Whitman who "sought ceaselessly in his verse to bridge the gap." Whitman became the "singer of loneliness," the poet who "ran away to the whole world." It was this picture of the Existentialist intellectual, "preoccupied with his own dreary doubts and anxieties,"[158] that James set out in the prospectus to counter with an alternative political vision. In what is one of the most evocative passages of the entire text, James writes: "Whitman is alone, he has no sense of belonging to any section of society, no class to which he belongs, no class which he is against."

The event that was to trigger James's preoccupation with this phenomenon of the isolated intellectual was the release in 1948 of Laurence Olivier's film of *Hamlet,* a dramatic masterpiece that was widely acclaimed by American critics, described by one of them as "the greatest show on earth."[159] Hailed in America as one of the greatest pictures of all time, *Hamlet* established the record as the first foreign film to be awarded an Academy Award for Best Picture, in addition to being awarded four other Oscars, including the award to Olivier for Best Performance by a male actor.

Olivier's *Hamlet* stirred a great deal of controversy. In James's view, however, the film was a disaster. "Have you noticed the colossal failure of Olivier's Hamlet, with his thesis that Hamlet's trouble was his love for his mother?" James inquired in his letter to Jay Leyda in 1953. "You are startled, I am sure. I have begun, so I must finish. Let us, bearing Ahab in mind, stick to Hamlet. Why is he the character he is?" James answers: "He is a new type of man – the modern intellectual." "Olivier cut down Hamlet" by imposing a social interpretation that distorted the character. Olivier's interpretation was predicated upon a view of Hamlet as governed by his oedipal striving for his mother. For James, however, Hamlet was an estranged, tortured intellectual due to the nature of the age that produced him. In a letter written a couple days later to another literary critic, Meyer Schapiro, James reiterates this basic point:

Hamlet is an intellectual, the first of the moderns, in drama what Descartes, Hobbes and Locke are in philosophy. His virtue (and his vice) is his love of intellectual speculation, and that in a world where his special business is to think primarily of his social responsibilities. Hamlet *questions* every accepted canon of his day in the light of his own individual response to it.[160]

The single reference to Hamlet found in *American Civilization* occurs in the section dealing with Melville. As always, James has his eyes fixed on the crew of the *Pequod.* "Now the question that Melville poses," James writes, "is: 'Why did [the] ship's crew not revolt, put Ahab in irons or kill him, and thus save the ship and crew?" It is a problem that James views as symptomatic of the present age: "No generation but our own could have appreciated this," he asserts, which is also what he believed regarding the character of Ahab. James quotes Melville to the effect "that the crew were not only mongrel, renegades, castaways and savages, but that they were 'morally enfeebled also by the incompetence of mere unaided virtue or rightmindedness in Starbuck, the invulnerable jollity of indifference and recklessness in Stubb, and the pervading mediocrity of Flask.'"

If the character of Ahab in *Moby Dick* was a prevision of the modern totalitarian dictator, the significance of Hamlet for James was that he symbolizes the prototypic dilemma of the modern intellectual, caught between serving competing tyrannies and bureaucracies or else retreating into existentialist dread and isolation. "In the breast of *every* modern intellectual," writes James, "exists powerful tendencies to existentialist emotions and ideas. But equally present are the authoritarian complement." He explains their dilemma thus:

Both are inherent in the history of modern production and the rationalism which has sprung from it, particularly since Rousseau. And they will swing between these forces, often combining both, until they have mastered an integrated humanism in which man as producer becomes the center of human theory and practice.

Fearful or fanatical, the intellectual becomes in James's perspective a necessary partner of the totalitarian bureaucracies of the twentieth-century. Symbolically, therefore, Hamlet supplies the theoretical half that James uses to complement Ahab. "How great passions could shake men who had escaped the rigid roles of feudalism – this more than anything else was what interested Shakespeare," James decides. The wavering that American intellectuals would experience as a result of the shaking produced by the crisis of capitalism greatly interested him. It was the political basis of his interest in "the tragedy above all of Hamlet, who could not decide."

> . . . that these men
> Carrying, I say, the stamp of one defect,
> Being nature's livery, or fortune's star,
> His virtues else, be they as pure as grace,
> As infinite as man may undergo,
> Shall in the general censure take corruption
> From that particular fault.[161]

XXXIV

America was where James found a solution to his prolonged quest in the "altogether exceptional capacity for free association, in industry, in politics and for any other purpose." In America he felt liberated in his ideas and in his great gift of expression. Finally, it was in America that he found a way to overcome the peculiar estrangement that comes with being a colonial intellectual. If cricket was a metaphor of vindication, America became a metaphor of personal and cultural validation.

While it was in the United States that James overcame his intellectual isolation, it must be emphasized that it was only achieved through a special form of political activity that was developed by James and his American colleagues as part of their political organization. The importance of their achievement is now becoming more widely known. Primarily, this activity took as its major goal the major reorganization of Marxist theory amidst the shambles in which it became mired after the Second World War. It was not by any means the personal achievement of James, however, as much as something made possible through association with a remarkable group of colleagues, "a small body of Marxists" who, during the years of his American sojourn, developed and sustained contact with and thus learned from "what is always the main source of any advance in Marxist theory – the actions and ideas of the proletariat itself."[162] Looking back on "the tasks and methods which we set ourselves in 1941," James declares: "*In this work I found the only way that I could live with energy, peace and satisfaction with the rest of the world, with my comrades, my family and myself.*"[163]

Through the looking glass of *American Civilization*, and from his encounter with the rich contours and complex dimensions of America society, James would catch a glimpse of his own colonial self-reflection, captured in the poignant question – "Why has the United States failed to produce men who planted flags in unexplored territory?" The vindicationist imprint of the question is obvious.

The problem that the question addresses is the phenomenon of mastery. The equation that James draws between civilization and cultural mastery reflects a unique blending of Marxism and the cultural imperative of the colonial subject. For cultural mastery rather than mimicry was the way of achieving a modicum of freedom within a colonial world predicated upon the denial of intellectual competence.

Besides American civilization, the quest for mastery was most graphically symbolized for James in the story of West Indian cricket that he celebrates so wonderfully in *Beyond a Boundary*. With all of its many examples of brilliant mastery exhibited in batting, bowling, fielding, the strategy and tactics of play, etc., the book ends with this captivating prose portrait, one of James's greatest, of the first innings of Garfield Sobers batting in the

Brisbane test-match in 1961:

. . . [it] was the most beautiful batting I have ever seen. Never was such ease and
certainty of stroke, such early seeing of the ball and such late, leisured play, such
command by a batsman not only of the bowling but of himself. He seemed to be
expressing a personal vision. I had thought of him as having too much bowling to
do, but after that innings I knew that such batting can come only at moments, and
until they come the unfortunate artist has the disruptive task of adjusting himself to
what he can do in relation to what he knows is possible. This is a sphere beyond the
unfailing self-mastery of a Bradman or a Hutton.[164]

Beyond a Boundary addresses the question *"What do they know of cricket
who only cricket know?"* James's answer has since become the anthem of
Caribbean cultural and intellectual identity: "To establish his own identity,
Caliban, after three centuries, must himself pioneer into regions Caesar
never knew." *American Civilization* is not only the locus for the posing of
the question; it is also the source of validation for the answer that would form
the capstone of James's literary career.

> 'Ban, 'Ban, Ca – Caliban
> Has a new master. Get a new man![165]

XXXV

To the question asked by Kant in 1784, "Do we presently live in an
enlightened age?" the philosopher answered, "No, but we do live in an age of
enlightenment."[166] On this view, James's *American Civilization* forms part of
the struggle for enlightenment of an unenlightened era. Cast out once before
by the metaphoric Ahab from America, the West Indian Ishmael finally
returns with his twice-told tale. Its publication thus marks a figurative sort
of literary homecoming.

Some will find James's prospectus vexing, undoubtedly, but, mainly, it
should give us reason to pause. Written nearly a half-century ago, the
questions that it poses seem even more timely today in 1993 than they would
have in 1950. Fundamentally, it is about who and what will save America.
"Who is to begin it? And who is to begin what?" James asks. These are not
abstract questions. They go to the heart of the social question, which springs
from "the permanent struggle as to who will rule production." In addition
to being still a timely work, therefore, *American Civilization* is also a caution-
ary tale of intellectual courage, written at a time of deepening moral and
political crisis. Probing deeply into America, searching for the roots of its
present discontents and the way out, it finally offers a countervailing vision

deriving from the genius of American civilization – free association.

Ever the colonial Jacobin, James writes as the spiritual descendant of the American Abolitionists and Transcendentalists of a century earlier. The emancipatory impulse that underlay their vision of American civilization reasserts itself in James, affirmed throughout his prospectus in his belief in the survival of that powerful, regenerative force that remains the most vital part of America – "the creative power inherent in the masses of the American people." We forget this at our peril.

Robert A. Hill
Literary Executor of C.L.R. James
Los Angeles, California
February 26, 1993

NOTES

American Civilization: An Introduction

1   C.L.R. James, *Beyond a Boundary* (London: Stanley Paul/Hutchinson, 1963).
2   C.L.R. James, *World Revolution 1917–1936: The Rise and Fall of the Communist International* (London: Secker & Warburg, 1937); C.L.R. James, *The Black Jacobins: Toussaint L'Ouverture and the San Domingo Revolution* (London: Secker & Warburg, 1938); C.L.R. James, *A History of Negro Revolt* (London: *Fact* Monograph No. 18, 1938).
3   James, *Beyond a Boundary*, p. 71.
4   "La Divina Pastora" (1927) and "Triumph" (1929), reprinted in C.L.R. James, *The C.L.R. James Reader*, ed. A. Grimshaw (Oxford, UK and Cambridge, Mass.: Blackwell, 1992); "Turner's Prosperity" (1929) reprinted in C.L.R. James, *Spheres of Existence* (London: Alllison & Busby, 1980); "Revolution" (1931) and "The Star That Would Not Shine" (1931) reprinted in C.L.R. James, *At the Rendezvous of Victory* (London: Allison & Busby, 1984).
5   C.L.R. James, *Minty Alley* (London: Secker & Warburg, 1936).
6   Interview with Anna Grimshaw, 1986.
7   C.L.R. James, *The Case For West Indian Self-Government* (London: L. and V. Woolf, Day to Day Pamphlets No. 16, Hogarth Press, 1933).
8   "'Civilizing' the 'Blacks:' Why Britain Needs to Retain her African Possessions," *New Leader*, May 29, 1936.
9   Interview with Anna Grimshaw, 1985.
10 C.L.R. James, *Mariners, Renegades and Castaways: The Story of Herman Melville and the World We Live In*, published privately in New York, 1953 (London: Allison & Busby, 1984), p. 167.
11 C.L.R. James, *American Civilization*, below, p. 197.
12 James to Constance Webb, August 26, 1943.

13   C.L.R. James with F. Forest and R. Stone, *The Invading Socialist Society* (New York: Johnson–Forest Tendency, 1947); (C.L.R. James, *et al.*), *State Capitalism and World Revolution* (New York: Johnson–Forest Tendency, 1950).

14   C.L.R. James, *Notes on Dialectics: Hegel, Marx, Lenin* (written in 1948), (London: Allison & Busby, 1980).

15   Cited in A. Grimshaw and K. Hart, *C.L.R. James and The Struggle for Happiness* (New York: C.L.R. James Institute, 1991), pp. 41-2.

16   James to Constance Webb, October 7, 1947.

17   see note 10.

18   Ibid., p. 17.

19   Ibid., p. 112.

20   Ibid., p. 89.

21   James to "G & S" (Grace Lee and Selma Weinstein), December 14, 1953.

22   C.L.R. James, with G. Lee and P. Chaulieu, *Facing Reality* (Detroit: Correspondence, 1958).

23   James, *American Civilization*, below, p. 69.

24   C.L.R. James, "Rising voices of women with a world to gain," *Times Higher Education Supplement*, March 24, 1989.

25   C.L.R. James, "Dialectical Materialism and the Fate of Humanity" (1947), *Spheres of Existence* (London: Allison & Busby, 1980), p. 80.

26   James to Maxwell Geismar, April 11, 1961 (reprinted in *The C.L.R. James Reader*).

27   C.L.R. James, *Modern Politics* (Port of Spain: PNM Publishing Co., 1960).

Chapter 2   The American Intellectuals of the Nineteenth Century

1   From *The Death Carol:*

Come, lovely and soothing Death,
Undulate round the world, serenely arriving, arriving,
In the day, in the night, to all, to each,
Sooner or later, delicate Death. . . .

"Approach, strong Deliveress! . . .

"From me to these glad serenades. . . ."

From *Out of the Cradle Endlessly Rocking:*

Whereto answering, the sea,
Delaying not, hurrying not,
Whisper'd me through the night, and very plainly before daybreak

Lisp'd to me the low and delicious word DEATH;
And again Death – ever Death, Death, Death,
Hissing melodious, neither like the bird nor like my arous'd
    child's heart,
But edging near, as privately for me, rustling at my feet,
Creeping thence steadily up to my ears, and laving me softly all over
Death, Death, Death, Death, Death.

Chapter 5   Popular Arts and Modern Society

1   In the same article *Life* rightly calls *The Best Years of Our Lives* a "172 minute catalogue of bromides about the postwar world" for frustration not only satisfies itself by murderous explosion but needs bromides as well. But that is not our main theme.
2   By synthetic characters I do not mean anything offensive. Many of these characters are some of the most attractive human beings that have been seen on any stage. But the character is synthetic because it is the character which dominates and not the part played.
3   Shakespeare comes closest in majestic tragic *concentration*. But Melville is closer to it than he because Melville was more conscious of the relation of the individual to the mass.

Chapter 7   Negroes, Women and the Intellectuals

1   The question of regionalism has not been developed. But it dominated the Civil War period and is so far decisive in political relations as they are.
2   For the future Reuther's new power can mean almost anything. In his own union he has been called the leader of the right wing. But this description is only relative; by standard definitions Reuther is a far left-winger himself. He was once a Socialist and still thinks in socialistic terms. His harshest words with executives in Detroit have been over his attempts to get the union a voice in management, a "look at the books" and a limit on profits. At the end of the war, in fact, it was one of Detroit's little ironies that R. J. Thomas, the U.A.W. left-winger, should be trying to help the Kaiser–Frazer Corp. take over the old Willow Run bomber plant as a private industry, while "right-winger" Reuther was urging the government to run the plant (pre-fabricated housing) with the union playing a big part in the management. There is no doubt that Reuther's philosophy, if carried to its logical conclusion, would mean some sort of nationalization of industry such as is now being tried by the Labour Party in England.
    At any rate Reuther has a program for labor – and his program is more concerned with politics than with the old-fashioned picket line. Now that he is safe from Communist undermining, the auto-makers will find him a

tough customer. (As far as mere bargaining goes, many of the manufacturers would rather deal with the Communists, who are usually more interested in the party line than in advancing the cause of the union.) But tomorrow's biggest headlines about Reuther may well be in the political field. Neither the Communists, John L. Lewis nor Henry Wallace could ever form a labor party or make labor a really potent factor in the present parties. If the trick is to be turned by anyone in this generation, Reuther looks like the man to do it. He also looks willing enough. At the convention a news photographer started to take a profile of Reuther from the right side, which Reuther considers unflattering. The redhead seemed to have more on his mind than just the affairs of the moment when he ordered: "Take it from the other side."

3   More than any philosopher in the modern world, Whitehead, who died about a year ago, was responsible for training a school of anti-pragmatic, anti-rationalist metaphysicians in the United States.

4   Signet has also issued Erskine Caldwell's *Tobacco Road*, 23 printings, 2,530,000 sold; *God's Little Acre*, 33 printings, 5,169,000 sold; *Tragic Ground*, 16 printings, 2,270,000 sold; *Journeyman*, 18 printings, 2,690,000 sold; *George Boy*, 1st Signet edition, over a million sold. Caldwell's books, as is well known, deal with the poor whites in the South. It is not at all excluded that there is a connection, but for the time being we leave it. Signet authors include Richard Wright, D. H. Lawrence, Chester Himes, Thomas Wolfe and James M. Cain et al.

5   The report appears in *La Pensee*, theoretical organ of the French Stalinists, which has on its Comité Directeur and its Comité de Patronage 10 professors at the Sorbonne, two at the Collège de France (including Frederic Poliot-Curie) and 32 other leading intellectuals, scientists and professionals.

Literary Executor's Afterword

1   C.L.R. James, *At the Rendezvous of Victory* (London: Allison & Busby, 1984).

2   C.L.R. James, *Beyond a Boundary* (London: Stanley Paul, 1963), p. 29.

3   Ibid., p. 125.

4   L. Trotsky, *History of the Russian Revolution*, tr. Max Eastman (3 vols, New York: Simon & Schuster, 1933, 1936).

5   O. Spengler, *The Decline of the West*, tr. C.F. Atkinson (2 vols, New York: Knopf, 1926, 1928).

6   C.L.R. James, *The Life of Captain Cipriani: An Account of British Government in the West Indies* (Nelson, Lancs: n.p., 1932).

7   Ibid., p. 10.

8   H. Steele Commager, *America in Perspective: The United States through Foreign Eyes* (New York: Random House, 1947).

9   E. W. Blyden, *A Voice from Bleeding Africa* (Monrovia, 1856).

10 H. S. Wilson, "Edward Wilmot Blyden," in *Abroad in America: Visitors to the New Nation, 1776–1914*, ed. M. Pachter (Reading, Mass.: Addison-Wesley in assoc. with the National Portrait Gallery, Smithsonian Institution, 1976), pp. 157–66.

11 E. W. Blyden, *Christianity, Islam, and the Negro Race* (London, 1887).

12 M. Lerner, *America as a Civilization: Life and Thought in the United States Today* (New York: Simon and Schuster, 1957), ch. 2.

13 V.I. Lenin, *State and Revolution* (New York: International Publishers, 1932, 1943), p. 7.

14 H. P. Vincent, *The Trying-Out of Moby-Dick* (Boston: Houghton Mifflin, 1949).

15 C.L.R. James to H. P. Vincent, Kent State University Library, Special Collections and Archives, Howard P. Vincent Papers, February 3, 1953.

16 Ibid., H. P. Vincent to C.L.R. James, April 3, 1963.

17 C.L.R. James, *Notes on Dialectics* (London: Allison & Busby, 1948, 1980), p. 153.

18 Ibid., p. 38.

19 L. Trotsky, "An Open Letter to V. F. Calverton," *The Militant*, December 31, 1932.

20 W. Wilkie, *One World* (New York: Simon & Schuster, 1943).

21 C. A. and M. R. Beard, *The American Spirit: A Study of the Idea of Civilization in the United States* (New York: Macmillan, 1942).

22 Ibid., 529.

23 Ibid., p. 535.

24 C.L.R. James, *Education, Propaganda, Agitation: Post-War America and Bolshevism* (New York, Oct. 1944).

25 L. Wilcox, *V. F. Calverton: Radical in the American Grain* (Philadelphia: Temple University Press, 1992).

26 V. F. Calverton, *The Liberation of American Literature* (New York: 1932).

27 V. F. Calverton, *For Revolution* (New York: John Day, 1932).

28 V. F. Calverton, *The Awakening of America* (New York: John Day, 1939).

29 C.L.R. James, "The Tasks of Building the American Bolshevik Party," *Bulletin of the Workers Party*, March 28, 1946.

30 James, *Notes on Dialectics*, p. 224.

31 Ibid., p. 221.

32 Ibid., p. 224.

33 Ibid., p. 150.

34 Ibid., p. 139.

35 Ibid., p. 225.

36 James, *Notes on Dialectics*, p. 180.

37 C.L.R. James, *State Capitalism and World Revolution* (Detroit, Mich: Facing Reality, 1969), p. 107.

38   James, *Notes on Dialectics*, p. 180.
39   Ibid., p. 148.
40   Ibid., p. 224.
41   A.C.H.C. de Tocqueville, quoted in André Jardin, *Tocqueville: A Biography*, tr. L. David with R. Hemenway (New York: Farrar Straus Giroux, 1988), p. 273.
42   M. Glaberman, *Wartime Strikes* (Detroit, Mich.: Bewick Editions, 1980).
43   James, *Notes on Dialectics*, p. 223.
44   Ibid., p. 15.
45   C.L.R. James, *The American Worker* (New York: n.p., 1947).
46   E. Mayo, *The Human Problems of an Industrial Civilization* (Cambridge, Mass.: Harvard University Press, 1946).
47   K. Marx, *Essays by Karl Marx Selected from the Economic-Philosophic Manuscripts* (New York: n.p., 1947).
48   K. Marx, *Economic and Philosophic Manuscripts of 1844* (New York: International Publishers, 1964).
49   T. Bottomore, *et. al.* (eds) *A Dictionary of Marxist Thought*, 2nd. rev edn (Oxford: Blackwell Publishers, 1991), p. 165.
50   H. Marcuse, *Reason and Revolution: Hegel and the Rise of Social Theory* (New York: Oxford University Press, 1941), p. 258ff.
51   K. Marx, *Karl Marx-Friedrich Engels: Historische-Kritische Gesamtausgabe*, tr. G. Lee Boggs (Frankfurt and Berlin, 1932, Abt. 1, Bd. 3).
52   K. Marx, *Grundrisse: Foundations of the Critique of Political Economy*, tr. M. Nicolaus (Harmondsworth: Penguin/New Left Review, 1973).
53   C.L.R. James, *Marxism and the Intellectuals* (Detroit: Facing Reality Publishing Committee, 1962), p. 12.
54   C.L.R. James, "After ten years: On Trotsky's *The Revolution Betrayed*," *New International*, vol. XII, no. 8, Oct. 1946, p. 237.
55   K. Marx, *Karl Marx-Frederick Engels Collected Works* (New York: International Publishers, 1975), Vol. 3, p. 275.
56   Ibid., p. 277.
57   C.L.R. James, *Mariners, Renegades and Castaways: The Story of Herman Melville and the World We Live In* (New York, C.L.R. James, 1953), pp. 104-5.
58   J. P. Diggins, *The Rise and Fall of the American Left* (New York: W.W. Norton, 1973), p. 200.
59   James, *Notes on Dialectics*, p. 48.
60   Marx, *Marx-Engels Collected Works*, Vol. 3, p. 296.
61   Alexis de Tocqueville, *Democracy in America*, ed. J. P. Mayer and M. Lerner, tr. G. Lawrence (New York: Harper & Row, 1966), Bk II, pp. 485-8.
62   James, *Beyond a Boundary*, p. 161, fn. 1.
63   F. J. Turner, *The Frontier in American History* (New York: Henry Holt, 1920), p. 343.

64 Ibid., pp. 344-5.
65 Marx, *Marx-Engels Collected Works*, Vol. 3, pp. 298-301.
66 K. Marx, *Capital: A Critical Analysis of Capitalist Production*, ed. by Frederick Engels (Moscow: Foreign Languages Publishing House, 1957-59), Vol. 3, p. 800.
67 James, *Mariners, Renegades and Castaways*, p. 30.
68 E. P. Thompson, "The Moral Economy of the English Crowd in the Eighteenth Century," *Past and Present*, no. 50 (1971), pp. 76-136, repr. in E. P. Thompson, *Customs in Common* (New York, The New Press, 1991), pp. 185-258.
69 James, *Notes on Dialectics*, p. 140.
70 Ibid., p. 141.
71 James, *Marxism and the Intellectuals*, p. 19.
72 James, *Beyond a Boundary*, p. 29.
73 W. Phillips, *Speeches, Lectures, and Letters* (Boston, 1864), pp. 265-6.
74 James, *Mariners, Renegades and Castaways*, p. 11.
75 Ibid., p. 63.
76 Ibid., p. 149.
77 C.L.R. James, *Facing Reality* (Detroit, Mich.: Correspondence, 1958).
78 James, *Beyond a Boundary*, p. 203.
79 W. H. Auden, *Portable Greek Reader* (New York: Viking, 1948).
80 James, *Beyond a Boundary*, pp. 155-6.
81 Ibid., p. 183.
82 E. F. Goldman, *The Crucial Decade and After: America, 1945-1960* (New York: Vintage, 1960), p. 41.
83 P. Watrous, "Dizzy Gillespie, Who Sounded Some of Modern Jazz's Earliest Notes, Dies at 75," *New York Times*, Jan. 7, 1993.
84 E. Roosevelt, *This I Remember* (New York: Harper, 1949).
85 M. Mead, *Male and Female: A Study of the Sexes in a Changing Society* (New York: William Morrow, 1949).
86 G. Swain, "The Cominform: Tito's International?," *Historical Journal*, vol. 35, no. 3 (Sept. 1992), pp. 641-663.
87 E. F. Frazier, *The Negro in the United States* (New York: Macmillan, 1949).
88 James, *Mariners, Renegades and Castaways*, p. 202.
89 C.L.R. James, *World Revolution 1917-1936: The Rise and Fall of the Communist International* (London: Martin Secker & Warburg, 1937).
90 D. Rousset, *L'univers concentrationnaire* (The Other Kingdom), tr. R. Guthrie (New York: Reynal and Hitchcock, 1947).
91 G. Orwell, *Nineteen Eighty-four* (New York: Harcourt, Brace, 1949).
92 H. Arendt, *The Origins of Totalitarianism* (New York: Harcourt, Brace, 1950).
93 T. Adorno, et. al., *The Authoritarian Personality* (New York: Harper & Row, 1950).

94   G. Orwell, *Homage to Catalonia* (London: Secker and Warburg, 1938).
95   James, *Notes on Dialectics*, p. 186.
96   C.L.R. James, "Cromwell and the Levellers," *Fourth International*, May 1949, pp. 143–148.
97   C.L.R. James, "Ancestors of the Proletariat," *Fourth International*, Sept. 1949, pp. 251-255.
98   James, *Notes on Dialectics*, pp. 184–94.
99   C.L.R. James, *The Black Jacobins: Toussaint L'Ouverture and the San Domingo Revolution* (New York: Vintage, 1963).
100 Ibid., p. 384.
101 R. Cobb, *A Second Identity: Essays on France and French History* (London: Oxford University Press, 1969), p. 96.
102 James, *The Black Jacobins*, p. 276.
103 D. Guérin, *La Lutte de classes, sous la première république, bourgeois et "bras nus"* (2 vols, Paris: Gallimard, 1946; 2nd ed., 1968).
104 James, *Mariners, Renegades and Castaways*, p. 188.
105 James, *The Black Jacobins*, p. 384.
106 D. Guérin, interview, Paris, France, Oct. 18, 1982.
107 D. Guérin, *Fascisme et grand capital* (Paris: Gallimard, 1936).
108 D. Guérin, *Fascism and Big Business* (New York: Pioneer, 1939).
109 L. Ménard, review of C.L.R. James, *Les Jacobins noirs, Les Temps Modernes*, no. 52, pp. 1527-9.
110 D. Guérin, interview, Paris, France, Oct. 18, 1982.
111 D. Guérin, *Où va le peuple Américain?* (Whither the American People?), Vols 1 and 2 (Paris: Julliard, 1950–51).
112 D. Guérin, excerpts from *Où va le peuple Américain?* (Whither the American People?), Vol. 3, *Les Temps Modernes*, nos 51-3, 1950.
113 Guérin, *Où va le peuple Américain?*, Vol. 1, p. 351.
114 D. Guérin, *Negroes on the March: A Frenchman's Report on the American Negro Struggle* (New York: Weissman, 1951, 1956).
115 M. J. Herskovits, *The Myth of the Negro* (New York: Harper, 1941).
116 Guérin, *Negroes on the March*, p. 188.
117 Guérin, *Où va le peuple Américain?* Vol. 1, p. 12.
118 Guérin, "Civilisation de classe ou civilisation de masse," *Révolution Prolétarienne*, no. 110, 1930.
119 James, *Facing Reality*, p. 173.
120 K. Ohashi *et al.*, *Amerika no bunka* (American Civilization), 7 vols (Tokyo: Nan'undo, 1969-71).
121 A. Kaspi, *et al.*, La civilisation américaine (Paris: Presses Universitaires de France, 1979).
122 H. Laski, *The American Democracy* (New York: Viking Press, 1948).
123 Ibid., 724.
124 Ibid., 723.

125 Ibid., 756.
126 Ibid., 760
127 D. W. Brogan, *The American Character* (New York: Viking Press, 1948).
128 G. Gorer, *The American People: A Study in National Character* (New York: W.W. Norton, 1948).
129 W. Lewis, *America and Cosmic Man* (London: Nicholson & Watson, 1948).
130 B. Kuklick, "Myth and Symbol in American Studies," *American Quarterly*, Vol. 24 (Oct. 1972), 435–50.
131 G. Lipsitz, "Listening to Learn and Learning to Listen: Popular Culture, Cultural Theory, and American Studies," *American Quarterly*, vol. 42, no. 4 (December 1990), p. 625.
132 Ibid., p. 626.
133 C.L.R. James, *The C.L.R. James Reader*, A. Grimshaw ed. (Oxford, UK and Cambridge, Mass.: Blackwell, 1992), p. 147.
134 Ibid.
135 F.O. Mathiessen, *American Renaissance: Art and Expression in the Age of Emerson and Whitman* (New York: Oxford University Press, 1941).
136 R. H. Brodhead, *The School of Hawthorne* (New York: Oxford University Press, 1986), p. 210.
137 Mathiessen, *American Renaissance*, p. xv.
138 Ibid., pp. 371–514.
139 Ibid., p. 447.
140 James, *Mariners, Renegades and Castaways*, p. 8.
141 Ibid., p. 50.
142 H. Melville, *Moby Dick* (New York: Penguin Books, 1992).
143 Ibid., p. xxiii.
144 H. Melville, *Pierre or, The Ambiguities* (New York: Hendricks House, 1949).
145 N. Mailer, *The Naked and the Dead* (New York: Rinehart, 1948).
146 James, *Mariners, Renegades and Castaways*, p. 149.
147 D. H. Lawrence, *Studies in Classic American Literature* (New York: Thomas Seltzer, 1923; reissued, New York: Viking Press, 1964).
148 G. Wise, "'Paradigm Dramas' in American Studies: A Cultural and Institutional History of the Movement," *American Quarterly*, vol. 31 (1979), p. 298.
149 R. W. Emerson, "American Civilization," in *The Complete Works of Ralph Waldo Emerson*, Vol. XI (Boston: Houghton Mifflin, 1903-4), pp. 300, 304.
150 V. H. Parrington, *Main Currents in American Thought: An Interpretation of American Literature from the Beginnings to 1920*, 3 vols., (New York: Harcourt, Brace & World, 1927, 1930).
151 James, *Notes on Dialectics*, p. 138.
152 James, *Mariners, Renegades and Castaways*, p. 7.
153 W. Shakespeare, *King Lear*, III. iv. 107.
154 E. Long, *The American Dream and the Popular Novel* (Boston: Routledge & Kegan Paul, 1985).

155 D. Wakefield, *New York in the 50's* (New York: Houghton Mifflin/Seymour Lawrence, 1992).
156 W. Benjamin, "The Work of Art in the Age of Mechanical Reproduction," *Zeitschrift für Sozialforschung*, Vol. V (1936), in W. Benjamin, *Illuminations*, ed. with an introduction by H. Arendt, trans. H. Zohn (London: Collins/Fontana Books, 1973), pp. 219-254.
157 T. W. Adorno, "On the Fetish Character of Music and the Regression in Listening," *Zeitschrift für Sozialforschung*, Vol. VII (1938), repr. in *The Essential Frankfurt School Reader*, ed. A. Arato and E. Gebhardt (New York: Continuum, 1992), pp. 270–299.
158 James, *Facing Reality*, p. 172.
159 Quoted in A. Holden, *Olivier* (London: Sphere Books, 1988), p. 269; see also J. Cottrell, *Olivier* (Englewood Cliffs, NJ: Prentice-Hall, 1975), pp. 220-232.
160 James, *The C.L.R. James Reader*, p. 239.
161 W. Shakespeare, *Hamlet*, I. iv. 30.
162 James, *Marxism and the Intellectuals*, p. 21.
163 Ibid.
164 James, *Beyond a Boundary*, p. 251.
165 W. Shakespeare, *The Tempest*, II. ii. 192.
166 I. Kant, *Perpetual Peace and Other Essays*, tr. T. Humphrey (Indianapolis, Indiana: Hackett, 1983), p. 44.

Index of Names

Adam, 81
Adams, B., 183
Adams, J. D., 216-218, 331
Adorno, T., 336, 359-360
Aeschines, 32
Aeschylus, 32, 36, 129, 149, 152-158
Ahab, 15-16, 70-72, 75-84, 156, 267, 315, 324, 351-354, 362-363, 365
Alger, H., 135, 169
Alinsky, S., 269
Althusser, L., 313
Annie, L. O., 120
Aphrodite, 143-144
Arbuckle, F., 142
Archer, M., 124
Arendt, H., 336
Aristophanes, 32, 124, 133, 135, 149-150, 152, 157
Aristotle, 32, 152, 155, 241
Armstrong, L., 35
Arnold, M., 34, 54, 295-296, 299
Aron, R., 238
Aspasia, 221
Attlee, C., 278
Auden, W. H., 128, 149, 151, 153, 156, 266, 326

Bacon, F., 262

Ball, L., 144
Balzac, H., 76, 266-267
Baruch, B., 232
Baudelaire, C., 51
Beard, C., 172, 186, 305, 346-347, 357
Beard, M., 305, 346-347, 357
Beck, D., 253
Bedaux, 107
Beethoven, L., 46, 242, 262, 302
Bel Geddes, B., 146
Belinsky, 284
Bell, 197, 356, 361
Benda, J., 265
Benjamin, W., 46, 358-360
Bennett, 177-179, 181
Benny, J., 135, 150
Bergman, I., 145
Blondie, 138
Blyden, E. W., 299
Blyth, A., 137
Boas, F., 346
Bogart, H., 119, 126, 132, 145
Boggs, J., 312, 314
Bovary, M., 51
Boyer, C., 145
Braun, K., 113
Brennan, T., 147
Brogan, D. W., 30-31, 263, 306, 347

Anna Grimshaw is a lecturer in visual anthropology at the University of Manchester, and was C.L.R. James's personal assistant for the last six years of his life; Keith Hart is Director of the African Studies Center at Cambridge University.